THE FEDERAL REPUBLIC OF GERMANY SINCE 1949

Politics, Society and Economy before and after Unification

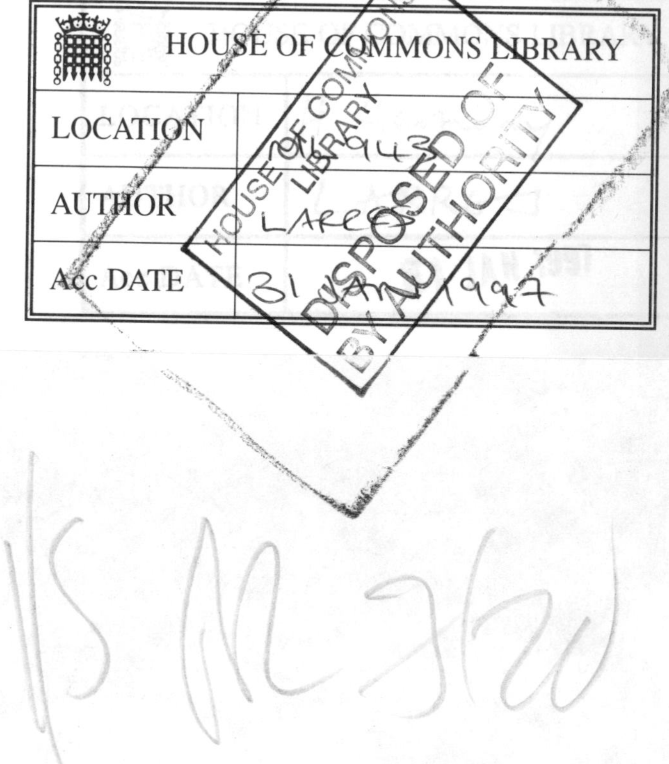

THE FEDERAL REPUBLIC OF GERMANY SINCE 1949

Politics, Society and Economy before and after Unification

Edited by Klaus Larres and Panikos Panayi

Longman
London and New York

Addison Wesley Longman Limited,
Edinburgh Gate,
Harlow, Essex CM20 2JE, England
and Associated Companies throughout the world.

*Published in the United States of America
by Addison Wesley Longman, New York*

First published 1996

ISBN 0 582 23890 0 CSD
ISBN 0 582 23891 9 PPR

British Library Cataloguing-in-Publication Data

A catalogue record for this book is available from the British Library

Library of Congress Cataloging-in-Publication Data

The Federal Republic of Germany since 1949: politics, society, and economy before and after unification/edited by Klaus Larres and Panikos Panayi.
p. cm.
Includes bibliographical references and index.
ISBN 0–582–23890–0 (CSD). — ISBN 0–582–23891–9 (PPR)
1. Germany–Economic conditions–20th century. 2. Germany–Social conditions–20th century. 3. Germany–Politics and government–20th century. 4. Germany–History–Unification, 1990. I. Larres, Klaus. II. Panayi, Panikos.
HC286.5.F43 1996
943.087—dc20 96–346
CIP

Phototypeset by 20
Produced by Longman Singapore Publishers (Pte) Ltd.
Printed in Singapore

Contents

List of Maps

Acknowledgements

We have attempted to trace the copyright owners of Map 2.1 but have been unsuccessful and would appreciate any information that would enable us to do so.

Introduction

The fall of the Berlin Wall in November 1989 and the subsequent unification of Germany in October 1990 have resulted in an explosion of academic interest in the internal and external politics of the Federal Republic of Germany (FRG) as well as the country's social, economic and political-diplomatic history. The essays in the current volume reflect this development.

However, instead of merely jumping onto the bandwagon of an academic growth industry by considering all the many dramatic events since 1989, the articles in this volume place the transformations which have taken place within the context of the long-term historical structures of the twentieth century, and in particular post-Second World War Germany, focusing upon the Federal Republic of Germany both before and after unification.

The individual authors were asked to consider the following three aspects when researching and writing their respective contributions. Firstly, the development of the general political, economic and social framework of the Federal Republic which has characterized the country's internal and external politics since its creation in 1949; secondly, the long-term changes in the FRG's constitutional set-up which have become apparent since unification in 1990 and are likely to be of a more permanent character. Thirdly, authors were asked to analyse their respective topics within the context of the long-term structures of the post-war West German state. Thus, it is the aim of the book to deliver a comparative analysis of the economic, social as well as domestic-political and political-diplomatic continuities and changes within the Federal Republic before and after unification. To this end, the book considers the German political tradition in general as well as the characteristics of the West German state which evolved between 1949 and 1989 and the continuities and likely long-term changes in the years since unification. As the Federal Republic since unification has largely emphasized the development and adaptation of West German political, economic and social structures while those of the former East German state (GDR) have been largely ignored or deliberately rejected, most of the articles do not concentrate on the political characteristics of the GDR between 1949 and 1989. The latter have not played any decisive part in the evolving political, economic and social features of the FRG since unification, though some of the contributions do touch upon the GDR's political structures.

The book is divided into two parts. The articles in Part One outline the main developments which have taken place post-war within the four major basic areas of contemporary German politics: economic, social, domestic-political and political-diplomatic. Richard Overy writes about the FRG's post-war economy and concentrates on the reasons for the so-called 'economic miracle'. Hartmut Berghoff considers population changes and the impact of the various migratory waves. He particularly analyses the role of refugees from the East, 'guestworkers' from Southern Europe and, most recently, the arrival of asylum-seekers. Torsten Oppelland, Matthias Siekmeier and Klaus Larres analyse the domestic and party political developments during the times of Adenauer, the Grand Coalition, the Social Democratic–Liberal years under Brandt and Schmidt, and, finally, the Kohl era. Imanuel Geiss looks at the German question and the role of the FRG in international politics. The underlying theme of his article is that German political interests and loyalties have always been torn between East and West.

Part Two contains essays upon individual subjects within the four themes, varying in specificity. Graham Hallet looks at the intervention of the state in the post-war German economy. He tackles the concept of *Soziale Marktwirtschaft* and, above all, deals comprehensively with the economic consequences of unification. Panikos Panayi focuses on the central importance of race, in terms of immigration, ethnicity and racism, for the development of the modern German nation-state. Throughout the twentieth century immigrants have played a crucial role in German economic growth while almost all governments have practised some form of more or less overt racism. David Childs considers the neo-nationalist scene since 1949. Above all he concentrates on the National Democratic Party (NPD), whose heyday was in the 1960s and early 1970s, and the *Republikaner* party, which was relatively successful immediately after unification. Stephen Padgett looks at the development of the Social Democratic Party since 1945. In particular, he focuses on the post-1982 years after Schmidt's resignation as Chancellor as well as on the effects of unification on the party's identity and the SPD's difficulties in the new *Länder*. Terry McNeill writes about West German–Soviet relations between 1945 and 1991 when the USSR ceased to exist. He differentiates between five phases characterized by different aims and tactics which the Soviet Union employed to either take over or, since the mid-1950s, come to an acceptable *modus vivendi* with the Bonn governments. He particularly concentrates on Gorbachev's policy of *glasnost* and *perestroika* and Moscow's eventual acceptance of a united Germany fully integrated into the Western Alliance. Klaus Larres writes on Germany's relations with the West. He analyses to what extent the so-called 'Rapallo factor' – traditional Western fears about a close alliance between Germany and the Soviet Union to the exclusion of the West – influenced Bonn's relations with Washington, London and Paris. After a brief outline of the circumstances of the Treaty of Rapallo in 1922, he looks at the Western reaction to Adenauer's journey to Moscow in 1955, to Brandt's *Ostpolitik* in the late 1960s/early 1970s and to the Kohl government's new and somewhat more assertive foreign policy towards eastern Europe and the EU since unification.

As a whole, taking Parts One and Two together, the book offers a thorough thematic (and often within the individual themes chronological) introduction to the history of the Federal Republic of Germany before and after unification.

Without the support and infinite patience of Andrew MacLennan, the Editorial Director at Addison Wesley Longman, this book would never have seen the light of day. Consequently, we are very grateful for his understanding concerning the many problems we encountered when embarking upon editing this volume. We would also like to thank Patricia McCourt, Belfast, and Bill Cory, London, for their very helpful editorial assistance. The supportive attitude to this project by Bob Eccleshall, Head of the Politics Department of the Queen's University of Belfast, is also gratefully acknowledged.

Klaus Larres and Panikos Panayi
Belfast and London
August 1995

Notes on the contributors

Hartmut Berghoff is a researcher in economic and social history at the University of Tübingen. His publications include *Englische Unternehmer, 1870–1914: Eine Kollektivbiographie führender Wirtschaftsbürger in Birmingham, Bristol und Manchester* (Göttingen, 1991).

David Childs is Professor of German politics at the University of Nottingham. He has written on both Britain and Germany since 1900 and his publications include *Germany in the Twentieth Century* (London, 1991) and, with Richard Popplewell, *The STASI: East Germany's Security and Intelligence System* (London, 1996).

Imanuel Geiss, who holds a chair at the University of Bremen, is one of Germany's leading historians. His numerous books have covered a diverse range of subjects which have included German foreign policy, Pan-Africanism, German historiography and world history ('Geschichte griffbereit', 6 vols, new edition, Dortmund, 1993).

Graham Hallett is an honorary lecturer in the Department of City and Regional Planning at the University of Wales, Cardiff, and a former Alexander von Humboldt research fellow. He is the author of various books and articles on agricultural, urban and housing policy.

Klaus Larres is a lecturer in Politics at the Queen's University of Belfast. He has written on superpower relations in the Cold War and on American, British and German domestic and foreign policy. His publications include *Politik der Illusionen: Churchill, Eisenhower und die deutsche Frage, 1945–1955* (Göttingen, 1995; English edition is in preparation). Currently, he is writing a book on the collapse of *détente* in the 1970s.

Terry McNeill holds a chair in Politics at the University of Hull. He is head of department and has published extensively on Western–Soviet relations during the Cold War and in the post-Cold War years.

Torsten Oppelland is a lecturer in Politics at the University of Jena. His publications include *Reichstag und Aussenpolitik im Ersten Weltkrieg: Die deutschen Parteien und die Politik der USA 1914–1918* (Düsseldorf, 1995). He is currently writing a biography of the former West German Foreign Minister Gerhard Schröder.

Richard Overy is Professor of Modern History at King's College, London. His books include *The Nazi Economic Recovery* (2nd edition, Cambridge, 1986) and *War and Economy in the Third Reich* (Oxford, 1994). His most recent publication is *Why the Allies Won* (London, 1995). He is currently writing a history of the Nazi economy and a textbook on Nazism.

Stephen Padgett is Professor of Politics at the University of Liverpool. He has published extensively on Germany since 1945 and is one of Britain's leading scholars on the history and politics of the Federal Republic of Germany. He is one of the editors of the journal *German Politics*.

Panikos Panayi is a senior lecturer in history at De Montfort University in Leicester. He has written widely on the history of minorities and his publications include *German Immigrants in Britain during the Nineteenth Century, 1815–1914* (Oxford, 1995).

Mathias Siekmeier is a history graduate of the University of Cologne. He has written his Ph.D. thesis on the role of the Free Democratic Party in post-war West German politics. This work will be published shortly.

Glossary

ABM	Anti-Ballistic Missile
AfA	Arbeitsgemeinschaft für Arbeitnehmerfragen (Working Group for Labour Affairs): the labour wing of the Social Democratic Party
APO	Ausserparlamentarische Opposition (Extra-Parliamentary Opposition); the student movement of the 1960s
ANR	Aktion Neue Rechte (New Right Action Group)
APUZ	*Aus Politik und Zeitgeschichte*
ASF	Arbeitsgemeinschaft sozialdemokratischer Frauen (Working Group for Social Democratic Women); women's group in the Social Democratic Party
ATM	Anti-Tactical Missile
BDI	Bundesverband der Deutschen Industrie
BHE	Bund der Heimatvertriebenen und Entrechteten (Bloc of Expellees and Disenfranchised)
BMD	Ballistic Missile Defence
BND	Bundesnachrichtendienst (Federal Intelligence Service)
Bundesrat	Upper house of the German parliament
Bundestag	Lower house of the German parliament
Bundeswehr	Armed forces of the Federal Republic of Germany
CDU	Christlich-Demokratische Union (Christian Democratic Union)
COCOM	Co-ordinating Committee of the Paris Consultative Group of Nations [on East–West trade]
COMECON	Council for Mutual Economic Assistance
CSCE	Conference on Security and Cooperation in Europe
CSU	Christlich-Soziale Union (Christian Social Union)
Deutscher Sonderweg	'German special path'

DGB	Deutscher Gewerkschaftsbund (German Trades Union Association)
DKP	Deutsche Konservative [Konservative] Partei (German Conservative Party). Later, the same abbreviation was used for the West German Communist Party
DM	Deutsch Mark
DN	*Deutsche Nachrichten*
DNZ	*Deutsche National-Zeitung*
DNZSZ	*Deutsche National-Zeitung und Soldaten-Zeitung*
DP	Deutsche Partei (the German Party)
DRep	Deutsche Rechtspartei (German Rights Party)
DRP	Deutsche Reichspartei (German Reich Party)
DVU	Deutsche Volksunion (German People's Union)
ECSC	European Coal and Steel Community (precursor of the EEC)
EDC	European Defence Community
FBIS-SOV	*Foreign Broadcast Information Service – Soviet Section*
FDP	Freie Demokratische Partei (Free Democratic Party)
FRG	Federal Republic of Germany
FRUS	*Foreign Relations of the United States*
Gastarbeiter	Guestworker
GATT	General Agreement on Trade and Tariffs (1947)
GDP	Gross Domestic Product
GDP	Gesamtdeutsche Partei (All-German Party)
GDR	German Democratic Republic (former East Germany)
GNP	Gross National Product
Historikerstreit	'Historians' Quarrel'
ICBM	Intercontinental Ballistic Missiles
ICE	Inter-City Express
INF	Intermediate-Range Nuclear Forces
JUSO	Jungsozialisten (Young Socialists); youth wing of the Social Democratic Party
KPD	Kommunistische Partei Deutschlands (Communist Party of Germany)
Lastenausgleich	Equalization of Burdens
Mitsbestimmung	Co-determination
NPD	Nationaldemokratische Partei Deutschlands (National Democratic Party of Germany)
NSDAP	Nationalsozialistische Deutsche Arbeiterpartei (National Socialist German Workers' Party)

OECD	Organization for Economic Cooperation and Development
OEEC	Organization for European Economic Development (1948)
Ostpolitik	Willy Brandt's Eastern policy
PDS	Partei des Demokratischen Sozialismus (Party of Democratic Socialism, East Germany)
Politikverdrossenheit	Party-political Apathy
PRO	Public Record Office, London
RAF	Rote Armee Fraktion (Red Army Faction)
REP	*Die Republikaner* (the Republican Party)
RIIA	Royal Institute of International Affairs
RM	Reichmark
SALT	Strategic Arms Limitations Treaty
Schaukelpolitik	Seesaw policy; policy of the swing
SED	Sozialistische Einheitspartei (Socialist Unity Party, East Germany)
Soziale Marktwirtschaft	Social market economy
SLBM	Submarine Launched Ballistic Missile
SPD	Sozialdemokratische Partei Deutschlands (Social Democratic Party of Germany)
SRP	Sozialistische Reichspartei (Socialist Reich Party)
Stasi	East German secret police
Volkskammer	East German parliament
Volkspartei	Peoples' Party or 'catch-all' party; a political party bridging traditional class or confessional divisions
WAV	Wirtschaftliche Aufbauvereinigung (Economic Construction Association)
Weltanschauung	world view
Wende	Turning-point
Westbindung	Commitment to the West
Wirtschraftswunder	Economic miracle
WTO	Warsaw Treaty Organization

PART ONE

The Development of the Federal Republic: a Survey

CHAPTER ONE

The Economy of the Federal Republic since 1949

Richard Overy

Shortly after the collapse of the communist regime in East Germany an article in the West German journal *Wirtschaftsdienst* explored the options open to its neighbour as the command economy crumbled. Reform was out of the question. There was, the article continued, only one acceptable course: abolition of the old system 'and replacement with a market economy'. More precisely it should be a market economy constructed along the lines of the Federal Republic, 'functionally efficient' with autonomous, highly competitive enterprises, free prices, and an effective monetary and currency system.[1] Here, in a nutshell, was the recipe for the startling success of the West German economy since the state's foundation in 1949. 'Capitalist restoration' had worked then; the assumption widely held in German circles in 1990 was that it would work again in the east.

Such a view is hardly surprising. The success of the market economy has been one of the defining features of the Federal Republic almost from its inception. To the outside world German strength is economic strength, and German revival a paradigm of the transforming power of modern capitalism. The very term 'economic miracle' has entered the vocabulary of modern political economy as first and foremost a German phenomenon. It is entirely plausible to argue that the political and social stability enjoyed by the Federal Republic for half a century owes a great deal to a solid foundation of economic success, in contrast to the economic stagnation of the inter-war years which spawned a violent radical nationalism.

There is no doubt that a remarkable economic revival did occur in the 1950s, and that high levels of growth were sustained, with small deviations, through to the 1990s. Between 1950 and 1970 the rate of growth was on average double the rate achieved in the years of rapid industrialization between 1871 and 1913. Growth during this period –

1. D. Lösch, 'Marktwirtschaft für die DDR: Chancen und Probleme der Systemtransformation', *Wirtschaftsdienst* 70 (1990), 3.

the core of the 'economic miracle' – was faster than all the other major industrial states save Japan.[2] Even with slower rates of growth in the 1970s and 1980s, the Federal economy on the eve of unification had grown at an average of 4.4 per cent a year for almost 40 years, the highest rate in Western Europe. The underlying long-term trend is an important indicator of the real strength of the Federal economy. In the 1950s high growth reflected recovery from the crisis conditions of the immediate post-war years; but from the 1960s growth was sustained well beyond the level of readjustment to more normal market conditions.

This distinction should act as a warning against any attempt to explain economic performance over the whole period with a common set of causes. The circumstances governing economic development in the early years of the new republic were not the same as those of the 1960s or the 1980s. Even the much-vaunted free market has been through a series of stages where state regulation or assistance has acted to push the market in the right direction, or to alter the terms of market competition. Nor has economic performance been entirely the product of forces developed within the Federal Republic; exogenous factors have also played a part in shaping German success. There is no simple recipe to explain German economic performance since 1949, as the citizens of Germany's new eastern provinces have since discovered.

THE 'CAPITALIST RESTORATION'

The development of the economy of the Federal Republic after 1949 must be understood in the context of what went before. It has always been a temptation to argue that economic revival in the 1950s was the product of a new beginning, like the construction of an effective parliamentary democracy. But only a few years before the birth of the new state, Germany was the second largest industrial economy in the world behind the United States. The German population enjoyed a high skill ratio in international terms. German science and technology boasted a large establishment and its practitioners worked in a whole range of vanguard technologies. After 25 years of war and economic crisis it was not a wealthy economy, but it was richly endowed with physical assets and manpower capable, under the right conditions, of generating high levels of prosperity.

2. H. Giersch, *Im Brennpunkt: Wirtschaftspolitik* (Stuttgart, 1978), p. 15.

At the end of the Second World War those conditions could not be met for reasons that are obvious. The bombing of Germany left much of the industrial and urban areas in ruins. In the major cities, an average of 50 per cent of the built-up area was destroyed and 45 per cent of the housing stock rendered uninhabitable.[3] Germany was occupied by Allies who could not decide the long-term future of the area, but who were anxious to reduce Germany's economic potential. German firms were seized as reparation, or limited in what they could produce. The 'Level of Industry' plan adopted by the Allies in 1946 was designed to restrict Germany to roughly half the industrial output of 1938. German firms were prohibited from producing aircraft, ships, ball-bearings, radio transmitters and a host of other products deemed to have a military significance. Steel production was limited to 7.5 million tons in a country capable of producing three to four times as much.[4] Germany was physically divided into four zones, each with its own economic organization. Even when the western zones were linked together into a single economic unit in 1947, economic life remained fragmented and insecure. Hunger and poverty were widespread; neither inflation nor the black market could be suppressed. A loaf of bread that cost 50 Pfennigs under Allied price controls cost 25 Marks on the black market in 1947.[5] After two years of occupation industrial production was only 44 per cent of the level achieved in 1936.

These conditions, over which German politicians and businessmen had little control, masked the real potential of the German economy. Labour was plentiful and cheap, and much of it highly trained. Bombing and reparations eliminated some of Germany's capital stock, but in 1945 the aggregate value of the buildings and plant that survived was greater in the western zones than it had been in 1936, 62 billion Marks against 51 billion Marks. Reparation accounted for a loss of a further 2 billion Marks of equipment, but a large number of machines, many of them hidden in caves or mines to avoid bomb damage, emerged intact and workable from the war.[6] Much of this capacity remained under-utilized

3. J. M. Diefendorf, *In the Wake of War: The Reconstruction of German Cities after World War II* (New York, 1993), p. 11.

4. S. Lieberman, *The Growth of European Mixed Economies 1945–1970* (New York, 1977), p. 34; H.-J. Braun, *The German Economy in the Twentieth Century* (London, 1990), pp. 148–9; I. Turner, 'British Policy Towards German Industry 1945–9', in idem, ed., *Reconstruction in Postwar Germany* (Oxford, 1989), pp. 81–4.

5. A. Kramer, *The West German Economy 1945–1955* (Oxford, 1991), p. 86.

6. W. Abelshauser, *Wirtschaftsgeschichte der Bundersrepublik Deutschland 1945–1980* (Frankfurt am Main, 1983), pp. 20–7; W. Stolper and K. Roskamp, 'Planning a Free Economy: Germany 1945–1960', *Zeitschrift für die gesamte Staatswissenschaft* 135 (1979), 379.

because of Allied controls restricting production and trade and the poverty of much of the German population. In 1949, when the western zones became the new Federal Republic, manufacturing industry operated at only 63 per cent of its capacity.[7]

Most historians are agreed that the revival of the post-war economy depended not on material conditions but on political and psychological adjustment. Under the occupation German businessmen were reluctant to invest until they knew the long-term prospects for expansion. Producers and consumers resented the command economy imposed on them, and feared inflation and economic disorder. This situation was reversed in 1948 when the western zones were given a new currency – the Deutschmark – and the limited restoration of a free market. The currency reform of 20/1 June 1948 provided a foundation for stable prices and wages, and a framework for the revival of the productive industrial economy. Debts, including over 400 billion Reichsmarks of debt accumulated from the war, were wiped out and savings sharply reduced. The reform favoured work and production against creditor interests. In the six months following the reform, industrial output increased by 50 per cent, and the length of the average working week also increased significantly.[8] The following year the Federal Republic was established and the network of controls and regulations imposed since 1945 was gradually unravelled. Restrictions on trade remained in force until 1950, and prohibitions on the production of certain goods for longer, but by 1951 economic sovereignty was fully restored. Both government and people welcomed the increased liberalization of the economy, and embarked on a rush for growth.

The change in the political framework was clearly an essential first step, not because the Allies prevented growth – revival began even before the currency reform – but because there was an overwhelming desire among the German public to control their own economic affairs. The practical effects of the change should not be exaggerated. The Federal economy faced serious problems in 1949. Currency reform produced short-term unemployment, made worse by the yearly influx of refugees and expellees from Eastern Europe. The balance of payments remained heavily in the red. Capital was in very short supply. Wages and labour productivity remained low. Although the 1936 level of overall industrial

7. Kramer, *West German Economy*, p. 168.

8. R. Klump, *Wirtschaftsgeschichte der Bundesrepublik Deutschland: zur Kritik neuerer wirtschaftshistorischer Interpretationen aus ordnungspolitischer Sicht* (Wiesbaden, 1985), p. 59. Average hours worked per week were 39.1 in 1947, 42.4 in 1948 and 46.5 in 1949. On the wider impact of currency reform see W. Carlin, 'Economic Reconstruction in Western Germany, 1945–1955', in Turner, ed., *Reconstruction*, pp. 53–8.

production was reached in 1950, the rest of Western Europe produced one-fifth more than in 1936. By 1952 trade was back to the 1938 level, but in Britain it was 40 per cent higher and in France 60 per cent.[9] The new economy needed foreign funds to expand production and between 1948 and 1950 $2,031 million was made available from relief and reconstruction funds, mainly from the United States, including $714 million of Marshall Aid.[10] There were fears that the stagnation of the 1920s might be repeated, along with the dangerous dependence on American money exposed by the slump of 1929.

The Federal economy was saved from stagnation by the buoyant growth of the world economy during the 1950s and the sustained demand this generated for Germany's traditional high-value exports, machinery, chemicals, electro-technical equipment and vehicles. After almost 40 years of reduced export demand and growing dependence on the poorer home market, the Federal economy experienced an export boom in the 1950s and 1960s that dragged the rest of the economy along with it, and solved the problems of unemployment, trade deficits and capital shortage inherited in 1949. High levels of foreign trade released the potential in the Federal economy that the home market, with low wages and low savings, could not.

Of course there was a great deal more to the revival in the 1950s than a favourable world market. The promotion of trade became a government priority, 'the highest and most fundamental concern of every German economic and trade policy', as one Economics Ministry official put it in 1955.[11] German producers enjoyed a number of advantages over their competitors. With under-utilized capacity and low wages, German industrial goods were cheaper on world markets; in addition, German industry was geared to producing the kind of high-quality, high-value capital goods and equipment that both the developing world and a reviving European economy wanted. These were all areas of high growth potential, and they were given tax concessions and subsidies to maximize that growth.

Export-led growth reflected the priorities of the new regime in 1949. Federal economic policy was dominated by the views of the so-called

9. H. Studders, *Zur Integration der europäischen Arbeitskraft: Bevölkerungs- und arbeitsstatistische Unterlagen* (Frankfurt am Main, 1952), p. 68; H. J. Jung, *Die Exportförderung im wirtschaftlichen Wiederaufbau der deutschen Bundesrepublik* (Cologne, 1957), p. 128.

10. Stolper and Roskamp, 'Planning a Free Economy', 390–1; M. Knapp, 'Reconstruction and West-Integration: The Impact of the Marshall Plan on Germany', *Zeitschrift für die gesamte Staatswissenschaft* 137 (1981), 421–4. Knapp estimates that the total of all aid granted to Germany after the war was $3.157 billion. About one-third of this sum was paid back to the United States by 1966.

11. Jung, *Exportförderung*, p. 129.

Freiburg school of political economists, who argued for the restoration of a strong market mechanism, vigorous and unrestricted competition, and a state apparatus designed to promote the market rather than distort or inhibit it. At the heart of this economic outlook was a concern with social development, a belief that a healthy and efficient market economy was the best way to secure social stability and effective welfare provision. This was not a full liberal or *laissez-faire* economy by any means. Walter Eucken, one of the leading spokesmen of the theory of the 'social market economy', suggested that the state took responsibility to provide the conditions for a 'viable and humane economic order', but should not actually direct the economic process itself.[12] Over the course of the 1950s, under the guidance of Ludwig Erhard, Minister of Economics from 1949 to 1963, the state gradually relinquished its remaining physical controls, including the privatization of most state-run industry inherited in 1949, while at the same time restrictions on free competition retained by German industry from the protectionist inter-war years (cartels in particular) were reduced.

The 'social market economy' as it developed in the 1950s was far from being a free market in any liberal sense, while the low level of wages and social expenditure made it a relatively poor social model too. But what the Erhard years did provide was the stable environment for growth lacking since the early 1900s. Underlying the trade boom was a commitment to a stable price level, low wage increases and high levels of productive investment. Foreign earnings and tax concessions made it possible for firms to make exceptionally high profits by the 1950s. Until 1960, private business was the most important source of savings, much of which was ploughed back into productive investment. Between 1949 and 1957 over DM28 billion was granted to industry in tax concessions. The net effect of high profits and generous subsidy was an exceptionally high investment ratio, over a quarter of the national product between 1955 and 1965.[13] Consumption was squeezed in favour of investment during the growth years. Ordinary Germans saved in preference to spending in the belief, encouraged by official publicity, that future prosperity depended on the rapid development of the productive economy.[14]

High export growth, price stability and exceptional levels of domestic

12. Stolper and Roskamp, 'Planning a Free Economy', 377. On the impact of the Freiburg school see A. J. Nicholls, *Freedom with Responsibility: The Social Market Economy in Germany 1918–1963* (Oxford, 1994), esp. pp. 136–55.

13. W. Glastetter, G. Högemann and R. Marquardt, *Die wirtschaftliche Entwicklung in der Bundesrepublik Deutschland 1950–1989* (Frankfurt am Main, 1991), p. 89.

14. Lieberman, *Mixed Economies*, pp. 52–4.

Table 1.1: Selected statistics on economic development, 1950–60

Year	Real national income (per capita, 1913 prices [DM])	Unemployment (millions)	Index of industrial production (1950 = 100)	Balance of trade (billion DM)
1950	845	1.58	100	–3.0
1951	922	1.43	118	–0.15
1952	993	1.38	126	0.7
1953	1,065	1.25	139	2.5
1954	1,138	1.17	155	2.6
1955	1,272	0.93	178	1.2
1956	1,350	0.76	192	2.8
1957	1,414	0.66	202	4.2
1958	1,442	0.68	208	5.8
1959	1,514	0.54	224	5.3
1960	1,633	0.27	249	5.2

Source: H.C. Wallich, 'Thirty Years of German Surpluses', *Zeitschrift für die gesamte Staatswissenschaft* 135 (1979), 481; W. Stolper and K. Roskamp, 'Planning a Free Economy: Germany 1945–1960', *Zeitschrift für die gesamte Staatswissenschaft* 135 (1979), 375, 379, 393; A. Kramer, *The West German Economy, 1945–1955* (Oxford, 1991), p. 183.

investment turned the German economy in ten years back to the trajectory of high growth interrupted in 1914 (see Table 1.1). But much of the 'economic miracle' involved the recovery of past growth levels, or the utilization of idle resources, or the reconstruction of wartime damage. Steel production, for example, was 23 million tons in 1938, but only 9 million in 1949. Not until 1956 was the pre-war figure recovered.[15] House construction and the rebuilding of Germany's shattered cities played a key part in sustaining those sectors of the domestic economy not engaged in export; between 1949 and 1959 5 million new dwellings were built. Even in the 1960s house construction ran at over half a million per year.[16] High growth also owed a good deal to the state of the labour market. Unemployment reached over 10 per cent of the workforce in 1950, and did not decline significantly until 1955. During the 1950s a net inflow of 2.8 million immigrants boosted labour supply. Between 1953 and 1958 2.2 million refugees, expellees and returning prisoners of war crossed into the Federal Republic from the east.[17] The

15. Statistisches Bundesamt, *Die Eisen- und Stahlindustrie: Statistische Vierteljahreshefte* (Düsseldorf, 1959).

16. Diefendorf, *In the Wake of War*, pp. 18–42; J. Rohwäder, *Die Geldpolitik der Deutschen Bundesbank zwischen 1969 und 1982 im Lichte von Monetarismus und Keynesianismus* (Hamburg, 1990), Table 18.

17. Statistisches Bundesamt, *Die Wanderungen im Jahr 1958* (Stuttgart, 1959), pp. 19–20; H. Körner, *Der Zustrom von Arbeitskräften in die Bundesrepublik Deutschland 1950–1972* (Frankfurt am Main, 1976), pp. 322–3.

new workers accepted lower wages, which in turn helped to hold down German prices. Labour also flowed into industry from agriculture, where a programme of state-sponsored modernization raised yields and reduced labour requirements.

Once the period of reconstruction was over and resources more fully utilized, the Federal economy was faced with a new set of problems more characteristic of a mature industrial economy. By 1958 the Federal Republic achieved full employment, and the economy was faced with problems of labour scarcity for the first time. The upward pressure on wages, which began to rise faster than levels of productivity between 1958 and 1962, threatened the strategy of price stability and revived fears of inflation. While the overall rate of growth of the economy and the trade surplus slowed down, prices began to edge upwards. Between 1960 and 1965 the Federal Republic was overtaken by France and Italy as the growth leader in Europe. These changes, while not critical, coincided with the period in which residual state controls and trade restrictions were lifted in the name of market economics. Just when the neo-liberal ambition to free the economy from intervention reached its apogee, a number of pressures forced the state to assume a much larger role in the economy than hitherto. Increases in welfare provision, education and health expenditure produced a doubling of the state budget between 1955 and 1965. By 1970 state expenditure was three times the level of 1955. The state debt, which had been progressively reduced during the 1950s as a proportion of Gross National Product (GNP), began to rise steeply in the mid-1960s.[18]

It would be wrong to argue that the Federal economy faced a serious crisis in the mid-1960s, but in a state with memories of inflation and the slump still fresh, the economic slow-down carried risks which German statesmen felt bound to respond to. During 1966 both the national product and industrial production grew at their lowest level since 1949; the following year both actually fell in real terms for the first time, while inflation and unemployment both rose. For Ludwig Erhard, who had become German Chancellor in 1963, the recession was a political body-blow from which he failed to recover. In December 1966 he was replaced as Chancellor by Kurt Kiesinger, who led a 'Grand Coalition' of right and left pledged to tackle economic crisis and restore growth.

The fall of Erhard brought a sharp change in the relationship between state and economy. The strategy of liberalization and microeconomic regulation gave way to a period of increased state regulation and macro-

18. Braun, *The German Economy*, pp. 199–201.

economic steering. The strategies adopted in the 1950s had been appropriate for an economy with large under-used resources riding the back of a world boom. In the 1960s the boom slowed down, competition increased in export markets, and the domestic economy moved from a situation where it absorbed spare capacities to one in which new capacity had to be created by raising productivity and encouraging structural changes in the economy. The change in economic strategy in 1967 was closely associated with the Economics Minister of the coalition, Professor Karl Schiller. A Keynesian in outlook, Schiller rejected the self-regulatory, free market model of the Freiburg school in favour of state economic management to smooth out the business cycle, maintain monetary stability and establish external equilibrium. He was not opposed to the market mechanism, but he recognized its limitations. His principle was 'as much competition as possible, as much planning as necessary'.[19]

In 1967 Schiller launched the first government anti-cyclical financial programme with the aim of reviving domestic demand and cutting unemployment. Tax incentives, selected state investment programmes and interest rate manipulation produced an immediate response and within a year the economy was growing again at an accelerated rate. Schiller also favoured more state planning to fix the medium-term conditions for economic growth, and to control money markets, prices and wages. In June 1967 parliament passed a Law to Promote the Stability of Economic Growth to allow the Federal authorities to operate the new strategy of economic management. In December 1967 a further law introduced five-year fiscal planning, and the co-ordination of federal, provincial and municipal budgets. A new corporativism was introduced, with government, business leaders and trade union representatives meeting regularly to agree on incomes policies that would maximize stability.

From 1967 to 1982 the Federal economy maintained a commitment to state economic steering with the aim of maintaining stability while encouraging growth. Though growth rates were considerably lower than the 1950s – an average of 3.5 per cent from 1968 to 1975, and 2.3 per cent from 1976 to 1982 – the trajectory of growth remained steadily upward. By 1980 the Gross Domestic Product (GDP) of the Federal Republic measured in constant prices was three-and-a-half times the size it had been in 1950 (see Table 1.2).[20] But greater state management came at a price. The public debt, which remained low by international standards in the 1950s and 1960s, rose sharply during the 1970s. The economic downturn in 1974–75 produced by the international oil price

19. Ibid., p. 184; Nicholls, *Freedom with Responsibility*, pp. 365, 372–4.
20. Glastetter *et al.*, *wirtschaftliche Entwicklung*, pp. 43, 50.

Table 1.2: Growth rates in the Federal German economy, 1950–89

Years	GDP	Exports	Capital stock	Labour productivity (output per man-hour)
		(1980 prices) (percentage change, yearly average)		
1950–58	8.2	—	4.5	6.8
1959–67	4.8	6.9	6.5	5.6
1968–75	3.5	7.0	5.1	4.8
1976–82	2.3	5.3	3.5	2.5
1983–89	2.5	3.2	2.7	2.7

Source: W. Glastetter, G. Högemann and R. Marquardt, *Die wirtschaftliche Entwicklung in der Bundesrepublik Deutschland 1950–1989* (Frankfurt am Main, 1991), pp. 50, 191.

crisis of 1973 marked the point at which public authorities adopted the practice wholeheartedly of spending their way out of recession. In 1970 public debt was 16 per cent of GNP; by 1975 it was 26 per cent; by 1982 over 40 per cent. With high education and welfare costs and higher levels of state investment, the share of the state (both Federal and local authorities) in GNP rose from 31 per cent in 1960 to reach 49 per cent by 1982. Public sector employment rose 250 per cent between 1950 and 1985. It is, of course, no coincidence that the period in which the state once again increased its economic role was a period dominated politically by the Social Democrats. There was widespread public hostility towards the Erhard model of growth, which had in practice emphasized market capitalism at the expense of social concerns. During the 1970s the ideal of the 'social market' was shifted in favour of social goals – low unemployment, adequate social opportunities, income redistribution. Under Helmut Schmidt, first as Economics Minister, then as Chancellor from 1974 to 1982, a balance was struck between market forces and the wider interests of the West German population.

State intervention was not enough on its own to sustain growth after 1967, though the mix of interventionist policies did succeed in keeping German inflation below world levels, and running a lower level of unemployment. What was also needed was the means to raise output and productivity levels in an environment of full employment and slower world growth. A particular concern was to maintain the momentum of exports against strong competition. By the 1970s the Federal economy was heavily dependent on exports. Almost one-quarter of the national product and one-fifth of the workforce derived from the export trade.[21]

21. Abelshauser, *Wirtschaftsgeschichte*, pp. 148, 164. Exports as a share of net national product were 9.3 per cent in 1950, 17.2 per cent in 1960, 23.8 per cent in 1970 and 26.7 per cent in 1980.

To maintain the competitiveness of exports another legacy of the Erhard years was gradually removed. Where the neo-liberals had favoured the dismantling of cartels and market restrictions and were hostile to industrial concentration, the trend after 1967 was in the opposite direction. A wave of mergers in the 1970s produced a sharp structural shift in German industry towards large firms and oligopolistic markets. The top 50 enterprises in 1960 controlled one-third of Federal industrial output; by 1980 they controlled one-half.[22] Many German firms began to invest heavily abroad, reproducing the modern multinational in an economy that had had very low levels of overseas investment since 1914. In 1955 only DM420 million was invested abroad; between 1966 and 1974 German businesses invested DM27 billion outside the Republic.[23]

Larger firms brought their own advantages. Research, development and marketing were conducted in general more efficiently. They could respond to market changes more easily; they cooperated more directly with government; they encouraged the shift, evident across the economies of the developed world, towards professional managerial structures and rational organization. The German banking system underwent the same transformation, offering a wider range of services, concentrating in larger and larger financial units, rationalizing the conduct of the private capital market.[24] The structural changes were matched by the state's ambition to encourage productivity growth as the only way to avoid the 'stagflation' – stagnant growth and high inflation – experienced by other mature economies. Levels of technical training were raised and an ethos of efficiency stimulated by the regime. The popular term for Federal society in the 1970s, the *Leistungsgesellschaft* or society based on performance and competence, reflected the deeper needs of the economy to encourage higher skill ratios in the workforce and a more productive commercial sector. The emphasis on achievement helped to compensate to some extent for the sharp fall in investment activity in the Republic during the 1970s and 1980s. High levels of investment peaked between 1959 and 1967 (26 per cent of GNP), and declined to only 20 per cent of GNP between 1983 and 1989, with particularly sharp falls in investment activity in the mid-1970s and the early 1980s.[25] This decline went hand-

22. E. O. Smith, *The West German Economy* (London, 1983), p. 287; J. Cable, J. Palfrey and J. Runge, 'Economic Determinants and Effects of Mergers in West Germany 1964–1974', *Zeitschrift für die gesamte Staatswissenschaft* 136 (1980), 226.

23. H. Schröter, 'Aussenwirtschaft im Boom: Direktinvestitionen bundesdeutscher Unternehmen im Ausland 1950–1975', in H. Kaelble, ed., *Der Boom 1948–1973* (Opladen, 1992), pp. 82–90.

24. L. Mülhaupt, *Strukturwandlungen im westdeutschen Bankwesen* (Wiesbaden, 1971), pp. 391–2.

25. Glastetter *et al.*, *wirtschaftliche Entwicklung*, pp. 79, 96.

in-hand with a steady fall in the productivity of capital. Crude labour productivity, on the other hand, expressed in terms of hourly output per worker, continued to grow steadily across the whole period from 1967 to 1989, at a rate that closely matched the overall performance of the Federal economy.[26]

German growth since the late 1960s was based on higher levels of state economic management, coupled to structural changes in the industrial economy and the enhanced efficiency of the German workforce. State deregulation, high investment and increased labour input were the components of the initial phase of recovery. Some historians have detected a third phase in the development of the Federal economy dating from 1982 and the return of a conservative Christian-Democrat government under Helmut Kohl. The new government announced an economic *Wende*, or turning-point, to indicate a move away from state economic management and high social spending. Germany's version of Thatcherism brought limited privatization of state assets, reductions in some social services, and a streamlining of the bureaucracy. But the desire to maintain employment with low inflation required a strong state presence in the economy. The same factors that sustained growth in the 1970s – high exports, industrial restructuring, price stability, improved labour productivity – sustained growth in the 1980s, if at a lower level.

The problems of the Federal economy were the problems of success. With the arrival of widespread prosperity German wage costs became the highest in the world. Where ordinary Germans had accepted the need in the 1950s for wage restraint and high savings, by the 1970s and 1980s they wanted high social spending and the fruits of a wealthy consumer society. With high export surpluses the Deutschmark had to be regularly revalued, forcing German exporters to compete against foreign economies with lower wage costs and weaker currencies. It was in the context of slowing growth and high state spending that the Federal economy was united with the East German provinces in the summer of 1990. The immediate effect was to bring a sharp down-

26. Ibid., p. 50. The figures are as follows:

Years	Labour productivity (output per man-hour)	Capital productivity
	(average annual % change)	
1950–8	6.8	3.5
1959–67	5.6	–1.6
1968–75	4.8	–1.5
1976–82	2.5	–1.1
1983–89	2.7	–0.1

turn in both economies: the former Federal economy was faced with the enormous costs of absorbing a weak and relatively less developed region against a background of world recession, while the former East German economy was exposed to market pressures which its old-fashioned and less-productive industrial structure could not cope with. Between June and September 1990 the industrial output of the eastern provinces fell to less than half the level of 1989.[27] Unemployment rose in both the eastern and western areas. The Federal economy entered a period of stagnation as it transferred high social expenditure and large funds for investment into the eastern provinces. State expenditure was just over DM1,000 billion in 1989; in 1993 it reached DM1,682 billion, or 59 per cent of the national product.[28] The same year German exports fell 6 per cent, and the overall growth rate by 2.4 per cent. 'Capitalist restoration' was finally achieved in eastern Germany at precisely the time that its wealthy western partner was trying to come to terms with the slackening of capitalist momentum.

EXPORTS: THE ECONOMIC PACE-MAKER

In the 40 years of the Federal economy the performance of the export sector was consistently favourable. In every year from 1952 there was a trade surplus, often of generous proportions. Historically Germany had experienced persistent balance of payments difficulties. Germany's export performance since 1914 had failed to regain the position enjoyed before the war. During the period of the Third Reich trade was restricted by world-wide protectionism and by the preferences of the regime for strategies of self-sufficiency and economic isolation. After 1949 the regime sought a revolution in Germany's relationship with the wider world economy: integration rather than isolation, open trade rather than a siege economy. This was an understandable choice. The desire to forge close trading links with the Western world paralleled the development of political and military integration.[29] It also made economic sense in a world-wide climate of trade liberalization provoked by American insist-

27. H. Klodt, 'Wirtschaftshilfe für die neuen Bundesländer', *Wirtschaftsdienst* 70 (1990), 619.

28. *Statistisches Jahrbuch für die BRD 1994* (Wiesbaden, 1994), p. 515; unemployment figures in *Wirtschaft und Statistik* 3 (1995), 158.

29. W. Hankel, 'Germany's Economic Nationalism in the International Economy', in W. L. Kohl and G. Baseri, eds, *West Germany: A European and Global Power* (Lexington, Mass., 1980), pp. 23–7.

ence that the post-1945 economic order should turn its back on the narrow economic nationalism of the 1930s. German exporters could work within a stable world environment for trade for the first time for almost 40 years.

This does not explain why German exporters were able to exploit the favourable trade climate so successfully. In the early 1950s they faced a number of obstacles. There was a natural prejudice against the revival of German trade in markets which were now dominated by American or British exports. Germany had almost no overseas assets as a base to facilitate a trade drive. For more than a decade German businesses had been cut off from the wider world economy by war and occupation. Two factors combined to set aside these disadvantages. During the 1950s the Deutschmark was undervalued in terms of other currencies and German goods enjoyed a price advantage against major competitors. In the second place there developed buoyant world-wide demand for just those products which the Federal economy was in a position to provide – capital equipment, machinery, electro-technical goods. The trigger for this demand is usually ascribed to the Korean war boom from 1951 to 1953, when demand for heavy equipment usually secured in the United States was switched to German producers. But the effects of the boom should not be exaggerated. It did allow an entry back into international markets for German firms, but the sustained growth of exports in the 1950s and 1960s owed much more to the industrial development of the rest of Western Europe, and a wider circle of states outside Europe where economic modernization was beginning in earnest. By the 1960s approximately 85 per cent of German exports went to the developed states, two-thirds to other European countries.

The structure of Federal exports reflected the traditional areas of German industrial strength. Exports were overwhelmingly based on manufactured products. In 1959 manufactures made up 82 per cent of all exports by value; in the 1980s the proportion averaged 85 per cent.[30] In 1959 chemicals, machinery, vehicles, electro-technical goods, precision instruments and metal goods represented 78 per cent of manufactured exports.[31] German firms developed a reputation for providing complex, customized engineering products which exploited the depth of technical competence and traditions of innovation in Germany's heavy industrial sectors. Yet the goods did not simply sell themselves. The major strength of the German export sector from the 1950s can be

30. *Statistisches Jahrbuch 1994*, p. 297; Bundesminister für Wirtschaft, *Die wirtschaftliche Lage in der BDR* (Wiesbaden, Jan. 1960), pp. 36–7.

31. *Die wirtschaftliche Lage*, p. 37. Machinery was the largest sector (22 per cent of manufactured exports), followed by vehicles (16 per cent) and chemicals (15 per cent).

found in the marketing strategies adopted to ease German businesses back into world markets.

German firms were under greater pressures than their rivals to sell vigorously because they were competing against established competitors. They made careful research of foreign markets and matched the product range and advertising campaigns to perceived gaps. A large and well-trained commercial workforce was sent abroad to establish effective promotion and after-sales networks. Money was invested long term, even in markets where German export penetration was low, on the basis that an established network would eventually pay dividends. German firms acquired the enviable reputation for punctual delivery times and the regular supply of spare parts. They were able to supply generous credit terms as the export boom developed. In the case of Krupp in the 1960s these terms were so generous for contracts in Eastern Europe that the firm was brought to the brink of bankruptcy because of poor levels of repayment. So successful was the commercial drive abroad that one German firm, Volkswagen, was able to do what no other European car firm had done, to sell in volume in the United States in competition with the largest mass-production motor industry in the world. Volkswagen was a classic example of careful market research. The car was targeted at specific sections of the population – students, young professionals – or it was promoted as a second car for successful families. Strong promotion of the image (not an easy task given its Nazi origins) included the establishment of 500 dealerships selling only Volkswagen, which produced half a million sales by 1960. In the 1960s annual sales averaged 400,000.[32]

The history of the Volkswagen abroad shows that there was nothing miraculous about the export boom. German firms produced good-quality products that customers wanted to buy, and they sold them through aggressive marketing techniques and intelligent attention to customer service. They also benefited from conditions in the German home market. Government commitment to price stability meant that German prices rose more slowly than world prices, improving the competitive position of German products. Low labour costs had the same effect. Exporters were also the beneficiaries of more direct state assistance. Credit facilities were supplied by public bodies; tax concessions and subventions were directed at key export sectors; the state pursued an active economic policy abroad aimed at reducing market restrictions and encouraging stable conditions for trade. The Federal government

32. F. Vogl, *German Business after the Economic Miracle* (London, 1973), pp. 111–13; W. Nelson, *Small Wonder: The Amazing story of the Volkswagen* (London, 1967), pp. 218–26.

played a major role in GATT negotiations, and in liberalizing trade within the OEEC and, from 1957, within the Common Market.[33] The government also acted to reduce the inflationary pressures produced by large export earnings. In 1961 the Deutschmark was finally revalued to take account of almost a decade of high foreign earnings and to pacify the objections of trading partners who found they could sell much less in Germany than they bought from it.

The revaluation temporarily made German goods more expensive, but it made little long-term difference to export growth, partly because of gains in domestic productivity, partly because German prices continued to lag behind world prices, so that German goods once again became highly competitive. But the revaluation highlighted a problem that became characteristic of trade growth in the 1970s and 1980s: large surpluses and price stability made the Deutschmark a strong currency and aggravated the long-term trend of currency revaluation and higher German export prices. In this second period businesses in the Federal Republic had to find new ways to maintain their competitive edge. The turning-point came in 1969 when, following both a British and French devaluation, the Deutschmark was revalued against major currencies. Despite widespread fears that German exporters would be unable to maintain high sales, the trade surplus reached record levels in the 1970s, averaging almost DM32 billion a year against DM8.75 billion in the 1960s.[34] Further revaluations in the 1970s, and a strong currency in the European Monetary System in the 1980s, similarly failed to dent German export strength. In the 1980s the export surplus averaged DM75 billion a year.[35]

There are a number of explanations for the success of German export industries in the context of an appreciating currency after 1969. Despite increased prices for German exports, the German price level remained below the world inflation rate, and considerably lower than inflation in Britain or the United States (see Table 1.3). Each currency revaluation was soon compensated for by lower levels of domestic inflation, which helped to make German products more competitive. The striking expansion of exports following revaluation also reflected the nature of many German products whose sale was not acutely price-sensitive. Many German products relied on quality, after-sales service or technical complexity to maintain market shares. Customers bought German goods on

33. Jung, *Exportförderung*, pp. 126–32; W. Hager, 'Germany as an Extraordinary Trader', in Kohl and Baseri, eds, *West Germany*, pp. 3–4.

34. H. Wallich and J. Wilson, 'Thirty Years (Almost) of German Surpluses', *Zeitschrift für die gesamte Staatswissenschaft* 135 (1979), 483.

35. *Statistisches Jahrbuch 1994*, p. 297.

Table 1.3: German and world prices, 1973–78

Year (1972 = 100)	World market prices	German export prices	German cost of living	DM/$ parity
1973	150	106.4	106.0	83.4
1974	251.7	124.5	114.4	81.2
1975	229.2	129.4	121.2	77.2
1976	241.6	134.3	126.7	78.9
1977	266.4	136.6	131.7	72.8
1978	265.3	137.7	135.5	65.4

Source: W. Hankel, 'Germany's Economic Nationalism in the International Economy', in W. L. Kohl and G. Baseri, eds, *West Germany: a European and Global Power* (Lexington, Mass., 1980), p. 28.

grounds other than price alone. In product sectors where price mattered more, German producers accepted considerably lower profit margins in the 1970s to maintain output and sales, and passed on these losses to their domestic customers.[36] Levels of research and development spending were raised to maintain German technical leads. As the growth of demand for capital goods slackened in Europe, German exporters switched to the developing world, which was generating a new wave of demand for the goods necessary for modernization. Between 1969 and 1975 the proportion of exports going to the developing countries rose from one-fifth to one-quarter.[37]

The greatest change came about in marketing. In the more competitive environment of the 1970s and 1980s German businesses, many of which were small in scale and highly specialized by international standards, began a process of amalgamation and concentration to increase their power in the market and to share the escalating costs of research, development and foreign marketing networks. This was particularly the case with the German machine-tool industry, where 50 per cent of products were exported. The specialized custom-built machinery which the industry supplied was produced by a large number of small and medium-sized firms. Revaluation and rising domestic wage rates forced the businesses to merge in order to cut costs and rationalize production

36. Wallich and Wilson, 'German Surpluses', 486–9; Braun, *The German Economy*, pp. 246–8, who emphasizes technological competitiveness; Hager, 'Germany as an Extraordinary Trader', pp. 4–6, who emphasizes marketing skills and the structural adaptability of German industry.

37. H. Dicke, *Strukturwandel im westdeutschen Strassenfahrzeugbau* (Tübingen, 1978), Appendix Table A36; on research and development see Smith, *West German Economy*, p. 52. In 1978 the Federal Republic was second only to the USA in R & D expenditure per head, DM388 to DM409. Expenditure in France was DM289 per head, in Britain only DM184.

and sales. Other sectors sought to merge with foreign competitors to match the size and marketing power of large American or Japanese corporations. The Agfa camera company merged with the Belgian firm of Gevaert to avoid collapse; Siemens merged in 1972 with the Dutch firm Philips and the French firm Compagnie Internationale pour L'informatique to rationalize the selling of computers in the European market. Some businesses failed to respond effectively. Zeiss, Agfa's main German rival, was forced out of the mass camera market by Japanese competition; the Federal ship-building industry survived a serious crisis early in the 1970s only by seeking state subsidies and restoring what were in effect cartel practices.[38]

Adaptation to the new market conditions, though it brought its share of business casualties, and higher levels of state assistance than the freer market of the 1960s, did produce a strong surge of exports in the mid-1970s, and again in the mid-1980s, when in 1986 and 1987 the Federal Republic became the world's largest exporter, and trade surpluses ran annually at more than DM100 billion (see Table 1.4). Success on such a scale revived the problems of the 1950s, when surpluses threatened to fuel domestic inflation or to produce retaliation from other traders. But from the 1970s the pattern of the Federal Republic's balance of payments served to counteract the potential problems of a strong balance of trade. From 1970 the balance on invisibles (services, tourism, etc.) produced a rising deficit with the rest of the world, caused largely by the flood of German holidaymakers abroad. Transfer payments also produced a strong deficit. Foreign workers in Germany (almost three million by the early 1970s) sent wages back to their home countries, while German businesses began to invest heavily abroad. By the mid-1970s over DM36 billion was invested abroad, 60 per cent of it in Europe; by the mid-1980s German firms had DM44 billion in the United States alone.[39] These movements out of the Republic produced much lower current account surpluses than the raw balance of trade figures suggest. This helped to reduce domestic inflationary pressures, and to keep German products competitive. Above all it provided other countries with the means to purchase German goods. Without high export sales the Federal Republic would almost certainly have experienced higher unemployment and lower growth after 1970.

Exports have played a critical part in the development of the Federal economy since the early 1950s. They help to explain the strength of

38. Vogl, *German Business*, pp. 114–17.

39. Schröter, 'Aussenwirtschaft', pp. 90, 99; Wallich and Wilson, 'German Surpluses', 484–6; H. E. Scharrer, 'Die Finanzierung deutscher Direktinvestitionen im Ausland', *Wirtschaftsdienst* 70 (1991), 43–50.

Table 1.4: Trade and current account statistics, 1950–93

Year	Exports	Imports	Balance of trade	Current account balance
			(billion DM)	
1950	8.4	11.4	–3.0	–0.2
1951	14.6	14.7	–0.1	–0.4
1952	16.9	16.2	0.7	2.5
1953	18.5	16.0	2.5	3.9
1954	21.9	19.3	2.6	3.7
1955	25.6	24.5	1.1	2.2
1956	30.7	28.0	2.7	4.5
1957	35.8	31.7	4.1	5.9
1958	36.8	31.1	5.7	6.0
1959	41.0	35.8	5.2	4.2
1960	47.8	42.7	5.1	4.8
1961	51.0	44.4	6.6	3.2
1962	53.0	49.5	3.5	–1.6
1963	58.3	52.3	6.0	1.0
1964	64.9	58.8	6.1	0.5
1965	71.7	70.4	1.3	–6.2
1966	80.6	72.7	7.9	0.5
1967	87.0	70.2	16.8	10.0
1968	99.6	81.2	18.4	11.9
1969	113.6	98.0	15.6	7.5
1970	125.3	109.6	15.7	3.2
1971	136.0	120.1	15.9	3.1
1972	149.0	128.7	20.3	2.5
1973	178.4	145.4	33.0	11.5
1974	230.6	179.7	50.9	25.4
1975	221.6	184.3	37.3	9.8
1976	256.6	222.2	34.4	9.7
1977	273.6	235.2	38.4	8.6
1978	284.9	243.7	41.2	16.1
1979	314.5	292.0	22.5	–11.2
1980	350.3	341.4	88.9	–28.5
1981	396.9	369.2	27.7	–12.4
1982	427.7	376.5	51.2	8.2
1983	432.3	390.2	42.1	10.5
1984	488.2	434.3	53.9	17.7
1985	537.2	463.8	73.4	48.3
1986	526.3	413.7	112.6	85.1
1987	527.4	409.6	117.8	82.5
1988	567.7	439.6	128.1	88.7
1989	641.0	506.5	134.5	107.6
1990	642.8	550.6	92.2	77.4

Source: *Statistisches Jahrbuch für die BRD*, 1953–92.

the long boom through to the 'Erhard recession' of 1966. They helped to sustain the high levels of output and employment, and the financial strength, that turned the Republic by the 1980s into an economic superpower. It has sometimes been argued that exports – which by the 1980s accounted for one-quarter of GNP – produced a dangerous dependence on the world economy during a period of relative economic instability after the oil crisis of 1973. This high level of dependence helps to explain why the Federal Republic took a major part in developing international market frameworks to secure long-term trade stability, and has continued to do so since unification in 1990. But the latent dangers of over-commitment to foreign trade have been offset by the cushion exports have provided in maintaining domestic output and employment and ending Germany's half-century of balance of payments problems. If export levels had stabilized at a much lower level, or if German trade had slumped dramatically following revaluations, the Republic would have run the much greater risk of emulating its weaker competitors, with high levels of unemployment, long periods of stagnant output and higher inflation.

PRICES, WAGES AND MONETARY STABILITY

The healthy export performance owed a good deal to the second plank of Federal economic strategy laid down in the 1950s: the pursuit, under all circumstances, of a stable currency and domestic price stability. There were sound historical reasons for the choice. Twice during the century Germany had suffered high inflation and currency collapse; twice, in 1924 and 1948, a new currency was established under the supervision of other powers. In the 1950s inflation was economic enemy number one. Price stability was economically desirable and politically necessary.

The initial commitment to monetary stabilization was associated with the first Federal Finance Minister from 1949 to 1957, Fritz Schäffer. He made his priority the fight against depreciation: 'the road to inflation goes over my dead body'.[40] The government promoted public awareness of the dangers of inflation, while monetary instruments – tax levels, interest rates, etc. – were used to keep the level of prices down, and to divert resources away from consumption towards investment in the productive

40. A. Zischka, *War es ein Wunder? Zwei Jahrzehnte deutschen Wiederaufstiegs* (Hamburg, 1966), p. 519.

economy. People were encouraged to save rather than spend; saving produced a high investment ratio and high gains in productivity; improvements in the efficiency of the productive economy in turn produced lower or stable prices in a world context of rising inflation. The high level of unemployment and under-utilized capacity in the domestic economy made the strategy of price stabilization a realistic ambition. Between 1955 and 1960 the price index of industrial goods rose only 6 per cent, an average of 1 per cent a year. In 1962 the Deutschmark was worth 86 per cent of its value in 1952, but the pound was worth only 75 per cent and the franc 70 per cent. Over the period from 1949 to 1960 the cost of living index rose 12 per cent, again at 1 per cent a year.[41]

The success of the strategy also relied on the attitude of workers and consumers. The government did not want to introduce a comprehensive prices and wages policy, with its echoes of Nazi *dirigisme*, yet it was essential in the early years of recovery to keep wage costs down and to divert resources away from consumption to savings and investment. The influx of immigrants in the 1950s, many of them willing to take work at low wages, helped to keep down the general level of wage costs. The new trade union organization, anxious to cooperate with government in creating a secure foundation for long-term growth, exercised constraint in the 1950s in wage negotiation. Wage levels rose more slowly during the 1950s than the growth of output and productivity (see Table 1.5). The same desire for economic security produced high savings ratios during the 1950s. The savings of private households expanded from DM2 billion in 1950 to almost DM15 billion in 1960.[42] The level of domestic consumption as a proportion of GNP fell sharply over the 1950s, from 68.8 per cent to 57.3 per cent. Consumers postponed expenditure in favour of high exports and high investment. The combination of modest wage settlements and a reduced propensity to consume complemented the practical efforts of the regime to achieve price stability.

In the 1960s the conditions governing that stability changed sharply. Wage rates under full employment began to move upwards at an accelerated pace. State expenditure rose substantially. A new generation of young workers and consumers, less affected by memories of past economic crises, was less inclined to accept voluntary wage restraint and modest consumption. The regime's commitment to monetary stability now came to rely less on conditions in the domestic economy, and more on the steady appreciation of the Deutschmark abroad. The external strength of the Deutschmark kept down import prices and maintained

41. Bundesminister für Wirtschaft, *Die wirtschaftliche Lage in der BRD* (Wiesbaden, 1960), p. 31; Zischka, *War es ein Wunder?*, p. 520.

42. Stolper and Roskamp, 'Planning a Free Economy', 389.

Table 1.5: Wages, productivity and industrial output, 1950–60

Year (1950 = 100)	Index of industrial production	Labour productivity (sales/workforce)	Earnings (wages/workforce)
1950	100	100	100
1951	118	123	115
1952	126	129	123
1953	139	131	128
1954	155	139	133
1955	178	152	141
1956	192	159	153
1957	202	165	159
1958	208	168	169
1959	224	183	178
1960	249	199	196

Source: E. von Knorring, *Lohn- und Beschäftigungsstruktur. Eine empirische Analyse für den industriellen Sektor der Bundesrepublik Deutschland im Zeitraum 1950–74* (Berlin, 1978); H. Jaspers, *Die Lohnstruktur in der Bundesrepublik Deutschland* (Essen, 1966).

strong domestic confidence in the currency. Between 1960 and 1988 the Federal Republic enjoyed on average a lower annual inflation rate than any other major developed economy.[43] The effect was to keep the growth of German export prices well below levels of world inflation despite regular revaluation. During the period of accelerating world inflation in the 1970s, triggered by the oil crisis of 1973, German export prices grew at 4.9 per cent a year. Only Switzerland had a better record (4.6 per cent). British prices rose on average by over 10 per cent a year, American and French prices by over 7 per cent, Japanese by 5.8 per cent.[44]

Nevertheless, even modest inflation rates alarmed the Federal government. In the period of the Grand Coalition after 1966 price stability remained a primary goal, and government policy was geared to reducing inflationary pressures through a combination of interventionist fiscal and monetary policies, and renewed efforts to keep wage settlements within the levels permitted by increases in productivity. Both business and labour broadly shared these ambitions. Productivity growth was regarded as the key to sustained income growth for the workforce and a low level of inflation. Over the whole period from 1950 to 1989 real per capita income in the Republic grew more slowly than the real rate of hourly productivity. As a result, the real burden of wage costs remained below

43. Glastetter *et al.*, *wirtschaftliche Entwicklung*, p. 170. The German average was inflation of 4 per cent a year; in Japan the figure was 5 per cent, USA 4.9 per cent, Britain 8.1 per cent, France 7 per cent.

44. Ibid., p. 193.

the 1950 level throughout the Republic's history.[45] Without the sustained productivity growth of labour, low levels of inflation would have been more difficult to achieve. As it was, German businesses accepted lower profit levels after 1960 in order to remain competitive abroad and to maintain employment and output. For both business and labour, price stability was in general preferred to high short-term income growth.

Though there are economic explanations for the long-term achievement of monetary stability, political and social factors have also played a significant part. The self-restraint shown by consumers and workers in the 1950s, like the acceptance later of lower profit margins and productivity-related wage settlements, reflected a consensus that the long-term stability of the Federal economy was worth the sacrifice. The long history of economic crisis and poverty before 1949 helped to create a psychological predisposition to accept sacrifices for the general health of the economy, and in the belief that long-term prosperity would result. The public discourse on economic development in the Republic was dominated by fears of inflation, and a loss of international competitiveness. The force of that fear may well have been sufficient to avert any need to adopt price or wage controls in an economy committed to a free market. Its effects are, of course, impossible to quantify, but the consequences of a popular commitment to price stability produced some of the defining characteristics of the Federal economy – high savings, sustained productivity growth and a strong currency.

INDUSTRY AND LABOUR

German industry entered the new Republic with a good deal of historical baggage. For almost 40 years market conditions had been exceptional; for the period from 1933 to 1949 businessmen had been forced to operate under more and more stringent economic controls. Their response had been in many cases defensive. Trade associations and cartels, designed to secure economic survival by restricting the operations of the market, became a central feature of German business life. During the Third Reich isolation from world markets and high levels of state contracting removed many of the usual pressures of the market and discouraged risk-taking. More than 2,000 cartels existed between the wars. The Nazi regime

45. Ibid., pp. 115, 117. The gap between real income growth and productivity growth actually widened faster after 1970.

made cartelization compulsory. Having relatively little control over the conditions governing the performance of individual firms, German businessmen became absorbed with conserving what they had, cautiously opportunistic rather than flamboyantly entrepreneurial. A whole generation grew up with the idea that price fixing and limited competition were to be preferred to the unfriendly conditions of liberal markets.

This tradition was entirely out of temper with the free market outlook of the Federal regime after 1949. The Western Allies, and in particular the American occupying authorities, were hostile to the cartel system. It was perceived to be a barrier both to freer international trade and to the effective revival of a liberal capitalist economy in the western zones. Major German businesses were broken up into smaller companies – IG Farben was reduced back to its three component firms, Bayer, BASF and Hoechst – and the big vertical trusts, mainly to be found in the iron, coal and steel sectors, were compelled to disintegrate. The occupying powers outlawed cartel agreements and restrictive practices of all kinds.[46] Erhard was also opposed to limitations on trade, particularly cartels, but he also needed to cooperate with the business community after 1949 in achieving economic revival. Much of the business community representing large-scale firms was hostile to the idea of outlawing cartels, and still favoured some form of 'organized capitalism' to counteract what they saw as the potentially damaging effects of an unregulated industrial market. The leading industrial association, the Bundesverband der Deutschen Industrie (BDI), orchestrated a campaign in the early 1950s for the restoration of traditional methods of market control.

The contest over the nature of industrial organization was a critical one in the long-run development of the Federal economy. Erhard, with American backing, saw anti-cartel legislation as the economic equivalent of the Basic Law setting up the new state in 1949. He wanted industry to reject the protectionist cast of mind inherited from the pre-war years and to embrace the American ideal of the modern, rationalized, market-orientated corporation. In 1952 a law banning cartels was introduced into the *Bundestag*. It was fiercely contested by business lobby groups and failed to become law until 1957. In the interim something of a compromise was reached. A younger generation of managers from German big business was attracted to the idea of integration with the

46. On IG Farben see R. G. Stokes, *Divide and Prosper: The Heirs of I. G. Farben under Allied Authority 1945–51* (Berkeley, 1989). On the process in general see V. Berghahn, *The Americanisation of West German Industry* (Leamington Spa, 1986), pp. 84–110. On the coal and steel industry see A. Diegmann, 'American Deconcentration Policy in the Ruhr Coal Industry', in J. Diefendorf, A. Frohn and H.-J. Rupieper, eds, *American Policy and the Reconstruction of West Germany, 1945–1955* (New York, 1993), pp. 198–214.

Western economy and freer markets, which reduced the power of the BDI to argue for unqualified restoration. Erhard did not want a long-running battle with business circles in the early years of a still unpredictable recovery. He conceded a number of clauses in the bill giving exemptions and emergency provisions for cartels, while the BDI accepted the formal banning of cartels and market restrictions.[47] A government cartel office monitored the operation of the legislation, but did so with a degree of flexibility.

It is arguable whether the anti-cartel movement of the 1950s was the factor chiefly responsible for turning German business away from its protectionist past. It is more likely that the extraordinary success of the Federal economy in its efforts to integrate with the Western world, with high profits, large export sales and selective state assistance, broke down the conservatism of the older business community, which was at last faced with a functioning market economy with prospects for long-run stability. Since the 1880s there had been an inverse correlation between the number of cartels in existence and the pace of economic growth: the more cartels, the lower the growth.[48] Whether the formation of cartels was a response to low growth, or a cause, is open to speculation. What is evident is that the decade when cartels were formally banned, the 1950s, saw the highest annual growth of the economy this century.

Successful economic growth also generated another change. The balance in the industrial economy tilted away rapidly from the traditional areas of manufacture towards the cluster of new industries – radio and television, motor vehicles, kitchen appliances, modern synthetic materials – which had no choice but to ape the production processes and marketing strategies of successful Western firms if they were to succeed. Iron, steel and coal were losing ground before 1939; by 1960 they supplied only 11.5 per cent of industrial output. Germany's largest industry in the 1970s was the motor industry.[49]

47. Berghahn, *Americanisation*, pp. 156–81; Smith, *West German Economy*, pp. 22–4.

48. Klump, *Wirtschaftsgeschichte*, p. 68. The figures are as follows:

Years	GNP growth rate (%)	Number of cartels
1880–90	3.4	50–60
1890–1910	2.7	400–500
1925–29	2.4	2,500 (1925)
1952–57	8.0	0*
1957–62	6.9	111 (1962)

* This represents official anti-cartel policy. Some unofficial cartel agreements were still in force.

49. A. Diekmann, *Die Automobilindustrie in der Bundesrepublik Deutschland* (Cologne, 1979), p. 18. Size is expressed in sales volume; in terms of employment the machinery sector was larger, 1,006,000 workers against 766,000 in the motor vehicles industry.

The German motor car industry was in many ways typical of the changing character of the industrial structure in the 1950s and 1960s. Because of the weaknesses of the inter-war German economy, the level of motorization in Germany was low compared with other developed states. The Hitler regime encouraged the development of the sector, but it was limited by low levels of exports and the competition for resources with rearmament. In the 1940s the vehicle stock declined.[50] In the following decade the situation was transformed. The level of motorization increased at 21 per cent a year, three times the level of GNP growth (see Table 1.6). Part of the explanation is that the German economy was simply catching up with the level of other developed states, but the success of the industry, in an international context of established volume vehicle producers, depended on keeping prices low and investing heavily in new plant and in new production techniques. State subsidies to business boosted vehicle demand in the early years. The industry also benefited from its close links with American experience. Two of the volume car producers, Ford in Cologne and the General Motors subsidiary, Adam Opel AG, obtained funds and expertise from their parent firms. The modernization of vehicle production generated exceptional levels of labour productivity – between 1953 and 1961 productivity expanded 127 per cent at Opel, 73 per cent at Daimler-Benz and 59 per cent at Volkswagen.[51] The industry made rapid strides in export markets. In 1951 one-third of car production was sold abroad; by 1963 the proportion was one-half. By the early 1960s the Federal motor industry exported more cars than any other country.[52] In the 1970s the industry exported two million vehicles a year and generated a large fraction of the trade surplus.[53] The success of the industry depended upon integration into the wider Western economy, open trade and modern methods of production and organization. The controlled trade and marketing agreements of the 1930s were left behind; open competition and a liberal trading environment were demonstrably more effective than protectionism in securing growth.[54]

50. F. Blaich, 'Why Did the Pioneer Fall Behind? Motorisation in Germany Between the Wars', in T. Barker, ed., *The Economic and Social Effects of the Spread of Motor Vehicles* (London, 1987), pp. 148–64; Diekmann, *Die Automobilindustrie*, p. 10. In 1938 there were 30 vehicles in Germany per 1,000 population; in 1950 only 11.

51. K. Busch, *Strukturwandlungen der westdeutschen Automobilindustrie* (Berlin, 1966), p. 72.

52. Ibid., pp. 40, 58.

53. Diekmann, *Die Automobilindustrie*, p. 18.

54. For a discussion of the issues explaining the success of the motor industry see S. Reich, *The Fruits of Fascism: Postwar Prosperity in Historical Perspective* (London, 1990), esp. chapters 4–5.

Table 1.6: Selected statistics on motorization in the Federal Republic

A Total vehicle stock 1950–90

Year	('000)
1950	1,149
1952	3,274
1954	4,699
1956	5,672
1958	6,498
1960	7,651
1962	9,714
1964	11,284
1966	13,146
1968	14,391
1970	16,783
1972	19,025
1974	20,633
1976	22,329
1978	24,814
1980	27,116
1982	28,452
1984	28,905
1986	31,748
1988	33,764
1990	35,748

B Output of cars and commercial vehicles 1950–70

Year	('000)
1950	301
1951	370
1952	424
1953	484
1954	674
1955	902
1956	1,070
1957	1,206
1958	1,488
1959	1,711
1960	2,047
1961	2,139
1962	2,343
1963	2,654
1964	2,897
1965	2,963
1966	3,035
1967	2,468
1968	3,091
1969	3,711
1970	3,825

Source: Statistisches Bundesamt, *Lange Reihen zur Wirtschaftsentwicklung* (Wiesbaden, 1982); idem, *Statistisches Jahrbuch für die BRD*, 1980–92.

The motor industry underwent what one historian has called the 'Americanization' of German industry. This was a process which owed something to the sudden increase in the number of American firms establishing subsidiaries in the Republic. Until June 1950 direct American investment in Germany was prohibited. By 1955 there were only 51 American-owned firms. By 1963 there were 186, by 1968 418 and in 1974 520, with a total capital of almost DM14 billion.[55] A great many German firms made the reverse trip. In 1949 Federal business had virtually no assets in America, but by the mid-1950s it had placed over 50 per cent of its overseas investment in the United States. In the early 1970s the capital value of investment by German industry in the United States was more than DM8 billion, by 1985 the figure was DM44 billion.[56] These figures reveal an important structural change. As German industry abandoned the defence of cartels and protection, it moved in the 1960s towards new forms of organization to cope with the competitive pressures of the world market.

In the domestic economy there developed a strong trend towards the concentration of industrial and banking activity in larger units, more capable of withstanding international competition, and better equipped to organize research, marketing and efficient labour use. Some of this reorganization was achieved through the reconstitution of cartel practices. By 1970 some 200 had been approved. But most of the restructuring occurred through merger. Until 1968 merger activity was low in German industry, running at only 30–40 a year. In the years 1968–70 there were 538, and throughout the 1970s they averaged almost 400 a year. Between 1960 and 1980 the top 50 enterprises in the Republic expanded their share of total industrial turnover from one-third to one-half, a process assisted by the traditional cooperation of Germany's largest banks, which by 1974 supplied directors in 75 of the 100 largest companies, and board chairmen in 37 cases.[57] Such developments were common to all developed economies, though more marked in Germany where there had been fewer giant companies in the 1960s. The merger movement also coincided with the accelerated growth of multinational business, as high-cost firms in the developed world transferred manufacture to developing countries, or bought up production facilities in developed economies to maintain volumes of sales and output. This

55. H. Kiesenwetter, 'Amerikanische Unternehmen in der Bundesrepublik Deutschland 1950–1974', in Kaelble, ed., *Der Boom*, pp. 74–5.

56. Schröter, 'Aussenwirtschaft', p. 99; Scharrer, 'Die Finanzierung', 43.

57. Klump, *Wirtschaftsgeschichte*, pp. 82–3; Cable *et al.*, 'Economic Determinants', 226, 246; W. Eckstein, 'The Role of Banks in Corporate Concentration in West Germany', *Zeitschrift für die gesamte Staatswissenschaft* 136 (1980), 466–70.

proved to be a comparatively successful adaptation for German industry, which shifted from growth based largely on expanded levels of domestic investment in modern production facilities, to growth based on structural and organizational changes produced by the international division of labour. De-industrialization was less pronounced in the Federal Republic than elsewhere. In 1980 44 per cent of the workforce was still engaged in industry, but in France the figure was 36 per cent and in the United States only 30 per cent.[58]

Labour entered the Federal Republic with historical baggage too. After years of enforced powerlessness, and a long history of confrontation with Germany's employer class and the German state, the relationship between labour and the new Republic was a critical element both for the recovery of a workable parliamentary system and for a successful industrial economy. Organized labour, like German business, was subject to considerable American pressure to avoid a political lurch to the left, and to reconstruct the trade union system on more modern, functional lines. The final outcome was a compromise between labour leaders who would have preferred a more socialized economy, and business leaders and the state who wanted to integrate labour on terms favourable to capitalist restoration. In 1947 a new trade union association was formed, the Deutscher Gewerkschaftsbund (DGB), and a single white-collar union set up, the Deutsche Angestelltengewerkschaft. Each of the 17 unions established represented a whole industry, to simplify wage negotiation and issues of demarcation. Under the influence of the veteran union leader Hans Böckler, the first chairman of the DGB, agreements were reached in 1949 on a national basis for collective bargaining. Two years later an agreement was reached under the *Mitbestimmungsgesetz* (Co-determination Law) to allow workers to provide half the directors in the iron, steel and coal sector. A year later in 1952, a supplementary law allowed workers to make up one-third of the board in other joint-stock companies. Any firm of more than five workers was entitled to a *Betriebsrat*, or works council. A further law in 1976 extended the original co-determination legislation for the steel and coal industry to cover any enterprise of more than 2,000 employees. Workers could make up to 50 per cent of the board of directors, though every board had a shareholder chairman with a casting vote to prevent full workers' control.[59]

58. H. van der Wee, *Prosperity and Upheaval: The World Economy 1945–1980* (London, 1987), p. 168.

59. P. Schwerdtner, 'Trade Unions in the German Economic and Social Order', *Zeitschrift für die gesamte Staatswissenschaft* 135 (1979), 456–62; M. E. Streit, 'Germany: Economic Developments, Problems and Policies', in J. Payne, ed., *Germany Today* (London, 1971), pp. 124–8; P. Hubsch, 'DGB Economic Policy with Particular Reference to the British Zone, 1945–49', in Turner, ed., *Reconstruction*, pp. 284–300.

Table 1.7: Days lost in strikes and lockouts, selected countries, 1972–75

Country	Days lost ('000)			
	1972	1973	1974	1975
USA	27,066	27,948	47,991	31,237
Italy	17,060	23,419	19,467	22,189
Britain	23,909	7,197	14,750	6,012
Japan	5,147	4,604	9,663	8,016
France	3,755	3,915	3,380	3,869
W. Germany	66	563	1,051	69

Source: P. Schwerdtner, 'Trade Unions in the German Economic and Social Order', *Zeitschrift für die gesamte Staatswissenschaft* 135 (1979), 464.

The effect of the integration of workers' representatives and unions was to create a climate for much more effective cooperation between the two sides of industry than existed elsewhere in Europe. Cooperation almost certainly explains why labour did not present greater resistance in the 1950s to low wage rates and high profits. Wage rates and earnings developed steadily over the whole period, but they were determined within a framework of productivity growth. Real wage growth between 1953 and 1982, given the relatively low wages of the recovery years, was modest in relation to other high-growth economies, such as Japan.[60] Wage restraint did produce clear long-term advantages. It helped to reduce inflation and maintain living standards, and it helped to maintain high levels of employment through to the 1980s. Above all it helped to avoid the damaging effects of industrial confrontation. The low level of strike activity in the Federal Republic is no myth. In 1960 there were only 17,000 workers involved in strikes, and only 38,000 working days lost. In 1965 only 6,000 workers struck throughout the entire year. The state of German labour relations can perhaps best be illustrated by looking at the strike record of leading industrial states in the mid-1970s, the high point of post-war labour militancy (see Table 1.7). Between 1972 and 1975 1.7 million working days were lost in the Federal Republic; in Italy the figure was 82 million, in Britain 51.8 million.[61] It would be rash to generalize about the economic effects of low strike activity, but it is difficult to avoid the conclusion that it gave German industry a competitive advantage in terms of price and reputation.

Stable labour relations were maintained against a background of structural change in the Federal workforce which also contributed to raising its productive performance. Between 1957 and 1980 agriculture declined as a share of employment from 16.3 to 5.6 per cent, moving workers

60. Van der Wee, *Prosperity and Upheaval*, p. 237.
61. Schwerdtner, 'Trade Unions', 464.

from low-paid, low-skill jobs to more skilled and better rewarded industrial labour. Over the same timescale the proportion of the workforce in the tertiary sectors rose from 35 per cent to 50 per cent.[62] The skill ratio was steadily improved over the same period. This was partly a product of social pressures in the 1950s and 1960s which encouraged the acquisition of formal qualifications in order to improve prospects for employment. It was also a result of the introduction of new payment methods in industry first begun during the war.[63] Instead of the traditional division between skilled, semi-skilled and unskilled wage rates, a more finely graded system of wage bands was introduced, based on eight separate achievement levels. Workers were given incentives to improve their productive performance and move from a lower pay band to a higher. The system allowed managers to organize the workforce more rationally and to reward merit. These changes within industry were matched by government efforts to increase the proportion of technically skilled workers in recognition of the importance of training as a contribution to economic development. The 1969 Vocational Training Law and the 1971 Promotion of Training Law were framed with the object of increasing the number of apprentices across all sectors of the economy. During the 1970s approximately 1.4 million apprentices were trained each year and 80 per cent of 15–18 year olds given some form of higher qualification. By 1990 Germany had the highest education participation rates in Europe, with 100 per cent of 17 year olds in academic or technical training.[64] The tendency since the 1970s has been to over-train the workforce. For example, an estimated one-third of journeymen were forced to take jobs at a lower skill level than their training had prepared them for.

It is impossible to ignore the impact on economic growth produced by high levels of training, though it is difficult to quantify. The correlation between skill levels and economic success can be inversely demonstrated. Britain has had the lowest growth record among the developed economies, and also the lowest participation rate in training and education for 16–19 year olds, well under half the German figure in 1990. The constant process of upgrading the achievement levels of German labour worked in symbiosis with the structural shifts in German industry and services towards specialized high-quality products and organizational

62. Van der Wee, *Prosperity and Upheaval*, p. 168.

63. On the origins of the system see R. Hachtmann, *Industriearbeit im 'Dritten Reich': Untersuchungen zu den Lohn- und Arbeitsbedingungen in Deutschland 1933–1945* (Göttingen, 1989), pp. 207–12.

64. D. Sadowski, 'Finance and Governance of the German Apprenticeship System', *Zeitschrift für die gesamte Staatswissenschaft* 137 (1981), 234–6; M. Stewart, *Employment Conditions in Europe* (London, 1976), pp. 88–90.

systems. This was a traditional German strength, which only required a stable economic and political climate at home and a healthy world market for its potential to be released.

AN ECONOMIC MIRACLE?

The success of the economic revival in Germany after the disasters of war and occupation, though it had demonstrable economic causes, cannot be separated from the political context in which recovery took place. The state's new leaders recognized that there was no question of returning to the pre-war years of protectionism, state control and economic imperialism. The prospects for democracy were bound up with economic freedoms. 'Only when every German can freely choose what work he will do and where, and can freely decide what goods he will consume', said Erhard in a speech on the currency reform in 1948, 'will our people be able to play an active part in the political life of their country.'[65] Konrad Adenauer, the first Federal Chancellor, recalled in his memoirs his determination to rid the new state of the legacy of Nazi economic controls, and to establish the principle that in a democracy 'the individual and his well-being must be the goal'.[66] Welfare capitalism was widely welcomed in West German society as a fundamental underpinning to political reform and a new direction in German foreign policy.

The economic record that followed was not an 'economic miracle' in the sense that it defies explanation. Federal economy and society had a range of inherited advantages – a high skill ratio, a strong scientific and technical tradition, a large stock of modern capital-equipment and a favourable set of circumstances abroad in the 1950s. Above all there existed a powerful psychological predisposition to set the past aside and to concentrate the energies of the population on the achievement of material well-being. There is more than a grain of truth in the popular perception of federal Germany as a country where people worked hard, saved hard and trained hard. In the post-war world there were few options for federal society other that to embrace western materialism with open arms in the hope that it would generate political stability and social peace.

65. Quoted in A. Grosser, *Germany in Our Time: A Political History of the Postwar Years* (London, 1971), p. 277.

66. K. Adenauer, *Memoirs 1945–1953* (London, 1965), p. 164.

CHAPTER TWO

Population Change and its Repercussions on the Social History of the Federal Republic

Hartmut Berghoff

Population change is a key variable for all social, economic and political processes which is vital for social planning of any kind, from education to welfare systems, and from housing to pensions schemes. Economists know that demographic trends determine the structure of labour markets and demand patterns. Politicians among others have to cope with the financial effects of uneven population growth and to secure political stability in the face of dynamic demographic changes such as mass migration. Dissatisfaction with political and economic conditions, on the other hand, can trigger off emigration on a scale which might even threaten the existence of political systems, as the last chapter in the history of the German Democratic Republic (GDR) has demonstrated. As a mass exodus gathered momentum in the autumn of 1989, the collapse of the regime passed the point of no return.

Because of its paramount importance, population change has recently become a major political issue in the Federal Republic of Germany (FRG), as in most member states of the European Union. In these debates rational reasoning is often overshadowed by emotional arguments. Thus it might be worthwhile looking back on the demographic history of the Federal Republic. This essay outlines the major trends and effects of population change in West Germany between 1949 and 1992. As several waves of immigration left their distinct marks on the demographic structure and social history of the FRG, this article is subdivided into four periods which are determined by its immigration history. Major turning-points were the erection of the Berlin Wall in 1961, the oil crisis of 1973 and the start of the collapse of the Eastern Bloc in 1987. Each of the four sections asks the following three questions: first, what were the reasons for, and the quantitative dimensions of, immigration into the FRG, and how far did it affect the overall demographic structure in the context of natural population change and emigration? Second, how did the resident population react to the influx from outside? To what degree did processes of integration or separation occur, and which role did governmental action play? Third, in what way did immigration leave an imprint on post-war German society as a whole? In other words, what were its main social, economic and political effects?

REFUGEES, EXPELLEES AND THE FORMATION OF WEST GERMAN SOCIETY, 1945/49–61

At first glance it might seem surprising that in the year of the FRG's foundation considerably more people lived within its territory than in 1939. Despite nearly seven million war-related deaths, the new state came into existence with a population surplus of about eight million inhabitants. This massive gain was the result of the five East–West movements, which were part of the biggest population transfer in modern German history. First, it was a key element of Hitler's scheme for reshaping Europe by racist criteria to repatriate ethnic Germans, mainly from the Baltic. They were primarily sent into German-occupied areas but were soon forced to join the hordes fleeing the Red Army. This second movement began in 1944 and lasted until the end of the war. After the capitulation a third phase commenced which was characterized by indiscriminate and brutal expulsions in revenge for German wartime atrocities. It affected those Germans who had remained in former German and German-occupied territories east of the Oder–Neisse line and in Czechoslovakia. These ad hoc measures were legalized by the Potsdam Treaty signed by Britain, the US and the Soviet Union in August 1945. In paragraph XII it specifies: 'The Three Governments . . . recognise that the transfer to Germany of German populations . . . , remaining in Poland, Czechoslovakia and Hungary, will have to be undertaken.'[1] The political rationale of these bare words was to eliminate the problem of ethnic minorities, which had played a crucial role in stirring up pre-war hostilities, once and for all. Back in 1944 Churchill

1. Protocol of the Proceedings of the Berlin Conference, 2 August 1945, in Rohan Butler and M. E. Pelly, eds, *Documents on British Policy Overseas* (London, 1984), p. 1275.

had explained in the Commons that he favoured 'the total expulsion of the Germans from the area to be acquired by Poland. . . . For expulsion is the method which . . . will be most satisfactory and lasting. There will be no mixture of populations to cause endless trouble, as has been the case in Alsace-Lorraine. A clean sweep will be made.'[2]

Although the Potsdam Treaty emphasized 'that any transfers . . . should be effected in an orderly and humane manner',[3] in reality there was no discernible difference between spontaneous expulsions and planned resettlements, both of which constituted an apocalyptic nightmare for the people affected. In most cases they were driven out of their houses by force and exposed to brutal acts of revenge. Moreover, they had to leave most of their belongings behind and to provide their own food and transport, which regularly meant starving and walking for several hundred miles to the West. According to one estimate about two million people died in the course of their flight and expulsion.[4]

The fourth movement into West Germany originated from the Soviet-controlled part of Germany, which became the GDR in 1949 (see Map 2.1). Contrary to the other processes described above, here people decided to leave for the West of their own will. In terms of migration theory, the FRG's political pluralism as well as its economic lead over the GDR acted as strong pull factors. At the same time Stalinism, which began to incapacitate East Germans in more and more respects, constituted an equally powerful push factor. A second major difference must be seen in the fact that the influx of refugees from East Germany was a rather permanent feature of the 1950s, whereas the population transfer from Eastern Europe had virtually been completed by 1947. There was no year between 1950 and 1961 in which official figures indicated fewer than 170,000 GDR refugees. This does not include, however, the enormous number of unreported cases that occurred. Peaks, directly reflected in Figure 2.1, were reached in 1953 (408,100), when strikes and revolts in East Germany were crushed by Soviet military forces, in 1956 (396,300), and in 1957 (384,700) under the influence of the Hungarian rising. In 1961 155,402 people had already left the GDR between January and August, mainly in reaction to a rigorously intensified policy of compulsory expropriation and

2. *Hansard* (Commons), 5th ser., CDVI, 15/12/1944, col. 1484.

3. Ibid.

4. Wolfgang Benz, 'Fremde in der Heimat: Flucht-Vertreibung-Integration', in Klaus J. Bade, ed., *Deutsche im Ausland – Fremde in Deutschland. Migration in Geschichte und Gegenwart* (Munich, 1992), p. 381.

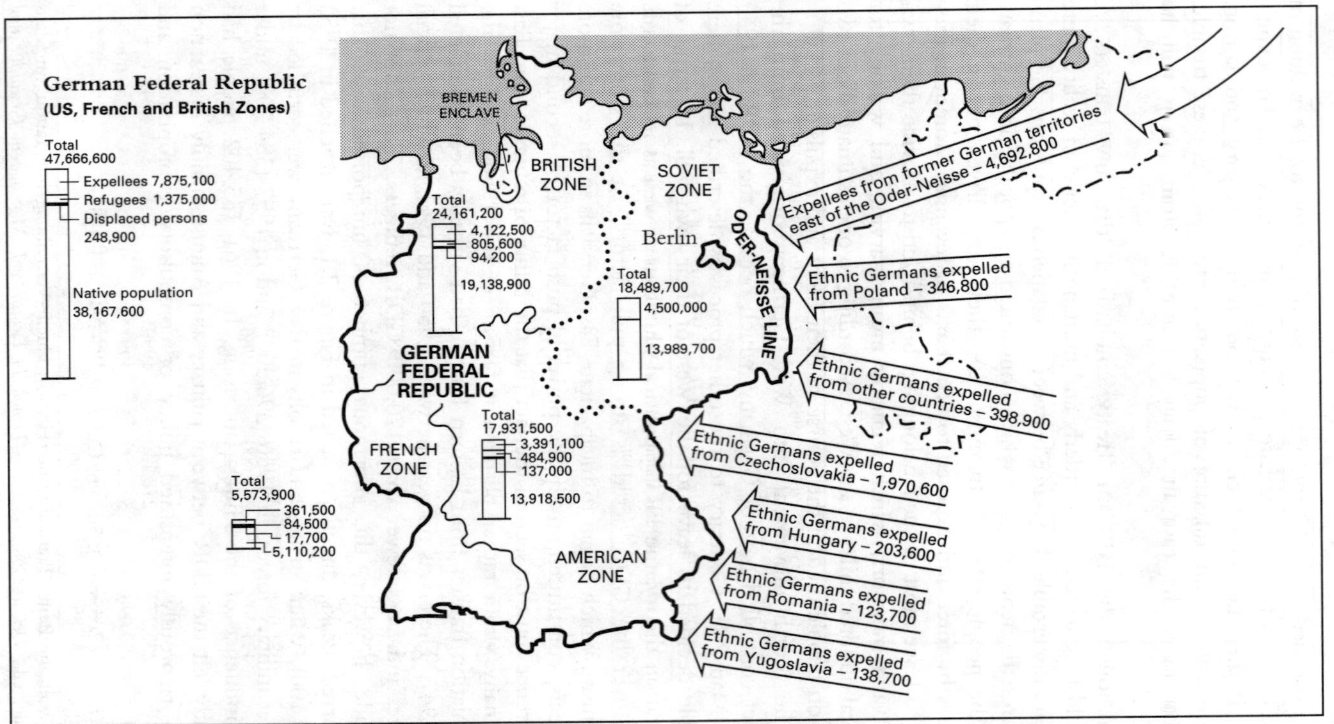

Map 2.1: Population movements, 1945–50
Source: Office of the US High Commissioner, *5th Quarterly Report*, 1950.

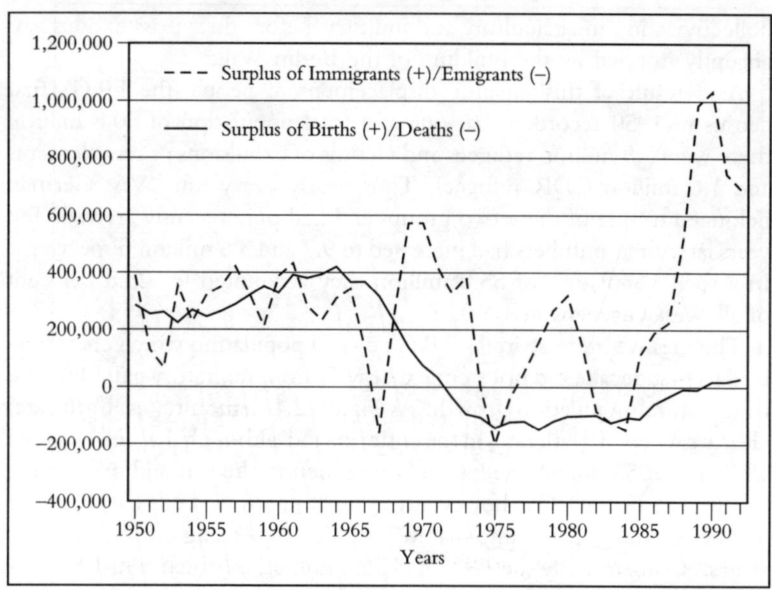

Figure 2.1: Population change in the FRG, 1950–92 ('000)

Years	Surplus of births (+)/deaths (–)	Surplus of immigrants (+)/emigrants (–)	Years	Surplus of births (+)/deaths (–)	Surplus of immigrants (+)/emigrants (–)
1950	284.088	378.000	1972	–30.050	330.775
1951	251.711	137.600	1973	–95.395	384.033
1952	253.117	64.900	1974	–101.138	–9.350
1953	218.069	348.900	1975	–148.748	–199.178
1954	260.569	221.200	1976	–130.289	–72.221
1955	238.256	310.800	1977	–122.578	32.652
1956	256.474	339.500	1978	–146.750	115.376
1957	277.212	416.600	1979	–129.748	246.002
1958	307.160	329.000	1980	–93.460	311.947
1959	346.438	210.700	1981	–97.635	152.334
1960	325.667	364.000	1982	–94.684	–75.391
1961	385.126	431.100	1983	–124.160	–117.135
1962	373.733	284.000	1984	–111.961	–151.147
1963	381.054	237.000	1985	–118.141	83.400
1964	421.309	301.000	1986	–75.927	188.400
1965	366.700	343.752	1987	–45.409	213.700
1966	364.024	131.619	1988	–10.257	481.900
1967	332.110	–176.919	1989	–16.193	977.200
1968	235.777	278.140	1990*	13.864	1.041.100
1969	159.096	572.299	1991*	13.432	756.086
1970	75.965	574.045	1992*	25.526	699.208
1971	47.856	430.667			

* Without former GDR. Borders as before 3 October 1990.

Source: *Statistische Jahrbücher der Bundesrepublik Deutschland* and Gert Hullen and Reiner Schulz, 'Bericht 1993 zur demographischen Lage in Deutschland', *Zeitschrift für Bevölkerungswissenschaft* 19 (1993–94), 3–70.

collectivization in agriculture and industry, before their mass exodus was abruptly stopped by the building of the Berlin Wall.[5]

As a result of this gigantic displacement of people the FRG's first census in 1950 recorded that out of a total population of 50.8 million there were 7.9 million refugees and victims of expulsions or resettlements and 1.6 million GDR refugees. Thus nearly every fifth West German belonged to one of these two groups and had only recently arrived. Ten years later their numbers had increased to 9.7 and 3.6 million respectively. In a total population of 55.8 million they accounted for 23.8 per cent of all West Germans in 1960.

The massive increase in the FRG's overall population which characterized its first decade did not stem exclusively from migratory gains but also from natural population growth. As Figure 2.1 demonstrates, birth rates clearly exceeded death rates in the entire period, although they fell between 1949 and 1953 due to the loss of young men in the war and grim living conditions. From 1955, however, the birth rate increased sharply as the 'economic miracle' became manifest and led to a rising number of marriages.[6] Consequently the FRG had 56.2 million inhabitants in 1961, 5.4 million (10.6 per cent) more than in 1950. Compared with 1939, when only 43 million people lived on its territory, the increase amounted to 13.2 million (30.7 per cent). Thus within 22 years, which included the most devastating war in history, the West German population had increased by nearly one-third. It goes without saying that a demographic change of this scale left a deep imprint on the society it affected.

In 1945–47 the influx of millions of refugees and expellees was by no means welcomed by a resident West German population struggling for survival, for it obviously aggravated all the problems of the post-war chaos. Although living conditions had improved by 1949, unemployment and housing shortages were two major bottlenecks which remained a problem throughout the 1950s and kept alive the hostility and rejection that many refugees had encountered during their first years in West

5. Siegfried Bethlehem, *Heimatvertreibung, DDR-Flucht, Gastarbeiterzuwanderung. Wanderungsströme und Wanderungspolitik in der Bundesrepublik Deutschland* (Stuttgart, 1982), p. 26; Dietrich Staritz, *Die Gründung der DDR* (Munich, 1984), pp. 126–38; Christoph Klessmann, *Zwei Staaten, eine Nation. Deutsche Geschichte 1955–1970* (Göttingen, 1988), pp. 303–24.

6. Statistisches Bundesamt, ed., *Bevölkerung gestern, heute und morgen* (Mainz, 1985), p. 13; Wolfgang Köllmann, 'Die Bevölkerungsentwicklung der Bundesrepublik', in Werner Conze and M. Rainer Lepsius, eds, *Sozialgeschichte der Bundesrepublik Deutschland. Beiträge zum Kontinuitätsproblem* (Stuttgart, 1983), pp. 66–74, 101–9; Ralf Rytlewski and Manfred Opp de Hipt, *Die Bundesrepublik Deutschland in Zahlen 1945/49–1980* (Munich, 1987), pp. 29–30; Hermann Korte, 'Bevölkerungsstruktur und -entwicklung', in Wolfgang Benz, ed., *Die Geschichte der Bundesrepublik, Vol. 3: Gesellschaft* (Frankfurt, 1989), pp. 12–20.

Germany. Full employment was only reached in 1961 after years of high though constantly declining unemployment rates.[7] In 1950 the FRG had a deficit of around five million dwellings. Despite massive investment in housing programmes, demand still exceeded supply in the late 1950s. Overcrowding and even living in camps had not disappeared by the mid-fifties. House rationing, the confiscation of dwellings and state-controlled rents were only abolished in 1960. Under these circumstances the memory of the late 1940s, when many refugee families had had to move into West German houses against the owners' will, virtually 'under the protection of machine guns',[8] remained only too vivid. During this time the compulsory sharing of kitchens and bathrooms created persisent causes for domestic unrest. It is no wonder that refugees were initially perceived mostly as intruders and unwanted competitors for scarce jobs and dwellings.

Sociocultural differences constituted an additional source of conflict and misunderstanding. The new neighbours spoke their own dialects, adhered to their own ways of life and values, and often found themselves in a denominational diaspora. The resident population took this situation as an outright attack on its own identity. Consequently, refugees and expellees were initially stigmatized and fell victim to all sorts of prejudices. People called them criminals, gypsies, foreigners, have-nots, dirty, lazy, and so on. *Flüchtling* (refugee) became a common swearword, just as the very pejorative *Polacke* (Pole) was used indiscriminately for all expellees no matter where they came from. Housing estates for refugees were deliberately built well outside existing residential areas, and for quite some time their inhabitants felt somewhat out of place.[9] In 1951 a *Schutzverband der Westdeutschen* (Protection Association) was even founded, the main object of which was defence against *unberechtigte Überfremdung*[10] (unlawful infiltration) by expellees and refugees and their alleged preferential treatment by the authorities.

Initial obstacles to integration did not stem exclusively from the inimical reactions of the host society but also lay on the side of the new immigrants themselves. They had left behind nearly all of their property and began life in West Germany impoverished and incapable of looking

7. The FRG's unemployment rate was 11 per cent in 1950, 8.4 per cent in 1953, 4.4 per cent in 1956, 2.6 per cent in 1959 and 0.8 per cent in 1961: Rytlewski and Opp de Hipt, *Die Bundesrepublik Deutschland*, p. 78.

8. Marion Frantzioch, *Die Vertriebenen. Hemmnisse, Antriebskräfte und Wege ihrer Integration in der Bundesrepublik Deutschland* (Berlin, 1987), pp. 117–20.

9. Ibid., pp. 127–9; Albrecht Lehmann, *Im Fremden ungewollt zuhaus. Flüchtlinge und Vertriebene in Westdeutschland 1945–1990* (Munich, 1991), pp. 20–54.

10. Quoted in *Trossinger Zeitung*, 8/9/1951 (my translation). This association, however, did not become very influential.

after themselves. Integration into the labour market often had to be payed for by social deprivation. It was quite typical to be forced to move from self-employment into wage earning, from agriculture into industry, and to have to restart one's professional career in very low-paid jobs. This degrading loss of status led to a psychologically as well as an economically difficult situation,[11] which was further enhanced by the fact that it coincided with sociocultural uprooting. To experience the forced and permanent loss of one's native home and the transplantation to strange and inhospitable surroundings was an extremely painful process that took some time to come to terms with. At first, many people clung to hopes of an eventual return to their *Heimat* (homeland), although the impossibility of these projections was more than obvious. Traumatic memories of one's escape and expulsion often combined with insecurity, anxiety about one's future, nostalgia and the feeling of being victimized. This state of mind led not only to bitterness but also to a latent or open reluctance to accept one's fate and thus to make a genuine effort to integrate. Instead many remained sceptical, socialized primarily with people from their own native region, and intensified the maintenance up of their traditions and customs. 'Whoever is forced to leave his home arrives full of resentment. He is not receptive to the new . . . , which gives him a hard start.'[12]

Widespread fears that millions of impoverished and embittered refugees could become a breeding-ground for social unrest and political radicalism[13] proved unfounded. Instead a swift and peaceful process of integration into West German society began in the 1950s and was eventually completed in the 1960s. The most important factor in surmounting the difficulties outlined so far was the FRG's economic dynamism which more than tripled industrial output between 1950 and 1965 and completely absorbed the population surplus into the labour market before 1960.[14] Although initially refugees and expellees remained mark-

11. Paul Lüttinger, 'Der Mythos von der schnellen Integration', *Zeitschrift für Soziologie* 15 (1986), 20–36.

12. Elisabeth Pfeil, *Der Flüchtling. Gestalt einer Zeitenwende. Europäische Stimmen* (Hamburg, 1948), p. 13 (my translation). See also Frantzioch, *Die Vertriebenen*, pp. 66–73.

13. In 1950 the US High Commissioner, McCloy, feared for the worst: 'inadequately housed, homesick, and feeling themselves strangers in a sometimes hostile environment, they form a group which might readily be swayed by political extremists who offer a plausible solution to their problems'. Quoted in Dennis L. Bark and David R. Gress, *A History of West Germany, Vol. 1: From Shadow to Substance 1945–1963* (Oxford, 1989), p. 307.

14. Gerold Ambrosius, 'Das Wirtschaftssystem', in Woldgang Benz, ed., *Geschichte der Bundesrepublik, Vol. 2: Wirtschaft* (Frankfurt, 1989), p. 36; Ulrich Herbert, *Geschichte der Ausländerbeschäftigung in Deutschland 1880 bis 1980. Saisonarbeiter, Zwangsarbeiter, Gastarbeiter* (Berlin, 1986), pp. 190–4.

edly over-represented among the unemployed, and work normally had to be taken up outside one's own profession, these disadvantages were soon overshadowed by the effects of unexpectedly fast rising living standards. The 'economic miracle' created a new society whose cohesion and consensus was mainly based on the experience of ever-increasing levels of consumption. More than anything else, the economic buoyancy of the 1950s pacified and unified West German society, which had been deeply fragmented and in complete turmoil in the late 1940s.[15]

Secondary factors supporting integration were manifold. One of them was the unambiguous legal status of former refugees and expellees, who held full German citizenship. Moreover, the Cold War climate ensured that no-one could realistically think of returning millions of refugees to their native regions in the foreseeable future. Consequently it was clear that they had to become an integral and permanent part of West German society.[16] Furthermore, and despite all differences, there was a great deal of common cultural ground between the resident and immigrant population. Problems of dialects and divergent patterns of behaviour, after all, are easier to overcome than those of foreign languages and ethnic heterogeneity. In addition, the rise of a mass-consumer society in the late 1950s levelled out many class-specific and regional traces in people's ways of life and created a more homogeneous society whose members did not feel so strongly attached to certain milieux but distinguished themselves primarily by their professional status and financial resources. Finally, refugees by no means represented a socially homogeneous group or even a class. On the contrary, they comprised a wide spectrum reaching from former *Junker*, i.e. large-scale landowners, to agricultural labourers, from industrial magnates to workers, and from civil servants to office clerks. For this reason internal cohesion was fragile and very much challenged by diversity in social status. The effects of financial compensation under the *Lastenausgleich* (Equalization of Burdens) scheme and the highly uneven distribution of wealth in the FRG enhanced the social stratification within the refugee community so that refugee status increasingly lost its function of defining its bearer's place in society.[17]

15. Bethlehem, *Heimatvertreibung*, pp. 45–7; Lüttinger, 'Der Mythos', 23–4; Hans-Peter Schwarz, *Die Ära Adenauer, Vol. 1: Gründerjahre der Republik 1949–1957* (Stuttgart, 1981), pp. 387–9; Arnold Sywottek, 'Konsum, Mobilität, Freizeit. Tendenzen gesellschaftlichen Wandels', in Martin Broszat, ed., *Zäsuren nach 1945. Essays zur Periodisierung der deutschen Nachkriegsgeschichte* (Munich, 1990), pp. 96–110.

16. Herbert, *Geschichte*, p. 185.

17. Josef Mooser, *Arbeiterleben in Deutschland 1900–1970* (Frankfurt, 1984), pp. 213–16; Schwarz, *Die Ära Adenauer, Vol. 1*, pp. 394–405; Stefan Hradil, 'Individualisierung, Pluralisierung, Polarisierung: Was ist von den Schichten und Klassen geblieben?', in

Nevertheless, former refugees and expellees formed a wide range of cultural and political organizations of their own. These served as highly efficient political pressure groups which managed to register and mobilize a membership of a size that no-one in politics was able to ignore, let alone antagonize. In 1963, when they were past their peak, their umbrella organization still had 2.2 million members. Some of them even formed their own political party, which received 1.6 million votes (5.9 per cent) in 1953, the first time it stood for the *Bundestag*. It then joined Adenauer's Christian Democratic Union (CDU) in a coalition government, before it failed to gain re-election in 1957 and fell into political insignificance in the 1960s. Moreover, refugees were well represented among the members, functionaries and parliamentarians of all the major parties. Between 1949 and 1957 nearly every fifth seat (18 per cent) in the *Bundestag* was occupied by a member of a refugee organization.[18] Their political strength facilitated resolute, sometimes aggressive lobbying. Apart from this, the urgency and scale of the refugee problem guaranteed that it received special political attention and was, with full justification, treated as a question of paramount national importance. Thus Adenauer established a *Ministerium für Vertriebene* (Ministry for Expellees) in 1949 which created a multitude of programmes promoting their integration. First of all it organized a massive resettlement within the FRG to transfer people from rural to industrial regions and helped with the replacement of lost household goods. Then it set up extensive housing, retraining and job creation schemes. Those who wanted to found their own businesses had access to low interest loans. The elderly and those unable to work received a new type of pension, because they were not covered by normal social insurance provisions. Finally, financial compensation for property losses could be claimed under the *Lastenausgleich* Act, which was passed in 1952 to balance the extremely uneven distribution of war burdens, a defect further magnified by the currency reform of 1948. Although this complex legislation was not restricted to expellees and refugees, it was first and foremost for their benefit, as collectively they had suffered the highest property losses. Compensation payments were linked to the value of the damage in inverse proportion. Fortunes under RM5,000 were

Robert Hettlage, ed., *Die Bundesrepublik. Eine historische Bilanz* (Munich, 1990), pp. 112–18; Axel Schildt and Arnold Sywottek, '"Wiederaufbau" und "Modernisierung". Zur westdeutschen Gesellschaftsgeschichte in den fünfziger Jahren', *APUZ* 6–7 (1989), 25–8; Alan Kramer, *The West German Economy, 1945–1955* (New York, 1991), pp. 214–19; Peter Waldmann, 'Die Eingliederung der ostdeutschen Vertriebenen in die westdeutsche Gesellschaft', in Becker *et al.*, eds, *Vorgeschichte der Bundesrepublik. Zwischen Kapitulation und Grundgesetz* (Munich, 1979), pp. 178–89.

18. Klessmann, *Zwei Staaten*, pp. 136–8; Frantzioch, *Die Vertriebenen*, pp. 149–54.

compensated at 95 per cent, those in excess of one million at only 6.5 per cent.[19]

Historians of the *Lastenausgleich* are divided over whether its financial or its psychological effects were more important for the integration process. It is beyond doubt, though, that it turned refugees and expellees from objects of social aid and charity into holders of legally recoverable rights. In addition to considerable material benefits this change in status wiped out the stigma of being dependent on social security payments. Financially, the *Lastenausgleich* constituted one of the largest transfer operations in German history. The amount paid out under the scheme until 1978 totalled more than DM110 billion, of which about two-thirds was allotted to expellees and refugees.[20] It was raised by a special levy on land, capital goods and buildings in West Germany in order to burden those who had not suffered war-related property losses or not forfeited the lion's share of their assets through the currency reform. As this levy was spread over 30 years and real property systematically undervalued, tax revenue had to be utilized from the start to balance the fund's chronic deficit. Thus the *Lastenausgleich* failed in its original aim to spread war-related burdens more equally and to level out a highly unequal distribution of private wealth. Nevertheless, it succeeded in diminishing the severe problems that arose from the need to integrate more than 11 million otherwise poverty-stricken people.

Turning to the effects of the influx of refugees and expellees, it becomes obvious that, despite all initial scepticism and hostility, their presence proved highly beneficial to the social and economic development of the FRG. First of all, it balanced the uneven demographic structure of post-war Germany, whose main characteristic was a relative lack of men aged between 18 and 45 years. Cynical as it may sound, refugees filled up the ranks of those who had suffered most from the war and who at the same time were in high demand from employers. Among refugees from Eastern Europe, people aged between 14 and 45 were over-represented in comparison to the native population, and among former GDR citizens this was true even for those between 14

19. The *Lastenausgleich* gave rise to a wave of envy. Adopting one of the most popular prejudices against refugees, the *Schutzverband der Westdeutschen* formulated a 'protest against fraudulent claims'. Quoted in *Trossinger Zeitung*, 8 September 1951 (my translation).

20. This figure includes payments made under the *Soforthilfegesetz* of 1949 which preceded the law on *Lastenausgleich* of 1952. For a general survey, see Dietrich Hilger, 'Die mobilisierte Gesellschaft', in Richard Löwenthal and Hans-Peter Schwarz, eds, *Die zweite Republik. 25 Jahre Bundesrepublik Deutschland – eine Bilanz* (Stuttgart, 1974), pp. 95–122; Reinhard Schillinger, 'Der Lastenausgleich', in Wolfgang Benz, ed., *Die Vertreibung der Deutschen aus dem Osten. Ursachen, Ereignisse, Folgen* (Frankfurt, 1985), pp. 183–92.

and 30.[21] They not only improved the sex ratio and age structure of West German society but also moulded its predominant attitudes and mentalities. As they had left behind most of their possessions and experienced a drastic loss in social status, they had to build up their property and livelihood from virtually nothing. This situation mobilized energies of despair and, at the same time, set free a particularly strong dedication to work and to material wealth. Considering the numerical weight of the refugee population, it is no exaggeration to conclude that their willingness to regain lost social ground through a strong commitment to their jobs had sizeable effects on the national economy and was filtered through to the rest of the workforce. This accords very well with the observation that in industry refugees were often charged with sabotaging piece rates. Furthermore, the absence of local ties in the FRG provided them with an exceptional readiness to change their places of work and residence in compliance with the needs of the labour market. This high geographical mobility, which of course decreased over the years, meant a huge step towards a flexible, demand-orientated allocation of the workforce. In short, refugees made a very strong contribution to the establishment of a highly competitive and mobile West German society.[22]

According to Kindleberger, the expansion of labour supply is an indispensable precondition of sustaining economic growth over long periods. Thus he very strongly emphasizes the fact that in the 1950s this variable grew much faster in the FRG than in any other European country. Among other things this reduced pressure in the labour market, diminished unions' strength, and kept wage increases in check. As a result pay rises never exceeded productivity gains in the 1950s, and the FRG enjoyed relatively low labour costs by comparison with its international competitors. This was a major advantage as extensive self-financing on the basis of high profits and competitiveness on foreign markets constituted central elements of the FRG's 'economic miracle'. The other side of the coin was living standards markedly below those in Britain and America. Pre-war levels of food consumption were only

21. Bethlehem, *Heimatvertreibung*, pp. 35–7; Herbert, *Geschichte*, p. 180; Uwe Kleinert, 'Flüchtlinge als Arbeitskräfte – zur Eingliederung der Flüchtlinge in Nordrhein-Westfalen', in Klaus J. Bade, ed., *Neue Heimat im Westen. Vertriebene, Flüchtlinge, Aussiedler* (Münster, 1990), pp. 50–1.

22. Kleinert, 'Flüchtlinge als Arbeitskräfte', p. 57; Frantzioch, *Die Vertriebenen*, p. 133; Waldmann, 'Eingliederung', pp. 188–9; Hellmut Körner, *Der Zustrom von Arbeitskräften in die Bundesrepublik Deutschland von 1850–1972. Auswirkungen auf die Funktionsweise des Arbeitsmarktes* (Frankfurt, 1972), pp. 153–73; Schwarz, *Die Ära Adenauer, Vol. 1*, pp. 389–94; Schildt and Sywottek, ' "Wiederaufbau" ', 23–5.

reached in 1955/56.[23] Without refugees, the trade unions would certainly not have displayed the remarkable moderation characteristic of wage negotiations in the 1950s.[24] Refugee businessmen often brought with them large parts of their former workforce as well as their technological know-how. By 1950 about 50,000 businesses with 300,000 jobs had already been founded or refounded by refugees and expellees. The majority of these firms were predominantly located in southern Germany and were rather small and highly specialized as well as being export-orientated. Although they represented only a minor part of the national economy, these companies improved its geographical structure by bringing industrial jobs into regions that had so far been neglected. Thus the so-called refugee industries promoted processes of regional development as well as sectoral diversification.[25]

GDR citizens leaving their country in the 1950s could be treated separately from those who came earlier and from those from Eastern Europe. Their integration posed fewer problems because economic recovery was already under way. Sometimes they did not leave the GDR until friends or relatives had fixed up a new job in the FRG. Besides, on average they were younger and far better qualified. Among them were many skilled industrial workers, technicians and graduates. According to one estimate, the GDR lost about one-third of its graduates. Another source gives figures of 20,000 engineers and technologists, 4,000 medical doctors and 1,000 university teachers. As their education and training had been paid for by the GDR, their immigration was a bonus for the FRG. While the former suffered a severe brain drain that deprived the country of the most ambitious part of its future elites, the latter's economy benefited strongly from the supply of highly qualified and motivated personnel who could be absorbed into its labour market without any additional investment into its educational system. Attempts

23. Charles P. Kindleberger, *European Postwar Growth. The Role of Labor Supply* (Cambridge, Mass., 1967), pp. 28–36; Körner, *Zustrom*, pp. 340–5; Rainer Klump, *Wirtschaftsgeschichte der Bundesrepublik Deutschland. Zur Kritik neuerer wirtschaftshistorischer Interpretationen aus ordnungspolitischer Sicht* (Wiesbaden, 1985), p. 104; Gerold Ambrosius, 'Flüchtlinge und Vertriebene in der westdeutschen Wirtschaftsgeschichte', in Raimer Schulze *et al.*, eds, *Flüchtlinge und Vertriebene in der westdeutschen Nachkriegsgeschichte* (Hildesheim, 1987), p. 219; Kramer, *West German Economy*, pp. 217–18.

24. Between 1951 and 1960 only 949,000 working days were lost due to industrial disputes, which compares favourably with France (2.9 million), Britain (3.4 million) and Italy (5.3 million). Werner Abelshauser, *Die langen fünfziger Jahre. Wirtschaft und Gesellschaft der Bundesrepublik Deutschland 1949–1966* (Düsseldorf, 1987), p. 83.

25. Idem, 'Der Lastenausgleich und die Eingliederung der Vertriebenen und Flüchtlinge – Eine Skizze', in Schulze *et al.*, eds, *Flüchtlinge*, pp. 234–8; Franz J. Bauer, 'Aufnahme und Eingliederung der Flüchtlinge und Vertriebenen. Das Beispiel Bayern 1945–1950', in Benz, ed., *Die Vertreibung*, p. 160.

to calculate the value of the human capital transferred from East to West Germany show that it amounted to at least DM30 billion, a sum that considerably exceeded capital input under the Marshall Plan.[26]

In exchange for these gains very few drawbacks had to be endured. One negative economic consequence of immigration was that it enabled industry to return more or less to its pre-war sectoral structure and to rely on conventional techniques and labour–capital ratios. In this respect the fast-growing labour supply delayed the adaptation and modernization of the FRG's industrial structure which took place in the 1960s and 1970s at enormous social and economic cost. Apart from this, the integration of refugees and expellees proved very conducive to dynamic change. For example, it accelerated one of the most prominent processes of social and economic restructuring that occurred in the 1950s and 1960s, namely the transfer of labour from agriculture into manufacturing and service industries. While the primary sector still employed 25 per cent of the population in 1950, its share had fallen to 11 per cent by 1965. Although this sectoral redistribution had been going on since the nineteenth century, the forced migration of millions of people from predominantly rural to industrial regions speeded up this long-term process enormously. The magnitude of this sectoral redistribution, however, must also be accredited to the fact that native West Germans increasingly took up non-agricultural jobs. Although this decision was primarily due to the appeal of higher incomes and shorter working hours in industry and services, refugees often served as a model that was adopted by young West Germans from agricultural regions. Especially in confrontations with their parents, who were often urging them to carry on with the family farm, they were able to refer to the example of refugees who had initially lived in their neighbourhood but had then moved into industrial towns. The fact that refugees had lost not only their property but with it the opportunity to rely on traditional patterns of behaviour, especially in choosing their occupation or residence, acted as a powerful agent of social modernization inside as well as outside their communities.[27]

The impact of refugees on the society they were becoming part of cannot be overrated. Sometimes change became obvious in a literal sense as their arrival triggered off extensive urban development. In many districts population figures grew by more than one-third, often changing the face of the area completely. Many small towns and villages, for

26. Werner Abelshauser, *Wirtschaftsgeschichte der Bundesrepublik Deutschland 1945–1980* (Frankfurt, 1983), pp. 96–7; Lüttinger, 'Der Mythos', p. 30.

27. Ambrosius, 'Flüchtlinge', pp. 220–1; Rytlewski and Opp de Hipt, *Die Bundesrepublik Deutschland*, p. 79.

example, lost their rural character for good. The most important processes, however, went on below the surface. The massive scale of the influx from outside made the confrontation, the cooperation and finally the mixing of newcomers and locals inevitable. Along the way, formerly closed milieux were opened and eventually broken up. First of all, this can be observed in respect to religion. Many purely or predominantly Protestant or Catholic areas were transformed into regions with a more balanced denominational structure. The result was that the grip of parish priests on their congregations was loosened. Hence, the secularization of West German society advanced at a greater speed than it would have done in its traditional structures.[28]

It seems to be one of the main features of the FRG in the 1950s that, in comparison to Weimar Germany, the segmentation and differentiation of its society had lost some of its rigidities, although in terms of incomes and wealth it was a far cry from a classless society.[29] Four main reasons underlie the relative uniformity of lifestyles and the increased degree of social mobility. First is the legacy of the Nazi regime, which had destroyed the labour movement's distinctive culture and dissolved or suppressed all organizations unwilling to integrate fully into the system. It also claimed to unify the German people and to level out social differences. As it is hard to fathom out the success and long-term effects of this policy, it is hotly debated as to whether, and to what degree, National Socialism advanced social modernization.[30] Second, the rise of a modern consumer society in the late 1950s began to dismantle many traces of regional as well as class-specific ways of life and to produce more uniform patterns of behaviour. Third, as we have already seen, the integration of millions of expellees and refugees contributed to the decline of traditional attitudes and lifestyles as well as to the dissolution of hermetically closed milieux. Fourth (and this was another conse-

28. Waldmann, 'Eingliederung', pp. 168–9, 188; Schwarz, *Die Ära Adenauer, Vol. 1*, p. 392; Christoph Klessmann, *Die doppelte Staatsgründung, Deutsche Geschichte 1945–1955* (Bonn, 1982), p. 42; Bauer, 'Aufnahme und Eingliederung', p. 160.

29. M. Rainer Lepsius, 'Soziale Ungleichheit und Klassenstrukturen in der Bundesrepublik Deutschland', in Hans-Ulrich Wehler, ed., *Klassen in der europäischen Sozialgeschichte* (Göttingen, 1979), pp. 166–209; Kramer, *West German Economy*, pp. 215–16; Hradil, 'Individualisierung', pp. 111–21.

30. David Schoenbaum, *Hitler's Social Revolution. Class and Status in Nazi Germany 1933–1939* (New York, 1968); Michael Prinz and Raimer Zitelmann, eds, *Nationalsozialismus und Modernisierung* (Darmstadt, 1991). Highly critical, however, is Bernhard Schäfers, 'Die Gesellschaft der Bundesrepublik: auch ein Fall der Modernisierung?', in Hettlage, ed., *Die Bundesrepublik*, pp. 284–5; Hans Mommsen, 'Nationalsozialismus als vorgetäuschte Modernisierung', in idem, *Der Nationalsozialismus und die deutsche Gesellschaft* (Reinbek, 1991), pp. 405–27; Norbert Frei, 'Wie modern war der Nationalsozialismus?', *Geschichte und Gesellschaft* 19 (1993), 367–87.

quence of escape and expulsion), a considerable part of Germany's traditional upper class, the East Elbian landed aristocracy, had been dispossessed. On their arrival in the West their social position did not differ greatly from that of other refugees. Through this unprecedented process of downward social mobility the *Junker* class lost the economic foundation of its former claim to social and political leadership. Apart from the broadening of the West German middle classes, the expropriation and dislocation of the old Prussian elites spared the FRG a political burden that had weighed very heavily upon the Weimar Republic.[31]

Although for the first time in German history industrialism and democracy became universally accepted, the 1950s witnessed a strange contrast between social modernity on the one hand and political and cultural conservatism on the other. This paradox can at least be partly explained by the mentality of the refugees and expellees, whose integration was once described as 'modernization under conservative principles' which 'combined progressive behaviour, especially in an economic sense, with sceptical and antiquated attitudes in politics and culture'.[32] Indeed the majority of them subscribed to conservative views in every respect. In doing so they adapted to and enhanced a main feature of the political and intellectual climate of the 1950s. Adenauer, who in a way embodied the predominant spirit of this era, pinpointed this mentality by choosing the slogan 'No Experiments' for his 1957 election campaign, which secured his greatest political victory and an absolute majority. In the atmosphere of the Cold War, 'experiments', i.e. far-reaching reform initiatives, were easily equated with 'communism'. For refugees this word evoked memories of the degrading circumstances of their escapes from or their experiences with Stalinism in the GDR. Moreover, as they had to concentrate on the difficult process of professional and social integration, their centre of gravity leaned towards job promotion, housing and other personal concerns, not to politics, industrial disputes or intellectual issues. Thus refugees and expellees strengthened existing individualistic and materialistic tendencies as well as a general conservatism.[33] In the 1950s it was no contradiction to be a stabilizing factor in

31. Schwarz, *Die Ära Adenauer, Vol. 1*, p. 394; Anselm Doering-Manteuffel, *Die Bundesrepublik Deutschland in der Ära Adenauer* (Darmstadt, 1983), p. 15.

32. Waldmann, 'Eingliederung', pp. 188–9 (my translation). See also Schwarz, *Die Ära Adenauer, Vol. 1*, p. 390; Frantzioch, *Die Vertriebenen*, pp. 155–60.

33. Bark and Gress, *From Shadow to Substance*, pp. 410–25; Doering-Manteuffel, *Bundesrepublik Deutschland*, pp. 206–11; Falk Wiesemann, 'Flüchtlingspolitik und Flüchtlingsintegration in Westdeutschland', *APUZ* 28 (1985), 44–5; Arnold Sywottek, 'Flüchtlingseingliederung in Westdeutschland. Stand und Probleme der Forschung', *APUZ* 51 (1989), 42–4.

cultural and political affairs and at the same time to act as a major force for social and economic change.

THE ARRIVAL OF THE GUESTWORKER AND THE MODERNIZATION OF WEST GERMAN SOCIETY, 1961–73

The erection of the Berlin Wall in August 1961 cut off the FRG from the constant supply of additional manpower that had fuelled its economic boom in the fifties. The resulting labour shortage was further increased by other factors. After 1960 employers began to feel the effects of the war years' low birth rates as this generation now entered the labour market and the overall workforce consequently decreased. Furthermore, with an unemployment rate of 0.9 per cent in 1961, no domestic labour reserve was available any more. Finally, the five-day working week had been introduced in 1956/57, although actual working hours were only slightly reduced. To ease the problems facing the FRG's still buoyant economy, recruitment treaties, mainly with Mediterranean countries, were concluded. Italy had been the pioneer, sending mainly agricultural workers since 1955 and industrial labour from 1960 onwards. In this year agreements with Spain and Greece were also signed. The next country to join the scheme was Turkey in 1961. Morocco followed in 1963, Portugal and Tunisia in 1964, Yugoslavia in 1968 and Korea in 1970. In the search for cheap labour, the FRG opened more than 500 recruitment offices in these countries. Applicants had to undergo several thorough medical check-ups. The international treaties gave to so-called *Gastarbeiter* (guestworkers) a specific legal status which included temporary work permits for an initial period of one year, pay and social insurance provisions in strict accordance with German standards, and the possibility of bringing over their families.[34]

Looking at Figure 2.2 one can detect three distinct phases in the pre-

34. Herbert, *Geschichte*, pp. 194–7; Bethlehem, *Heimatvertreibung*, pp. 116–35; Klaus J. Bade, *Vom Auswanderungsland zum Einwanderungsland? Deutschland 1880–1980* (Berlin, 1983), pp. 67–79; Schild and Sywottek, ' "Wiederaufbau" ', 28; Hartmut Esser, 'Gastarbeiter', in Benz, ed., *Die Geschichte der Bundesrepublik, Vol. 2: Wirtschaft*, pp. 329–48; Ray C. Rist, *Guestworkers in Germany. The Prospects for Pluralism* (New York, 1978), pp. 61–74, 109–14; Christoph M. Schmidt and Klaus F. Zimmermann, 'Migration Pressure in Germany: Past and Future', in Klaus F. Zimmermann, ed., *Migration and Economic Development* (Berlin, 1992), pp. 209–17.

1973 history of foreigners in the FRG. In the 1950s their numbers were very low, hardly ever exceeding 1 per cent of the total population. Their share in the labour force, however, increased from 1957 onwards, bringing it to 1.5 per cent (329,300) in 1960. After 1961 the guestworkers' influx accelerated considerably. In 1963 their numbers had almost trebled compared with 1960. A constant flow continued until 1966, when a slight recession led to a massive return movement. The third phase set in with economic recovery in 1968. In the following five years the number of guestworkers rocketed from 1,089,900 to 2,595,000. In 1973 their share in the labour force reached an all-time high of 11.9 per cent. Figure 2.1 underlines the very close correspondence between foreign labour supply and German business cycles. During the recessions of 1966/67 and 1973/75 guestworkers left the FRG on a scale that resulted in net emigration. On the resumption of economic growth this movement was immediately and drastically reversed. This graph also demonstrates another fundamental event in the population history of the FRG: the influx of foreign workers coincided with a dramatic decline in the birth rate. From 1964 to 1973 the number of births per year fell from 1,065,000 to 635,633, mainly due to the changing role of women in society. Moreover, under conditions of labour scarcity women were needed to fill gaps in the workforce, and thus it became increasingly acceptable for women to keep on working after marriage.

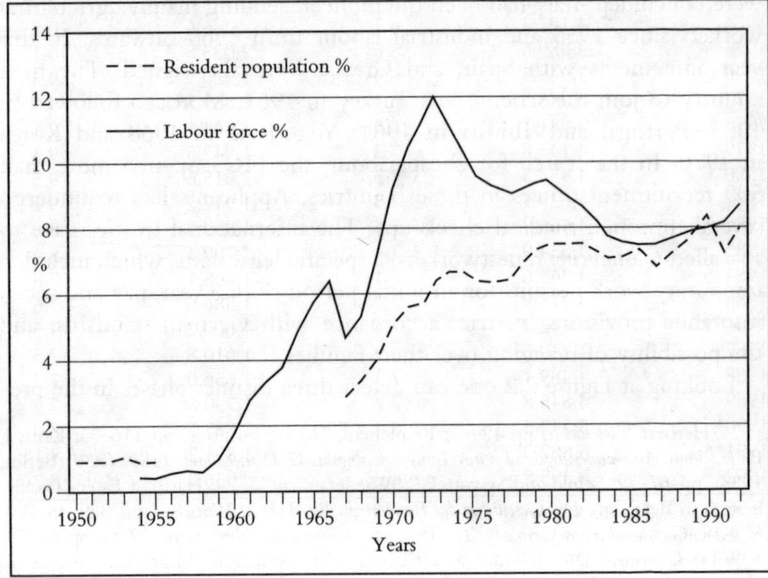

Figure 2.2: Foreigners in the FRG, 1950–92

Figure 2.2: Foreigners in the FRG, 1950–92

Years	Resident population		Labour force°	
	'000	%	'000	%
1950	567.9	0.9	—	—
1951	506.0	0.9	—	—
1952	466.2	0.9	—	—
1953	489.7	1.0	—	—
1954	481.9	0.9	72.9	0.4
1955	484.8	0.9	79.6	0.4
1956	—	—	98.8	0.5
1957	—	—	108.2	0.6
1958	—	—	127.1	0.6
1959	—	—	166.8	0.8
1960	—	—	329.4	1.5
1961	686.1	1.2	548.9	2.5
1962	—	—	711.5	3.2
1963	—	—	828.7	3.7
1964	—	—	985.6	4.4
1965	—	—	1,216.8	5.7
1966	—	—	1,313.5	6.3
1967	1,806.7	2.8	991.3	4.7
1968	1,924.2	3.2	1,089.9	5.2
1969	2,381.1	3.9	1,501.4	7.0
1970	2,976.5	4.9	1,949.0	9.0
1971	3,438.7	5.6	2,240.8	10.3
1972	3,520.6	5.7	2,359.4	10.8
1973	3,966.2	6.4	2,595.0	11.9
1974	4,127.4	6.7	2,286.6	10.9
1975	4,089.6	6.6	2,038.8	10.1
1976	3,948.3	6.4	1,920.9	9.5
1977	3,948.3	6.4	1,869.5	9.3
1978	3,981.1	6.5	1,864.1	9.1
1979	4,143.8	7.2	1,947.5	9.3
1980	4,453.3	7.5	2,015.6	9.5
1981	4,629.7	7.5	1,917.2	9.1
1982	4,666.9	7.6	1,809.0	8.8
1983	4,534.9	7.4	1,709.1	8.4
1984	4,363.6	7.1	1,608.1	7.8
1985	4,378.9	7.2	1,586.6	7.6
1986	4,512.7	7.4	1,600.2	7.5
1987	4,240.5	6.9	1,610.8	7.5
1988	4,489.1	7.3	1,656.0	7.7
1989	4,845.8	7.7	1,730.8	7.9
1990*	5,342.5	8.4	1,837.7	8.0
1991**	5,882.3	7.3	1,891.2	8.1
1992**	6,495.8	8.0	2,036.0	8.7

° As registered by the Ministry of Labour
* Excluding former GDR
** Including former GDR

Source: *Statistische Jahrbücher der Bundesrepublik Deutschland* and G. Hullen and R. Schulz, 'Bericht 1993 Bundesminister für Arbut, *Auslanderdaten*.

In 1972 the death rate exceeded the birth rate for the first time in post-war history. Although in this period a marked decline in fertility can also be observed in most other industrial countries, it occurred to a unique degree in the FRG, making it the only industrial society with a natural population decrease in the 1970s.[35]

Despite the enormous speed and dimension of the guestworkers' influx into the FRG, they encountered hardly any open hostility. With unemployment rates well below 1 per cent during most of the years between 1961 and 1973 they were not perceived as job-hunting competitors. As their recruitment was vehemently demanded by employers and carried out by the Ministry of Labour on the basis of international treaties, there was nothing to worry about. The employment of foreigners was universally accepted and looked upon as an officially monitored, temporary and above all economically necessary measure. It was obvious to anyone that guestworkers were needed to do the lowest-paid, dirtiest and most strenuous jobs which were becoming increasingly unpopular with Germans. As they lived in mass accommodation, either in camps or in overcrowded hostels, no-one could blame them for occupying dwellings urgently needed by Germans or intruding into 'normal' residential areas. This set-up offered no breeding-ground for xenophobia but rather created a climate of sociocultural segregation and mutual strangeness. Attitudes in a small Württemberg town might be characteristic. In 1960 the local newspaper commented on the arrival of the first guestworkers under the headline: 'Italians keep more than expected.' The article praises them as useful but exotic characters who are compliant, hard-working and happy with low wages. Besides, their language problems, curious eating habits, different mentalities and 'jet-black hair identifying them as south Europeans right away' are mentioned. Finally, their popularity with 'certain ladies' gives rise to the statement that 'not only the guest but also the host is responsible for correct moral behaviour', before the article concludes: 'We do expect the Italians to adapt to our ways of life and never to forget that they are guests after all.'[36]

As long as their inferior status remained unambiguous, foreign workers were able to count on the benevolence of their German 'hosts'. This constellation, however, rested on a very feeble foundation. During the 1966/67 recession a sudden change of attitude took place. An unemploy-

35. Korte, 'Bevölkerungsstruktur', pp. 15–30; Ute Frevert, *Frauen-Geschichte zwischen bürgerlicher Verbesserung und neuer Weiblichkeit* (Frankfurt, 1986), pp. 256–64; Rainer Geissler, *Die Sozialstruktur Deutschlands. Ein Studienbuch zur gesellschaftlichen Entwicklung im geteilten und vereinten Deutschland* (Bonn, 1992), pp. 265–91.

36. *Trossinger Zeitung*, 12/8/1960 (my translation).

ment rate of 2.1 per cent (1967) deeply shattered German confidence. The right-wing NPD (state) blamed foreigners for job losses among Germans and won seats in seven *Länder* parliaments. In 1966 the tabloid *Bild* published an article claiming 'guestworkers work harder than Germans', which led to hysteric protests and several token strikes. Obviously these words had struck right at the core of German identity, challenging the dogma of German 'superiority' over guestworkers. Thus for the first time they were seen as potential rivals on the labour market. This atmosphere was further stirred up by reports of guestworkers' alleged crimes and sexual escapades. With the speedy economic recovery, however, this first wave of hostility disappeared as suddenly as it had emerged, and the recruitment of guestworkers entered its peak period between 1968 and 1973, when an immigration of more than 5.6 million went virtually undisturbed by political debate and open hostility.[37]

The employment of *Gastarbeiter* proved to be the perfect solution to the FRG's labour market problems of the early 1960s. The shortage of workers was overcome by the influx of highly mobile and motivated staff who had been selected from large numbers of applicants by criteria of age, strength and reliability. Recruitment was restricted mainly to young men between 20 and 40 years of age without any health problems or criminal records. In the FRG they reduced pressure on wages and above all guaranteed that the most menial and undesirable jobs would be done, and without the need for bonus payments. Moreover, guestworkers facilitated a demand-elastic labour supply which was able to be reduced or expanded according to economic variations. In times of recession, guestworkers' numbers were drastically reduced by sending them home, i.e. by not renewing their work permits and turning them out of their accommodation. Thus they did not even claim unemployment benefit, and their unemployment rate was always minimal and much below the German quota. In boom periods their number could be increased very rapidly. At such times companies registered their detailed requests with the Federal Institute of Labour, which promptly recruited the exact number and kind of workers asked for. Further economic advantages resulted from the fact that guestworkers' tax payments and social security contributions far exceeded what they received in terms of public utilities and social services. The majority of their children still attended school back home, just as the guestworkers' own education had not been payed for by the FRG. Mass accommodation meant that there was no need yet for extra housing. As guestworkers were young and healthy, they did not claim pensions and only caused

37. Herbert, *Geschichte*, pp. 204–18.

modest medical bills. In effect, they subsidized the FRG's budget and welfare system.[38]

German workers profited overtly from these gains. Despite conditions of sustained labour scarcity, average working hours could be reduced from 44.4 per week in 1960 to 40.1 in 1972, and the retirement age was lowered from 1965 onwards. Simultaneously, social security provisions were substantially improved, either by raising old or by creating new benefits. Most of all, guestworkers increased chances of social mobility because they made it possible for more and more Germans to leave the lowest-paid jobs. In fact, they formed a new social stratum beneath the lowest segment of German society. This *Unterschichtung*, i.e. the emerging of an underclass, is a well-known side-effect of immigration. In pre-war USA, the employment of immigrants did not normally lead to redundancies among native workers, but 'the general tendency has . . . been to push the older labour up into better positions as the new took their place on the bottom rung of the economic ladder'.[39] Exactly the same happened in the FRG, when in the 1960s 2.3 million additional white-collar jobs were created and 2.7 million former wage-earners rose to the status of salaried employees.[40] Increased chances for upward social mobility were also found above the level of the lower-middle class because the most important event in the social history of the 1960s was the universal lowering of traditional class barriers in education. This decision, which in the long run considerably accelerated the dissolution of rigid class structures, was taken in the wake of the erection of the Berlin Wall. The inflow of highly qualified East Germans, which had rendered it possible to reconstruct an antiquated and by international standards underdeveloped educational system

38. Furthermore, guestworkers' high savings ratios slightly absorbed inflationary tendencies, just as their remittances eased the problems of the FRG's chronic trade and balance of payments surplus to a modest degree. Rudolph C. Beitz, 'A benefit–cost analysis of foreign workers in West Germany, 1957–1973', *Kyklos* 30 (1977), 479–502; Günter Schiller, 'Die Bedeutung der Ausländerbeschäftigung für die Volkswirtschaft', in K. J. Bade, ed., *Auswanderer, Wanderarbeiter, Gastarbeiter. Bevölkerung, Arbeitsmarkt und Wanderung in Deutschland seit der Mitte des 19. Jahrhunderts*, (2 vols; Ostfildern, 1984), pp. 625–34; Eugen Spitznagel, 'Gesamtwirtschaftliche Aspekte der Ausländerbeschäftigung', in Elmar Hönekopp, ed., *Aspekte der Ausländerbeschäftigung in der Bundesrepublik Deutschland* (Nuremberg, 1987), pp. 243–86; Rist, *Guestworkers in Germany*, pp. 109–20; Schmidt and Zimmermann, 'Migration Pressure', pp. 220–1; Bert Rürup and Werner Sesselmeier, 'Einwanderung: Die wirtschaftliche Perspektive', in Friedrich Balke *et al.*, eds, *Schwierige Fremdheit. Über Integration und Ausgrenzung in Einwanderungsländern* (Frankfurt, 1993), pp. 285–304.

39. D. Young, *American Minority Peoples* (New York, 1932), p. 116.

40. Friedrich Heckmann, *Die Bundesrepublik: Ein Einwanderungsland? Zur Soziologie der Gastarbeiterbevölkerung als Einwanderungsminorität* (Stuttgart, 1981), pp. 170–1; Herbert, *Geschichte*, pp. 199–202.

in the 1950s, had suddenly stopped. After a few years' experience with guestworkers it became clear that their lack of formal qualifications prevented them from fully replacing GDR refugees on the labour market. Now the almost total absence of educational innovation in the 1950s was realized and charged as a severe political failure. Heading the line of protesters was sociologist Ralf Dahrendorf, supported by theologian and education expert George Picht, whose 1964 book *The German Education Catastrophe* became famous as it was serialized by the popular *Stern* magazine. Indeed, the FRG spent only 3 per cent of its GNP on education in 1962, which was markedly below levels in most other industrial countries. Public spending on education had even fallen below the quotas of the 1920s.[41]

Thus comprehensive educational reform became both the motto of the day and at the same time the most potent force of social change in the late 1960s and early 1970s. In secondary education new *Gymnasien* (grammar schools) were founded and children from lower-middle- and even working-class families encouraged to enter these formerly elitist schools. Their overall attendance rose from 264,000 in 1960 to 495,000 in 1975. Students passing the *Abitur* exam (A-levels) represented only 6 per cent of the 18–20 year old population in 1960, whereas their proportion had risen to 15 per cent by 1975. In higher education, the capacities of existing colleges were greatly expanded and, in addition, 26 new universities opened between 1964 and 1974. These new foundations served not only the aim of creating more college places but also the aim of catering for regions and social groups traditionally neglected by the university system. Thus the Ruhr (Bochum 1965, Dortmund 1968, Essen 1972, Duisburg 1972) and Bavaria (Regensburg 1964, Augsburg 1970, Bamberg 1972, Bayreuth 1975) profited most from this massive investment in higher education, but also towns in peripheral regions such as Constance (1966), Bielefeld (1969), Kassel (1970), Bremen (1971), Paderborn (1972), Osnabrück (1973) and Oldenburg (1974). For many students the possibility of staying with their parents removed the financial barrier that had formerly prevented them from going into higher education. Students in need of financial assistance benefited from a comprehensive system of non-repayable grants. Night schools, aiming to enable people well into their twenties to make up for earlier educational disadvantages, also received special attention. An Open University with correspondence degree courses had already been set up in 1964. Higher technical and commercial colleges were upgraded to polytechnics in 1968, which involved academic recognition, more

41. Abelshauser, *Wirtschaftsgeschichte*, pp. 97, 99; Klessmann, *Zwei Staaten*, pp. 256–64.

state finance and an expansion of capacities. This policy succeeded in almost trebling student numbers in higher education, from 291,000 in 1960 to 836,000 in 1975, and raising the proportion of working-class students at universities from 5 per cent in 1962 to 12 per cent in 1973. Although this group remained strongly under-represented, their chances of social climbing via higher education had considerably improved because their share of the student population had more than doubled at a time of soaring enrolment figures.

Other groups who had been traditionally disadvantaged by the educational system also benefited from the extension and opening up of further and higher education. Female attendance in particular increased dramatically, and denominational differences virtually disappeared. Education reform also affected institutions beneath the grammar school level. Most federal states extended obligatory schooling to nine years in the late 1960s. In 1969 new apprenticeship laws improved the quality of vocational training. The overall teacher–student ratio could be reduced from 1:31 in 1960 to 1:19 in 1980 as 231,000 extra teachers had been appointed by 1970. All these measures required gigantic increases in expenditure on education, and indeed its share in public spending rose from 9.6 per cent in 1962 to 15.8 per cent in 1975. In relation to GNP the FRG now spent 5.5 per cent on education compared with 2.7 per cent in 1956.[42]

These expensive and comprehensive reforms had three main consequences. First, they lowered social barriers and improved overall chances of vertical mobility. Second, a general improvement in the educational level and the vocational qualification of the workforce took place. In economic terms, the import of highly trained personnel had been successfully replaced and even overcompensated for by massive gains in the quality of domestic human capital. Third, the transition from an industrial to a service society was advanced at the same time. The service sector's share of overall employment rose from 38.4 per cent in 1960 to 47.2 per cent in 1975, already ahead of industry (45.6 per cent). It is often overlooked that this fundamental modernization thrust would not have been possible without the almost unlimited availability of foreign labour, which allowed a significant extension of average education and training times in a period of labour scarcity and minimal unemployment.

42. Klaus Köhle, 'Bildungsrestauration, "Bildungskatastrophe", Bildungsexplosion: Die Entwicklung des Bildungssystems von 1945 bis heute', in Hettlage, ed., *Die Bundesrepublik*, pp. 234–49; Geissler, *Die Sozialstruktur Deutschlands*, pp. 216–26; Hellmut Becker, 'Bildungspolitik', in Benz, ed., *Geschichte der Bundesrepublik, Vol. 1: Politik* (Frankfurt, 1989), pp. 330–52; Dietrich Goldschmidt, 'Hochschulpolitik', in ibid., pp. 363–87; Klessmann, *Zwei Staaten*, p. 260.

In a literal sense, *Gastarbeiter* worked the additional hours Germans spent in schools and colleges. Furthermore, they moved into those jobs at the lower end of the labour market which Germans turned their backs on because of their improved qualifications. Without foreigners stabilizing the bottom part of the social ladder, Germans would not have been able to climb to the middle and top rungs. Finally, guestworkers contributed to the financing of educational and social reforms, as they reinforced the FRG's economic strength by acting as an industrial reserve army perfectly geared to the needs of its labour market, and by paying taxes and contributions strongly in excess of extra spending caused by them. All in all, it seems almost symbolic that many new schools and universities were built by foreign construction workers, as they in a literal and figurative sense laid the foundation for reforms that in the 1960s began to change the social fabric of the FRG with a vengeance.

THE END OF THE POST-WAR ERA AND THE TRANSFORMATION OF GUESTWORKERS INTO IMMIGRANTS, 1973–86

Nineteen seventy-three marked a watershed in the FRG's economic and social history. The post-war boom was finally over, and the collapse of the world's currency system together with the explosion of oil prices led the country into its first serious recession. Unemployment rates rose from an average of 1.0 per cent in 1961–73 to 4.8 per cent in 1974–81 and even 8.8 per cent in 1982–86, and the economy never regained its pre-1973 vigour. Under these circumstances the Bonn administration immediately changed its attitude towards the employment of foreign labour. Within weeks of the imposition of the oil embargo by Arab states, a recruitment ban on workers from non-EEC countries was declared. However, the incipient economic crisis was not the only reason for discontinuing the guestworker scheme. In the mid-1970s the first cohorts of the baby-boom generation, born between 1955 and 1966, moved into the labour market. Now the German workforce was growing for demographic reasons. There was 'a need for an additional 80,000 new jobs each year during the decade 1975–85 just to handle the German nationals coming of age'.[43] Moreover, the tendency of foreign

43. Rist, *Guestworkers in Germany*, p. 77.

workers to stay in the FRG for prolonged periods, to move out of mass accommodation and to bring over their families created a growing uneasiness among politicians. Although the vast majority (79 per cent) of foreigners entering the country between 1955 and 1973 had returned home,[44] the FRG now experienced a *de facto* immigration process that nobody had planned or anticipated, neither the government nor the foreigners themselves.

Their metamorphosis from guestworkers to immigrants had several causes, among them the bleak economic prospects in their home countries. Turks and Yugoslavs therefore displayed the strongest inclination to stay, while Italians and Spaniards often preferred to return home. Moreover, employers were anxious to avoid high fluctuation. In order to keep experienced staff on their payrolls they saw to the extension of their work permits. Despite the economic necessity, popular sentiment and politicians alike developed a diffuse feeling that the continued presence of large numbers of foreigners might be detrimental to the FRG. Chancellor Willy Brandt expressed his concern in a 1973 governmental declaration which stated that it was 'necessary . . . to consider . . . where our society's capacity for taking in [foreigners] is exhausted'.[45] A 1976 poll revealed that more than half the workforce believed that the last three years' increase in unemployment figures from 273,000 to 1,060,000 had been caused by foreigners snatching away jobs from Germans. At the same time the majority of jobless Germans were not prepared to take over the jobs vacated by foreigners. This *prima facie* paradox pinpoints the dilemma German policy towards foreigners has faced since the early 1970s. On the one hand, the economy found itself in strong need of foreign labour; on the other, the FRG was not willing to grant full integration into its society or even to accept that *de facto* immigration was taking place. Its policies were thus full of contradictions.[46]

Despite asserting again and again the principle that 'Germany is not an immigration country', the Bonn administration enacted a series of regulations which in fact engendered immigration. In 1971 rules were introduced making it possible for former guestworkers to receive an unlimited residence permit after a five-year stay. The 1973 recruitment ban ended fluctuation along the line of the business cycle. Returning home now meant leaving the FRG for good, as re-entries were

44. According to Klaus J. Bade, *Ausländer – Aussiedler – Asyl in der Bundesrepublik Deutschland* (Hanover, 1990), p. 14, official statistics recorded about 14 million arrivals and 11 million departures.

45. *Verhandlungen des Deutschen Bundestages*, 7. Wahlperiode, Stenographische Berichte, Vol. 81, 13/12/1972–16/2/1973, p. 131 (my translation).

46. Rist, *Guestworkers in Germany*, pp. 63–74, 82–3.

precluded under the ban. Therefore even unemployed foreigners recoiled from what would now be an irrevocable decision and preferred to stay, hoping to find jobs later on. As a consequence, the average length of residence in the FRG continued to rise and with it the wish to reunite families. Thus, ironically, a measure taken to reduce the number of foreigners produced the opposite effect. As Figure 2.2 demonstrates, the foreign population grew from 3.9 million in 1973 to 4.5 million in 1986, although the non-German workforce decreased from 2.5 to 1.6 million. In 1975 foreigners received equal rights to claim child benefit, provided their children lived in Germany. Of course, this condition acted as a further incentive to bring them over. In 1978 the legal status was again improved by granting foreigners the right of unlimited residence after eight years, superseding the 1971 regulation, which used the term 'permission' and left the final decision with the authorities. Now full protection from expulsion was given after eight years, and permission was normally granted after five years. In 1978 the 'Office for the Integration of Foreign Workers' was set up as an official government agency. Although politically not very influential, it acted as an advocate of foreigners' interests, proposing the official acknowledgement of *de facto* immigration and the introduction of less obstructive naturalization laws. Foreign children have been subject to compulsory education in German schools from the beginning. As a rule they were educated along with Germans of the same age. If necessary they would attend preparatory classes to learn German as a second language. In 1973 the concept of 'temporary integration', a contradiction in terms, was adopted. Its main aim was to prevent foreign children from losing the opportunity of leaving the FRG and becoming alienated from their own culture and language. Hence they received additional lessons in their mother-tongues, which of course did little to encourage remigration. For more and more youths this would in fact have meant emigration to an unfamiliar country, considering that by 1987 already 64 per cent of all foreigners under 18 had been born and raised in the FRG.[47]

This leads us to a second set of political measures which were designed to prevent integration and to promote repatriation. Some of them, indeed, impinged on foreigners' personal well-being and the integrity of their families. From 1973 employment permits were only renewed if

47. Uli Bielefeld, 'Strukturwandel des "Ausländerproblems" in der Bundesrepublik. Gesellschaftlich-politischer Ausschluss und ethnische Gemeinschaftsbildung', *Gewerkschaftliche Monatshefte* 40 (1989), 393–404; Regine Erichsen, 'Zurückkehren oder bleiben? Zur wirtschaftlichen Situation von Ausländern in der Bundesrepublik Deutschland', *APUZ* 24 (1988), 14–18; Dietrich Thränhardt, 'Die Bundesrepublik Deutschland – ein unerklärtes Einwanderungsland', ibid., 3–13; Herbert, *Geschichte*, pp. 222–32; Geissler, *Die Sozialstruktur Deutschlands*, p. 155; Esser, 'Gastarbeiter', pp. 334–55.

no German competed for the same job. Despite mass unemployment, this priority regulation hardly ever had to be applied because foreigners and Germans were rarely in the same segments of the labour market. In 1975 a restriction on foreigners' geographical mobility was instigated. To counteract their heavy concentration in certain regions – in some quarters they represented more than one-third of all inhabitants – towns with more than 6 per cent foreigners could apply for the status of an 'overburdened area' – which made it illegal for foreigners to move in and even hindered children from joining their parents. In 1977 45 towns had imposed this ban. Their names were stamped into foreigners' passports to remind them where it was forbidden to settle. It is interesting to note that Stuttgart, where every fourth employee was a foreigner in 1973, did not instigate the ban out of consideration for local industry, and that in many other places companies openly protested against it. High mobility was a major asset of foreign workers, and they were most needed in places which had already attracted large numbers of them. Therefore the residence restrictions were abolished in 1977. In 1981 it was made more difficult for families to live together by refusing entry to children older than 15, to wives whose husbands had been born or grown up in the FRG, and to children with only one parent living in the FRG. In 1983 cash premiums and refunds of contributions to pension schemes were handed out to those leaving the FRG. Although Figure 2.1 reveals a net emigration taking place in 1982–84, the law was repealed after 10 months, when it turned out that payments had only been claimed by those who would have left anyway. In fact many postponed their repatriation until the law was passed. Thus the remigration of 1982–84 was primarily caused by the recession of 1982.[48] This highly ambivalent policy not only confused foreigners and Germans alike but also produced results, i.e. a growing foreign population, inconsistent with its openly proclaimed goals. Worst of all, it left the impression that immigration was detrimental to the FRG and that the government was unable to monitor it.

Turning to the effects on German society as a whole, one is faced with the problem that very little research on the social history of the 1970s and 1980s has yet been undertaken. Nonetheless, five general tendencies are clearly visible. First, as more foreign children and wives came to live in the FRG and the first ex-guestworkers retired, the cost–benefit calculation of the 1960s had to be revised. Expenditure on additional school places, medical charges, pensions and other benefits

48. Rist, *Guestworkers in Germany*, pp. 78–88; Esser, 'Gastarbeiter', pp. 334–41; Herbert, *Geschichte*, pp. 220–36; Bade, *Ausländer*, pp. 14–17.

was growing fast. Altogether, foreigners' tax and contribution payments, however, still exceeded the capital outlay they caused. Other economic gains were also shrinking. Due to the move out of mass accommodation, the regional mobility of foreign labour was declining, and the recruitment ban had finally destroyed the elasticity of its supply. Foreigners' relatively low qualifications meant that they were hardest hit by recession, de-industrialization and rationalization. From 1974 their unemployment rate exceeded that of Germans: in 1983 it was 14.7 per cent compared with a German quota of 9.1 per cent. Thus they no longer subsidized this part of the social insurance system.[49]

Second, as Figure 2.1 shows, the FRG had been experiencing a natural population decrease since 1972. This situation, unique among Western nations until 1984, was closely linked with another fundamental change within West German society, namely the transformation of family structures. Immediately after the war many families were incomplete or highly unstable. Numbers of divorces, illegitimate children and employed mothers reached unprecedented peaks. To many observers the end of the traditional family seemed to be near. The 1950s, however, saw its successful restoration. It was only in the 1960s that its permanent dissolution began and in the 1970s and 1980s that this process was substantially accelerated. Now only a diminishing number of women still found it acceptable to define their social status through their husbands or their role as mother. The number of married women who were employed nearly doubled between 1950 (25 per cent) and 1990 (47.4 per cent). At the same time women made great progress in catching up with men in terms of educational and professional qualifications.

Greater participation and less disadvantages on the labour market were not the only indicators of change. There was also a marked trend towards more individualistic forms of life in general. Marriages tended to become less durable as the divorce rate trebled between 1960 and 1985, and a rising number of people preferred to live outside traditional families. In 1985 the average household size had fallen to 2.3 persons, and 33.6 per cent of all households were occupied by one person only. New 'family patterns' emerged and began to become socially acceptable, such as cohabitation, childless couples, single or unmarried parents, singles, long-distance, commuting families living apart yet together, and homosexual couples. There were two main driving forces behind these far-reaching transformations, first the wish for more individual freedom and second the demands of a dynamic society for a highly qualified

49. Erichsen, 'Zurückkehren', p. 17; Herbert, *Geschichte*, p. 225; Rürup and Sesselmeier, 'Einwanderung', pp. 296–300.

and mobile workforce. For women this situation meant that they increasingly preferred to have no children at all or to have them at a later stage in their lives. Thus motherhood tended to become the result of a deliberate decision rather than a matter of course. Moreover, official family politics failed to adapt to this new constellation and to create an adequate supply of crèche and kindergarten places, which made it difficult to combine family and professional life. Whatever the overall and lasting effects of these fundamental social changes will be, the resulting decline in the birth rate made the FRG a rapidly aging country and put an enormous burden on its welfare state. An increasing share of pensioners and patients now had to be provided for by a decreasing workforce, which simultaneously had to support rising numbers of jobless. At the same time, some segments of the labour markets were beginning to face recruitment problems. Although the foreign population was by no means large enough to reverse these trends, which had not yet reached their full extent, immigrants did absorb and delay them to some extent because of a more favourable age structure and higher birth rates. 'Between 1972 and 1976 the birth deficit . . . of the German population amounted to 941,187, whereas the surplus of births among the non-German population totalled 435,567; as a result the overall deficit . . . was cut by 46,3 per cent to 505,620.'[50]

Third, in the 1970s and 1980s the social history of the FRG was generally characterized by two main tendencies, the continuation of modernization processes embarked on in the 1960s and the emergence of structural mass unemployment. The overall qualification profile of the workforce improved steadily. Whereas only 11 per cent of all people aged between 18 and 20 had passed the *Abitur* in 1970, this figure had doubled by 1985. At the same time the number of students grew from 525,000 to 1,300,000. The service sector kept on growing at the expense of industry, exceeding employment in the primary and secondary sectors for the first time in 1980 and reaching 53.9 per cent in 1988 after 42.7 per cent in 1970. Between 1970 and 1986 2.5 million jobs in industry, i.e. nearly one-fifth (19 per cent) of total industrial employment, were lost. At the same time 2.5 million new jobs (22 per cent) were created in the service sector. This fundamental structural shift changed the qualifications and skills demanded by employers. Thus between 1970 and 1989 the share of

50. Wolfgang Köllmann, 'The Historical Background', in David Eversley and Wolfgang Köllmann, eds, *Population Change and Social Planning* (London, 1982), p. 15. See also idem, 'Bevölkerungsentwicklung', pp. 91–103; Bethlehem, *Heimatvertreibung*, pp. 132–8; and Figure 2.1. For the family since the 1950s see Merith Niehuss, 'Kontinuität und Wandel der Familie in den 50er Jahren', in Axel Schildt and Arnold Sywottek, eds, *Modernisierung im Wiederaufbau. Die westdeutsche Gesellschaft der 50er Jahre* (Bonn, 1993), pp. 316–48 and see note 35 above.

graduates among the total workforce almost doubled from 4 to 7 per cent, and the amount of skilled labour rose from 44 to 58 per cent. The quota of unqualified personnel meanwhile dropped from 41 to 23 per cent. This contraction at the lowest end of the labour market meant that a growing number of people were excluded from employment for structural reasons, i.e. lack of skills, rationalization or de-industrialization. As a consequence, their fate is largely independent of the business cycle, and their chances of ever finding a new job minimal. In 1986 50 per cent of the 2.2 million unemployed (9 per cent) had no formal qualifications at all, 32 per cent had been on the dole for more than one year, 31 per cent were older than 45, and an unspecified number were disadvantaged for health reasons. To sum up, the continued transition from an industrial to a service society drastically raised the qualification standards required by the labour market. While the majority of Germans adapted themselves successfully to this situation, a growing minority was pushed from the bottom rung of the occupational ladder into long-term unemployment, relative poverty and dependence on the welfare state.[51]

Fourth, part of this process was the dissolution of the relatively homogeneous guestworker underclass of the 1960s. Although foreigners were still over-represented in the lowest-paid jobs, a growing number of them responded to the economic challenge of the time, acquired better qualifications, and began to rise socially. Recently research on a representative panel of male Turks in 1988 recorded a rate of skilled labourers of only 8.8 per cent among the first generation, who had moved into the FRG before 1973. This figure had risen, however, among the second generation, i.e. their sons, to 23.1 per cent. Simultaneously, education had greatly improved. Some 11 per cent of the second generation held qualifications from further education, and 7 per cent had even passed the *Abitur.* Among a parallel Greek sample, 17 per cent of the second generation aged between 18 and 24 had been or were in higher education, having almost caught up with Germans of the same age (23 per cent). The number of self-employed foreigners almost trebled after 1973, reaching 140,000 in 1987. To sum up, processes of intra- and most of all intergenerational social mobility took place and greatly improved the incomes and living conditions of many foreigners. It must, however, be strongly emphasized that not all foreigners were able to participate in this upward movement. According to the 1988 study of Turks and Greeks, the transformation from guestworkers to immigrants produced not only 'winners' but also 'losers'. The latter joined the ranks of long-

51. Geissler, *Die Sozialstruktur Deutschlands*, pp. 198–205, 212–17; Statistisches Bundesamt, *Datenreport 1989. Zahlen und Fakten über die Bundesrepublik Deutschland* (Bonn, 1987), pp. 83–4, 92–7; and see note 47 above.

term unemployed Germans, the difference being that the foreign jobless were predominantly under 25. The 1988 Turkish sample identified 41 per cent of members of the second generation who had left school with no exam pass at all. Thus, roughly speaking, the foreign population began to differentiate itself at the extreme ends into one group of ambitious social climbers and another of jobless and frustrated youths.[52]

Fifth, all the phenomena described so far contributed to a rather ambivalent relationship between Germans and foreigners. On the one hand, processes of sociocultural integration and assimiliation proceeded at an enormous speed, while, on the other, open xenophobia emerged. According to the 1988 study, only 26 per cent of first-generation Turks met Germans outside work, whereas the second generation recorded a rise to 65 per cent. Fluency in German had increased from 23 to 73 per cent, and with it familiarity with customs and social norms. Trade unions opened themselves to foreign workers, who in some cases were better organized than their German colleagues. Membership of German clubs also increased in the 1980s, making more and more foreigners feel at home. In 1989 only 11 per cent of a foreign panel had made definite plans to leave the FRG, while 90 per cent of Turkish and Yugoslav youths asked in 1988 said they liked living in the FRG, and 55 per cent could envisage marrying a German. In fact, a rising number of foreigners have German relations, as more than 370,000 German–foreign couples married between 1973 and 1986. In 1989 9 per cent of all marriages fell into this category. Patterns of consumption were converging, which meant decreasing remittances and savings as well as increased spending on consumer goods and real property in Germany. Despite their passports, young foreigners often lost touch with the language and culture of their parents' native countries. All this demonstrates that the guestworker's perspective of a better life back home was gradually being replaced by the immigrant's outlook, who was beginning to put down roots in his new environment.[53]

Considering the speed and extent of integration, the simultaneous

52. Günther Schultze, 'Die Gesellschaft der Bundesrepublik Deutschland auf dem Weg zur multikulturellen Gesellschaft? Zum Eingliederungsprozess von griechischen Jugendlichen und Türken der ersten und zweiten Generation', *Archiv für Sozialgeschichte* 32 (1992), 253–67; Harald Schumacher, *Einwanderungsland BRD? Warum die deutsche Wirtschaft weiter Ausländer braucht* 2nd edn (Düsseldorf, 1993), pp. 38–44.

53. In 1986 29.4 per cent of all foreigners had taken out life insurances in the FRG and 14.6 per cent had been on long-term saving schemes with building societies. By 1993 11 per cent of all Turkish households lived in their own property. See Bade, *Ausländer*, pp. 12–17; Erichsen, 'Zurückkehren', pp. 21–5; Geissler, *Die Sozialstruktur Deutschlands*, pp. 153–61; Schumacher, *Einwanderungsland BRD?*, pp. 40, 99, 144; Schultze, 'Gesellschaft', 254–60.

rise of xenophobia is difficult to account for. There are, however, four tendencies which offer some explanation. To start with, the upward social mobility of foreigners provoked the envy of Germans who found themselves at the bottom of the social ladder or totally excluded from employment and with it the wealth of the FRG. Obviously many clung to the myth of German superiority and found it difficult to accept reality. At the same time, rising numbers of foreigners out of work stirred up anxieties and antagonistic attitudes. The concentration of disconcerted foreign youths in certain districts triggered fears of social unrest and crime which were grossly out of proportion to the real problems, however serious they were. Moreover, Turks became the largest foreign nationality in 1971. Islamic traditions are very different from the sociocultural background of most Germans. A lack of understanding of religious and everyday life created prejudices and intensified the rejection of foreigners in general, particularly in areas with high numbers of Turkish inhabitants. The rise of Islamic fundamentalism and hostilities between Turks and Kurds living in the FRG did little to foster mutual understanding. Finally, it has already been pointed out that the contradictory political line pursued by various governments failed to make it clear that the foreign population had become a permanent part of West German society. Open xenophobia emerged in 1979–83, when in the wake of the second oil crisis unemployment figures reached post-war records and asylum-seekers from Third World countries entered the FRG in tens of thousands. A series of newspaper articles demanded the repatriation of all foreigners. In 1981 eight professors published the Heidelberg Manifesto, an openly racist programme which conjured up the dangers of millions of foreigners infiltrating Germany and destroying its 'cultural and ethnic integrity'. At the same time, several right-wing splinter parties were founded, and racist jokes about Turks, closely modelled on antisemitic stereotypes, spread throughout the country. The wave of open hostility towards foreigners, however, ebbed away with the economic recovery of 1983, only to return with a vengeance to reveal its brutal face at the end of the decade.[54]

54. Bade, *Auswanderungsland*, pp. 110–16; Thränhardt, 'Bundesrepublik Deutschland', pp. 11–13.

ASYLUM-SEEKERS, ETHNIC GERMANS, RESETTLERS AND GERMAN UNIFICATION, 1987–92

Neither *perestroika* nor *glasnost* succeeded in surmounting the political and economic crisis in the USSR. Instead they heralded the disintegration of its empire, which was accompanied by a drastic deterioration of living conditions and the outbreak of fierce nationalism and ethnic violence. These historic transformations affected Germany in several ways. They caused the collapse of the GDR, its unification with the FRG, and mass migration of a scale unknown since the 1940s. Figure 2.1 shows that net immigration into West Germany[55] began to rise dramatically in 1986 and reached an all-time high in 1989–92, the absolute climax occuring in 1990 with a gain of over one million people. Figure 2.3 distinguishes between the most important groups of immigrants, asylum-seekers, ethnic Germans from Eastern Europe and former GDR citizens, and proves that in all three cases a stream turned into a flood in 1988–92.

Asylum was now sought mainly by refugees fleeing the chaos of the disintegrating Eastern Bloc, whereas in the 1970s and early 1980s refugees from Third World countries predominated. In 1992, when 438,191 asylum-seekers – more than double the number entering the FRG in the 25 years between 1953 and 1978 – were registered their origins were as follows: former Yugoslavia (28 per cent), Romania (23.7 per cent), Bulgaria (7.2 per cent), Turkey (6.5 per cent) and the former USSR (2.5 per cent). No other Western country was confronted with a refugee problem of similar proportions. In fact, the FRG had to deal with the majority of asylum-seekers entering the EC (now the EU),[56] for geographical as well as legal reasons. Not only is the FRG the only member to have common land boundaries with former Eastern Bloc countries, but in 1992 it also had the most liberal refugee laws. Remembering the fate of refugees from Nazi Germany, the Parliamentary Council of 1949 established article 16 of the FRG's constitution. It gave those who were persecuted for political reasons the unconditional right to claim asylum in the FRG. Border police were thus unable to refuse entry to anyone claiming refugee status. Then a lengthy investigation

55. Data for 1990–92 refer to the old FRG, thus movements between East and West Germany were treated as immigration and emigration respectively.

56. In 1991 compounded refugee numbers in Britain (58,000) and France (47,000) were less than half the FRG's contingent (256,000). See Schumacher, *Einwanderungsland BRD?*, p. 19; Der Bundesminister für Arbeit und Sozialordnung, *Ausländerdaten*.

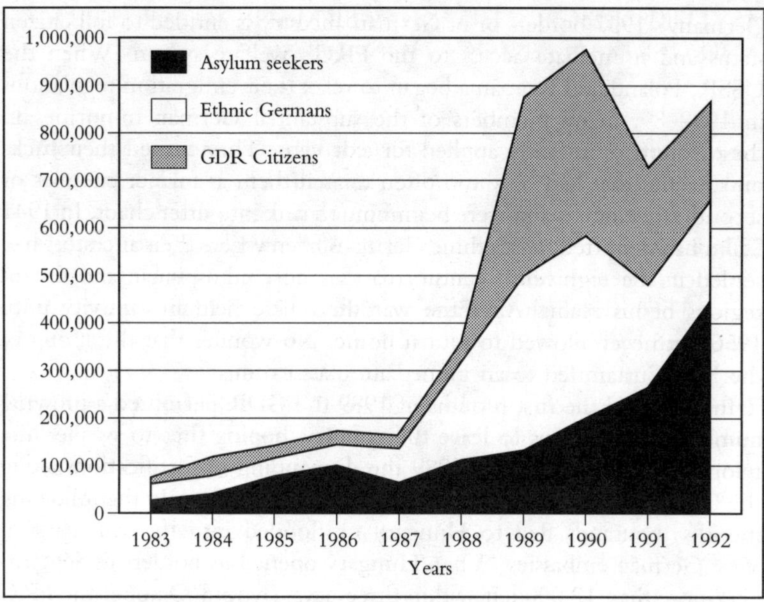

Figure 2.3: The influx of asylum-seekers, ethnic Germans and former GDR citizens into the FRG, 1983–92

Year	Asylum-seekers ('000)	Ethnic Germans from Eastern Europe ('000)	GDR citizens/ former GDR citizens ('000)	Total ('000)
1983	19.737	37.844	13.400	70.981
1984	35.278	36.459	42.316	114.053
1985	73.832	38.968	26.346	139.146
1986	99.650	42.788	26.191	168.629
1987	57.379	78.523	18.961	154.863
1988	103.076	202.673	39.832	345.581
1989	121.318	377.055	388.400	886.773
1990	193.063	397.075	395.300	985.438
1991	256.112	221.995	249.743	727.850
1992	438.191	230.565	199.170	867.926

Source: *Statistische Jahrbücher der Bundesrepublik Deutschland* and G. Hullen and R. Schulz, 'Bericht 1993.

into each individual case would follow, after which, irrespective of the outcome, only a small proportion of applicants would be repatriated. In 1993 the refugee laws were amended, making it much more difficult to claim asylum.

The majority of immigrants from Eastern Europe, however, were ethnic Germans. According to citizenship laws, anyone born inside

Germany's 1937 borders or of German ancestry is entitled to full citizen status and immediate access to the FRG's welfare system. When the USSR, Poland and Romania began to relax their emigration regulations in 1988–89, many members of the substantial German minorities in these countries instantly applied for exit visas. They turned their backs on societies that had only too often treated them as former enemies or second-rate citizens and were beginning to sink into utter chaos. In 1941 Stalin had deported most ethnic Germans from where their ancestors had settled in the eighteenth century to the most inhospitable and distant regions of his realm. After the war they were held in captivity until 1956 but never allowed to return home. No wonder that the lifting of the Iron Curtain led to an immediate mass exodus.[57]

In 1988 and the first months of 1989 the GDR permitted a growing number of its citizens to leave the country, hoping thus to weaken the reform movement. In May 1989 the dismantling of fortifications along the Hungarian–Austrian border intensified this outflow. In the following months thousands fled to Hungary or flooded into the sanctuary of West German embassies. When Hungary opened its borders in September, more than 12,000 left within three days. By mid-October the FRG had registered 132,075 GDR refugees. The following weeks saw a mounting wave of refugees, 60,000 alone in the first six days of November, and mass demonstrations demanding fundamental reforms. After the opening of the Berlin Wall on 9 November, the collective exodus gathered further momentum, and early in 1990 more than 2,000 a day left for the FRG. In fact, emigration acted as a main stimulus to reforms within the GDR but eventually exceeded their speed. Later the same year neither currency reform nor economic and political union managed to stop the flow of people from East to West. Thus the migration pattern of the 1950s re-emerged in 1990 and young, well-trained people left for the West, too impatient to wait for the economic reconstruction of East Germany and determined to participate in Western prosperity right away.[58]

So far one can discern six effects of these parallel immigration movements. First of all, their coincidence and gigantic scale aggravated the problems of German unification as well as those which had developed within the old FRG during the 1970s and 1980s. In 1987–92 a surplus

57. Klaus J. Bade, 'Aussiedler – Rückwanderer über Generationen hinweg', in idem, ed., *Heimat*, pp. 128–49; D. L. Bark and D. R. Gress, *A History of West Germany, Vol. 2: Democracy and its Discontents 1963–1991* 2nd edn (Oxford, 1993), pp. 563–4, 763–4.

58. Bark and Gress, *Democracy and its Discontents*, pp. 588–659. In 1989–92 1.2 million people moved from East to West, but only 232,964 from West to East Germany. Gert Hullen and Reiner Schulz, 'Bericht 1993 zur demographischen Lage in Deutschland', *Zeitschrift für Bevölkerungswissenschaft* 19 (1993–94), 22–3.

population of more than four million people had to be housed and fed. Very few towns and villages were without mass accommodation. When their occupants moved out to vacate places for new arrivals, West Germany's chronic housing shortage was further increased. In 1992 a deficit of about two million dwellings was recorded. Especially at the lower end of the market, i.e. flats with modest rents, it became extremely tight. According to one survey, 800,000 people were homeless in West Germany in 1991 and living in hostels, shelters or on the streets. Another 700,000 had to put up with inadequate or overcrowded accommodation. This situation deteriorated further in 1991 and 1992.[59]

Second, ethnic Germans, asylum-seekers and all West Germans dealing with them were faced with enormous sociocultural barriers. Many ethnic Germans had language problems, speaking no or only basic German or having grown up with antiquated dialects. Moreover, being transplanted from the backwaters of Poland or Central Asia into the hustle and bustle of a modern capitalist society can be a difficult experience to cope with. Many obviously did not find the Germany they had dreamt of. Asylum-seekers encountered even bigger problems but received less help from the authorities. The total strangeness of the host country, the ambivalence of their status and uncertainty about their future put them in an extremely precarious position. Living conditions in hostels, overcrowded with people adhering to different cultural, religious and social rules, put an additional strain on them.

Third, the integration of former GDR citizens and ethnic Germans into the West German labour market progressed with amazing speed. A survey of all immigrants in 1988–92 found that more than one-third had already found jobs by the end of 1992. Among them, former GDR citizens (61 per cent) stood the highest chances of taking up employment, but ethnic Germans (31 per cent) also did very well. Asylum-seekers (6 per cent) had the greatest difficulties, caused by language problems, low qualifications and above all legal restrictions. They were forbidden to work during their first five years in the FRG. In January 1991 this ban was reduced to one year and abolished in July. Without it the overall rate of jobs taken up by immigrants would have been even higher, and in 1988–92 the FRG probably would not have recruited more than 200,000 guest-workers from Eastern Europe for temporary jobs in building, agriculture and catering. Despite continued mass unemployment it was impossible to fill them with jobless Germans. This also explains the success of former GDR citizens and ethnic Germans. They proved to be highly flexible as

59. Schumacher, *Einwanderungsland BRD?*, pp. 91–5; Geissler, *Die Sozialstruktur Deutschlands*, pp. 176–7.

well as motivated and were prepared to accept work below the level of their qualifications. Finally, demand was brisk with 2.2 million new jobs being created in 1988–92 by the post-unification boom.

Fourth, the same study undertook an econometric cost–benefit analysis of immigration in 1988–92. Its surprising finding was that extra revenue from taxes and social insurance contributions exceeded expenditure by DM14 billion in 1991 and 1992 respectively. However, immigrants did not only reduce the FRG's public debt but also stimulated economic growth, which on average reached 3.5 per cent a year in 1988–92. Without them a figure of only 2 per cent would have been possible.[60]

Fifth, none of the social problems that had emerged since the 1970s had been solved by 1987. According to recent sociological research, only 75 per cent of all West Germans lived in financially stable conditions in the 1980s, while 15 per cent were threatened by temporary and 10 per cent were faced by permanent or long-term poverty. Although West Germany's unemployment rate dropped from 8.7 per cent in 1988 to 5.9 per cent in 1992, overall social tensions increased after unification. At the end of 1992, 3.1 million jobless were recorded in the new FRG, and another 0.9 million were to join the dole queue over the next 13 months. Some 4.2 million people received social security benefits in 1991. A geographical breakdown of statistics reveals that despite political unification Germany remained a socially as well as an economically divided country. While employment grew in the West, 57 per cent of all jobs in East German industry were axed between January 1991 and August 1992. In 1992 the unemployment rate in the former GDR (15.5 per cent) was almost three times as high as in West Germany (5.9 per cent). Other indicators also emphasize the depth of the rift between both Germanies and the extent of the social catastrophe taking place in the East. Dismal economic prospects caused, for example, a dramatic fall in marriages. Within four years the birth rate dropped by 54 per cent to a historic low in 1992, which was less than half the minute West German birth rate. Most depressing of all, suicide rates in the East exceeded those in the West by almost 40 per cent in 1991.[61]

60. Bundesminister für Arbeit, *Ausländerdaten*; György Barabas *et al.*, 'Gesamtwirtschaftliche Effekte der Zuwanderung 1988 bis 1991', *RWI-Mitteilungen* 43 (1992), 133–54; Arne Gieseck *et al.*, 'Wirtschafts- und sozialpolitische Aspekte der Zuwanderung in die Bundesrepublik', *APUZ* 7 (1993), 29–41; Volker Ronge, 'Ost–West-Wanderung nach Deutschland', *APUZ* 7 (1993), 21.

61. Lutz. Leisering 'Zur Wissenschaftssoziologie der Armut in der bundesrepublikanischen Gesellschaft', *Soziale Welt* 44 (1993), 499–502; Hullen and Schulz, 'Bericht 1993', pp. 6–18 – the dramatic fall in the East German birth rate from 12.0 per 1,000 inhabitants (1989) to 5.5 (1992) brought it below the West German birth rate of 11.1 (1991), already one of the lowest in Europe; *Der Spiegel*, No. 52, 1993, p. 83; *Die Zeit*, No. 2, 1992, No. 7, 1994.

Sixth, developments in both parts of the united Germany widened the gulf between the top and the bottom of its society. Furthermore, the exclusion and poverty of a fast-growing minority came to be tacitly accepted by the majority, who enjoyed relative security or even prosperity. Under these circumstances the victims of this process tried to draw society's attention to themselves and at the same time began to look for scapegoats. A 1991 poll revealed that every other German believed that foreigners were responsible for high unemployment. Two-thirds blamed them for exploiting the social system. Right-wing organizations thus had easy play in finding audiences prepared to listen to simplistic anti-foreigner messages like: 'Turkey for the Turks, Germany for the Germans!' In 1989–92 they succeeded in being elected to four *Länder* parliaments, collecting their votes mainly from the lowest social strata, in which frustration about being pushed to the periphery of a rich society was mounting. Some went beyond protest at the ballot box. Although racial violence had been rising all through the 1980s, it was only after unification that the floodgates opened. In 1983–90 an average of 180 acts of right-wing violence per year had been reported. In 1991 their number reached 1,483 and in 1992 2,583, some of them open pogroms, such as the 1992 burning of a Rostock multi-storey building packed with asylum-seekers to the applause of hundreds of onlookers and the eyes of passive police. Waves of blind hate swept the country, making not only asylum-seekers and Turks, but also in some cases foreign visitors, disabled, Jews and ethnic Germans victims of racial violence.[62] Yet it is too early to pass a final judgement on the years 1987–92, especially on the effects of immigration and the integration of two German societies which had not only been geographically separated, but had lived under different political, economic and social structures for 40 years.

62. For a list of events in Germany from 1987 to 1992 see Schumacher, *Einwanderungsland BRD?*, pp. 118–33. The data were gathered from Albert Mühlum, 'Armutswanderung, Asyl und Abwehrverhalten. Globale und nationale Dilemmata', *APUZ* 7 (1993), 12; *Der Spiegel*, No. 27, 1993, p. 82. See also Chapter 7 in this book.

CHAPTER THREE

Domestic Political Developments I: 1949–69

Torsten Oppelland

THE CONSTITUTIONAL FRAMEWORK

On 23 May 1949, with the passing of the Basic Law, the new constitution, the history of the second German democracy in the twentieth century began.[1] The Basic Law would soon become one of the most influential features and unique characteristics of the new West German state. The authors of the new constitution expressly intended to avoid repeating the experience of the Weimar constitution that had lasted only 14 years before succumbing feebly to the Nazi dictatorship. The attention given to human and civil rights – the first 19 articles of the new constitution were devoted to these – was clearly in reaction to the experiences of the recent past. The whole institutional edifice of the Basic Law was designed to ensure stability in the government. The instability that had plagued the Weimar Republic (20 cabinets in only 14 years) had to be avoided.

In sharp contrast to the position in the Weimar Republic, the position of the very powerful President was limited to a representative role while the position of Chancellor was correspondingly strengthened. This was accomplished by the adoption of the 'constructive vote of censure'. This made it impossible to depose the Chancellor unless an absolute majority

1. For some reason this date has never captured the collective imagination of the German people; from the mid-fifties to 1990 the national holiday commemorated the uprising in East Germany (GDR) against communist rule (17 June 1953). Since 1990 Germans commemorate the date of the official reunification (3 October 1990). The most memorable date in recent history remains 9 November: 1918 revolution, 1923 Hitler's attempted *coup d'état*, 1938 the first organized riots against German Jews (the infamous *Reichskristallnacht*), 1989 the opening of the Berlin Wall. See Johannes Willms, ed., *Der 9. November: Fünf Essays zur deutschen Geschichte* (Munich, 1994).

of the *Bundestag* was (and is) prepared to elect another.[2] Together with a variety of other factors outside the constitution, this provision has been remarkably successful in promoting stability. The vote of censure has only been used twice: once, in 1972, unsuccessfully and then, in 1982, with success. All other governments have lasted until the end of their terms.

Another provision designed to promote the stability of a multi-party system was the famous '5 per cent' clause, which in the case of the first Federal elections in 1949 was also drafted by the same Parliamentary Council that deliberated and passed the Basic Law. In those first elections the 5 per cent clause applied only to the state level. A party would only be represented in the first *Bundestag* if it had won at least 5 per cent of the vote in at least one Federal state. Before the next elections in 1953, the electoral law was expanded to the Federal level. Henceforward, a party would only be represented in the *Bundestag* if it had succeeded in the difficult task of winning at least 5 per cent of the entire vote cast in the whole of the Federal Republic – not just in one Federal state as had been the case with the 1949 election. There was only one exception to this rule. If the party had gained a minimum of three constituency mandates it would also be represented in the next parliament even if it remained below the 5 per cent hurdle – a provision that saved the PDS (the successor to the East German SED) in 1994. This reform not only served to reduce the number of parties in the *Bundestag* but also ensured that the German Communist Party (KPD) would not gain representation in the second *Bundestag*.[3]

One lesson that was learned from the fall of the Weimar Republic was that a democracy needed the means to defend itself against its enemies. The newly founded Federal Constitutional Court (*Bundesverfassungsgericht*) was given the power to ban an anti-democratic party, provided the Federal government charged it with being 'inimical

2. If the majority of the *Bundestag* refuses to follow the Chancellor in a vote of confidence, the President has the option to dissolve the *Bundestag* and call general elections or to let the Chancellor continue without a stable majority; Basic Law Art. 68. This is one of the few remaining instances where the President has a decisive influence. Such a scenario has occurred only twice, in 1972 and in 1983, and in both cases the respective presidents decided to leave the decision to the people, i.e. to dissolve the *Bundestag* and call general elections.

3. For the debate on the electoral law that came up again in the late sixties under the Grand Coalition when a second attempt was made to introduce a British-type majority system, see Eckhard Jesse, *Wahlrecht zwischen Kontinuität und Reform: Eine Analyse der Wahlrechtsänderungen in der Bundesrepublik Deutschland 1949–1983* (Düsseldorf, 1983); Erhard H.M. Lange, *Wahlrecht und Innenpolitik. Entstehungsgeschichte und Analyse der Wahlgesetzgebung und Wahlrechtsdiskussion im westlichen Nachkriegsdeutschland 1945–1956* (Meisenheim, 1975).

to the constitution'. This self-defence became known as the concept of 'militant democracy' (*wehrhafte Demokratie*) when it was applied against a neo-Nazi party in 1953 and against the KPD in 1956. The antipathy of the founders against any sort of referendum can also be seen to be a result of the experience of the Weimar Republic and the Third Reich.[4]

Lastly it is important to mention another element in this constitutional framework: namely federalism. During the Third Reich, federalism had of course been, *de facto*, abolished. The Weimar version of federalism had been somewhat unbalanced because of the domination exerted by the state of Prussia, which at that time covered almost two-thirds of German territory. This had already been corrected during the military occupation after 1945, particularly in the British zone, which consisted basically of the western parts of Prussia and some new states. Northrhine-Westphalia and Lower Saxony had been founded by the British military government. Together with the states of the American and the French zones, this new federalism was much more balanced than before.[5] In the collective memory of Western Germany the domineering personality of the first Chancellor, Konrad Adenauer, and two or three other politicians such as Kurt Schumacher, the less successful but equally dominating leader of the Social Democratic Party (SPD), Theodor Heuss, the popular first President, and Ludwig Erhard, the father of the economic miracle (*Wirtschaftswunder*), have overshadowed the role of those statesmen in the state governments who, with their adninistrative experience and talent, played a great part in the reconstruction of West Germany. Their authoritative style formed the political culture of the era. Amongst these there were the mayors of the city-states: Wilhelm Kaisen of Bremen, Max Brauer of Hamburg and, best known, Ernst Reuter, Mayor of Berlin during the blockade; then there were the Minister-Presidents Georg August Zinn of Hessia and Hinrich Kopf of Lower Saxony (all SPD) and Reinhold Maier who managed the union of Baden and Württemburg. He was the only Minister-President ever to come from the small Liberal Party (FDP). Of course some were from the Christian Democrat Party (CDU): for instance Karl Arnold of Northrhine-Westphalia. The special case of Bavaria, where the preponderance of the

4. For the deliberations in the Parliamentary Council see Karlheinz Niclauss, 'Der Parlamentarische Rat und die plebiszitären Elemente', *APUZ* 45 (1992), 3–15.

5. The issue of federalism was a matter of contention between the Allied powers, particularly the French and the Americans, on the one hand, and the Parliamentary Council, particularly the SPD *Bundestag* group which was in favour of a more centralized type of federalism, on the other. See Hans-Jürgen Grabbe, 'Die deutsch–alliierte Kontroverse um den Grundgesetzentwurf im Frühjahr 1949', *Vierteljahrshefte für Zeitgeschichte* 26 (1978), 393–418.

Christian Social Union (CSU) (the CDU's sister party) soon developed, also deserves mentioning.[6]

When dealing with the first years of the 'Bonn Republic' one has to keep in mind three facts. Firstly, the new state, the Federal Republic of Germany (FRG), was not a sovereign state at that time. In 1949 the military government of the Allied powers was replaced by a High Commission and sovereign military rule by the Statute of Occupation. Foreign affairs and foreign trade were both controlled by the High Commission. All military matters (the FRG was of course still without any military forces of its own), reparations and the process of dismantling entire factories as industrial reparations (which absurdly continued after 1949, i.e. long after West Germany had become a beneficiary of Marshall Plan Aid) were fully under the control of the Allied powers. These measures were extremely unpopular with the German people who still suffered from high unemployment – the late fifties when foreign labour had to be imported to keep up the growth rate of the economy were still far away. Even matters that were, in other countries, clearly domestic, such as finances and taxation, fell within the competence of the High Commission or at least under its supervision.[7] The High Commission kept a large bureaucracy at its service whose support, together with the costs of the Allied troops stationed in West Germany, consumed more than a third of the Federal budget of 1949.[8] The transformation of German–Allied relations from complete dependence to real alignment remained one of the major goals of the first Adenauer governments. It was largely achieved in 1955 when the FRG entered NATO as a full member and regained its sovereignty (albeit with some remaining restrictions).[9]

Secondly, the Federal Republic was not a complete nation-state. The division of the German nation into two states had become fact, but a

6. For the early years of the new West German state see Parts I, II and III in Dennis L. Bark and David R. Gress, *A History of West Germany, Vol. I: From Shadow to Substance, 1945–1963* (Oxford, 1989).

7. Recently a considerable amount of research has been conducted on the policies of the American High Commission under John J. McCloy, whereas the British Commissioner, General Robertson, has been somewhat neglected. See Thomas Schwartz, *From Occupation to Alliance: John J. McCloy and the Allied High Commission in the Federal Republic of Germany, 1949–1952* (Ann Arbor, Mich., 1985); Hermann-Josef Rupieper, *Der besetzte Verbündete: Die amerikanische Deutschlandpolik 1949–1955* (Opladen, 1991).

8. See Hans-Peter Schwarz, *Adenauer, Vol. I: Der Aufstieg 1876–1952* (Munich, 1993), pp. 672–3 (paperback edn).

9. See the various articles in Ludolf Herbst *et al.*, eds, *Vom Marshallplan zur EWG: Die Eingliederung der Bundesrepublik Deutschland in die westliche Welt* (Munich, 1990).

fact nevertheless that was not yet an accepted reality. The West German Republic was expressly constructed as a provisional state, or, as Theodor Heuss called it, a 'Transitorium'. That is why inconspicuous Bonn became the capital and seat of government and not the old, traditionally important city of Frankfurt. Bonn was intended to be a provisional substitute for the real capital, Berlin. That is also why there was no referendum on the new constitution, the Basic Law. A 'real' constitution was to be adopted by all Germans (something that was conveniently forgotten in 1990). All politicians either shared or, at least, had to take into account that there existed widespread feeling that reunification was or had to be the primary goal of West German politics. Moreover, the preamble of the Basic Law required all West German governments to pursue reunification. This is why Adenauer consistently tried to sell his policy of integration with the West as the direct path to reunification. This referred not only to the GDR; there were the 'territories temporarily under Polish (or Soviet) administration' east of the Oder–Neisse line. The millions of German refugees had not at all accepted the fact that these territories, for which no final settlement had been reached at the Potsdam conference, were in fact lost for good. In domestic politics these refugees and their pressure groups remained an important factor until in 1990, with reunification, the borders with Poland and Czechoslovakia were finally recognized.[10]

Third and last, the Federal Republic was, at least during the fifties, the most important front-line state in the Cold War. This fact had an enormous impact not only on all foreign policy decisions but also on domestic politics. The FRG was, for instance, the only Western state where the Communist Party was outlawed; not even the United States in the McCarthy era went as far. The anti-communist conviction was shared by all democratic parties, especially the SPD, who had not forgiven the forced amalgamation of the Eastern SPD and the KPD which resulted in the establishment of the East German Socialist Unity Party (SED).[11] The implications of being on the front line of the Cold War were ambiguous. On the one hand there was throughout the era of reconstruction and economic miracle a persistent feeling of underlying insecurity, fear and depedence on the protection of the Allies and the Americans in particular. On the other hand the particular West German situation and the pro-active anti-communism was a factor that muffled

10. See Bark and Gress, *From Shadow to Substance*, pp. 305–10.

11. See Kurt Schumacher, *Reden – Schriften – Korrespondenzen 1945–1952*, ed. Willy Albrecht (Bonn/Berlin, 1985). The book gives many examples of Schumacher's anti-totalitarian views, which included anti-communism.

party strife and contributed to the remarkable stability of this second democracy in Germany.[12]

THE ADENAUER ERA (1949–59)

On 21 August 1949 Konrad Adenauer assembled a group of CDU and CSU notables at his villa in Rhöndorf, a small village on the east bank of the Rhine near Bonn. This 'Rhöndorf Conference', as it came to be known, took place one week after the first Federal elections in the FRG. The CDU/CSU had become the strongest party with 139 seats, only a few seats ahead of the SPD with 131 seats.[13] Numerous small parties were represented in the first *Bundestag*. Among them were the Liberals, who had overcome the historical split between their right and left wings; the German Party (DP), a conservative party with a strong regional bias from Lower Saxony; the old Centre Party, whose Catholic electorate was eventually swallowed up completely by the CDU/CSU; the Communist Party of Germany (KPD); and several other small and short-lived parties.

The CDU/CSU won the elections on the issue of its economic policies; its main spokesman in this field was Ludwig Erhard. He had been the director of the department of economy in the bizonal 'government' and had guided the West German people through the currency reform of 1948 that was in retrospect the real start of reconstruction.[14] Adenauer had been the leader of the CDU in the British zone. He had won some national renown as the President of the Parliamentary Council.

These two politicians had, through their political rhetoric, polarized the elections on the question of whether the FRG was to have a socialist-inspired, planned economy like Britain, which was at that time the model

12. In a very polemical essay on the world of the West Germans the prominent journalist Günter Gaus – from 1974 to 1981 the first diplomatic representative of the FRG in the GDR – has described this anti-communism as almost totalitarian. See *Die Welt der Westdeutschen: Kritische Betrachtungen* (Cologne, 1986), pp. 117ff., 193–4.

13. For Kurt Schumacher and his SPD this result was a great disappointment. They had expected to be the strongest party and to form the government. See Schumacher, *Reden*, pp. 147–8.

14. See Anthony J. Nicholls, *Freedom with Responsbility: The Social Market Economy in Germany, 1918–1963* (Oxford, 1994).

for German socialists, or a market economy favoured by the Americans.[15] During the Rhöndorf Conference Adenauer, who was the host of this informal assembly, recaptured the main theme of the electoral campaign and made it clear that he was against a 'Grand Coalition' between CDU/CSU and SPD. This was not at all as evident as it may seem.

The CDU was at this point a very heterogeneous party that existed only at state or (in the case of the British zone) at a zonal level. The party was ideologically mixed as well. There was a strong left wing led by Karl Arnold, the Minister-President from Northrhine-Westphalia, who happened to be the only important CDU notable not invited to the Rhöndorf Conference. This left wing had dominated the policy debate in the first phase of the CDU's history. The famous Ahlen programme of 1947 was anti-Marxist, denouncing the concept of class struggle and, at the same time, 'christian-socialist' in calling for the nationalization of key industries such as mining and steel. With the implementation of Erhard's policies in the bizonal government, this programme had to some extent become obsolete. Nevertheless, the CDU left wing remained strong and considered it essential to balance the market economy with a comprehensive welfare system. The new party was united only by the will to end the confessional split in German politics and to create a large, popular alternative to a (at least as far as rhetoric was concerned) still Marxist SPD. At Rhöndorf Adenauer succeeded in winning the support not only of Erhard and his followers, which was to be expected, but also of some of the trade union leaders in the CDU, most notably Jakob Kaiser, the famous leader of the East German CDU who had been ousted by the Soviet authorities in 1947, and Theodor Blank, who became one of Adenauer's most loyal supporters within the party's left wing. The previous day, Adenauer had secured the support of the Bavarian Minister-President and CSU leader Hans Ehard for the coalition with the other bourgeois parties.[16] When it became clear that his preference for the small coalition would prevail, he made his claim to the office of Chancellor. Thus at Rhöndorf the foundation for the 'Adenauer era' was laid.

Once the support of his own party was secured it was fairly easy to strike a deal with the other members of the coalition. For the conservative Deutsche Partei (DP) there was no other partner than the CDU

15. Erhard not only provided the most important issue of the campaign, he was also the most interesting man for the industrial interests, who, after all, financed the campaign to a large extent. See Udo Wengst, 'Die CDU/CSU im Bundestagswahlkampf 1949', *Vierteljahrshefte für Zeitgeschichte* 34 (1986), 40–47.

16. See Schwarz, *Adenauer I*, pp. 622–6 and Henning Köhler, *Adenauer: Eine politische Biographie* (Berlin/Frankfurt am Main, 1994), pp. 520–5.

available. As for the FDP, although it sometimes seemed closer to the SPD on the issues connected with the question of German unification, the differences with the socialists' economic policies could not be overcome. This dilemma kept the FDP tied to the CDU until 1956, and then again from 1961 to 1969 when for the first time a coalition of SPD and FDP was formed on the Federal level. The coalition between FDP, DP and CDU/CSU was cemented by a deal that gave Adenauer the chancellorship, Theodor Heuss, the FDP leader, the presidency, and the Bavarian Ehard the presidency of the *Bundesrat* (the second chamber of the legislative branch which represents the states at the Federal level).[17] On the whole the formation of his first coalition cabinet was a difficult job for Adenauer. This was because of the claims of the different coalition members. The two wings of his own party,[18] and the need for proportional appointments of both Catholics and Protestants, had also to be considered. But once the Chancellor was elected by the *Bundestag* and the cabinet was formally appointed by the President, *Kanzlerdemokratie* – democracy dominated by the Chancellor – soon became evident. Although Adenauer was elected with a majority of only one vote, this forced discipline on the coalition parties and in the end strengthened rather than weakened the coalition.[19]

Adenauer developed two strategies by which he controlled the cabinet. He monopolized contact with the Allied High Commissioners; thus he always stayed one step ahead of his ministers in matters concerning the intentions and policies of the Allies. This monopoly was reinforced following the first (albeit small) revision of the Statute of Occupation when the FRG was allowed to have a Secretary of Foreign Affairs. The position was at once filled by Adenauer himself, though this was not at all popular with some of the CDU leaders who wanted the office for

17. Actually it did not quite work out as planned, for Karl Arnold and not Hans Ehard was elected President of the *Bundesrat* – a bitter defeat for Adenauer which shows how his prestige rose only slowly to the heights he is usually credited with. See Schwarz, *Adenauer I*, p. 628.

18. His most notable defeat was that the party's Protestants forced Gustav Heinemann on him as Minister of the Interior (see Köhler, *Adenauer*, pp. 543–5). Only a year later Heinemann left the cabinet and the CDU because of his profound disagreement with Adenauer's rearmament policy. He founded a new party, the Gesamtdeutsche Volkspartei (All-German People's Party), a single-issue party whose sole political programme, as the name suggests, was reunification. The party was a complete electoral failure and it was dissolved after the general election of 1957. Most of its activists joined the SPD, where many rose to national importance (e.g. Johannes Rau, Erhard Eppler, etc.). See Josef Müller, *Entstehung und Politik unter dem Primat der nationalen Wiedervereinigung 1950–1957* (Düsseldorf, 1990).

19. See Karlheinz Niclauss, *Kanzlerdemokratie: Bonner Regierungspraxis von Konrad Adenauer bis Helmut Kohl* (Stuttgart, 1988); idem, 'Repräsentative und plebiszitäre Elemente der Kanzlerdemokratie', *Vierteljahrshefte für Zeitgeschichte* 35 (1987), 217–45.

themselves. Adenauer held the position until 1955 when the treaties concerning West Germany's membership of NATO and sovereignty were signed and ratified.

The Chancellor was not only a supreme political tactician, he also had the services of the controversial Hans Globke as the secretary of the chancellery.[20] This talented senior official provided Adenauer with a well-managed civil service, not only in the chancellery but also in many other departments. Thus Adenauer was usually well informed about what was going on inside the bureaucracy of his government and had access to the senior officials, thus often circumventing his ministers. In cabinet meetings, the Chancellor left no doubt that he was in charge.[21] Adenauer treated his party and the *Bundestag* coalition in exactly the same way. Since he held the office of Chancellor it was almost preordained that he become party chairman when the CDU was constituted at the Federal level in 1950. However this job was of secondary importance.[22] Over time Adenauer's authoritarian style evolved into a form that may have been best suited to the task of guiding the German people from totalitarianism into democracy.

Complementary to Adenauer's strong government was a strong opposition that crystallized around the SPD, which was led initially by Kurt Schumacher until his death in 1952, and afterwards by Erich Ollenhauer. This represented a true break with the Weimar tradition of broad coalitions, either centre-left or centre-right, that usually included at least three parties. When practically all of the available democratic parties were involved in government, the electorate was left with almost no alternative but to express its opposition to the democratic system itself. This had happened during the last years of the Weimar Republic when the extreme parties of the right and the left grew stronger and stronger. In 1949 the choice of a small coalition was accepted by the SPD along with its role as a loyal democratic and constructive opposition.[23] The Adenauer government's slim majority and the strong position of the SPD in several federal states and thus in the *Bundesrat* facilitated this

20. The problems that were connected with the appointment of Globke will be discussed below. Globke officially became secretary of the chancellery in 1952, but he was administratively the most important senior civil service member from 1949. For Globke's role in Adenauer's government see Arnulf Baring, *Im Anfang war Adenauer: Die Entstehung der Kanzlerdemokratie* 2nd edn (Munich, 1982), pp. 19–22; Klaus Gotto, ed., *Der Staatssekretär Adenauers. Persönlichkeit und politisches Wirken Hans Globkes* (Stuttgart, 1980).

21. Schwarz, *Adenauer I*, pp. 766–74; Köhler, *Adenauer*, p. 636, where the conflict between Adenauer and Heinemann is described.

22. Köhler, *Adenauer*, p. 43; and with a somewhat different interpretation Hans-Otto Kleinmann, *Geschichte der CDU 1945–1982* (Stuttgart, 1993), pp. 131–2.

23. Schumacher, *Reden*, pp. 151–2, 690–1.

choice. Had it been known that the SPD was to remain in opposition until 1966, the party would probably have pressed harder for a Grand Coalition; but as it was, the successful establishment of the pattern of majority government and a loyal democratic opposition in the *Bundestag* was a most important contributing factor to the gradual reduction of the number of parties in the West German parliament and thus to the strengthening of the party system and the stability of the second German democracy.[24]

In the public debate of the 1950s and again, with the rise of the New Left, in the historiography of the early 1970s, the Adenauer government was often criticized as being a regime of restoration instead of reform.[25] This is of course true, though only superficially if the only criterion is the ownership of the means of production. It is a truism to say that in West Germany an economy based on private capital was restored (with the support of the Americans who had vetoed nationalization in their zone of occupation). But this argument ignores the fact that although Adenauer's main interests were foreign relations and the retrieval of full sovereignty for the FRG, the reformist impulse of the early CDU programmes was not entirely lost during the fifties. Three examples in the field of domestic politics can illustrate this.[26]

Firstly, in 1950/51 the issue of *Montanmitbestimmung* (the joint participation of organized labour and management in decision-making in the companies involved in the coal-mining and the iron and steel industries) has to be mentioned.[27] Joint participation had been a major aim of the German trade unions since the Weimar Republic. It was seen as the foundation of economic democracy. The prime mover in drafting a law that would replace Allied regulations was the CDU group in the

24. Werner Kaltefleiter, 'Die Entwicklung des deutschen Parteiensystems in der Ära Adenauer', in Dieter Blumenwitz *et al.*, eds, *Konrad Adenauer und seine Zeit: Politik und Persönlichkeit des ersten Bundeskanzlers, Vol II: Beiträge der Wissenschaft* (Stuttgart, 1976), pp. 285–93.

25. The debate is documented in Hans-Joachim Rühl, ed., *Neubeginn und Restauration* (Munich, 1972).

26. Numerous other questions cannot be discussed here, for instance housing, which was of utmost importance for the people living in cities often largely destroyed in the war. See Günther Schulze, *Wiederaufbau in Deutschland: Die Wohnungsbaupolitik in den Westzonen und in der Bundesrepublik von 1945 bis 1957* (Düsseldorf, 1994).

27. A considerable amount of research has been carried out in this field. See for instance the excellent collection of documents (with a good introduction by the editor): *Montanmitbestimmung*, ed. Gabriele Müller-List (Düsseldorf, 1984). For the important role of the Allied powers in the reform of the iron and steel industry see the forthcoming book by Isabel Warner, *Steel and Sovereignity: The Deconcentration of the West German Steel Industry, 1949–1954* (Mainz, 1996).

Bundestag led by a young deputy from Düsseldorf, Gerhard Schröder.[28] He worked in the German branch of the British 'North German Iron and Steel Control'. Schröder and the CDU group wanted to avoid the mere restoration of pre-war ownership. Rather they wished to develop a new progressive form of industrial relations that gave labour an acceptable level of influence. There remained of course wide differences with the trade unions in the interpreation of what was acceptable. These reforms were designed to limit the effects of the class struggle and to act as a palliative against any communist wooing of the working class. Thus the Cold War had a major impact on domestic politics.

Adenauer disliked this initiative by the CDU group because he wanted to keep a low profile on this issue; he preferred to leave the negotiations to the so-called *Sozialpartner* (a new term describing the relations between capital and labour which shows how the new West German capitalism was perceived as being cooperative in nature). In the end, when these negotiations ended in stalemate, it was Adenauer who took the initiative and obliged the employers to accept a compromise that gave labour equal representation on the supervisory board (*paritätische Mitbestimmung*).[29] For Adenauer, foreign policy factors were more important than any liberal economic principles. Since it was essential for him to have the support of the unions for the realization of a European Coal and Steel Community (ECSC) – the uniting of the iron and coal industries of several European countries, the precursor of the EEC – he threw his considerable weight on their side in this matter.[30] In the end the legislation regulating the *Montanmitbestimmung* was passed in the *Bundestag* with the combined votes of the CDU and the SPD against those of the smaller coalition partners who put up fierce resistance against it but nevertheless did not dare to leave the coalition. Since it was clear from the beginning that this form of joint participation was not to be extended to the rest of industry, the issue continued to be hotly debated and came up again in the 1970s when the SPD led the government.[31]

One of the major domestic problems faced by the first Adenauer cabinet was the integration of about 13 million refugees from the former

28. No biography of Schröder exists. The author is currently working on such a project.

29. Gabriele Müller-List, 'Adenauer, Unternehmer und Gewerkschaften: Zur Einigung über die Montanmitbestimmung 1950–51', *Vierteljahrshefte für Zeitgeschichte* 33 (1985), 288–309.

30. John Gillingham, *Coal, Steel and the Rebirth of Europe, 1945–1955: The Germans and French from Ruhr Conflict to Economic Community* (Cambridge, 1991).

31. Karl Dietrich Bracher, Wolfgang Jäger and Werner Link, *Republik im Wandel 1969–1974: Die Ära Brandt* (Stuttgart, 1986), pp. 127–9, 313–16.

German territories east of the Oder–Neisse line and increasingly from the Soviet zone of occupation and, since 1949, from the GDR.[32] The problem was basically a question of national solidarity. The consequences of the war had hit different groups of the German population to varying degrees. In the West many people had lost hardly any possessions at all, while others had suffered a considerable loss of capital like, for example, houses or factories that were destroyed in Allied air raids. Still, these could be rebuilt if banks provided the necessary credit. The refugees who had been driven out of their homes in the East during the last months of the war or shortly after the end of the war, in accordance with the provisions of the Potsdam agreement, had lost everything they possessed. Moreover, they did not have the prospect of ever recovering their possessions. The question now was how to distribute more evenly the burden of the losses incurred by the war which, after all, had been initiated by the Germans themselves. Refugee pressure groups fought for a solution that would to some extent redistribute the capital owned in the western zones of Germany. And they fought hard. In 1952 when the law on the compensation of the refugees (*Lastenausgleichsgesetz*) was debated in parliament, Bonn saw its first mass demonstration with about 60,000 participants. The various pressure groups threatened the Adenauer government that all refugees would vote for the BHE, a short-lived special interest party that mostly appealed to the refugees from the East.[33] The Chancellor saw the parliamentary majority for his foreign policy endangered and consequently supported the refugees against his more cautious Minister of Finance, Hans Schäffer. However, in the end the demands of the refugee pressure groups were not completely met. Instead of a redistribution of capital in the Federal Republic, a special tax on capital income was levied. The revenue was used for the sole purpose of compensating the losses of the refugees. While smaller losses were compensated fully, bigger onces were compensated proportionally; thus former owners of large estates in the East would still receive a minimum of 2 per cent of the approximate value of their lost property. This was a socially well-balanced solution that contributed not only to the integration of the refugees but also – though to quite a moderate degree – to a certain levelling of the wealth of the West German population. The most important factor in the all-important integration

32. Hans-Peter Schwarz, *Die Ära Adenauer 1949–1957: Gründerjahre der Republik* (Stuttgart, 1981), pp. 166–9. For the specific problems regarding the East German refugees see Helge Heidemeyer, *Flucht und Zuwanderung aus der SBZ/DDR 1945/1949–1961: Die Flüchtlingspolitik der Bundersrepublik Deutschland bis zum Bau der Berliner Mauer* (Düsseldorf, 1994).

33. Franz Neumann, *Der Block der Heimatvertriebenen und Entrechteten 1950–1960* (Meisenheim, 1968).

of the refugees into West German society was, of course, the 'economic miracle' of the 1950s that provided the jobs the refugees needed to help themselves and regain some prosperity.

The third example of socially progressive legislation during this era is taken from the end of Adenauer's second term as Chancellor. In 1957 the cabinet undertook the reform of old age pensions.[34] This was of course a measure that was immensely popular with the elderly and contributed to the CDU's electoral success in 1957. Hans-Peter Schwarz has shown that Adenauer was not simply motivated by electoral concerns but that he had always believed in the principle of subsidiarity.[35] In short, the reform consisted of the principle of the 'contract of the generations'. This meant that each generation during its working life would supply the funds for its old age pensioners while its own pensions would be provided by future generations. The pensions rose automatically with the average wage of the people ('dynamic pensions'). This was an improvement and modernization of the old Bismarckian social security system, which, like the other examples, shows how the Adenauer era was not simply a time of mere restoration, but one of thorough modernization and the development of a modern, peaceful and cooperative type of market economy with a strong welfare and social system. A prerequisite for this modernization was of course economic success and the revenues flowing from it.

Adenauer's second term in office had begun in late 1953, after he had won his re-election with a much bigger majority than in 1949. The CDU/CSU won the majority of the seats in the *Bundestag* and came close to a majority of the popular vote.[36] In order to establish the two-thirds majority that was needed to change the constitution and thus to ensure the passing of the laws concerning West German rearmament, the Chancellor maintained a coalition government. This time even the short-lived refugee party was included in the cabinet. Adenauer's second term was dominated more than anything else by foreign policy issues,

34. The best work is still Hans Günther Hockerts, *Sozialpolitische Entscheidungen im Nachkriegsdeutschland: Alliierte und deutsche Sozialversicherungspolitik 1945–1957* (Stuttgart, 1980).

35. Hans-Peter Schwarz, *Adenauer. Vol. II: Der Staatsmann 1952–1967* (Munich, 1994), p. 282 (paperback edn).

36. This landslide victory had not been at all expected because at mid-term the Adenauer cabinet had been quite unpopular. Several factors had contributed to the success, most notably Adenauer's state visit to the United States in the spring of 1953 (everything American impressed German public opinion enormously in the fifties) and of course the uprising in the GDR against communist rule in June 1953. See Schwarz, *Adenauer II*, pp. 82–7, 95–105; Köhler, *Adenauer*, pp. 775–85; and Klaus Larres, 'Preserving Law and Order: Britain, the United States and the East German Uprising of 1953', *Twentieth Century British History* 5 (1994), 320–50.

and most of all by the Federal Republic's integration into NATO.[37] With his comfortable majority, Adenauer was able to triumph over all opposition from both inside and outside parliament. Only after 1955 and after membership in NATO had been achieved did the coalition with the FDP fall apart over the issue of reunification and over personal enmities between Adenauer and Thomas Dehler, the leader of the parliamentary FDP.[38]

The 1957 elections were another personal triumph for Adenauer. The CDU/CSU won the majority of the popular vote – to this day, the only time that a party has achieved such electoral success. These elections were clearly the climax of the Adenauer era, but a somewhat more turbulent time soon followed. Before this can be dealt with further, however, there is one issue that deserves a closer look.

The history of the Adenauer era in the matter of *Vergangenheitsbewältigung* (a very German term meaning the moral and practical way the nation deals and comes to terms with the Nazi past) is more than ambiguous. On the one hand there was the Treaty of *Wiedergutmachung* (providing for the generous financial and also moral compensation for Nazi crimes) with Israel in 1952 which was a prerequisite for a successful foreign policy, particularly in the United States.[39] On the other hand there was Adenauer's unfortunate hand in the choice of personnel. His closest adviser, the secretary of the chancellery Hans Globke, had written the official commentary to the Nuremberg racial laws in 1935 when he had been a senior civil service member in the interior department. Later he had been close to the resistance against Hitler and had provided the Catholic church with useful internal information. It was quite clear that there was no personal, or in any way criminal, guilt in his case: he had been cleared by the Allied de-nazification process and there had been no Allied objections against his appointment. Although Globke's competence was very valuable to Adenauer,[40] it has been justifiably argued that it was not necessary for such an official to work in such a high place. Adenauer never yielded to the criticism and clung to Globke until the end of his chancellorship. This was only one example; there were others such as the tainted ministers Oberländer and Seebohm. Neither belonged to the CDU but were in the cabinet. These examples

37. Saki Dockrill, *Britain's Policy for West German Rearmament, 1950–55* (Cambridge, 1991).

38. Köhler, *Adenauer*, pp. 912–21, 971–6.

39. An excellent description of Adenauer's position on this issue and his strategy to push the treaty through against considerable resistance is in Köhler, *Adenauer*, pp. 698–722.

40. See the discussion of the Globke case in Schwarz, *Adenauer I*, pp. 659–60, and, somewhat more critical, Köhler, *Adenauer*, pp. 725–33. See also Gotto, ed., *Der Staatssekretär*, pp. 230–82.

suggest that Adenauer's sensitivity in this field was not very well developed, to say the least.[41]

A different matter is the way the judiciary dealt with the crimes committed during the Nazi era. Here also the deficiencies are obvious.[42] The reasons were, on the one hand, a closing of ranks – in other words, a readiness to spare old colleagues – and, on the other hand, a widespread feeling that the Allied de-nazification had wrought a lot of unjustified evil on innocent people and that these practices should end.[43] Two events brought a profound change to this attitude. Towards the end of 1959 there occurred a series of antisemitic acts directed against synagogues that were denounced by all relevant parties and the government. However, these events reminded the public of Germany's dark past – not only in the Federal Republic, but throughout Europe and the United States.[44] The other event was the first major trial of some second-rank Nazis in Ulm in 1958. That led directly to the foundation within the Federal Ministry of Justice of a central office that had as its purpose the prosecution of Nazi crimes – particularly those connected to the Holocaust. Although the attitude of the judiciary did not change, the spirit of the times with regard to the Nazi past had altered profoundly by the time of the Eichmann trial in Jerusalem between 1960 and 1962.[45] The issue of *Vergangenheitsbewältigung* is still debated today, but it was particularly passionately discussed in the 1960s, culminating in the student revolt, which, although an international phenomenon, was given a special German context by a younger generation condemning its elders. This was epitomized on 7 November 1968 when Beate Klarsfeld publicly slapped Chancellor Kiesinger in the face because he

41. The issue of *Vergangenheitsbewältigung* has lately been debated in the historiography when Manfred Kittel (*Die Legende von der 'Zweiten Schuld': Vergangenheitsbewältigung in der Ära Adenauer*, Berlin/Frankfurt am Main, 1993) challenged the use of the phrase 'second guilt' coined by the journalist Ralph Giordano (*Die zweite Schuld oder Von der Last ein Deutscher zu sein*, Hamburg/Zurich, 1987).

42. This matter has been ignored in Kittel, *Die Legende*.

43. Rearmament was another factor that led to a wave of pardons for war criminals and to a general mood of forgiveness. See the excellent discussion in Peter Graf Kielmannsegg, *Lange Schatten: Vom Umgang der Deutschen mit der nationalsozialistischen Vergangenheit* (Berlin, 1989), pp. 42–7.

44. Manfred Kittel, 'Peripetie der Vergangenheitsbewältigung: Die Hakenkreuzschmirereien 1959/60 und das bundesdeutsche Verhältnis zum Nationalsozialismus', *Historische Politische Mitteilungen. Archiv für christlich-demokratische Politik* (1994), 49–67.

45. See the classic works by Hannah Arendt, *Eichmann in Jerusalem: The Report on the Banality of Evil* (London, 1963) and Alexander and Margarete Mitscherlich, *Die Unfähigkeit zu trauern* (Munich, 1967).

had been an ordinary Nazi Party member.[46] This event shows how every and even the smallest offence was perceived with hindsight in the light of the Holocaust.

WIND OF CHANGE (1959–69)

Generally, the end of the Adenauer era is assumed to have coincided with the end of his chancellorship in 1963. However, quite a few indications suggest that the change in the political climate had begun much earlier.[47] The new attitude towards the Nazi past has already been mentioned, but there were other more concrete political changes as well. It has to be remembered that Adenauer was 81 years old when he won the general election in 1957. Like the British Tories a few years before, the Christian Democrats were faced with the problem of how to remove an aging hero. After the election Ludwig Erhard, Economics Minister since 1949 and still extremely popular, was forced upon Adenauer as the Vice-Chancellor and, as it was perceived by many, as his designated successor. For Adenauer, who thought that Erhard was good at economics but bad at politics, especially foreign policy, this was unpalatable. What followed was, for the CDU, an agonizing feud between its two most eminent politicians.[48] The year 1959 might have been an opportunity to resolve the conflict when Heuss's second term as Federal President ended and Adenauer publicly announced that he would be a suitable successor. But after a short while, when he fully realized the representational character of the office and that Erhard would certainly be his successor, the Chancellor changed his mind and proposed Wilhelm Lübke as his candidate, who, as it later transpired, proved to be rather a liability. Adenauer's authority and his public image suffered a great deal through this affair.[49]

Even in politics Adenauer's instincts now seemed to be failing him.

46. Thomas Ellwein, *Krisen und Reform: Die Bundesrepublik seit den sechziger Jahren* (Munich, 1989), p. 20.

47. Hans-Peter Schwarz, *Die Ära Adenauer: Epochenwechsel 1957–1963* (Stuttgart, 1983), although this 'official' history of the FRG clearly sees the bigger incision in 1963. See also the introduction in Klaus Hildebrand, *Von Erhard zur Grossen Koalition 1963–1969* (Stuttgart, 1984), pp. 19–20.

48. This feud has been described in great detail by Daniel Koerfer, *Kampf ums Kanzleramt: Erhard und Adenauer* (Stuttgart, 1987).

49. Wolfgang Wagner, *Die Bundespräsidentenwahl 1959* (Mainz, 1972).

The bill introducing emergency powers into the Basic Law[50] did not obtain sufficient support to pass parliament. Similarly, the establishment of a second TV network, to be privately owned but under Federal government control,[51] could not be realized. Even in foreign affairs Adenauer was not as successful as before. The bedrock of his policy, the close relationship with Washington, was quickly dissolving with the advent of the Kennedy administration. Moreover, a large part of the CDU did not approve of Adenauer's sudden preference for de Gaulle's France and there ensued a rift in the party between the 'Atlanticists' – soon to be led by Gerhard Schröder, Minister of Foreign Affairs since 1961 – and the 'Gaullists', led by Franz-Josef Strauss, the leader of the Bavarian CSU, that lasted through most of the sixties.[52] When in 1961 the GDR government erected the Berlin Wall it became clear to many observers that Adenauer's argument that military and political integration into the Western Alliance was the shortest way to reunification would not, at least in the short run, prove to be true.

While the CDU was torn by internal rivalries concerning the succession, the SPD was well on its way to the famous *Godesberger programm.* The results of the 1957 elections had shown that there were no prospects for an unreformed SPD, but a new generation of leaders was ready to take the necessary steps towards a reform of the party. Foremost among them were Herbert Wehner, a communist renegade and, as such, highly vulnerable to suspicions and CDU propaganda, Fritz Erler, who had played an important role in drafting the legislation allowing democratic control of the *Bundeswehr* (as the new West German army was called),[53] and Carlo Schmid, who for a long time had been one of the most popular SPD politicians with a bourgeois background. These three were elected as deputy chairmen of the SPD *Bundestag* group. With the Godesberg programme the SPD tried to move beyond its traditional appeal to the working classes and open itself up to the middle classes

50. On the contrary, when Gerhard Schröder, Minister of the Interior since 1953, in defending the bill, called it 'the hour of the executive branch', he alienated the SPD. As ever since its defeat in 1957 the party had been distrustful of the authoritarian style of the Adenauer cabinet, Schröder managed to kill the bill, which needed a two-thirds majority to be passed by the *Bundestag*. Some of the SPD's resentment can be detected in the memoirs of Horst Ehmke, *Mittendrin: Von der Grossen Koalition zur Deutschen Einheit* (Berlin, 1994), p. 65.

51. Not even the CDU minister-presidents of the Federal states could be won for the project: See Schwarz, *Epochenwechsel*, pp. 167–9.

52. Reiner Marcowitz, *Im Banne des Generals: Unionsparteien, SPD und Charles de Gaulle* (Cologne: Ph.D. dissertation, 1992, soon to be published).

53. Hartmut Soell, *Fritz Erler: Eine politische Biographie* (Berlin/Bonn, 1976). Erler has been almost forgotten because he died before the SDP achieved its long sought goal, namely participation in government.

and other segments of society that shared some of the ideals of the left. It shed its outdated Marxist rhetoric and symbols like the red banner – in short, 'the ideological ballast', as Carlo Schmid put it.[54] Instead, from 1959 the Godesberg programme presented a modern, open, pluralistic left-wing party that basically accepted capitalism and particularly the West German version of the 'social market economy'. The break with tradition was completed in 1960 when Herbert Wehner in his *Bundestag* speech accepted, on behalf of the SPD, West Germany's membership of both NATO and the EEC. The SPD could no longer be portrayed as an opposition whose sole philosophy was 'No', as the CDU had succeeded in doing in 1957. The SPD reforms found resonance in many circles that before had found the party rather boring and dull. Among these were the intellectuals, important parts of the media and also the Protestant churches.[55]

The new SPD soon came to be personified by its young, almost Kennedy-like leader and the challenger to the 85 year old Chancellor in the elections of 1961: Willy Brandt. But it took longer to translate party reform into votes than either the party leadership or the rank and file had anticipated. The results of the election came, therefore, as a disappointment:[56] the CDU lost almost 5 per cent of its vote and came down to 45.3 per cent. The SPD, on the other hand, raised its share from 31.8 per cent to 36.2 per cent. The real winner in the elections, however, was the FDP, which almost doubled its share to an impressive 12.8 per cent. The FDP had led a campaign against the SPD and for the revival of the coalition with the CDU – but not with Adenauer. The CDU was put into an awkward position since the party wanted to remain in government but it could not just drop its leader. In the end, after almost three months of negotiations, Adenauer proved to be tougher than the FDP. He threatened, in a none too subtle manner,

54. Susanne Miller and Heinrich Potthoff, *Kleine Geschichte der SPD: Darstellung und Dokumentation* 7th edn (Bonn, 1991), p. 203.

55. Detlef Lehnert, *Sozialdemokratie zwischen Protestbewegung und Regierungspartei 1848–1983* (Frankfurt am Main, 1983), p. 187. The major work on the post-war development of the SPD is still Kurt Klotzbach, *Der Weg zur Staatspartei: Programmatik, praktische Politik und Organisation der deutschen Sozialdemokratie 1945 bis 1965* (Berlin/Bonn, 1982).

56. The disappointment was increased because Adenauer, who was already leading a slandering campaign against Willy Brandt by alluding to his illegitimate birth and his emigration during the Nazi era, had committed a blunder when he refused to go to Berlin when the Wall was built in 1961. This event occurred in the midst of the campaign. Adenauer later claimed that he had not wanted to escalate the situation but most observers agreed that he did not want to be seen together with Willy Brandt, then mayor of West Berlin. See Schwarz, *Adenauer II*, pp. 595–6, 661–2; Köhler, *Adenauer*, pp, 1088–92, 1106–11.

with a Grand Coalition. The FDP gave in and accepted Adenauer as Chancellor, but not for the full four-year term.[57]

These last years of the Adenauer chancellorship were again dominated by foreign policy issues, by Adenauer's desperate struggle against the emerging US policy of *détente* and his preferred option for de Gaulle. The major event in the domestic politics of the time was the so-called *Spiegel* affair of 1962. The weekly news magazine *Der Spiegel* published an article on 11 October on the situation of the *Bundeswehr* and NATO, especially on the intention of Minister of Defence Franz-Josef Strauss to supply the *Bundeswehr* with nuclear arms. This article was part of a long-standing feud between *Der Spiegel* and Strauss, who had been criticized for his policies, but also for alleged corruption. Strauss reacted by accusing the magazine of treason and having the editor, Rudolf Augstein, and the journalist responsible for the article, Conrad Ahlers,[58] arrested. Ahlers was in Spain when he was arrested by Spanish authorities at the request of the German embassy.

All of this caused an enormous row in West Germany. With the changing attitude towards the Nazi past, this affair seemed to reaffirm the deep suspicion that the past was beginning to reappear. All those who had long been dissatisfied with politics in the Adenauer era – pacifists who campaigned against rearmament, the SPD, the left and the left-wing/liberal media – were aroused by this clumsy attempt at censorship, and by the cooperation with the Franco regime and what was perceived as the repressive policy of the government in general. The trials that followed, and that ended with the acquittal of the journalists, could not restore confidence in the democratic system. This fear of the reappearance of the past and of the politics of repression set the stage for the students' rebellion in the late sixties. Apart from these long-term consequences, the *Spiegel* affair led also to political consequences in the short term. The FDP ministers resigned and broke up the coalition. Although the SPD was alienated by the affair, Adenauer for the first time officially negotiated with the opposition, whose delegation was led by Herbert Wehner, for an alternative to his centre-right coalition government. With this threat pending, the FDP came back, but under two conditions that were accepted by the CDU. Firstly, Strauss had to leave the cabinet, which led to lasting antagonism between the CSU leader and the FDP. Secondly, Adenauer was to 'retire' the following

57. Ellwein, *Krisen*, pp. 30–1.

58. For some anecdotes surrounding this episode and the juridical aspects of the scandal see Ehmke, *Mittendrin*, pp. 34–9.

year.[59] Adenauer may not himself have accepted this date, but he was living on borrowed time. The CDU *Bundestag* group, and the party as a whole, was starting to lose elections in the federal states and did not follow the old Chancellor any more. In April 1963 it was made clear to him that Erhard would succeed him after the summer break. Adenauer, who knew that his time to retire had finally come, did not hesitate to restate his views about Erhard. Indeed, only a few years later these views had become the common opinion. Moreover, although Adenauer retired as Chancellor he remained as CDU party chairman.[60]

With Erhard's nomination and election on 16 October 1963 the campaign for the general election in 1965 had practically begun. In this battle Erhard could not rely completely on his own party. To some extent this was his own fault. He tried to keep above party politics and refused to succeed Adenauer as party chairman. Also, being a liberal economist he had alienated the Gaullists in the CDU and CSU and the left wings of both parties. He had never agreed with Adenauer's French leanings and had especially criticized the protectionist tendencies in EEC policies and the exclusion of Britain from the Common Market.[61] For Strauss, the foremost enemy of the Liberal Party, this was unpalatable. And there were others from the younger generation, such as Rainer Barzel, the new leader of the CDU/CSU *Bundestag* group, who tended to see Erhard's government as transitional. A Grand Coalition with the SPD remained an enduring temptation for many in the CDU ranks. Under these circumstances the general election of September 1965 was a personal triumph for Erhard. Although the SPD did win a few extra percentage points, the CDU obtained 8 percentage points more than the Social Democrats.[62] In absolute terms, more people had voted for the popular Chancellor than had ever voted for Adenauer, and the CDU had even won in northern, Protestant areas. Half a year later, Erhard again succeeded Adenauer, this time as the CDU party chairman. The party had managed to live through a difficult period of adjustment and reform.[63]

However, despite all these successes, in the autumn of 1966 Erhard was forced to resign. The reasons for this were many. First of all,

59. The *Spiegel* affair and its consequences have been described many times. For a concise description see Ellwein, *Krisen*, pp. 33–7.

60. Köhler, *Adenauer*, pp. 1210–13.

61. For a comprehensive portrait of Erhard and his views see Hildebrand, *Von Erhard zur Grossen Koalition*, pp. 29–34.

62. The exact results were: 47.6 per cent CDU/CSU, 39.3 per cent SPD, 9.5 per cent FDP. No other party came even near the 5 per cent hurdle which needs to be overcome to gain representation in the *Bundestag*. See ibid., p. 474.

63. Kleinmann, *Geschichte der CDU*, pp. 250–3.

Erhard had won the election because of his success as Minister of Economics. He made ample use of this capital by delivering electoral bribes, mostly in the form of tax cuts.[64] By the spring of 1966 the signs of an economic recession were becoming more than obvious – although of course, compared to the crises of the seventies, times were still good. The iron and steel industry and coal-mining were the sectors most severely hit by the recession. The state elections in the summer of 1966 in Northrhine-Westphalia, where the Ruhr region was particularly stricken, were a disaster for the CDU. Not only did the party lose a considerable percentage of the popular vote, it soon became clear that the CDU/FDP coalition would not be able to survive the whole electoral term. All this was interpreted as a loss of prestige and authority on the part of the Chancellor, who had been much involved in the campaign and whose reaction to the recession seemed to be limited to calls for restraint. This meant that some of the 'electoral presents' had to be taken back. The situation suggested a crisis in the 'small coalition' of CDU/CSU and FDP.

The SPD, on the other hand, seemed a more modern but also the more competent party. Its spokesman for economic affairs, another professor of economics, Karl Schiller, was a rising star, and in foreign policy the SPD appeared not only as the party of peace and *détente* but also as being more in touch with US policies.[65] The SPD was said to have the 'Genosse Trend' (comrade trend) on its side while the CDU appeared antiquated. Paradoxically, the pending threat of the 'Grand Coalition', which had existed throughout Erhard's chancellorship,[66] made the FDP more difficult to deal with rather than easier, as might have been expected. All this gave the impression that in autumn 1966 the coalition and the Chancellor had reached the end of their political lives. A public debate followed regarding the succession within the CDU and undermined Erhard's authority even further. In the end it was the FDP who relieved the contenders of the responsibility for sticking the knife into Erhard's back. When the 1967 budget could only be balanced by a tax rise, the FDP *Bundestag* group refused to compromise on the issue, which had been made a matter of life and death for the coalition by Barzel and Strauss. In the end the FDP ministers resigned. Erhard struggled on for another month but it was obvious that a minority

64. Ellwein, *Krisen*, p. 38.

65. Hildebrand, *Von Erhard zur Grossen Koalition*, pp. 202–11.

66. When the SPD in 1964, under the leadership of Herbert Wehner, voted for the re-election of President Lübke, an ardent protagonist of the 'Grand Coalition', the party had signalled that it was available for participation in such a coalition. See ibid., pp. 138–9.

cabinet could not survive. On 30 November he resigned. Adenauer, his predecessor, lived to see his prophecy come true.[67]

In the CDU *Bundestag* group, it was the southern axis that decided the question of the succession. On the one hand there was Gerhard Schröder, Erhard's loyal Minister of Foreign Affairs, who had worked hard in the cabinet to reach a compromise with the FDP and stood for a renewed 'small coalition'. On the other hand there was a surprise candidate, Kurt Georg Kiesinger, Minister-President of Baden-Württemberg, who was in favour of the 'Grand Coalition'. While the CDU deputies divided their votes more or less evenly between both candidates, the CSU cast its vote unanimously for Kiesinger. Rainer Barzel, leader of the *Bundestag* group, hardly won any votes; he had to take too much of the blame for the overthrow of Erhard.[68]

Above all, economics, especially in connection with the recession of 1966/67, had been the *raison d'être* of the Grand Coalition, and in this it proved remarkably successful. Karl Schiller and Franz-Josef Strauss, who was in a way rehabilitated when he worked in the same cabinet as ex-communist Herbert Wehner, cooperated particularly smoothly. Together they introduced new Keynesian planning elements into economics and fiscal policy that perfectly suited the international fashion of the times. They inaugurated the *Konzertierte Aktion* (concerted action), which actually never amounted to more than a forum in which industry, labour and politicians could discuss economic policy and planning, but it seemed a perfectly logical tool in the cooperative, almost neo-corporate style of West German capitalism. And when the economy picked up again – in 1968 the growth rate was back to 7.3 per cent – both claimed credit for it.[69] Another major reform in this field was the reorganization of the financial relations between the Federal states and the government in Bonn.[70] It was the built-in two-thirds majority of the 'Grand Coalition' that enabled it to effect reforms which had long been delayed simply because any smaller coalition had had to deal with an opposition that could either choose to cooperate or not. The FDP as an opposition party did not matter.

Another issue that had been delayed since the late fifties was the problem of emergency provisions in the Basic Law. This matter was long overdue to be settled because certain Allied reserve powers restricting the

67. Moreover, Adenauer had actually played a part, albeit a minor one, in the decomposition of the Erhard government. See Kleinmann, *Geschichte der CDU*, p. 255.

68. For a detailed account of the end of Erhard's chancellorship, including an analysis of the reasons, see Hildebrand, *Von Erhard zur Grossen Koalition*, pp. 218–40.

69. For a more comprehensive account of the economic and fiscal measures and for further literature see Ellwein, *Krisen*, pp. 43–49.

70. Ibid., pp. 65–6.

national sovereignty of the FRG could only be overcome if these provisions were inserted in the Basic Law.[71] Again, after some internal compromises this issue was settled rather smoothly by the coalition.[72] The matter was managed by Kiesinger, who defined his role as Chancellor as a moderator of the coalition – the times of Adenauer's authoritarian *Kanzlerdemokratie* had already disappeared with Erhard.

A legislative project that did not necessarily need the two-thirds majority was the reform of the electoral law. Yet this was an extremely sensitive issue and consensus between CDU/CSU and SPD was necessary because the FDP would surely be opposed to any changes endangering its parliamentary existence. Both the CDU and the CSU – the archfoe of the FDP – wanted to reform the electoral law in accordance with the British model and the aim clearly was to establish a two-party system.[73] In the beginning, the SPD leaders seemed to be moving in a similar direction. Such a system appeared to give the SPD – aided by the 'Genosse Trend' – a good chance of one day leading a majority government, unimpeded by any FDP influence. By 1968 it had become clear that the reform of the electoral system was much more a matter of interest than of principle for the SPD.[74] Since it had never really been discussed within the coalition which system was to be adopted for the next general election in 1969 (actually, it was only for the 1973 elections that the British model was to be installed), it was tactically prudent to keep in touch with the FDP and to leave the door open for an alignment with this party. When the polls indicated that under the new system the SPD would have to return to the opposition, it was obvious that the reform was dead.

Despite this failure the Grand Coalition was on the whole remarkably successful. West German federalism had been reformed and modernized, the old problem of the emergency amendment of the Basic Law had been resolved and, most importantly, the economic recession had been overcome. The cooperative style, even the harmony between the two

71. See also note 50.

72. For the legislative process and the compromise within the coalition see Hildebrand, *Von Erhard zur Grossen Koalition*, pp. 369–70.

73. The CDU had favoured such a system since 1949 when it had supported such measures during the deliberation of the Parliamentary Council, but it did not prevail at the time. The difficulties with the FDP in 1962, and again in 1966, when the party had left the governing coalitions and had been able to impose certain conditions for rejoining the government, made the opportunity to avoid the recurrence of such events all the more attractive. See ibid., pp. 352–3.

74. The tactical considerations of Herbert Wehner above all, as well as the dilemma of the CDU, which had to deal with a new threat from the right – the neo-Nazi NPD had been very successful in some Federal state elections – are discussed in great detail in ibid., pp. 352–65.

great parties, fitted the German political tradition in which party politics and confrontation had never been popular. Still, this picture, centred on the parliamentary and governmental political process, does not do justice to the reality of the political situation in West Germany in the late sixties. After all, 1968 has come to symbolize a new political generation that celebrated its anniversaries in the late eighties and early nineties in various media outlets.[75] In terms of lifestyle, the most important event of 1968 even for West Germany was probably Woodstock, which epitomizes what the late sixties stood for. But in political terms it was the students' revolt that counted.[76]

The popular memory of the late sixties is not one of political harmony but of enormous student demonstrations that often turned into battles with the police. The long-term reasons for the student unrest, memories of the Nazi past that seemed to reappear, have been described above. The dominant issue that triggered the demonstrations was the emergency amendments to the constitution. A loose alliance of students, trade unions and Protestant churches that was unrepresented in parliament interpreted these provisions as ominous signs of an evolving repressive and authoritarian regime. The cooperation of the SPD in the adoption of this amendment to the constitution only served to intensify the resistance of an increasingly organized extra-parliamentary opposition (*Ausserparlamentarische Opposition – APO*). It seemed impossible to understand how the Social Democrats could participate in the government of Kiesinger, who had been a member of the Nazi party, albeit in no responsible position. But when the unions, whose objections to those provisions that curtailed the freedom of labour organizations in the event of a national emergency had largely been met, finally accepted the compromise, the alliance soon fell apart. The neo-Marxist rhetoric of student leaders such as Rudi Dutschke had never been popular with the working classes; students were supposed to study, not to demonstrate. The students' battle for more democracy in the universities and their fight against the popular conservative press of media tsar Axel Springer appealed to intellectuals but not to the masses. Thus, once the students were isolated, their revolt lost its political cohesion and the movement split into many different factions in the following years. The path that

75. Since German unification the generation of 1968 and everything it stands for has been under increasing attack by the so-called 'generation of 1989'. See for instance Rainer Zitelmann, *Wohin treibt unsere Republik?* (Frankfurt am Main/Berlin, 1994). See also Klaus Larres, 'Willy Brandt's Ostpolitik, Neo-Conservatism and the German Federal Elections of 1994', *German Politics* 4.1 (1995), 42–63.

76. Literature on the student movement in the late sixties is abundant; for a concise description and further literature see Ellwein, *Krisen*, pp. 11–21, 60–4; Arnulf Baring, *Machtwechsel: Die Ära Brandt–Scheel* (Stuttgart, 1982), pp. 71–94, 793–6.

was chosen by very few nevertheless received most attention in the seventies: terrorism.[77]

By the late 1960s the intellectual climate of the Federal Republic, the general atmosphere, in short, the *Zeitgeist* (spirit of the times), had changed. This had of course the greatest impact on the parties of the left.[78] The use of the plural is justified because by the late sixties the FDP had turned into a party of the liberal left.[79] The possibility that the parties of the left might cooperate was in the air. A first test for such cooperation between SPD and FDP was the presidential election of March 1969.[80] The SPD, who claimed the office after the first two Federal presidents had been members of the FDP and the CDU, was in doubt whom to present as a candidate. Georg Leber, the prominent member of the trade union wing, would have been acceptable to the CDU/CSU and was favoured by SPD delegates who wanted to continue the Grand Coalition. In the end those who wanted to test the feasibility of governmental cooperation between SPD and FDP prevailed and presented Gustav Heinemann, the Minister of Justice. This renegade[81] was unacceptable to the CDU and it nominated Gerhard Schröder as its candidate. It was known that Schröder favoured a CDU–FDP coalition and thus it was hoped that he could win enough liberal support to secure his election. In a dramatic contest Heinemann succeeded, though it was only after a third ballot that he was able to obtain a large enough majority. This was a triumph for Walter Scheel, the new leader of the FDP, who had worked hard to keep his party united behind Heinemann. Thus the dress rehearsal had proved successful and the stage was set for the SPD–FDP coalition government led by Willy Brandt. After the *Bundestag* elections in the autumn of 1969 this coalition came into being, though it commanded a majority of only 12 seats. The

77. Stefan Aust, *Der Baader–Meinhof Komplex* (Hamburg, 1985).

78. One strategy of the waning student movement was 'the long march through the institutions' and the foremost institution it turned to was of course the SPD, which changed profoundly in the following years as far as the structure of its membership was concerned. See Peter Lösche and Franz Walter, *Die SPD: Klassenpartei – Volkspartei – Quotenpartei. Zur Entwicklung der Sozialdemokratie von Weimar bis zur deutschen Vereingung* (Darmstadt, 1992), pp. 152–4.

79. Electorally, this amounted to a near-disaster for the FDP. The small party did not profit at all from being the sole parliamentary opposition party between 1966 and 1969. With just 5.8 per cent of the vote the party even found it difficult in 1969 to jump the hurdle of the 5 per cent clause. See Hildebrand, *Von Erhard zur Grossen Koalition*, p. 477.

80. On the basis of a large number of interviews with contemporaries, this prelude to the Social–Liberal coalition has been described in great detail by Baring, *Machtwechsel*, pp. 27–71, 94–123.

81. Heinemann had been a CDU member of parliament and Minister of the Interior in the first Adenauer cabinet before leaving both party and government. See note 18.

Machtwechsel, the transition of power from the CDU to the new Social–Liberal coalition, was achieved. This truly marked the end of an era in German politics.

CHAPTER FOUR

Domestic Political Developments II: 1969–90

Mathias Siekmeier and Klaus Larres

THE BRANDT ERA

In October 1969, Willy Brandt was elected to be the fourth Chancellor of the Federal Republic of Germany by the votes of the SPD and FDP. This was the first time in almost 40 years that a Social Democrat would lead the affairs of government of a German democracy.

His election was preceded by one of the most exciting and perhaps dramatic ballot decisions in the history of the Republic. Right until the evening of that fateful 28 September, everything pointed to the reinstatement of Kurt Georg Kiesinger (CDU) as Chancellor. The only question appeared to be whether the Grand Coalition of CDU/CSU and SPD would be continued or whether a Conservative–Liberal government would re-emerge as in the days of Konrad Adenauer and Ludwig Erhard. It was only just before midnight that the computers of the election experts calculated a possible lead of 12 mandates for a Social–Liberal reform alliance.[1] During the next 24 hours the course was set for a change of government in the Palais Schaumburg, the Chancellor's residence in Bonn at the time. Leading representatives of the SDP and the liberal FDP eventually agreed to form a government, despite the slim parliamentary majority.[2]

The SPD and FDP had already made one attempt three years before to end the domination of West German politics by the conservative CDU/CSU. When the Christian–Liberal Ludwig Erhard/Erich Mende government fell apart in late October 1966, all three major parties sat down to discuss a way out of the crisis. It was then assumed that a Social–Liberal alliance would be bound to fail, due to the precarious

1. The exact figures are as follows: SPD 42.7 per cent (+–3.4 per cent); CDU/CSU 46.1 per cent (−1.5 per cent); FDP 5.8 per cent (−3.7 per cent). See Arnulf Baring, *Machtwechsel: Die Ära Brandt–Scheel* (Stuttgart, 1982).

2. Ibid., pp. 166ff.

majority of mandates such a government would have. Moreover, there existed considerable doubts within the SPD leadership about the reliability of the Free Democrats.[3] The party and parliamentary party of the FDP was dominated by representatives of the conservative establishment who had joined forces with the CDU/CSU for many years and repeatedly and categorically rejected any form of alliance with the political left. Under these circumstances an SPD–FDP coalition was surely destined for failure. Therefore, in November 1966 the Grand Coalition was all that eventually remained as an option.[4]

In autumn 1969 the situation was radically different; the Free Democrats were above all responsible for this. Since the break-up of the Conservative–Liberal coalition in October 1966 the party had been torn apart by internecine conflict. The left wing sought to transform the FDP into a radical reform party to absorb the social protest potential. The main areas for reform were to be domestic, judicial and education policy as well as Bonn's Eastern policy including its relations with East Germany (the GDR). The eventual aim was the formation of a Social–Liberal coalition government. Yet those on the right of the FDP, around party chairman Erich Mende, believed that it was the natural function of the Liberals to operate as the corrective partner within the framework of a middle-class coalition. As a consequence, they strove for the restoration of the alliance with the CDU/CSU and categorically rejected any radical alterations to the party programme. A group of otherwise pragmatic reformists had established itself to the centre of the opposing factions. Their leading exponents were Mende's successor as party chairman, Walter Scheel, and his deputy, Hans-Dietrich Genscher. To keep inter-party tensions at a minimum they argued for only moderate alterations to the Liberal manifesto.[5]

Whilst outwardly attempting to keep the party on a course in the centre, Scheel also worked ambitiously behind the scenes for a change of power in Bonn. In his view only an alliance with the Social Democrats would lead to the realization of urgently needed reforms. At the same time Scheel was also exploring ways of securing new electoral support for the party from all social levels. In the medium term, he believed, this would allow the FDP to become the permanent 'third force' in the West German party system.[6]

3. Klaus Hildebrand, *Von Erhard zur Grossen Koalition 1963–1969* (Stuttgart, 1984).

4. On the politics of the Grand Coalition see Chapter 3 in this book.

5. See Hildebrand, *Von Erhard zur Grossen Koalition*, pp. 280ff.; J. Dittberner, *FDP – Partei der zweiten Wahl: Ein Beitrag zur Geschichte der liberalen Partei and ihrer Funktionen im Parteiensystem der Bundesrepublik* (Opladen, 1987).

6. Baring, *Machtwechsel*, pp. 124ff.; R. Zülch, *Die dritte Partei im Kräftefeld des Koalitionssystems: Von der FDP zur F.D.P.* (Cologne, 1971).

When the SPD candidate Gustav Heinemann was elected President of the Federal Republic in March 1969 with the votes of the Liberals, Scheel's strategy gradually began to take shape for the general public. It became more and more obvious that West Germany was heading towards a new political era. SPD and CDU/CSU had put up separate candidates in the race to elect President Heinrich Lübke's successor, a first signal that the Grand Coalition would not survive the federal elections.[7] Centrifugal tendencies in the government camp then strengthened progressively. Contrasting practical issues such as the revaluation of the Deutschmark and the implementation of the Hallstein Doctrine in the case of Cambodia were accompanied by tactical skirmishing for the most favourable vantage points in the general election campaign. Bitter personal animosities between the SPD's Willy Brandt, who had emigrated during the Nazi era, and Chancellor Kurt Georg Kiesinger, the one-time NSDAP member, were an additional burden upon the coalition.[8] By the middle of 1969 the Grand Coalition was more or less finished.

The small Liberal opposition was forced into a delicate position due to the continuous conflict within the CDU/CSU–SPD government. The party's election campaign in 1969 was totally fixed upon the fight against the Grand Coalition. The German public was repeatedly informed that only a vote for the Liberals could halt the black–red power cartel in Bonn.[9] However, the deteriorating image of the government increasingly contradicted this claim, and the FDP had still to answer how they hoped to bring about a change of power. The coalition question was deliberately left open to prevent an exodus of leading representatives from the conservative school of thought within the FDP in the run-up to the elections.[10] Only three days before election day the party leadership changed course in view of catastrophic opinion polls – the party lay well below the 5 per cent hurdle of entry into the *Bundestag*. Scheel now publicly spoke out in support of a Social–Liberal reform alliance.[11]

Scheel's last-minute coalition statement probably gave the Liberals their vital push over the 5 per cent hurdle; however, with only 5.8 per cent this was still the worst result in the history of the party. As a

7. For the presidential election of 1969 see the end of Chapter 3 in this book.

8. Baring, *Machtwechsel*, pp. 133ff.

9. Zülch, *Die dritte Partei*, p. 76; P. Seibt, 'Die Wahlwerbung der FDP im Bundestagswahlkampf 1969', in K. von Beyme, I. Fetscher and G. Lehmbruch, eds, *Demokratisches System und politische Praxis in der Bundesrepublik* (Munich, 1971), pp. 341–2.

10. Baring, *Machtwechsel*, p. 150.

11. R. Appel, 'Bonner Machtwechsel', in R. Klett and W. Pohl, eds, *Stationen einer Republik* (Stuttgart, 1979), p. 161.

consequence, criticism from within the party was fierce. It was chiefly Mende and his supporters who demanded the head of the party leader. Scheel's survival was due not only to the lack of credible alternatives, but also to the fact that in spite of the election débâcle, the Liberals were now able to participate in government again.

The FDP leader and future Foreign Minister finally achieved his objectives over the coalition without major stumbling blocks. Many of the conservatives within the FDP also conceded that the survival of their party was dependent upon the formation of a Social–Liberal coalition government; only an isolated minority around ex-leader Mende categorically rejected any form of alliance with the Social Democrats.[12]

Indicators in the SPD also pointed to a change of power. Willy Brandt, supported by the vast majority of his party, made no secret about his wish to become Chancellor. Sceptics like party deputy Herbert Wehner and the future parliamentary party leader Helmut Schmidt were largely left isolated.[13]

The coalition negotiations were over in a few days. Agreement existed mainly as far as Brandt's Eastern policy (*Ostpolitik*) and relations with the GDR were concerned. In previous years both partners had developed similar concepts so as to allow West German foreign policy to adapt to the main thrusts of a new international climate in the East–West conflict. It was hoped that West Germany's conclusion of non-aggression treaties would encourage a new era of relations with the Eastern Bloc. The GDR, which was to be officially recognized for the first time as the second state on German territory, was also to be bound into the process of *détente*.[14]

The coalition discussions were to prove more difficult in the traditional areas of conflict such as economic and monetary policy. As well as rejecting parity of decision-making by means of workers' equal representation on the supervisory board of large companies, the Liberals also indicated their intention to block extensive reforms in areas such as social policy and taxation.[15] The future role of the party as the instrument to slow down some of the SDP's radical reform proposals was thereby already well evident. The FDP saw itself primarily as a counter-check to the larger partner, just as it had been in the times of the Christian–Liberal

12. K. Bohnsack, 'Bildung von Regierungskoalitionen, dargestellt am Beispiel der Koalitionsentscheidung der F.D.P. von 1969', *Zeitschrift für Parlamentsfragen* 7 (1976), 414ff.

13. Baring, *Machtwechsel*, pp. 171ff.

14. See Chapter 11 in this book (particularly pp. 301–19).

15. W. Jäger, 'Die Innenpolitik der sozial–liberalen Koalition 1969–1974', in K. D. Bracher, W. Jäger and W. Link, *Republik im Wandel 1969–1974: Die Ära Brandt*, Geschichte der Bundesrepublik Deutschland 5/1 (Stuttgart, 1986), pp. 19ff.

coalition. Thus, following the election disaster there was no more talk of Scheel's much more ambitious concept of the 'third force'.

On 21 October 1969 Willy Brandt was elected Federal Chancellor. Three or four FDP delegates denied him their vote.[16] The CDU/CSU were exiled to the opposition benches for the first time in the history of the Federal Republic. The smooth nature of the changeover in Bonn, however, demonstrated the functional durability of West Germany's parliamentary democracy.

Only a week after the ballot, Willy Brandt announced his governmental programme to the *Bundestag*. Never before had the inaugural speech of a chancellor been awaited with so much anticipation and rarely were so many hopes and expectations pinned upon it. The government's declaration thus became the awaited 'manifesto of the new beginning and departure from the old'.[17] All of the great ideals and high expectations were manifested in the catchy slogan 'to dare more democracy; ('Mehr Demokratie wagen'), and this was subsequently regarded as Brandt's *Leitmotif* for his ideas regarding the transformation of West German politics. The extensive democratization of all political areas and the widening of opportunities for greater political participation in all areas was essentially the central theme of the declaration. The concept of the social state was to be expanded, far-sighted planning was to optimize concerted action by the state, organizational potential was to be improved, and financial resources were to be employed more efficiently.[18]

The reform projects included the most diverse political areas; yet the main emphasis remained on education and scientific research, structural and regional policy. In curious contrast to the extensive, though often unclear and vaguely held visions of reform in Brandt's inaugural speech was the lack of definite projects and detailed proposals for the restructuring of society. From the very outset the desire for change was not strongly represented within the ranks of the smaller coalition partner. This explains why quite a few reform proposals were nipped in the bud before they could even be incorporated into Brandt's speech.[19] All that was eventually left were general principles and objectives which, although highlighting the style and the direction of change, did not offer a detailed blueprint for reform.

16. E. Mende, *Von Wende zu Wende* (Bergisch-Gladbach, 1988), p. 393.

17. Jäger, 'Innenpolitik 1969–1974', p. 24.

18. Ibid., p. 26. On Brandt see particularly Terence Prittie, *Willy Brandt: Portrait of a Statesman* (London, 1974); David Binder, *The Other German: Willy Brandt's Life and Times* (Washington, DC, 1975); Barbara Marshall, *Willy Brandt* (London, 1990); and also his memoirs: Willy Brandt, *My Life in Politics* (London, 1992) and Horst Ehmke, *Mittendrin: Von der Grossen Koalition zur Deutschen Einheit* (Berlin, 1994).

19. Baring, *Machtwechsel*, pp. 183ff.

The success of all policies of massive state intervention is inextricably linked to the quality of administrative management and leadership. As such, the new government gave special attention to the expansion of its political machinery. It was possible in some areas to fall back upon innovations from the era of the Grand Coalition, such as Economics Minister Karl Schiller's concept of single taxation and medium-term monetary planning. Yet the reform principles of Brandt's cabinet were much more extensive, to say the least; the functions of state planning also reached a totally new dimension and intensity. Modern scientific methods of planning and organization now played a major role. It was intended to index all aims of the new government at an early stage and discuss and agree them among and within the various government departments dealing with the respective issues in question, thereby avoiding difficulties that would arise from friction in the process of implementation.[20]

Moreover, the time-scale for the realization of the government's programme was put back. Instead of middle-term planning in a five-year framework, long-term programmes of up to 15 years were now on the agenda. This was far too ambitious, as was soon to be seen. By the 1972 *Bundestag* elections this approach was shelved as having been too unsuccessful.[21] Within a relatively short time the once indestructible belief of the government in politically achievable tasks as well as the euphoria about progress and optimism for the future had all suffered a considerable set-back. The reasons for a sobering of attitudes were wide-ranging. Predictions about future development, which had been the basis for state planning, had proved to be much less reliable than expected. There were too many grey areas in the calculations; much had simply been impossible to forecast, like the oil crisis in 1973 which fundamentally transformed the basic conditions for economic management.[22] Furthermore, it was soon recognized that, even under the direction of economic guru Karl Schiller, the course of the economy could not be randomly manipulated. The instrument of single taxation simply was not able to overcome the cyclical ups and downs of the West German economy as was once believed in the euphoria of the new beginning.[23] Like its predecessors, the Brandt/Scheel government was also confronted with economic crises – particularly serious ones, the like of which West Germany had not experienced before.

As a result, the West German cabinet's room for manoeuvre was quite

20. Ibid., pp. 658–9.
21. See Jäger, 'Innenpolitik 1969–1974', p. 30.
22. Ibid., p. 31.
23. Baring, *Machtwechsel*, p. 647.

limited. Usually, reform does not come cheaply. A reduction in the intake of public revenue rapidly pushes the intention of the government to reorganize society to its limits. This was a problem that was to beset the Social–Liberal coalition from the very beginning, even when there existed no real crisis. Early in 1971 it was predicted that tax revenue in the coming years would be far below previously projected margins.[24] Alarm bells rang for SPD Finance Minister Alex Möller. He vigorously lobbied the cabinet to slow down the pace of the reform programme so as to harmonize expenditure with altered budgetary conditions. Nevertheless, government departments were impervious to his calls for tighter monetary control. In May 1971 Möller resigned from his post.[25]

His successor was the brilliant yet arrogant Economics Minister Karl Schiller, who as a consequence was now in charge of both ministries, and advanced to become the strong man in the cabinet. Yet only 12 months later he, too, was finished, brought down by the double burden of his offices, but also by his own personality, his hybrid ambition, his airs and graces and by his egocentricity. Moreover, Schiller also had to cope with the same problems as his predecessor, the ever-widening gap between the inflow of public revenue and the requests for expenditure from the various ministries.[26] Pressure for reform additionally came from below, from an SPD base which finally saw its chance to make a mark on West German society after 20 years of abstinence from power. It was above all the left wing of the party, now considerably stronger due to the influx of many younger supporters and the socio-structural shift of its membership in the direction of the new left-leaning middle class, which strove for radical change and soon even spoke of a 'structural revolution'.[27] The party leadership attempted to rechannel the *élan* of the forces of reform;[28] party commissions and committees were set up to work out a 'long-term socio-political programme'[29] on the basis of the Bad Godesberg programme, and to calculate the financial requirements for the reforms under consideration. Arguments over money worsened the conflict between the rival camps. The SPD left wing looked for massive tax increases to finance their reform plans, yet 'superminister' Schiller resisted the pressure from the avantgardists with a certain degree of success. However, this did little to enhance his popu-

24. Ibid., p. 646.
25. Ibid., pp. 650ff.
26. Ibid., pp. 662ff.
27. S. Heimann, 'Die sozialdemokratische Partei Deutschlands', in R. Stöss, ed., *Parteienhandbuch: Die Parteien in der Bundesrepublik Deutschland 1945–1980*, 4 vols (Opladen, 1986), p. 2078.
28. Jäger, 'Innenpolitik 1969–1974', p. 37.
29. Heimann, 'sozialdemokratische Partei', p. 2075.

larity within the party.[30] In July 1972, following a cabinet quarrel on currency matters, he resigned a disillusioned man.[31] His successor was Defence Minister Helmut Schmidt, who had been a long-standing rival of Schiller's.

The programme debate continued over the following years. Bitter arguments led to the agreement of a compromise formula which could be interpreted either way. It basically 'provided arguments for all opinions within the party without favouring any'.[32] The so-called 'Orientation Framework 85', agreed upon at the party conference in Mannheim in November 1975, had no more than an integrative function. As far as practical politics was concerned it was almost meaningless.[33] The downward spiral of the economy removed any basis for costly reform policies; crisis management was necessary instead.

The Free Democrats were also shaken by massive internecine conflict. Party leader Scheel was seriously weakened after the election débâcle of 1969. Additional negative headlines were provided by Scheel's poor start as Foreign Minister.[34] Above all, Chancellor Brandt himself was in charge of the government's 'New *Ostpolitik*'. Therefore, Scheel occasionally resembled an unimportant non-executive director who did not participate in the major decision-making process. This, of course, strengthened the opposition to Scheel within the FDP, which was naturally focused upon the irreconcilable Erich Mende and the boisterous lobbyist for the refugees from the East, Siegfried Zoglmann. Both regarded the new policy of *détente* as a needless sacrifice of German national interests. Additionally, the radical-socialist concept for reforming society submitted by the Young Democrats, the party's youth organization, nurtured traumatic fears within the circle around Mende that the FDP was on a steady drift to the left. It was only in the summer of 1970 that Scheel was able to consolidate his position.[35] Through their own over-excessive attacks, Mende and his supporters had manoeuvred themselves into a marginal position and were subsequently neutralized in the *Bundestag*.

The reform debate in the FDP eventually resulted in the so-called 'Freiburg Theses' of October 1971 which represented a departure from classic *laissez-faire* liberalism. 'A free run of economic forces would only be possible in the absence of imbalances', the new party programme stated, 'otherwise, specific measures should be implemented to organize

30. Baring, *Machtwechsel*, p. 666.

31. Jäger, 'Innenpolitik 1969–1974', p. 51.

32. W. D. Narr, H. Scheer and D. Spöri, *SPD – Staatspartei oder Reformpartei?* (Munich, 1976), p. 55.

33. Heimann, 'sozialdemokratische Partei', p. 2083.

34. Baring, *Machtwechsel*, pp. 269ff., 285ff.

35. Jäger, 'Innenpolitik 1969–1974', pp. 42ff.; Dittberner, *FDP*, p. 43.

the capitalized structure of society.'[36] Like the 'Orientation Framework 85', the 'Freiburg Theses' represented a compromise paper. The formulations were by and large vague and unclear. Programmatically the Liberals were now on a par with what had already been realized in practice by means of the political reorientation that had occurred as a result of the coalition negotiations with the SPD in late 1969.[37]

The CDU/CSU had considerable difficulties in adjusting itself to the unaccustomed role of opposition following the change of power in Bonn. Whereas in times of government it had often been no more than the election club for the future Chancellor, the party was now void of an efficient party apparatus that could compensate for having to work without the support of the state bureaucracy.[38] The party leadership was additionally plagued with no real sense of direction. Moreover, there were bitter arguments among the senior party leaders regarding the succession of fallen Chancellor Kiesinger. During the party conference in Saarbrücken in October 1971, CDU parliamentary party leader Rainer Barzel emerged as victor over Helmut Kohl, the Minister-President of Rhineland Palatinate. New CDU leader Barzel also became the party's candidate for Chancellor.[39]

Only a few months later Barzel signalled his first attempt to conquer the chancellorship. The Social–Liberal coalition had lost its slim parliamentary majority when several FDP right-wingers defected to the CDU/CSU. Public opinion also appeared to be drifting away from the Brandt government. Furthermore, the opposition had been able to notch up substantial gains in all of the regional parliamentary elections. Such a scenario led Barzel to decide to topple Brandt through a constructive vote of no confidence. But the coup misfired. When the ballot result was revealed to the *Bundestag* on 27 April 1972, Barzel had failed by two votes.[40] Rumours and speculation abound to this day as to the reasons for this defeat. Bribery played a part in at least one case. Facts show that both sides employed all means possible to destabilize the opposing camp; as is so often the case in politics, both parties seemed to believe that the end justified the means. Yet it is

36. Dittberner, *FDP*, p. 18.

37. H. Vorländer, 'Der Soziale Liberalismus der F.D.P.: Verlauf, Profil und Scheitern eines soziopolitischen Modernisierungsprozesses', in K. Holl, G. Trautmann and H. Vorländer, eds, *Sozialer Liberalismus* (Göttingen, 1986), p. 192.

38. K. H. Niclauss, *Kanzlerdemokratie: Bonner Regierungspraxis von Konrad Adenauer bis Helmut Kohl* (Stuttgart, 1988), pp. 134ff.

39. Jäger, 'Innenpolitik 1969–1974', pp. 55ff.

40. Baring, *Machtwechsel*, p. 397; Jäger, 'Innenpolitik 1969–1974' pp. 67ff.

evident that Barzel was let down by his own people at the decisive moment.[41]

Barzel's defeat did not, of course, change the basic fact that the Social–Liberal coalition was no longer in command of a parliamentary majority. Fresh elections were set for 19 November 1972. However, the government had an even more difficult hurdle to clear beforehand. The ratification of the so-called Eastern Treaties was planned for the middle of May. These treaties represented, after all, the core of the Social–Liberal reform policy of the previous few years.[42] Whether Brandt would be able to secure a majority in favour of the treaties was totally unclear. Everything rested upon the stance of the opposition. Parliamentary party leader Barzel had employed a sort of double strategy that involved pragmatic cooperation and rhetorical disassociation so as to unite the opposing views within his own camp without appearing to be too negative and obstructive. To ensure that the hardliners (above all in the CDU/CSU) would agree to the treaties, a joint *Bundestag* declaration was drawn up with the consent of the opposition, which would allow for a binding interpretation of the treaties according to international law, and which was to resolve central points of conflict. Yet, in the end, the leader of the opposition failed miserably.[43] The aims and interests of the individual party groups could not be reduced to a common denominator. Only a handful of opposition members supported the treaties; the majority abstained. Although the agreements could then be passed by the *Bundestag*, the gulf between government and opposition widened even more. CDU and CSU had proved themselves to be 'not capable of forming a coalition in foreign policy';[44] the chances for a speedy return to power were therefore very limited.

The general elections on 19 November 1972 were to be a triumphant success for the governing coalition. Following a bitter and highly charged election campaign the Social Democrats advanced to become the strongest political force in the Federal Republic for the first time (45.8 per cent). The Free Democrats also increased their share of the vote (8.4 per cent), whereas the CDU/CSU forfeited a good 1 per cent. The dominant theme of the election campaign had been the coalition's policy of *détente*; the election was eventually to become a plebiscite on Brandt's 'New *Ostpolitik*'.[45]

41. Klaus Larres, 'A Widow's Revenge: Willy Brandt's Ostpolitik, Neo-Conservatism and the German General Election of 1994', *German Politics* 4.1 (1995), 47–8.

42. See Chapter 11 in this book.

43. Jäger, 'Innenpolitik 1969–1974', pp. 62ff.

44. Ibid., p. 66.

45. Niclauss, *Kanzlerdemokratie*, p. 89.

Brandt's second government was confronted with difficulties from the very beginning. The SPD's left wing endeavoured to use the grand election success to realize radical and far-reaching social changes. Alongside Marxist anti-capitalist-inspired reform proposals, an ecological school of thought became evident for the first time. Concerns were now publicly aired regarding a philosophy of progress that paid no consideration to ecological principles, criticism that was largely directed against the purley growth-orientated economic concept of the conservative wing of the party gathered around new 'super-minister' Helmut Schmidt.[46] Permanent fighting between the opposing wings eventually undermined the authority of Chancellor and party leader Brandt who repeatedly had to facilitate compromise solutions between the warring factions. In poor physical condition and without the *élan* of the initial years, ever-increasing signs of wear and tear and a general weakness of leadership began to show in Willy Brandt.[47] Following his election triumph Brandt's decline from power took place at an almost breathtaking rate.

The relationship with the FDP was naturally affected by the growing pressure for reform from the SPD's left. Once Brandt's *Ostpolitik* had run its course – and *Ostpolitik*, after all, was the real binding force in the Social–Liberal coalition – centrifugal tendencies in the government increased slowly but surely.

The end of the Brandt era is a story quickly told. During the course of 1973 the economic situation degenerated considerably. The rate of inflation, which had already been troubling the coalition for a number of years, now reached record heights and high wage agreements frustrated the government's attempts to halt the downward slide of the economy. As a result of the oil crisis the West German economy slumped further into recession and unemployment reached record heights.[48] The government was never capable of solving these problems, especially as the man at the top appeared drained and without initiative. Open criticism soon came from within the party's own ranks, particularly from SPD parliamentary party leader Herbert Wehner, who did not hide his doubts about Brandt's suitability for the job of Chancellor.[49] The result was a process of dismantling by instalments. In the middle of the crisis the powerful trade union of public servants, transport and general workers went on strike and got its way in forcing the government to agree tamely to two-figure wage increases. For Brandt, who had called

46. Jäger, 'Innenpolitik 1969–1974', pp. 96ff.
47. Baring, *Machtwechsel*, pp. 509–10; Larres, 'Widow's Revenge', 47–9.
48. Jäger, 'Innenpolitik 1969–1974', pp. 107ff.
49. Larres, 'Widow's Revenge', 47–9; Baring, *Machtwechsel*, pp. 601ff.

for wage moderation all along, this represented both a personal defeat and the beginning of the end.[50] When a few months later a close adviser of the Chancellor's, Günter Guillaume, was revealed to be a spy for the East German secret police (*Stasi*), the head of government gave up in exhaustion. Willy Brandt resigned in May 1974.[51]

If a balanced view were to be taken of Willy Brandt's period of office, then the policy of *détente* would most certainly contribute to his credit. Twenty-five years after the end of the war the government succeeded in reaching a compromise with the main victims of Hitler's aggression, and in achieving a new orderly relationship in the complicated dealings with the other German state. It is much more difficult to arrive at a balanced conclusion with regard to the domestic reforms of the coalition.[52]

General political participation was increased through a reduction of the average voting age and the modification of the works council bill (*Betriebsverfassungsgesetz*). Social security was improved by pension and health insurance reforms. Increased environmental awareness led to diverse statutory provisions like the improvement of air quality levels. The criminal law reforms of the Brandt/Scheel era largely consisted of continuing the preliminary work begun by the Grand Coalition; the same applied to education policy. General opportunities for an academic education were increased through the extension and creation of new universities. Previously under-represented sections of the population now had much easier access to higher education than before. However, quite a few reform initiatives ended in (ideological) stalemate, with others remaining mere fragments; when viewed in light of the expectations of the early years, this was a major disappointment. The reasons are diverse. Political administration in itself often appeared to have been put under too much pressure by self-imposed tasks and objectives, thereby pushing the capabilities of administrative planning, and even of state intervention in general, to their very limits. A good deal became snared up in the machinery of conflicting coalition interests. The individual *Länder* were keen to have their say and the CDU/CSU opposition used its majority in the *Bundesrat*, the upper chamber, to block important reform proposals. However, above all the Brandt government's reform policies were strangled by empty coffers.

50. Jäger, 'Innenpolitik 1969–1974', pp. 111–12; Larres, 'Widow's Revenge', 49–50.

51. Niclauss, *Kanzlerdemokratie*, pp. 154–5; Willy Brandt, *Erinnerungen* (original German edn of his memoirs, *A Life in Politics*) (Frankfurt, 1989), pp. 315–29.

52. Jäger, 'Innenpolitik 1969–1974', pp. 127ff.; Ch. Fenner, U. Heyder and J. Strasser, eds, *Unfähig zur Reform? Eine Bilanz der inneren Reformen seit 1969* (Cologne, 1978).

THE SCHMIDT ERA

When Willy Brandt announced his resignation from the office of Chancellor on 6 May 1974 (he remained SPD party leader), a successor was already poised in the wings – Helmut Schmidt, the equally brilliant and ambitious Minister of Finance and Economics and SPD deputy leader. With Schmidt's arrival a different style of leadership was introduced to the cabinet. Schmidt was more decisive, more inclined towards efficiency than the decidedly anti-authoritarian Brandt, who was always ready to embark upon a discussion of the government's policies. But Schmidt's understanding of politics also differed greatly from that of his predecessor. He was no friend of grand designs or utopias. The new Chancellor was more a pragmatist and technocrat who viewed politics as the art of achieving the possible by way of small steps on the overall path towards social progress.[53]

Schmidt had inherited the most pressing problems from his predecessor: an ever-worsening economic crisis and high unemployment. Nineteen seventy-five was the lowest point in the recessional abyss; for the first time more than one million people were without work. The government sought to boost demand through economic programmes, but the slight upturn in 1976 had hardly any effect on the employment market.[54] Unemployment remained consistently high, notwithstanding economic ups and downs in the following years. A phenomenon became evident for the first time that was to burden West German politics increasingly until the present day. Growth periods largely made no impression on the employment market; jobs could simply not be won back. A renewed slump in the economy would lead to a higher base rate of unemployment. It was a clear indication that the problems were more of a structural than of a recessional nature; they were due to long-term changes in the West German economy.[55]

A lively debate began in the coalition as to the measures which could best be used to resolve this crisis. Large sectors of the SPD continued to argue for a traditional Keynesian economic policy. However, Chancellor

53. W. Jäger, 'Die Innenpolitik der sozial–liberalen Koalition 1974–1982', in K. D. Bracher, W. Jäger and W. Link, *Republik im Wandel 1974–1982: Die Ära Schmidt*, Geschichte der Bundesrepublik Deutschland 5/2 (Stuttgart, 1987), pp. 9ff.; M. Graf von Nayhauss, *Helmut Schmidt: Mensch und Macher* (Bergisch-Gladbach, 1990); J. Carr, *Helmut Schmidt: Helmsman of Germany* (London, 1985); H. D'Orville, *Perspectives of Global Responsibility: In Honor of Helmut Schmidt on the Occasion of his 75th Birthday* (New York, 1993).

54. Niclauss, *Kanzlerdemokratie*, p. 160; Jäger 'Innenpolitik 1969–1974', pp. 15–16.

55. W. Abelshauser, *Wirtschaftsgeschichte der Bundesrepublik Deutschland 1945–1980* (Frankfurt, 1983), p. 118.

Schmidt increasingly resorted to the use of supply-orientated measures such as improvement of investment conditions, the curbing of public expenditure and an attempt to reduce the public debt. The views of the Liberal Economics Minister Hans Friedrichs pointed in the same direction.[56] While Schmidt could only change West Germany's economic course slowly as he had to take SPD grass-roots opinion into consideration, the Free Democrats were relentlessly adhering to the recipe of supply-orientated policies. Increasingly, they gained a reputation as the party which believed most in the virtues of the free market economy.[57] The 'Freiburg Theses', with their critique of capitalism and underlying philosophy of state intervention, thus became more and more irrelevant. In November 1977 the new trend became manifest in the neo-liberal 'Kiel Theses'.[58]

Changes had meanwhile occurred in the party leadership. In July 1974 Walter Scheel had succeeded Gustav Heinemann as Federal President. Interior Minister Hans-Dietrich Genscher became new FDP leader and Foreign Minister. With Scheel's departure the coalition lost its second symbolic figure after Brandt. The friendly relationship between the two founding fathers was now followed by a more sober and businesslike state of affairs. Above all, conflicting economic policies ensured a considerable cooling down of the coalition climate. What once had been proclaimed as an 'historic alliance' now increasingly resembled a practical partnership on probation.

The growing alienation within the government led to a tentative rapprochement between FDP and CDU/CSU. Similarities in economic policy could not be overlooked and the past battles over the government's *Ostpolitik* gradually faded into the background. Once more, CDU/FDP coalitions in certain *Länder* became a distinct possibility.[59] FDP leader Genscher spoke of a 'relaxation . . . in the political climate in West Germany'.[60] In the course of 1975 speculations began regarding a new *Wende* (turning-point) in West German politics. However, these were no more than rumours for the time being; the 1976 *Bundestag* election campaign resulted in a renewed widening of the gulf between government and opposition.

In the CDU, meanwhile, reform-orientated forces had taken control. The central force was Rhineland-Palatinate Minister-President Helmut Kohl, who had replaced the luckless Rainer Barzel as leader of the party

56. Jäger, 'Innenpolitik 1974–1982', pp. 20–1.
57. Niclauss, *Kanzlerdemokratie*, p. 201.
58. Dittberner, *FDP*, p. 19.
59. Ibid., p. 47.
60. Jäger, 'Innenpolitik 1974–1982', p. 45.

in June 1973. An efficient party apparatus was developed.[61] In the mid-seventies a mass party had emerged from the one-time party of dignitaries. At the Mannheim party conference in June 1975 the CDU eventually announced its support for Brandt's Eastern Treaties. With its theses on 'The New Social Questions' – which were concerned with the lack of consideration for the interests of non-organized groups in German society – the CDU also attempted to portray a more progressive image.[62]

However, the new progressive thinking coming from its sister party appeared highly suspect to the Bavarian CSU. Additional discord was caused by the CSU's differing views on how to deal with the government. Whereas CDU leader Kohl worked on a strategy of constructive opposition to 'soften up' the coalition by attracting voters in the centre of the West German party spectrum towards the CDU/CSU, the leader of the CSU, Franz-Josef Strauss, was in favour of all-out confrontation. His aim was an absolute majority for the CDU/CSU as opposed to a restoration of the old-style middle-class bloc.[63]

Dispute within the ranks of the CDU/CSU was further caused by the nomination of the chancellor candidate for the 1976 *Bundestag* election. Strauss made no secret about his disdain for the CDU leader and soon announced his own ambition to take over the role as chancellor candidate.[64] Although the majority of the much larger CDU was to throw its weight behind Kohl, the conflict between the two sister parties smouldered on.

The 1976 *Bundestag* election campaign was fiercely waged by both opposition and government. The opposition campaign was entirely dominated by the CSU's confrontation strategy. The slogan 'Freedom, not Socialism' was exploited to convey the impression that the election would determine the future direction (democratic or communist) of West German politics. The governing coalition was quick to retaliate with equally damaging accusations; it fought fire with fire.[65]

After an election campaign devoid of the discussion of any serious topics, the CDU/CSU fell just short of an absolute majority with 48.6 per cent (+3.7 per cent) of the vote. The SPD suffered substantial losses (42.6 per cent, −3.2 per cent), and could only just remain in power thanks to the enormous popularity of Chancellor Schmidt. However,

61. U. Schmidt, 'Die Christlich Demokratische Union Deutschlands', in Stöss, ed., *Parteienhandbuch*, pp. 604–5.

62. Ibid., pp. 557ff.

63. Jäger, 'Innenpolitik 1974–1982', pp. 36ff.; Franz-Josef Strauss, *Erinnerungen* (Berlin, 1989), pp. 495ff. (paperback edn).

64. Jäger, 'Innenpolitik 1974–1982', pp. 39ff.

65. Niclauss, *Kanzlerdemokratie*, p. 182.

the Liberals were able to more or less maintain their position with 7.9 per cent (−0.5 per cent).[66]

In the end, the election result was only sufficient for the SPD–FDP coalition to secure a majority of four mandates. The daily affairs of government would become much more arduous and difficult in the future; a lot would depend on the unifying skills of the parliamentary party leaders and on cooperation between the government and the parliamentary parties.

A taste of the trouble to come was already evident in the coalition negotiations. During the election campaign, the government had promised a 10 per cent increase in pensions for July 1977, but due to the desolate financial state of the federal pension insurance scheme it was now agreed that the whole project should be postponed for a further six months. The result was widespread outrage in the Republic, and talk was of 'pension betrayal'. Opposition was especially fierce within the SPD parliamentary party. The government was forced to backtrack on its plans and Helmut Schmidt was seriously weakened before the new legislative period had even begun.[67]

The SPD found no rest in the following months. The 'Stamokap' debate (abbreviated for *Staatsmonopolkapitalismus*, state monopoly capitalism) opened a new chapter in the endless theoretical argument between orthodox Marxists and Godesberg reformers within the party.[68] In parliament the left used the slim majority of the coalition to emphasize its own position. A decisive event occurred in June 1977 when plans to reduce capital taxation were doomed to fail due to the veto of the left wing of the parliamentary party. It was only with great difficulty that parliamentary party leader Wehner succeeded in bringing the MPs to support the government's course. Fear of a premature end to the coalition proved to be the disciplining factor.[69]

The subject of domestic security also proved a serious test for the government. In autumn 1977 and spring 1978 a small group of delegates from the SPD left wing rejected a call to confront the terror of the 'Red Army Faction' (RAF) with special powers and to sacrifice liberal principles. Although they succeeded in creating a highly charged emotional atmosphere, they were to remain outsiders within the party.[70]

The beginnings of West German terrorism go back to the end of the

66. Jäger, 'Innenpolitik 1974–1982', p. 50.

67. Niclauss, *Kanzlerdemokratie*, p. 183.

68. P. Lösche and F. Walter, *Die SPD. Klassenpartei – Volkspartei – Quotenpartei: Zur Entwicklung der Sozialdemokratie von Weimar bis zur deutschen Vereinigung* (Darmstadt, 1992), pp. 279ff.

69. Jäger, 'Innenpolitik 1974–1982', p. 100.

70. Ibid., pp. 102–3.

1960s. The protest movement of the left fragmented into numerous smaller groupings. Some became radical and slipped into terrorism, the most significant being the RAF. Modelling themselves on South American urban guerillas, they attempted to destabilize the hated system through acts of terror directed against institutions and leading public figures, and to win the masses over to revolutionary change.[71] Policemen and American soldiers in particular were to fall victim to bombings and other attacks. In June 1972 the leaders of the first generation of terrorists were eventually arrested, but the violence continued and even visibly escalated. The terrorism reached its peak in 1977. In April the head of public prosecution, Sigfried Buback, was shot dead in the open. At the end of June the chairman of the board of the Dresdner Bank, Jürgen Ponto, was murdered after an attempt at abduction misfired. Then in Spetember an RAF squad abducted the president of the West German Association of Employers, Hans-Martin Schleyer, to pressurize the authorities into releasing imprisoned 'comrades in arms'. During these weeks the Republic became an armed fortress. It was hoped that a massive police contingent could trace the location of the kidnapped person – but all was in vain. On 13 October a Palestinian terror squad took control of a Lufthansa plane to add support to the demands of the Schleyer abductors. But the Schmidt government did not give in. Following a true odyssey, the plane was eventually stormed in Mogadishu, Somalia, by an elite unit of West German border police. The hostages were freed, while most of the terrorists were killed in the process. As a consequence three imprisoned terrorists committed suicide in a prison located in Stuttgart-Stammheim. Hans-Martin Schleyer was found murdered the next day.[72]

Police attempts to apprehend leading figures of the RAF and permanently weaken the guerilla infrastructure were slowly rewarded. Yet this was not the end of the Red Army Faction. After a period of relative calm, terrorist attacks, notably in the second half of the 1980s, were repeatedly to claim the lives of prominent political and economic figures.

During the second half of the 1970s the argument about the peaceful use of nuclear energy became the number one political topic. Atomic energy appeared to solve future energy problems once and for all and to reduce the risk of dependence on oil imports. Construction of nuclear power plants therefore boomed from the beginning of the decade onwards. But the enormous risks involved in such technology

71. U. Backes and E. Jesse, *Politischer Extremismus in der Bundesrepublik Deutschland* (Bonn, 1990), pp. 149ff.

72. Ibid., pp. 158ff.; Stefan Aust, *Der Baader–Meinhof Komplex* (Munich, 1989), pp. 9ff. (paperback edn).

increasingly affected its acceptability within West German society. Numerous citizen initiatives were created. Legal channels were used to correct political decisions and prevent the expansion of nuclear energy. Huge demonstrations organized by the large anti-nuclear movement would occasionally escalate into civil war-like confrontations with the forces of the state.[73] The consensus on energy policy soon crumbled within the coalition camp. Within sections of the FDP but above all within the left wing of the SPD, scepticism concerning the Schmidt government's atomic course was particularly well developed. The unanswered question of what to do with all the atomic waste produced by nuclear power plants became the main counter-argument of the opponents of nuclear energy. However, at the SPD's party conference in 1977 the problem was not properly addressed; instead a compromise formula was found: 'Priority for Coal', while the atomic energy option was left open.[74]

Civic protest now began to organize itself in the form of a new party. 'Green Lists' were soon to register first local successes[75] – all at the cost of the Social Democrats, who subsequently became entangled in an internal dilemma of massive proportions. To win back renegade voters the party needed not only to gain the environmental initiative, but also to abandon the primacy of a purely growth-orientated economic policy. But Chancellor Schmidt adhered rigidly to his course. As economic prospects improved in 1978–79 and unemployment sank well below the one million mark, his popularity even reached new heights. The downward trend of the Social Democrats appeared to have been halted, and the SPD went from one regional parliamentary election victory to another.[76]

Yet the FDP remained in a state of crisis. Conflicting coalition statements in the *Länder* led to disorientation of their supporters and to a credibility problem. The party therefore returned to a more defined Social–Liberal course; the strategy of distinct image-building of the previous years was withdrawn. In addition, the growth of the economy led to a defusing of the conflicting economic beliefs that existed within the coalition. By autumn 1978 the Liberals had eventually overcome their slump in popularity, and all rumours about an imminent end to the coalition had proved to be unfounded.[77]

73. Jäger, 'Innenpolitik 1974–1982', pp. 89ff.

74. Niclauss, *Kanzlerdemokratie*, pp. 193–4.

75. A. Hallensleben, *Von der Grünen Liste zur Grünen Partei? Die Entwicklung der Grün en Liste Umweltschutz von ihrer Entstehung in Niedersachsen 1977 bis zur Gründung der Partei DIE GRÜNEN 1980* (Göttingen, 1984), pp. 65ff.

76. Jäger, 'Innenpolitik 1974–1982', pp. 111–12.

77. Ibid., pp. 115ff.

Following its narrow defeat in the *Bundestag* election of 1976, strategic arguments once again flared up in the CDU/CSU. The CSU terminated all parliamentary party teamwork with its sister party in the *Bundestag*; an extension of the regional party from Bavaria to all other parts of the Federal Republic could no longer be ruled out. However, in the end the CDU kept the upper hand in the ensuing struggle for dominance. Internally torn apart and fearing the march of the CDU into Bavaria, the CSU surrendered and renewed its parliamentary links.[78] Nonetheless, the arguments persisted. The more stable Schmidt's coalition government became, the less likely was it that Kohl's strategy of winning back power with the help of the FDP would succeed. The CSU demanded tougher tactics be employed against the government as a whole; Kohl, the leader of the opposition, became increasingly caught up in a crossfire of criticism. Seriously weakened, Kohl desisted from a renewed chancellor candidature in May 1979. After a weary battle which lasted for weeks, the CDU/CSU nominated CSU leader Strauss as the challenger to Helmut Schmidt.[79]

As had already been the case four years earlier, the *Bundestag* election of 1980 led to a contest fought on ideological terrain.[80] Viewed in perspective, Strauss stood no real chance of winning the election and defeating the highly popular Chancellor. Numerous affairs had given the leader of the CSU the reputation of being an unscrupulous, power-hungry politician. He was even regarded by the left and many Liberals as being the ultimate personification of the enemy. The CDU/CSU eventually suffered an election débâcle by gaining only 44.5 per cent of the vote. Whereas the SPD could slightly increase its proportion of the vote, the Free Democrats, who to their coalition partner's frustration had depicted themselves as the real governing party, achieved one of their best results and polled 10 per cent.

The new party, 'The Greens', had failed in their first attempt to clear the 5 per cent hurdle. Founded at federal level in early 1980, they brought together a colourful array of very different non-parliamentary civil protest groups. The backbone of the party was comprised of ecological reformists of all political shades as well as of people of an anti-capitalist persuasion who wished to radically transform West Germany's political system; they often had a community background. Diverse groups and initiatives from the wide-ranging spectrum of people practis-

78. Niclauss, *Kanzlerdemokratie*, pp. 186–7.

79. Jäger, 'Innenpolitik 1974–1982', pp. 126ff.; P. Koch, *Das Duell: Franz-Josef Strauss gegen Helmut Schmidt* (Hamburg, 1979); Th. Enders, *Franz-Josef Strauss, Helmut Schmidt und die Doktrin der Abschreckung* (Koblenz, 1984); Strauss, *Erinnerungen*, pp. 566–7.

80. Jäger, 'Innenpolitik 1974–1982', pp. 167ff.; Niclauss, *Kanzlerdemokratie*, pp. 188–9.

ing 'alternative lifestyles' complemented the Green political mix.[81] Green political goals consisted above all of environmental change, pacifism and the fundamental democratic reorganization of West German society including the economy. In practice this became particularly manifest in the Greens' definite 'no' to nuclear energy and to other major technological projects, as well as in their battle against NATO's dual track agreement.[82]

In the two years following the quite satisfactory result of the 1980 *Bundestag* elections, the coalition experienced a rapid decline. The economy slumped yet again following a second explosion in the price of oil. Rising inflation and an enormous budgetary deficit were the grim signs of a rapidly worsening crisis. By autumn 1981 unemployment reached the new record level of almost 1.4 million. The expansive monetary policy of earlier years now left the government without the financial means to kick-start the economy with Keynesian measures. On the contrary: the economic problems carved even greater chunks from the federal budget.[83] The government had no choice but to return to a consolidation course which involved cuts to the social safety net as had been propagated by the FDP all along, and which the Chancellor also felt to be unavoidable. In the SPD, where the excessive influence of the FDP upon the coalition government had been criticized for years, the envisaged austerity measures created bad blood. To control the rapidly growing rate of unemployment it was suggested that the government should use a more active employment policy which was to be financed by a temporary supplementary contribution on income tax. However, this was rejected outright by the FDP. Helmut Schmidt, suffering from severe health problems and showing ever-increasing signs of leadership weakness, now came under attack from all sides. Compromise packages were constantly drawn up which satisfied no-one, and, worse still, did not solve any of the problems. The coalition atmosphere became increasingly frosty.[84]

Moreover, Chancellor Schmidt became increasingly an outsider within his own party as far as the government's security policy was concerned. It was not least Schmidt who was responsible for the Western

81. Jäger, 'Innenpolitik 1974–1982', pp. 152–3; F. Müller-Rommel and Th. Poguntke, 'Die Grünen', in A. Mintzel and H. Oberreuter, eds, *Parteien in der Bundesrepublik Deutschland* (Bonn, 1990), pp. 287–8.

82. Th. Poguntke, *Alternative Politics: the German Green Party* (Edinburgh, 1993); E. G. Frankland and D. Schoonmaker, *Between Protest and Power: the Green Party in Germany* (Boulder, Colo., 1992); M. Dittmers, *The Green Party in West Germany: Who Are They and What Do They Really Want*? 2nd rev. edn (Buckingham, 1988).

83. Jäger, 'Innenpolitik 1974–1982', pp. 193ff.

84. Ibid., pp. 208ff.

Alliance's controversial dual track decision in December 1979.[85] This was in response to the Soviet Union's ever-increasing production and deployment of medium-range missiles. In effect, the NATO alliance had issued an ultimatum to the Soviet Union. Unless Moscow scrapped all of its SS-20 missiles in the European theatre the West would start deploying Pershing II and similar missiles in Britain and on the European continent. Initially Schmidt found the support of most of the SPD rank and file for this strategy, though critical voices could already be heard.[86] After some time, opposition to the policy increased considerably. Peace movements took to the streets in opposition to NATO's intention of updating its nuclear weapons if the Soviet Union did not withdraw its missiles targeted at Western European cities. Large sections of the Chancellor's party sympathized openly with these protests. SPD leader Brandt sought to reconcile the opposing strands. At the same time he attempted to build a bridge to the non-parliamentary groups in order to integrate the protest movement into the SPD itself just as he had done at the end of the 1960s and in the early 1970s.[87] As a result the already tense relationship with the Chancellor deteriorated even further.

Until the spring of 1982 Helmut Schmidt succeeded, albeit through threats of resignation, in rallying the majority of his party behind him and thereby saving the coalition. Nevertheless, the end had only been postponed. A series of severe SPD defeats in regional parliamentary elections caused visions of doom within the ranks of the Free Democratic Party. The FDP feared being dragged into the abyss along with the Social Democrats. Matters of conflict in economic and budgetary questions were deliberately used to create a distance from the SPD[88] – always with the view to a possible change of partner.

The end for the SPD–FDP coalition government came closer when the FDP issued a coalition statement in favour of the CDU during the Hessian parliamentary election campaign – a statement that was given full backing by the party leaders in Bonn. However, the FDP did not yet dare to take the final step. To prevent accusations of political treachery it was agreed that the gulf between the Chancellor and his own party should be exploited. On the decisive day, the Social Democrats were to

85. W. Link, 'Aussen- und Deutschlandpolitik in der Ära Schmidt 1974–1982', in Bracher *et al.*, *Republik im Wandel 1974–1982*, p. 318; Christoph Bluth, *Britain, Germany and Western Nuclear Strategy* (Oxford, 1995), pp. 238–48; Herbert Dittgen, *Deutsch–amerikanische Sicherheitsbeziehungen in der Ära Helmut Schmidt: Vorgeschichte und Folgen des NATO-Doppelbeschlusses* (Munich, 1991).

86. Jäger, 'Innenpolitik 1974–1982', pp. 218; Barbara D. Heep, *Helmut Schmidt und Amerika: eine schwierige Partnerschaft* (Bonn, 1990).

87. Niclauss, *Kanzlerdemokratie*, pp. 195.

88. Jäger, 'Innenpolitik 1974–1982', pp. 225–6.

be made responsible in the eyes of the public as the guilty party who had initiated the break. In August 1982 Lambsdorff submitted a 30-page memorandum entitled 'Manifesto for the Market Economy' to Schmidt. Lambsdorff knew that the paper's underlying uninhibited free market philosophy would be unacceptable to the SPD's rank and file. Chancellor Schmidt, however, used the opportunity. He had realized that the FDP wished to avoid any major upheaval before the forthcoming *Land* elections in Hesse in late September. The Liberals feared that a premature end to the Social–Liberal coalition in Bonn might well lose them the votes of people who wished to see a continuation of this government, which in turn might push the FDP below the 5 per cent threshold in Hesse. The Chancellor therefore immediately called on the FDP ministers to disown Lambsdorff and his radical paper or to resign from his government.[89] Thus, Chancellor Schmidt thwarted the FDP leadership's tactical game. With diabolical finesse, he staged the end of the coalition as a dispute regarding a radical change of course in economic policy. The FDP leadership around party leader Genscher and Economics Minister Otto Graf Lambsdorff, who had eagerly awaited the most favourable opportunity to abandon the sinking ship, were brilliantly outplayed. The FPD ministers resigned from the government and the Social–Liberal coalition came to an end on 17 September 1982.[90] For almost two weeks Schmidt continued as Chancellor of a minority SPD government.

Following the high-flying reform plans of Brandt's early years as Chancellor, the governments led by Helmut Schmidt had been characterized by a more sober approach to politics. Although some reform projects were continued, the initial *élan* had by and large disappeared. Many projects were in need of correction, especially in view of the pressure that was caused by the precarious financial situation. Instead of imaginative ambitions, the chancellorship of Helmut Schmidt was characterized by crisis management and the eradication of permanent economic problems became talking point number one.

The end of the coalition placed the FDP in a dangerous position. The SPD's propaganda of betrayal found a wide public audience, and Chancellor Schmidt sought to use this opportunity to finish the Liberals once and for all by calling early elections. But the coup failed. FDP leader Genscher had long since forged political links with the leader of the opposition, Helmut Kohl, who had become the undisputed number one in the CDU/CSU following Strauss's election débâcle in 1980.

89. Michael Balfour, *Germany: The Tides of Power* (London, 1992), pp. 218–19; H. A. Turner, *Germany from Partition to Reunification* (New Haven, 1992), pp. 174–5; Klaus Bölling, *Die Letzten 30 Tage des Kanzlers Helmut Schmidt: ein Tagebuch* (Hamburg, 1982).

90. Bölling, *Die Letzten 30 Tage*; Niclauss, *Kanzlerdemokratie*, pp. 212–13.

Kohl and Genscher agreed that Schmidt should be toppled by a constructive vote of no confidence. To give the FDP time to recuperate from the widespread accusations of betrayal, fresh elections would only be arranged after a few months.[91]

For the Liberals the waiting period was a question of 'to be or not to be'. Its left wing rebelled against the change of coalition and accused the leadership of misleading the electorate.[92] However, such opposition stood no real chance of changing the strategy of the FDP leadership. Genscher could rely on a solid majority particularly within the parliamentary party.

THE KOHL ERA

On 1 October 1982 Helmut Kohl was elected Chancellor by the new CDU/CSU–FDP parliamentary majority. Foreign Minister Genscher and Economics Minister Lambsdorff retained their cabinet positions. CSU leader Strauss declined a ministerial post in Bonn and remained Minister-President in Bavaria.

The new Chancellor delivered his inaugural speech in the *Bundestag* two weeks later. The core of the speech basically dealt with the grave economic and budgetary situation. The new coalition partners had beforehand agreed to increase VAT and impose supplementary taxation on 'higher earners' – exactly what the Liberals had vehemently opposed when their old partner had suggested it. In addition to these measures, cuts in public services were envisaged to fill the deficit gap in the federal budget.[93] In the *Bundestag* Kohl fiercely attacked overblown expectations and excessive demands on the social security system at a time of economic crisis and empty coffers. Personal responsibility and self-help were to be the principles of the future.[94]

Kohl's inaugural speech also pointed to a fundamental change in economic policy. Whereas in the end the Schmidt government had relied on a mixture of supply and demand measures, the new government spoke out in favour of a clear improvement of the supply side: a reduction

91. Jäger, 'Innenpolitik 1974–1982', pp. 251ff.

92. Dittberner, *FDP*, pp. 52–3.

93. Niclauss, *Kanzlerdemokratie*, pp. 223.

94. *Archiv der Gegenwart*, 13/10/1983, p. 26046A; Dietrich Heissler, ed., *Der Weg zur Wende: von der Wohlfahrtsgesellschaft zur Leistungsgemeinschaft* (Husum, 1983).

in the economic activities of the state, cuts to social services, deregulation, improvement of profitability for entrepreneurs and restrictive control of the government's monetary policy were the instruments preferred by the new government.[95]

Apart from pointing to the economic and employment problems in the Federal Republic, the Chancellor also diagnosed a deep spiritual–political crisis, general disorientation and a feeling of insecurity. Kohl's solution was expressed in a confusing slogan that argued for the necessity of a 'spiritual–moral change' (*geistig–moralische Wende*), understood by some to be a recourse to traditional principles and by others to be an ideological roll-back to the 1950s.[96] But pragmatism largely triumphed in the end and the conservative counter-revolution only partly took place, much to the disappointment of the right wing of the CDU/CSU. The more moderate position of the FDP as well as the simple philosophy of holding on to power have to be given credit for this. Moreover, the fact that the CDU/CSU represented a genuine 'people's party' (*Volkspartei*) prevented any too radical experiments.

On 6 March 1983 the government put itself to the vote. Economic and budgetary questions together with the country's security policy were the main issues in the election campaign. The Social Democrats' position in all of these areas was difficult. The party was helplessly divided as far as the topic of NATO's dual track decision was concerned. Moreover, most Germans viewed the CDU/CSU as much more competent in economic and employment matters than the SPD. High levels of public debt did not help the SPD opposition either. People spoke of the CDU's 'inherited burden' (*Erblast*), which restricted its room for manoeuvre in the future.[97]

On election day the CDU and CSU polled the second best result in their history with a combined 48.8 per cent of the vote. The Liberals had by then overcome their electoral doldrums. A party conference in mid-November 1982 had sanctioned the change of coalition partner. When Genscher was clearly confirmed as party leader after a leadership ballot, many on the left of the party resigned their membership in

95. J. Gabriel, 'Das eingeschränkte Wirtschaftswunder', in W. Süss, ed., *Die Bundesrepublik in den achtziger Jahren: Innenpolitik, politische Kultur, Aussenpolitik* (Opladen, 1991), pp. 114–15.

96. W. Röhrich, *Die Demokratie der Westdeutschen: Geschichte und politisches Klima einer Republik* (Munich, 1988), pp. 158ff.

97. Niclauss, *Kanzlerdemokratie*, pp. 228; Röhrich, *Demokratie der Westdeutschen*, pp. 156–7.

embitterment.[98] On 6 March 1983 the FDP polled 7 per cent of the vote and was once again represented in the *Bundestag*.

The election had been a disaster for both the SPD and its chancellor candidate, ex-Minister of Justice Hans-Jochen Vogel. With only 38.2 per cent the party was thrown back to the levels of the 1960s.[99] Former SPD voters defected not only to the CDU/CSU, but also to the left, to the Greens, who, with 5.6 per cent of the vote, would be represented in the *Bundestag* for the first time.

Subsequently the relationship with the new Green party on the opposition benches in the *Bundestag* dictated strategic considerations within the SPD leadership.[100] If the party moved closer to the position of the post-materialist, ecologically orientated pacifists, further losses would threaten among the ranks of the workers, the SPD's traditional voters. If the party attempted to bind the traditional voters closer to it, the SPD would lose all appeal for the younger generation. The problem appeared intractable.

At the Federal level the Greens were initially approached at arm's length. The plain and often quite bourgeois SPD members found it difficult to come to terms with the anarchic, colourful clutter of old 68ers (those who had been active in the 1968 student rebellion), communists and conservative environmentalists. However, this relationship changed over time. The two parties discovered common ground and points for cooperation. For example, in November 1983, at a special party conference, the Social Democrats also opposed the stationing of American medium-range missiles in the Federal Republic in execution of NATO's dual track agreement – though this had been the brainchild of the SPD's own Helmut Schmidt.[101] Three years later the gradual withdrawal from the use of atomic energy was decided upon. Still, the SPD found it difficult to approach the question of an official alliance with the Greens. Although party leader Brandt had speculated as early as autumn 1982 on a majority 'this side of the CDU',[102] it was not until October 1985 that the first red–green coalition emerged in Hesse. However, a mere one and a half years later the red–green alliance in

98. Dittberner, *FDP*, pp. 55–6.

99. Niclauss, *Kanzlerdemokratie*, pp. 227–8.

100. S. Heimann, 'Zwischen Aufbruchstimmung und Resignation', in Süss, ed., *Die Bundesrepublik in den achtziger Jahren*, pp. 37–8.

101. Niclauss, *Kanzlerdemokratie*, pp. 252–3; also Th. Benien, *Der SDI-Entscheidungsprozess in der Regierung Kohl/Genscher (1983–1986): Eine Fallstudie über Einflussfaktoren sicherheitspolitischer Entscheidungsfindung unter den Bedingungen strategischer Abhängigkeit* (Munich, 1991).

102. Heimann, 'Aufbruchstimmung', p. 37.

Hesse broke up over arguments concerning the operation of the plutonium factory Alkem in Hanau.[103]

Like the Social Democrats, the Greens were anything but united over the question of whether or not to strive for a political alliance with the SPD. After all, at issue was the party's identity. 'Eco-socialists' and 'fundamentalists' believed above all in extra-parliamentary activities such as citizens' initiatives and the mobilization of mass social protest, so as to achieve a long-term change of attitudes in accordance with Green objectives. Radical, partly Marxist-inspired critique of the system thus became linked to a rigorism with moral–ethical undertones that viewed any coalition compromise with the established parties as a betrayal of true doctrine. However, the so-called 'Realos' tended to push for more parliamentary influence.[104] Although frequently agreeing with their opponents on the basic goals of the Greens, they represented a more pragmatic, compromise-orientated political school of thought which aimed for a transformation of society in smaller steps. The required majorities were to be organized via governmental pacts with the Social Democrats. At first, however, the 'Realos' had less influence in the party than the more radical wing, the so-called 'Fundis' (fundamentalists). Representatives of the fundamentalist-ecological-socialist wing dominated the highest party committee of the Greens between 1984 and 1988.

In the meantime, the CDU became again a sort of association for nominating the Federal Chancellor, as it had been in Konrad Adenauer's time. Secretary General Heiner Geissler's advocacy of party independence from Kohl's government was not able to change this.[105] Within the CSU the Strauss era continued throughout the 1980s. But following the arrangement of a multi-million loan for the GDR, the chairman was confronted with the discontent of the CSU's grass roots during the party conference in 1983. Two CSU members of parliament even resigned and founded a new party, *Die Republikaner*, which subsequently fought for votes to the far right of the CSU.[106]

Kohl's first parliamentary term was dominated by security policy and economic policy. In the middle of November 1983, the *Bundestag* passed

103. Müller-Rommel and Poguntke, 'Die Grünen', p. 280; D. L. Bark and D. R. Gress, *A History of West Germany, Vol. 2: Democracy and its Discontents, 1963–1988* (Oxford, 1989), p. 398.

104. Müller-Rommel and Poguntke, 'Die Grünen' pp. 292–3.

105. Niclauss, *Kanzlerdemokratie*, pp. 243–4; B. Vogel, ed., *Das Phänomen: Helmut Kohl im Urteil der Presse 1960–1990* (Stuttgart, 1990).

106. Niclauss, *Kanzlerdemokratie*, pp. 245–6; M. Rowold, 'Im Schatten der Macht: Nicht-etablierte Kleinparteien', in Mintzel and Oberreuter, eds, *Parteien in der Bundesrepublik Deutschland*, p. 331.

a resolution to allow new American medium-range missiles to be stationed on West German soil. The SPD opposition voted against it.[107] The previous week had been dominated by the protests of the peace movement which brought more than one million people onto the streets in opposition to the deployment of new Cruise missiles on German soil. Prominent SPD figures such as Willy Brandt appeared as speakers at the events.

Alarmingly high unemployment was, however, to become increasingly the number one domestic policy subject. The economic crisis had peaked in 1982. With a gradually recovering economy, growth rates lay between 1.5 per cent and 2.5 per cent. Rigid austerity measures helped the government to consolidate the Federal budget; the rate of inflation sank from over 5 per cent to approximately 2 per cent. Yet economic recovery largely bypassed the employment market. Corporate investments grew again in 1983. However, these financial resources were primarily used for rationalization measures and not for expanding production. Thus, by 1987 the number of unemployed had grown to over 2.2 million.

The government acted by instigating so-called job promotion measures (*beschäftigungsfördernde Massnahmen*) and an early retirement law allowed older employees to benefit prematurely from their pension scheme. In the summer of 1984 the trade unions secured a reduction from 40 to 38.5 hours which employees in the metal and printing trades were required to work per week. Although this helped to create several hundred thousand new jobs, the poor employment situation was largely unaffected by it.[108]

The high rate of unemployment was without doubt the decisive factor in the slump of popularity of the Kohl/Genscher government in the middle of its parliamentary term. In addition, a series of minor blunders and scandals led to further negative headlines.[109] Kohl himself was largely blamed for mismanagement and leadership weakness; the Chancellor's inclination to wait until the problems solved themselves led the German public repeatedly to doubt whether the CDU leader was really suitable for the position of Chancellor.

In the first half of the 1980s the so-called 'party donations affair' became one of the enduring problems that simply would not go away.[110] During the previous decades representatives of all the established parties had smuggled millions of donations from industry through secret chan-

107. Niclauss, *Kanzlerdemokratie*, p. 232.
108. Ibid., pp. 236–7; Gabriel, 'Wirtschaftswunder', p. 110.
109. Niclauss, *Kanzlerdemokratie*, p. 238.
110. See H. W. Kilz and J. Preuss, *Flick: Die gekaufte Republik* (Reinbek, 1983).

nels past the finance authorities and into the coffers of their respective parties. The affair had been revealed by the news magazine *Der Spiegel* when Helmut Schmidt was still Chancellor. The matter became even more controversial when FDP Minister Lambsdorff was accused of exempting the Flick Corporation from substantial tax payments after receiving financial donations for the FDP.[111] Towards the end of 1983 the prosecution authorities in Bonn brought charges against the main individuals involved who came from the worlds of both politics and commerce. In June 1984, shortly before the court procedures were to begin, Lambsdorff resigned from his post as Economics Minister.[112] Less than three years later Lambsdorff and others were sentenced for tax evasion. However, corruptibility and bribery could not be proved. In the meantime the political parties had attempted to rid themselves of the numerous pending court cases in the matter by introducing a general amnesty. But the FDP grass roots rebelled and the coup failed in the middle of July 1984 – just as the first attempt at conveniently solving the matter had failed three years before. Then, all the established parties had initially been in favour of such a law before the SPD parliamentary party pulled the plug on the project at the last minute.[113] The party donations affair and the attempt to push through an amnesty for the culprits plunged the parties as a whole into a serious credibility crisis; soon the fashionable phrase 'party-political apathy' (*Politikverdrossenheit*) was to become the buzz word.

An affair of a totally different nature is associated with the small Eifel town of Bitburg. In early May 1985 US President Reagan used the commemorations for the 40th anniversary of the German surrender in the Second World War to pay a state visit to the Federal Republic. Federal Chancellor Kohl, with his special preference for staging symbolic events in arenas of historical significance, had planned to round off the visit with a demonstrative gesture of reconciliation; the small military graveyard in Bitburg was chosen as the destined place. This was most controversial when it became known in the run-up to Reagan's visit that SS members lay buried in Bitburg. In spite of massive national and international protests the government adhered firmly to its plans, so as not to lose favour with the nationalist-conservative section of the electorate. To undermine the general criticism, a visit to the concentration camp Bergen-Belsen was now also included in the official programme for Reagan.[114]

111. Jäger, 'Innenpolitik 1974–1982', pp. 227ff.
112. Niclauss, *Kanzlerdemokratie*, pp. 239–40.
113. Jäger, 'Innenpolitik 1974–1982', pp. 231ff.
114. Niclauss, *Kanzlerdemokratie*, p. 235.

Bitburg became the symbol for the West Germans' still uneasy relationship with their Nationalist Socialist past. Too much had been covered up and not spoken about in previous decades; those with political responsibility had certainly not disregarded election campaign considerations in underpinning desires amongst large sectors of the population to suppress past memories. Commemorations, however, pushed a past with which people had not come to terms back into conscience with a vengeance. Was 8 May primarily a day of liberation or merely a stop-over on the way to new injustices such as the mass expulsions of Germans from the East and the beginning of Stalinist repression in Eastern Europe? In a highly significant speech 40 years after the end of the war Federal President Richard von Weizsäcker attempted to put the various conflicting interpretations into perspective and clarify the responsibilities. Much to the dislike of the nationalist-conservative camp he declared that the cause for the mass expulsion of Germans from the East could not be found in the events at the end of the war but in Hitler's aggressions, which, after all, had started the Second World War.[115]

The so-called 'Historians' Quarrel' (*Historikerstreit*) in 1986 was also a reflection of contemporary West German society.[116] The 1980s were characterized by a general renaissance of German nationalism. A new sense of national awareness secured conservative dominance in the country; the interpretation of the past became an instrument in the battle for cultural hegemony. To allow for an unconditional identification with one's own nation, the historical picture had to be cleansed of dark areas; conservative historians began to put the Nazi era into historical perspective. However, the comparison of national-socialist crimes with other crimes in history (e.g. Stalin's purges) made those crimes appear less outstanding and thereby more acceptable. Nevertheless, anti-revisionist forces could eventually rally a considerable degree of support in opposition to nationalist-apologist tendencies.[117]

The Social Democrats profited from the unpopularity of the govern-

115. *Archiv der Gegenwart*, 8/5/1985, p. 28743A.

116. See *Forever in the Shadow of Hitler? Original Documents of the Historikerstreit, the Controversy Concerning the Singularity of the Holocaust*, trans. James Knowlton and Truett Cates (Atlantic Highlands, NJ, 1993); also Richard J. Evans, *Im Schatten Hitlers? Historikerstreit und Vergangenheitsbewältigung in der Bundesrepublik* (Frankfurt, 1991); Hans-Ulrich Wehler, *Entsorgung der deutschen Vergangenheit? Ein polemischer Essay zum Historikerstreit* (Munich, 1988); Charles S. Maier, *The Unmasterable Past: History, Holocaust, and German National Identity* (Cambridge, Mass., 1988).

117. R. D. Müller, 'Geschichtswende? Gedanken zu den Ursachen, Dimensionen und Folge des "Historikerstreits" ', in G. Erler *et al.*, *Geschichtswende? Entsorgungsversuche zur deutschen Geschichte* (Freiburg, 1987), pp. 128ff.

ment in mid-term. In the regional parliamentary elections in Northrhine-Westphalia and Saarland both Johannes Rau and Oskar Lafontaine achieved the absolute majority in spring 1985.[118] Optimists believed in an imminent return to power in Bonn. But attitudes changed in the course of 1986. Economic prospects improved and the coalition recaptured the thrust of public opinion in central questions concerning the economy and the budget. Moreover, the Chancellor was lucky as far as some changes in his cabinet were concerned. The CDU/CSU–FDP government became clear favourite in the run-up to the *Bundestag* elections in 1987.[119]

This time round the Social Democrats sent Johannes Rau into the race as their chancellor candidate. As well as having gained the absolute majority in the election in Northrhine-Westphalia, Rau had also kept the Greens under the 5 per cent margin. This recipe for success was now to be applied to the whole of the Republic. A clear SPD majority was the goal – but this had little to do with reality.[120] Rau was, nevertheless, able to sidestep the tiresome strategic debate on the relationship with the Greens, as well as to counter successfully the propaganda campaign of the government. Kohl and his party were busy painting a horror scenerio of 'red–green chaos' should the SPD and the Greens form the next coalition government.

In an election campaign marked by relatively low levels of conflict and substance, the Social Democrats relied entirely on the personality factor, especially as Kohl could hardly fall back upon the usual 'Chancellor bonus'. Rau's election manifesto was complemented by the classical SPD themes such as social justice and solidarity, whereas the government pushed the idea of optimistically looking towards the future by marketing positively the encouraging economic prospects.[121]

Polling day was 25 January 1987. It saw the generally expected victory of the government parties. While the vote of the CDU/CSU was reduced to 44.3 per cent, the Liberals polled 9.1 per cent. The FDP had finally overcome the legacy of having changed its coalition partner in 1982/83. Martin Bangemann, Lambsdorff's successor as Minister of Economics, was also the new party leader. Hans-Dietrich Genscher had become the target for considerable criticism, not least because of the government's amnesty project in connection with the 'party donation'

118. Niclauss, *Kanzlerdemokratie*, pp. 241–2.
119. Ibid., pp. 256–7.
120. See Röhrich, *Demokratie der Westdeutschen*, p. 182.
121. Ibid., p. 183; Niclauss, *Kanzlerdemokratie*, pp. 261.

affair; Genscher's resignation as party leader in 1985 was the logical consequence.[122]

The *Bundestag* election of 1987 was yet another disaster for the Social Democrats. With only 37 per cent of the vote they fell behind their already disastrous 1983 margin. They were now further away from power than ever before. The Greens, however, increased their vote to 8.3 per cent.

The beginning of the new parliamentary term was anything but promising for the government parties. Squabbling broke out during the coalition negotiations when Liberals and delegates from the left wing of the CDU/CSU clashed over details regarding the envisaged tax reform. The atmosphere got worse and worse because of constant bickering about personnel questions and departmental appointments, during which the head of government performed very badly. Fifteen members of the coalition government retaliated for Kohl's poor conduct of the negotiations by denying him their vote when Kohl was elected Chancellor by the *Bundestag* a short time later. With only four votes above the necessary majority, Kohl had escaped a personal débâcle by a whisker.[123]

The decline of the CDU/CSU, which had already been hinted at during the general elections, continued at an almost breathtaking pace. Whereas the CDU suffered great losses in all of the 1987 regional parliamentary elections, the Liberals increased their vote. This was hardly a positive development for the coalition climate in Bonn. FDP and CSU became particularly involved in incessant domestic security arguments, especially regarding the so-called *Vermummungsverbot*, i.e. the law which prohibited people from disguising themselves at demonstrations. The contemplated tightening of demonstration laws as a whole also led to huge controversies within the government. In the end the Liberals gave in.[124] FDP leader Bangemann sought to preserve peace within the coalition by embarking on a conciliatory course. But the conflicts continued. The CSU now demanded the tightening of abortion paragraph 218. Disagreement also prevailed in respect of foreigner and asylum laws.

The government's reform plans remained mere patchwork. In particular the grandly announced tax reforms were responsible for an endless series of debates on how to finance them and how the burden should be distributed between the central government in Bonn and the regional governments in the individual *Länder*. In addition, the *Länder* used their

122. Niclauss, *Kanzlerdemokratie*, pp. 247–8.

123. *Der Spiegel*, No. 6, 2/2/1987, pp. 21–2; No. 7, 9/2/1987, pp. 19ff.; No. 8, 16/2/1987, pp. 17ff.; No. 10, 2/3/1987, pp. 17ff.

124. Ibid., No. 21, 23/5/1987, pp. 25–6; *Archiv der Gegenwart*, 13/1/1988, p. 31810A.

veto position in the *Bundesrat*, the upper chamber, to change some of the proposed new tax laws – SPD and CDU minister-presidents were now seen pushing in the same direction for the first time. The overall negative public impression worsened when the coalition set out in June 1988 to claw back the benefits of the income tax reform by increasing indirect taxation and social security contributions.[125]

The government did not fare much better in its attempts to reduce national health service expenditure. Endless arguments broke out regarding the distribution of the burden. In the end the FDP succeeded in its argument that the health reform should largely be paid for by the patient; the providers of goods and services, such as the pharmaceutical industry, remained unaffected by the reforms.[126]

Dramatic losses in the regional elections led to heated arguments within the CDU about the party's future course of action. Secretary General Geissler wished to target new voters for the party from within the Social Democrat catchment area so as to secure a long-term majority. But the envisaged opening to the left was met with fierce resistance by the right, especially by the CSU in Bavaria.[127]

Election defeats and permanent factional bickering led to a progressive loss of authority for the Chancellor and CDU leader. Kohl's leadership became a serious problem for the party; a loss of power could no longer be ruled out. The elections to the Hamburg senate in September 1987 led to the reinstatement of a Social–Liberal coalition for the first time since the fall of Helmut Schmidt;[128] by the end of the year, talk began about another turn-around of the FDP. The Free Democratic camp now feared that the decline of the CDU/CSU could prove to be contagious; former party leader Genscher worked behind the scenes for a subtle rapprochement with the SPD.[129] However, any realistic opportunity for a change of coalition was still absent. The Social–Liberal influence remained marginal within the FDP parliamentary party. Moreover, there were hardly any concrete political issues which the FDP and SPD viewed similarly. When one of the protagonists of the 1982 change of coalition, Otto Graf Lambsdorff, was elected party chairman in October 1988 a Social–Liberal renaissance appeared more unlikely than ever.

The Social Democrats could only capitalize marginally on the weakness of the CDU/CSU. Substantial victories were nonetheless gained in

125. D. Webber, 'Das Reformpaket', in Süss, ed. *Die Bundesrepublik in den achtziger Jahren*, pp. 160–1; Th. Ellwein, *Krisen und Reformen: Die Bundesrepublik seit den sechziger Jahren* (Munich, 1989), p. 135.

126. Webber, 'Das Reformpaket' pp. 156–7.

127. *Der Spiegel*, No. 14, 4/4/1988, pp. 22–3; No. 15, 11/4/1988, p. 19.

128. Ellwein, *Krisen*, p. 134.

129. *Der Spiegel*, No. 16, 18/4/1988, p. 22.

various regional elections. As a consequence of the so-called Barschel affair in Schleswig Holstein,[130] the party even succeeded in conquering yet another CDU-controlled Federal state in May 1988.[131] However, in Bonn the SPD still struggled to find its feet following the Rau election débâcle. Since 1984 the party had been working on the development of the Godesberg Manifesto under the auspices of Willy Brandt. The SPD leader sought to bring his party 'back onto the offensive'[132] and to activate wide-ranging discussions on questions most relevant to the future of West German society. An initial draft was presented by the programme commission in June 1986. The party declared therein its commitment to an 'ecologization of production and consumption',[133] and to an 'ethically-based control of technology and the means of production as a whole', whilst at the same time fundamentally rejecting the principle of unrestricted economic growth. It was no surprise that the so-called 'Irseer Draft Programme' became associated with the stigma of being hostile to progress. As a consequence the proposals were ditched following the *Bundestag* election in 1987.

A short time later Willy Brandt resigned as party chairman following a scandal involving his unilateral decision to appoint a personal friend, Margerita Mathiopolis, a Greek political scientist entirely unfamiliar with SPD politics, as the party's new spokesperson. Brandt's successor was parliamentary party leader Hans-Jochen Vogel. The administration of the programme commission was now taken over by the Minister-President of the Saarland, SPD deputy leader Oskar Lafontaine. Lafontaine, the SPD's new political star, realized that the party could only return to power in Bonn if it shelved its anti-modernist image. He believed the SPD should not just concentrate on the risks but also highlight the opportunities technological progress presented and acknowledge the general increase in the desire for individuality and flexibility.[134] In doing so new upwardly mobile and performance-orientated voters could be won over to the party; the SPD deputy leader viewed the SPD's traditional concentration on the interests of the socially deprived as being a lost cause. With provocative theses such as the reduction of working hours at reduced wages, Lafontaine additionally sought to rid the party of its image of being subservient to the trade unions, break through the old domestic political fronts and profile the

130. See N. F. Pötzel, *Der Fall Barschel: Anatomie einer deutschen Karriere* (Reinbek, 1988).

131. Ellwein, *Krisen*, pp. 134–5.

132. Lösche and Walter, *Die SPD*, p. 125.

133. Ibid., p. 126.

134. Ibid., p. 128.

SPD as economically competent and trustworthy. However, in the end Lafontaine failed. The traditionalists in the party accused the exalted idealist of treason. To make matters worse, work on proposals for a new party manifesto allowed the old theoretical argument between market economists and protagonists of state intervention to resurface. At times even a relapse into pre-Godesberg days could not be ruled out. Eventually the modernizers within the party won the day but for the time being the general public continued to view the SPD with suspicion.[135] The SPD was still regarded as being unsuited to coping with the problems of the future – irrespective of the desolate state of the government.

The Greens also wallowed in the mud of deep crisis in spite of their brilliant election result in 1987. The principal argument between the 'Fundis' (fundamentalist wing) and the 'Realos' (more pragmatic wing) escalated progressively; the Green model of politics was faced with self-destruction. A way out of the hopeless situation only became a reality towards the end of 1988. A grouping covering the centre ground of the party, the so-called 'Zentralos', was successful in defusing the opposing views. The fundamentalist party executive was voted out at the Karlsruhe party conference in December 1988. The new majority of 'Realos' and 'Zentralos' opened the way for a pragmatic policy of internal reform; government alliances with the SPD were no longer taboo.[136] Soon, following the election to the West Berlin senate at the end of January 1989, this change resulted in the Republic's second red–green coalition.

The regional elections in the city-state of West Berlin ended in yet another election disaster for the CDU/CSU as well as for the FDP. The Liberals remained below the 5 per cent hurdle and the CDU vote was reduced by 9 per cent. The right-wing extremist *Die Republikaner* polled 7.5 per cent of the vote and entered the West Berlin House of Representatives for the first time.[137] As a protest party with a decidedly anti-pluralist, anti-modernist tone its message was viewed favourably by voters of a lower social status. Unemployment, insufficient housing, fear of a decline in social status and the general feeling of unease in view of a rapidly changing world were all factors that created the culture for the emergence of the 'Rep's' xenophobic slogans. It also nurtured the desire for simple solutions characteristic of the political ideas of the right-wing party. Foreigners resident in West Germany, and especially asylum-seekers who had come to the Federal Republic from the Third World in great numbers since 1984,[138] were made to suffer as scapegoats for

135. Ibid., pp. 129–30.
136. Müller-Rommel and Poguntke, 'Die Grünen', p. 294.
137. *Archiv der Gegenwart*, 29/1/1989, p. 33005A.
138. Rowold, 'Im Schatten der Macht', pp. 332–3.

the country's economic problems. The question of asylum-seekers entering West Germany legally and illegally was increasingly to become the number one subject in domestic policy. Sections of the CDU and CSU argued for a change in the respective article in the Basic Law that offered asylum to anyone fleeing from political or religious persecution. Initially a change of the law was categorically rejected by FDP, SPD and the Greens.[139]

The election success of the *Republikaner* above all placed the CDU/CSU in a most precarious position. A large proportion of so-called 'Rep' voters came from their ranks. To win back renegade clientele in the forthcoming elections, CDU/CSU politicians began increasingly to play upon people's fears of becoming a minority in their own country.[140] Moreover, language hostile to foreigners gradually became part of the basic political repertoire. The asylum debate was closely linked to an overall increase in xenophobia in the Republic. Racist-motivated criminal acts had already been on the increase since the beginning of the 1970s.[141] Voter initiatives like the 'Kiel Group for the Restriction of Foreigners' achieved some successes in local elections; the tabloids made sure that the heat was kept on.[142] Neo-Nazi splinter groups began organizing at underground level; in addition to Red Army Faction terrorist attacks the authorities were now forced to deal with terror from the right.[143]

The downward trend of the Christian–Liberal coalition government continued throughout 1989. Speculations circulated regarding a change of Chancellor. Lothar Späth, the Minister-President of Baden-Würtemberg, was increasingly mentioned as Kohl's possible successor.[144] In April 1988 Späth had emerged from the regional elections in Baden-Würtemberg, fought on a clear anti-Bonn platform, with an absolute majority. He seemed to be the obvious man to become the next Chancellor. Meanwhile, Helmut Kohl's attempts to reverse the downward slide with a cabinet reshuffle were not successful. The CDU/CSU lost a further 8 per cent of the vote at the European elections in June 1988; a change in Kohl's and the party's political fortunes was not on the horizon. Not even promising economic predictions were able to help the government, irrespective of the fact that GNP grew to 4 per cent in 1988–89 and unemployment fell by 200,000 in 1989. Instead, the internal arguments

139. *Archiv der Gegenwart*, 12/10/1986, p. 30363A.
140. *Der Spiegel*, No. 7, 13/2/1989, pp. 28–9.
141. Backes and Jesse, *Politischer Extremismus*, pp. 78–9.
142. Röhrich, *Republik der Westdeutschen*, p. 179.
143. Backes and Jesse, *Politischer Extremismus*, pp. 161–2.
144. *Der Spiegel*, No. 13, 28/3/1988, pp. 18–19.

about the future of Kohl and his party continued. The Chancellor was now determined that CDU Secretary General Heiner Geissler, who had all along urged the party to emancipate itself from the government, should be replaced at the forthcoming party conference.[145] Kohl's position both as leader of the CDU and as Chancellor was seriously threatened by the circle around Geissler, Späth and others from the left wing of the party. However, at the party conference in mid-September the CDU did not dare to solve the crisis with a big bang. Kohl left the arena as clear victor.[146] Kohl and his government were thrown a much-needed lifeline by the process of German unity which was to follow the opening of the Berlin Wall on 9 November 1989 and the subsequent attempt to come to terms with the economic and social consequences of German unification on 3 October 1990. This emergency situation allowed Kohl to make a comeback as Chancellor and solidify his position. Without the turmoil created by the 'velvet revolutions' in the GDR and other Eastern European countries, Kohl might well have been ousted as Chancellor by his own party.

The events of late 1989/90 constitute a juncture in (West) German history. This date therefore presents itself as an ideal point for an evaluation of Helmut Kohl's Christian–Liberal coalition before unification. The greatest achievements of the Kohl/Genscher government between 1982 and 1989 are unarguably represented by the consolidation of the budget and by the government's economic policy. The traditionally most important indicators – the rate of inflation and GNP growth rate – consistently point towards a positive trend. Only unemployment remained alarmingly high, in spite of the fact that 1.2 million new jobs had been created since 1983.[147] However, the coalition's most important reform plans, such as tax reform and measures for consolidating the social security system, remained fragmentary in essence. Cause for criticism was also provided by the ill-balanced distribution of financial responsibility between the Federal government in Bonn and the individual *Länder*. Moreover, environmental matters were largely neglected in the 1980s, just as they had been during Helmut Schmidt's era. However, the Chernobyl nuclear plant disaster in the Soviet Union prompted the creation of a Ministry of the Environment in June 1986. Still, its sphere of influence remained tightly restricted; environmental concerns continued to be the casualty of the central conflict between ecology and economy. Although the government could claim success in specific areas

145. Ibid., No. 32, 7/8/1989, pp. 16ff.; No. 36, 4/9/1989, pp. 24–5.
146. Ibid., No. 35, 28/8/1989, pp. 14–15; No. 38, 18/9/1989, pp. 26ff.
147. Gabriel, 'Wirtschaftswunder', p. 110.

such as in the statutory safeguarding of air and water quality,[148] the political will to enforce fundamental reform was simply lacking in areas such as transport or energy policy. In the end the state ultimately restricted itself to its role as an ecological repair shop. An imaginative, natural resource-preserving environmental policy was practically non existent in the Kohl era.

The coalition's election successes were undoubtedly attributable to the positive development of the economy. The prosperity of the general public was the guarantee for secure majorities in Bonn; an increasing lack of solidarity in society throughout the Kohl era also contributed to the fact that homelessness and the growing numbers of poor were no longer regarded as causes for grave social concern. West German voters failed to punish the numerous blunders and affairs, conceptional deficiencies and weakness of leadership that were so characteristic of the Kohl era before unification. However, the SPD did not seem to be a serious alternative to the rule of the CDU/CSU. In the end it was the weakness of the opposition which became the greatest source of strength to those in power in Bonn. This has largely remained the case in the years since unification in October 1990.[149]

148. H. Weidner, 'Umweltpolitik', in Süss, ed., *Die Bundesrepublik in den achtziger Jahren*, p. 142.

149. On the post-unification years see Chapters 2, 5, 6, 7, 8, 9 and 11 (pp. 319–26).

CHAPTER FIVE

The Federal Republic of Germany in International Politics Before and After Unification

Imanuel Geiss

The Federal Republic of Germany before and after unification on 3 October 1990 is only superficially the same state. In fact, Germany was changed dramatically by the event: although Western values have triumphed so far, the East Germans are bound to make their impact on united Germany, one way or the other. Historical perspectives on German history as part of the 'German question' since 1945 have changed correspondingly. In particular, the worn-out quarrel about the 'primacy' of 'foreign' or 'domestic' policy has become even more sterile. Developments in the old Federal Republic also have to be seen in contrast to those in the GDR, if only because the collapse of the communist regime opened the way to German unification.

Forty years of historical developments will not be presented here in any detail. Rather, I will attempt to sketch broader outlines under the headings of both history and world politics. For the old Federal Republic was a product of German, European and (through the agencies of two world wars) world history and world politics since 1945, usually summed up as the Cold War.

HISTORICAL BACKGROUND: CONTINUITIES OF THE GERMAN QUESTION BETWEEN FRAGMENTATION AND HEGEMONY

The immediate background to the old Federal Republic is the Second World War and its immediate sequel: the division of a territorially amputated Germany, first into four occupation zones, then from 1949 into two rival German states. The foreign and domestic policy of the Federal Republic became a function of what is loosely called the 'German question' or 'problem'[1] and is part of the curious concept of the so-called *Deutscher Sonderweg*, which has never been properly defined by its protagonists.

Germany between East and West before 1945

Germany's miserable position in 1945–49 was, to a certain extent, also the inexorable consequence of its geographical situation in the centre of Europe – basically torn between Latin West and Orthodox East. The West, represented by England and France, had been industrializing under more or less liberal auspices since the Industrial Revolution in England and the political revolution in France.[2] The East had been represented by autocratic Tsarist Russia since it reached the status of the great hegemonic power in Eastern Europe at the end of the Nordic War (1700–21), leading to the partitions of Poland (1772/93/95, 1814/15). But the Bolshevik October Revolution in 1917 had dramatically changed the ideological colours of the 'East' – from autocratic Tsarism on the extreme right to totalitarian Soviet communism on the extreme left in the spectrum of European possibilities.

Even before Germany had been pulled by both poles of the ideological spectrum, wavering uneasily between them in terms of culture and, by and large, of economics, it belonged, undoubtedly, to the Latin West, particularly since the great age of German classical culture from Bach to Kant, Goethe, Schiller and Beethoven. But already the so-called 'second serfdom', roughly east of the River Elbe from 1492–98 onwards, had made its eastern half slip, in socioeconomic terms, increasingly under the shadow of expanding Tsarist Russia. Agrarian serfdom in East Elbian Germany made Eastern Germany partly akin to autocratic Russia, along with the rest of East Central Europe (Poland, Hungary, Bohemia, Saxony). Socioeconomic affinity paved the way for further Russian expansion, under whatever ideological guise. Since Russia had saved Prussia three times – in 1762 with a separate peace at the end of the Seven Years War, followed by the first Russo-Prussian Alliance in 1764,

1. For a historical definition see Imanuel Geiss, *Die deutsche Frage 1806–1990*, Meyers Forum No. 1 (Mannheim, 1992), English version is forthcoming.

2. In greater detail, especially for the importance of Europe's division into Latin and Orthodox Europe, and Germany's place in it, see idem, *Europa – Vielfalt und Einheit. Eine historische Erklärung*, Meyers Forum No. 12 (Mannheim, 1993).

in 1807 with the Peace of Tilsit, and in 1813 with the massive and decisive pursuit of Napoleonic France after Napoleon's disaster in the winter of 1812 – Prussia had been a kind of Russian client-state. Only the founding of the new Reich in 1871 emancipated Prussia–Germany from Russian tutelage.

On the other hand, one of the shattering consequences of the German problem made itself felt soon after 1871: by uniting into one national state, following the spirit of the time, even Germany became too strong for any balance of power within the European system, which had been defined, since Utrecht 1713, by Britain's naval prevalence. The result was the First World War, at the end of which Georges Clemenceau at Versailles in 1919 burst out in despair over the sheer number of high-powered Germans in the critical central position of Europe: if only there were 20 million fewer, they would be more manageable. But, partly because of German resentment against Versailles and the 'arch-enemy' France, which had sought security against its daunting neighbour in the east by sometimes rough methods, Germany fled into its Third Reich under Hitler, who made it even more powerful by massive rearmament soon after 1933 and by consummating the Greater Germany in 1938, which led to the Second World War only one-and-a-half years later.

What began to be called the German *Sonderweg* by the late nineteenth century – the constitutional monarchy of the Second Reich – turned out to be a constitutional cross between the West and East of the time: Germany lay exactly between the British parliamentarian monarchy and the French parliamentarian republic to the west and autocratic Tsarism, a kind of absolute absolutism, to the east. The October Revolution did not change the basic German dilemma, because Germany was now wedged in between the liberal West and the left-wing totalitarian East, with the strongest communist party outside Soviet Russia reproducing the same kind of tension at home. That delicate position crystallized into Rapallo 1922 and the Berlin Treaty of 1926, which established the special relations of the Weimar Republic between the West and the Soviet Union, directed against Poland, which were to be consummated by the Hitler–Stalin Pact in 1939. But the right-wing, totalitarian Third Reich also broke that ambivalence by attacking the Soviet Union in 1941, for international socialism was the real enemy of National Socialist Germany, not only for ideological but for strategic reasons, as it sought new *Lebensraum* for Germany to the east.

With the inevitable defeat of Germany's second 'bid for world power' (Fritz Fischer) within 25 years, it was no historical coincidence that the dividing line of 1945–90 between the new world systems of West and East followed almost exactly the line of 1492–98, which, in its turn, reproduced with uncanny accuracy the eastern frontier between Christian Proto-Germans and heathen Slavs of around 800, at the height of Charlemagne.[3] The structural divide of 800 and 1492–98 became a new world structural divide in 1945, now between the 'Free West', led by the USA, and the communist East, led by the Soviet Union. Germany's structural inability to commit itself wholly to the West or the East (however defined ideologically) led logically to it being split in 1945 by and between the two world blocs.

Options in the West – Adenauer and Schumacher, 1945

During the collapse of 1945 there was an elementary stampede, both of civilian refugees and of *Wehrmacht* soldiers, from the Eastern front to reach the western provinces of the dying Reich and captivity with the Western Allies, because the rigours of Soviet rule and prisoner-of-war camps were feared, and justly so. By and large, fighting was less heavy in western Germany than in eastern Germany. Thus, there was an instinctive preference of most Germans for the west. But any clear political or historical thinking about the deeper causes of the traumatic defeat, and the essentials of what the 'West' stood for, was absent, and has more or less continued to be so to the present. The option for the 'West' was largely pragmatic – hoping for a better deal in the sheer struggle for survival.

Into this intellectual and political vacuum stepped Konrad Adenauer. Seen against the historical background, he really personified the political factors that came to the foreground after 1945 in West Germany. This is why analysing his political role is no historical hero worship, but the easiest way in to understanding West German politics after 1945, because he left his stamp on the foreign policy of the Federal Republic: Adenauer was a liberal Catholic from the Rhineland, fully conscious of 2,000 years of Latin civilization since the coming of the Romans, a moderate German Reichspatriot, at least in his rhetoric, but full of distrust against East Elbian Prussia. When he had to travel to Berlin as President of the Prussian *Staatsrat* during the Weimar Republic and crossed the River Elbe at Magdeburg, he would draw the curtains of his railway compartment, declaring: 'We are now entering heathen country!' After the First World War he had been prepared to accommodate French security jitters

3. Jeno Szücs, *Die drei historischen Regionen Europas* (from the Hungarian) (Frankfurt am Main, 1990), p. 15.

by pleading for a federal Rhineland state outside Prussia but within the Reich; he was charged with being 'separatist' for that.

Adenauer had never been a soldier, and he became the perfect embodiment of the new civilian Germany in its more conservative version. His two dismissals as Mayor of Cologne, by the Nazis in 1933 and by the British occupation authorities in 1945, turned out to be blessings in disguise for him, for they saved him valuable energies. When he entered national politics as the first Chancellor of the Federal Republic at the age of 73 he seemed to be going strong forever.[4]

In the general confusion after the Second World War, Adenauer, with his conservative instincts, quickly grasped the historical situation, in particular the outlines and consequences of the emerging Cold War for prostrate Germany. His was an astonishing intuition and clarity for one who had been, until then, mainly engaged in local or at most provincial politics. The Stalinist Soviet Union would try to keep – apparently for good – what German defeat had given to it, while the West would become dependent on Western Germany to close the gap between Denmark and Italy in order to prevent communism from spreading even further, mainly via France and Italy which had the strongest communist parties in Western Europe. Furthermore, he did not see France as the 'natural' 'arch-enemy'. But, as a student of law, he appreciated the French influences that in the past had had the effect of softening the harshness of the Prussian regime in his homeland Rhineland after the French Revolution, above all the *code Napoléon*, which remained in force after 1815 in all the German territories that had belonged to the Rhine Confederation under Napoleon. In the mid-twenties he had favoured a first attempt by German and French heavy industries to cooperate in an effort to overcome traditional enmities. Now he pleaded for a second attempt, which this time was more successful.

The contrast with his first real political opponent, Kurt Schumacher from the SPD, was almost pathetic. Born and raised in the German East, in West Prussia with its one-third Polish population, Schumacher was a passionate German Reichspatriot, tempered by his socialism. Crippled as a front-line officer in the First World War, embittered and almost broken by his time in the Nazi concentration camps, he fought for the rest of his life with his remaining incredible energies, both against communism within Germany, as a whole and in the West, and against Adenauer's 'European' line in foreign matters. Schumacher read

4. For a more recent study see Kurt Sontheimer, *Die Adenauer-Ära. Grundlegung der Bundesrepublik* (Munich, 1991).

the lessons of the rise of German National Socialism in his own way – not to leave the national cause as a monopoly to right-wing elements.[5]

The net result was a curious cross of traditional political alignments in West Germany after 1945, which in fact shaped its foreign policy both before and after the formal installation of the Federal Republic. The more conservative–liberal right vaguely opted for the West and 'Europe', whatever that may have meant for them at the time, even to the point of being a clever subterfuge for reclaiming strength for Western Germany to see what might happen after. In contrast, the SPD stood for the speedy reunification of Germany on more national lines, against both Soviet communism and integration into the West. In an abstract way, Schumacher's stance could be summed up as a German social-democratic nationalism – anti-Nazi, anti-communist and anti-Western all at the same time. When Adenauer as the first Federal Chancellor made his first moves to shed the Allies' sovereignty over West Germany by the Petersberg Agreements in November 1949, Schumacher called Adenauer 'Chancellor of the Allies', causing an uproar in parliament.

The Founding of the Federal Republic and the GDR, 1949

Even before the founding of the Federal Republic, basic decisions had set the course for West Germany: the fusion of the three western occupation zones in 1947–48 foreshadowed the future Federal Republic. The currency reform of June 1948, economically upheld by West Germany's inclusion into the Marshall Plan, inaugurated economic recovery and escalated, thanks to the 'Korea boom' after 1950, into the dazzling *Wirtschaftswunder* (economic miracle). France was against any central authority for Germany, whereas Britain and the USA were for a loose confederation of the *Länder*; German politicians, certainly the SPD, preferred more centralism. As a compromise solution, the provisional constitution emerged, the *Grundgesetz*, with its federal structure and a fairly strong central federal government.

The Federal Republic was founded in national competition with East Germany, whose Stalinist regime of the SED also cultivated a national rhetoric, while hoping to take over West Germany somehow during the impending collapse of capitalism and the progress of World Revolution. Thus, the SED accused West German politicians of splitting the

5. For a more critical view from a New Left perspective, see W. Albrecht, *Kurt Schumacher* (Bonn, 1985).

Fatherland by founding a West German state, while the communists themselves did all they could to camouflage a shadow state for East Germany, run by themselves under the supervision of Stalin and the Soviet Union. By clever timing, the SED appeared only to react to Western moves, including the founding of the Federal Republic, while the apparatus for a communist system was in fact already at hand, in particular the police and the *Kasernierte Volkspolizei*, as the nucleus of the future *Nationale Volksarmee*.

In one respect, history seemed to have turned full circle after a thousand years with a vengeance. The territory of the Federal Republic, which alone could act relatively freely and speak for the rest of the Germans under a Stalinist dictatorship, was roughly the same as that of Germany in 911–25, when its national history started. East Germany took the part of the 'Elbe Slavs' between the rivers Elbe and Oder, while Poland in 1945 had almost returned to the frontiers of its own national beginnings in 960–66. With the eastern provinces lost to Poland and the Soviet Union (Königsberg/Kaliningrad) and the division of Germany hardening with the consolidation of both German states, the Rhine was once more the economic and political backbone of Germany, given flesh by the Ruhr area close by, then West Germany's powerhouse. In social and political terms, the loss of the eastern provinces destroyed the *Junker* strongholds in East Elbian Prussia, the manors of the Prussian gentry still carrying their medieval name, *Rittergüter*. Their eclipse as a social and political power, doomed by the Second World War and the failure of the conservative resistance amongst aristocratic circles against Hitler, was ratified by the Allied decision to dissolve Prussia formally in 1947.

For structural reasons, Adenauer's choice of Bonn as the 'provisional' capital was not just the purely personal whim of an old man wanting to stay close to his home at Rhöndorf, just outside Bonn. Bonn reflected a dramatic swing in Germany's centre of gravity: away from Prussian, East Elbian Berlin, surrounded by the predominantly agrarian east, and back to the more industrial west, which now also opened itself politically to the 'West', both in European and global terms. Germany once again had a 'capital' problem, which rose to the surface in all bitterness, ironically, only with unification in 1990. While Berlin remained, in the national rhetoric of political parlance, the former *Reichshauptstadt* and the future capital of a Germany to be reunified at some uncertain date, Bonn was close to the Ruhr area and Frankfurt am Main. Frankfurt, the seat of the first pre-Federal institutions since the establishment of the US–British 'Bizone' in 1947, had wanted to become the new 'provisional capital' of the future Federal Republic. When that project fell through in favour of Bonn, Frankfurt found some consolation for its wounded pride by returning after 1949 to its former position as Germany's prime finance and banking city, which it had lost to Berlin in 1866 after being annexed by Prussia.

'Geopolitically' (to use with some reservation a paradigm that has become respectable again internationally, particularly in France), the Federal Republic, representing the only Germany left to the 'West', had been cut down to handy quantitative sizes, in both territory and population. Losses in population through war were more than offset, numerically at least, by the influx of refugees from the east and south-east. Yet the problem of German strength and the balance of power in Europe persisted, for both France and Britain. One of the sore points of the German problem or *Sonderweg* remained, namely that the Germans, once united into one national state, are propelled into the position of the strongest power in the region, literally overnight.

France, opposed to any central authority for post-war Germany, could live with a truncated Germany that seemed to have answered Clemenceau's sigh to the heavens at Versailles. West Germany was about equal to France at least in population, and post-war France encouraged an increase in the birth rate to keep up with the formidable Germans. Even when the Federal Republic grew in stature, both in economic and, because of the Korean War, also in military terms, France remained one of the Great Four, with a nuclear *force de frappe* of its own, independent of NATO and the Americans. Comparable fears and resentments were besetting Britain, which had declined from its proud British Empire through two world wars, both started by powerful Germany, to become just a European power, though with nostalgia for lost imperial grandeur, bursting out, once a year, in the 'Last Night of the Proms'.

THE OLD FEDERAL REPUBLIC, 1949–90

Since the old Federal Republic has won out in the 'competition of the systems' (*Wettstreit der Systeme* – Krushchev), an emphasis on the Western state is well justified. The GDR's history can now be summed up as one of defeat and failure because of its own totalitarian structures and principles,[6] though problems persist with the apparent 'victor'. Strictly speaking, the old Federal Republic had no proper 'foreign' policy of its own: everything was subordinated – more or less, directly or indirectly, openly or latently – to the problem of German unity. Until 1989, the 'foreign policy' of the old Federal Republic was, in effect, *Deutschlandpolitik*, whether it was acknowledged as such or not.[7]

Commitment to the West, 1949–55

A historical analysis of the old Federal Republic[8] can follow the major debates at crucial points of decision in its 'foreign policy' (as defined above). The first one was about the commitment to the West (*Westbindung*). From the pragmatic character of West Germany's option for the 'West' flowed some practical consequences: the energetic will to overcome stifling international isolation, on both the personal and the collective level, led to a search for admission into the emerging Western Europe. Behind it lurked the emotional controversy about how to define Germany's national identity and which priorities were to triumph – European or German unification. Here, Schumacher was Adenauer's first protagonist with the biggest parliamentary batallions of the SPD. But his real intellectual opponent in the founding years turned out to be an almost exact Protestant version of his own Catholic liberalism, first from within, later from outside his own party, the Christian Democratic Union (CDU): Gustav Heinemann,[9] who ended up as the SPD's first (and so far only) President of the Federal Republic in the stormy post-Adenauer years 1969–74.

The whole debate revolved around how best to achieve the unification of Germany in a democratic context. All were agreed on this. Adenauer's big point, which he drove home with persistent simplicity, was to join the West, making the West and West Germany so strong that one day the Soviet Union would give way and grant German unification in her own interest. Although the precise formulation came first from Schumacher, in its substance the 'magnet theory' neatly sums up Adenauer's concept. In that respect, Adenauer's policy won the day – 40 years later though, which meanwhile had changed both Germanies.

6. Written from the perspective of its collapse, see Hermann Weber, *DDR. Grundriss der Geschichte, 1945–1990* (Hanover, 1991).

7. Just the same, see Frank R. Pfetsch, *Die Aussenpolitik der Bundesrepublik 1949–1992. Von der Spaltung zur Vereinigung* (Munich, 1993).

8. For the most detailed historical treatment see Karl-Dietrich Bracher *et al.*, eds, *Geschichte der Bundesrepublik Deutschland*, 5 vols (Stuttgart, 1981ff.).

9. Dieter Koch, *Heinemann und die Deutschlandfrage* (Munich, 1976).

Although the Federal Republic remained under the sovereignty of the three Western occupation powers, foreign policy was so important to Adenauer that he made himself his first Foreign Minister on becoming Chancellor in 1949, and remained so until 1955 when the Federal Republic achieved a substantial degree of sovereignty. But all steps made in the field of foreign policy basically also affected the status of the Federal Republic and Germany as a whole. The first bone of contention, therefore, was how best to regain sovereignty. Adenauer sought it by an arrangement with the Western powers, including going to 'Europe'.

The Korean War at the end of June 1950 raised the spectre of a communist military advance in Europe. Pressures from America to provide some contribution to the defence of Western Europe and Adenauer's offer to supply a West German military contingent sparked off bitter controversies about the rearmament of the Federal Republic. Adenauer wanted to use West German divisions as a lever to regain sovereignty for the Federal Republic.[10]

The basic problem was finding some way to appease French and British apprehensions about the potential threat to their security from too powerful a West German military contribution to their common defence. The result was the European Defence Community (EDC), into which German troops were to be integrated from the level of divisions. When the EDC foundered in the French National Assembly in August 1954, after admitting defeat in Vietnam, Germany's military 'contribution' was made in the form of the Federal Republic joining NATO directly in 1955.

The opposition to 'remilitarization' was split. The SPD stood for more political rights for the Federal Republic, Schumacher's social-democratic nationalism would have amounted to a variation of Adenauer's concept, as the general agreement over the 'magnet theory' suggests. But vociferous quasi-pacifist groups within the Protestant churches, in particular around Martin Niemöller, pleaded for some kind of settlement with the Soviet Union, because unification via Europe might take too long and harden Germany's division. Approaching unification in the context of the Cold War was seen as foreclosing the options of speedy unification. Heinemann, not keen on any nationalist power politics, sought a compromise in a neutralized Germany to the Oder–Neisse frontier, with sufficient defensive armed forces and with a democratic constitution and peaceful intentions. He had not minded the apparent concordance with the Soviet line ever since Stalin's famous note of 10

10. The earliest German study is still very useful: see Kurt von Schubert, *Wiederbewaffnung und Westintegration. Die innere Auseinandersetzung um die militärische und aussenpolitische Orientierung der Bundesrepublik* (Stuttgart, 1970).

March 1952. While Stalin tried to torpedo West German rearmament as another concrete step to the integration of the Federal Republic into Western Europe, Heinemann hoped that a unified democratic Germany would be strong enough to resist communist attempts to take over all Germany from within, as was undoubtedly the long-term strategic intention behind the apparently 'generous' offer coming from Stalin.

Yet Heinemann's concept, for all his well-wishing sincerity, was naive on two counts: firstly, a neutralized Germany was so much according to Soviet liking that even a staunch democrat such as Heinemann would have found it difficult to preserve the political and ideological independence of a united neutral Germany under the onslaught of a concerted communist offensive. Secondly, Heinemann underrated the tremendous dynamics and at least latent power of any united Germany, as has been shown since 1989/90.

Because Adenauer rejected Stalin's offer out of hand, the controversy about the allegedly 'missed' opportunity for achieving German unification at a much earlier date, when the two Germanies had not drifted as far apart as they had done by 1989, poisoned public debate for many years to come.[11] The uprising of 17 June 1953 in East Berlin and East Germany, the first of comparable turmoils shattering the *Imperium Sovieticum*, destroyed, unwittingly, all chances for early German unification, which Berjia apparently had aimed at.[12]

Quasi-sovereignty, 1955

Against bitter resistance from the West German opposition parties, the Federal Republic achieved near-sovereignty through the agency of the West German *Wehrbeitrag* or 'rearmament', after France's baulking over the EDC led to Germany joining NATO directly in 1955. The Federal Republic became an ally of the Western powers, who now left their troops stationed in West Germany in order to protect the Federal Republic and Western Europe against the threat of a Soviet attack. The three Western powers reserved for themselves only the final decisions over the status of West Berlin and of German unification as a whole. The latter reservation was both confirmed and abolished by the Act of German Unity with the agreement of all four occupation powers in 1990.

The consequences were far-reaching: since the Federal Republic

11. Hermann Graml, 'Die Legende von der verpassten Gelegenheit. Zur sowjetischen Notenkampagne des Jahres 1952', *Vierteljahrshefte für Zeitgeschichte* 29 (1981), 307–41.

12. For an early analysis see Arnulf Baring, *Der 17–Juni 1953* (Cologne, 1965).

claimed to be the only truly legitimate German state, she tried to isolate the communist GDR by the Hallstein Doctrine. All states that recognized the GDR would be punished by breaking off diplomatic relations with the Federal Republic. An exception had to be made with the Soviet Union, because it held the key to any German unification; Bonn resumed diplomatic relations with the Soviet Union and achieved, during Adenauer's visit to Moscow in August 1955, the release of the last 10,000 prisoners of war, who had been held back as 'war criminals'.

Controversies about Germany's status between East and West reached new heights with the *Kampf dem Atomtod*, the highly emotional movement against atomic weapons for West Germany organized by the SPD, trade unions, pacifist groups and Heinemann in 1958. In its substance, it was a sequel to the rearmament debate, but now against a higher quality of armaments and on an even higher moral pitch. It was provoked generally by Franz-Josef Strauss's ambitious drive for nuclear weapons, certainly to satisfy a high degree of power politics, and specifically by Adenauer's belittling the impact of nuclear weapons as a new kind of 'artillery'. The steam was taken out of the campaign when the *Bundestag* adopted a resolution which demanded 'equality' for the Federal Republic in the domain of nuclear weapons. But, in fact, nothing ever came of it, certainly because Germany's Western allies, including the USA, were just as wary of nuclear weapons in German hands as were the Soviet Union and the Eastern European states under its suzerainty. The continued presence of Western forces was seen by Poles no longer as a Cold War threat, but as a guarantee against German unification on West German terms.

Another consequence of the near-sovereignty of the Federal Republic in May 1955 was that the GDR, at least formally and on paper, achieved a comparable status within the communist Eastern Bloc. It became a member of the newly formed Warsaw Pact in January 1955, which camouflaged Soviet imperial power in its *Imperium Sovieticum*. But the GDR, in spite of its internal weaknesses, rose to become the second strongest military, economic and political factor within the Soviet Bloc, usually subservient to Soviet wishes except for the final years of its precarious existence. Meanwhile, in critical moments, such as Berlin 1961 and Poland 1980, it gathered sufficient strength to exert its weight even on Moscow – the tail wagging the dog.

Bonn Goes European

Parallel to pressing for a West German military contribution within the West in order to achieve sovereignty for his Federal Republic, Adenauer used his newly won freedom of action to commit West Germany firmly to Europe in the economic sphere. After the Schuman Plan for a measure of coordination between the French and German coal and steel industries in 1950, the principle of controlling German economic power through European integration was institutionalized and widened by the European Economic Community (EEC) in 1957, which broadened the original Franco-German arrangement to include Italy and the Benelux countries. At the same time, economic gains for West Germany from the European Common Market were great and contributed to the German 'economic miracle' that was apparently going on, as a new economic *perpetuum mobile*, from economic strength to political power for the Federal Republic. Since success was breeding more success (and problems, which emerged only later), the Common Market was expanded by more countries joining – Britain, Ireland and Denmark (1973), Greece (1981), Portugal and Spain (1986), Austria, Sweden and Finland (1995), while Norway joined twice (1972, 1994). Post-communist countries are demanding membership as well, as soon as possible.[13]

The Berlin Crisis and the Berlin Wall, 1958–61

The next great crisis was over Berlin. Still in the dawn of the Adenauer era, Krushchev's Berlin Ultimatum of 1958 indirectly provoked the building of the Berlin Wall on 13 August 1961. Refugees from the GDR had kept slipping over to West Berlin through the borders of East Berlin – borders that were controlled by the East German police but were in principle open, as long as discontented East Germans were able to cross them. When, in a last-minute mood of despair (*Torschlusspanik*) the number of refugees to West Germany rose to unprecendented heights, Ulbricht wanted to eliminate West Berlin by a military coup, but was deflected from this by the compromise solution advanced by Krushchev – sealing off the intra-Berlin boundaries between West and East Berlin.[14]

While both the Federal government, still under Adenauer, and the SPD local government under Willy Brandt acted with the utmost restraint, the Berlin Wall came as a deep shock for German society as a

13. For an analysis which is already out of date see Werner Weidenfeld, *30 Jahre EG. Bilanz der europäischen Integration* (Bonn, 1987).

14. Vladislav M. Zubok, 'Khrushchev and the Berlin Crisis (1958–1962)', in *Cold War International History Project*, Woodrow Wilson International Center for Scholars, May 1993, pp. 13f., 20, 22; still without those new post-Soviet sources, but already from a post-communist perspective, see K.-A. Aanderud, *Die eingemauerte Stadt. Die Geschichte der Berliner Mauer* (Recklinghausen, 1991).

whole, with far-reaching consequences. Adenauer's mild reaction – in the midst of an election campaign, he even refused to go to West Berlin – finally broke his charisma as a political leader after his confused and abortive attempt to become Federal President in 1959 in order to control from (supposed) higher authority his unwanted successor, Ludwig Erhard, as Chancellor. From then onwards, he was a 'lame duck' in his rapidly declining last two years as Chancellor.

For the East Germans, the Berlin Wall forced most of them into an arrangement of some sort with the SED regime. In West Berlin, the shock of the Berlin Wall caused hard rethinking for Willy Brandt and his crew, who had inherited the strictly anti-communist line of West Berlin's popular SPD *Bürgermeister* Ernst Reuter. From this emerged the origins of the new *Ostpolitik* – seeking limited arrangements with the SED regime to ease the burden of Germany's division (*Politik der kleinen Schritte*).[15]

Storm in the Western Tea Cup: 'Atlanticisists' v. German 'Gaullists', 1963–66

But before the new *Ostpolitik* would come into its own, Adenauer had made another move with the Elysée Treaty of 1963, with which he hoped to forge unbreakable links between France and Germany as his political legacy. It made sense enough in the purely (Western) European context and the logic of Franco-German relations since 1950, because both countries had become the nucleus for any meaningful integration of Europe. But de Gaulle had drifted further into his own peculiar brand of nationalism with its striking mixture of *bonapartiste* and *boulangeriste* strains (of course, without any *revanche* against Germany, because France was, formally, on the side of the victors). He had vetoed Britain's entering the European Economic Community in 1961, pulled out of NATO in 1966, cultivated his own national nuclear *force de frappe*, had his quarrel with Israel and followed a course of almost headlong collision with the USA, the real protector of West Germany.

Such a close tête-à–tête on a sentimental journey between towering figures in both France and the Federal Republic was bound to conjure up hosts of suspicions and misunderstandings between the Federal Republic and the United States. The next controversy about 'foreign policy' raged amongst the ruling Christian Democrats themselves,

15. For a monumental analysis, also under broader European perspectives, see Timothy G. Ash, *In Europe's Name. Germany and the Divided Continent* (London, 1993).

between the 'Atlanticists' and the 'Gaullists'. This was provoked, ironically enough, by Adenauer himself with his Elysée Treaty. The 'Gaullists', led by Defence Minister Strauss, and the 'Atlanticists', led by Foreign Minister Gerhard Schröder, had to find an uneasy balance between the superpower beyond the Atlantic and their closest and greatest immediate neighbour on the Continent. Commitment to the 'West' was no longer so easy to define and practise, if the 'West' itself was a divided house, almost rent by conflicting interests. At the same time, German 'Atlanticists' and 'Gaullists' were jockeying for power in a post-Adenauer Federal Republic.

The controversy between 'Gaullists' and 'Atlanticists' became irrelevant, however, due to another consequence of US global policy: after the height of Cold War confrontation between the superpowers in the Cuban Missile Crisis in autumn 1962, which might easily have escalated into a Third World War, the US and the USSR both shrank away from the yawning abyss and opened a phase of de-escalation or even *détente*. De-escalation in the Cold War, however, cut away much of the ground beneath the feet of Adenauer or his successor. It was partly in reaction against that threat from unexpected quarters that Adenauer fled into the Elysée Treaty in January 1963, in order at least to retain a firm hold on de Gaulle's France. Adenauer was too old and already too much on his way out of office to adapt to world changes that threatened his life's work in politics – committing the Federal Republic as a partner of the West. He sensed new risks on the way ahead, but was able neither to define them clearly nor to find constructive answers.

Adenauer's Exit, 1961–63

Thus, Adenauer was pushed aside by younger forces which were confident enough to take up the challenges implied. Strauss, the would-be strong man of the future, tried to sell to the wary Soviets his version of peaceful unification: they would grant to him, as the new Bismarck, the triumph of German unification, while he would guarantee to them that unification would not spill over the Oder–Neisse frontier.

After the 1961 elections, the liberal FDP entered a coalition with the CDU/CSU only on condition that Adenauer would resign after two years to make room for Erhard, an avowed 'Atlanticist'. Meanwhile, the *Spiegel* affair in November 1962 clouded even Adenauer's last year in office, and painfully demonstrated the paralysis of his last government in an issue intimately connected with foreign policy – alleged treason (*Landesverrat*) in sensitive defence matters. When the first serious recession seemed to threaten the *Wirtschaftswunder* in 1966 with disastrous losses for the CDU in regional elections and the rise of the right-wing National Democratic Party (NPD), Erhard had to go. He was unceremoniously replaced by the Grand Coalition between the CDU/CSU and SPD.

The Beginnings of the New Ostpolitik

As we have already seen, in West Berlin, Willy Brandt and his crew had been shocked by the appearance of the Berlin Wall into seeking limited arrangements with the SED regime to ease the burden of Germany's division. The new turn remained hidden for some time behind a resurgence of social-democratic nationalism in Schumacher's tradition, which reached its height in 1965 with SPD posters showing the frontiers between the Federal Republic and the GDR plus the Oder–Neisse frontier, given additional force by the caption: 'Germany three-fold divided? Never!' (*Deutschland dreigeteilt? – niemals!*). But, in line with the SPD Godesberg programme of 1959 and the acceptance of the *Westbindung* since Herbert Wehner's solitary foray in the *Bundestag* in 1960, the SPD prepared to join the government once the impending post-Adenauer crisis had come to a head.

Willy Brandt as Foreign Minister cautiously applied his new Berlin line to German foreign policy in general by discreetly preparing the ground for what later emerged as his new *Ostpolitik*. Bonn waived the Hallstein Doctrine for the first time in 1967 in favour of Romania, which was just starting to steer clear of Moscow in foreign affairs under its new leader Ceauşescu. Economic Legations (*Handelsmissionen*) were also established in communist Poland and Hungary.

The Grand Coalition and the Internal Crisis of the Federal Republic, 1966–69

The Grand Coalition under Kurt-Georg Kiesinger as Chancellor (CDU) and Brandt as Vice-Chancellor tackled the economic crisis with rapid success by sheer economic crisis management and the introduction of major reforms, above all under Heinemann as Minister of Law.[16] But the price was high. But for the weak liberal FDP, which took a turn to the left while out of office, there was no opposition to speak of. The

16 R. Schmoekel and B. Kaiser, *Die vergessene Regierung. Die grosse Koalition 1966 bis 1969 und ihre langfristige Wirkungen* (Bonn, 1991).

vacuum was partly filled by the *Ausserparlamentarische Opposition* (APO), which quickly adopted Marxist to communist positions of various shades.

While the new opening to the East, in accordance with the general trend towards co-existence and *détente*, was gradually feeling its way, the Federal Republic ran into its most serious domestic crisis so far, which had serious repercussions on its foreign policy. Starting from riotous incidents sparked off by the Shah of Iran's visit to West Berlin, possibly planned by East Berlin, on 2 June 1967, the students' revolt broke out and quickly spread to West Germany like bushfire, catching up with similar movements in other Western countries, including Japan and South Korea.

In Germany, the students' revolt was also a protest against the political stagnation of Adenauer's last years of office, against the Grand Coalition with its legislation for the State of Emergency (*Notstandsgesetze*), and the long-delayed radical reaction against Nazism and the partial silence about it in German society. (As we can see today, however, after the demise of the GDR, the rooting out of Nazi personnel from public office had been much more thorough and sincere in the Republic than in the GDR with its ostentatious but cynical 'anti-fascism'. West Germany had also made a more honest effort to square the ugly Nazi past, both on the part of its historians and through trials before courts, whereas in the GDR the SED just buried the whole problem with its anti-fascist pathos of democratic self-righteousness.) Part of the APO and the students' movement followed the call of the SPD and joined the party, making a long-term impact and pushing the SPD further and further to the left in the following decades.

The New Ostpolitik *1969–89: From Common Sense to Appeasement*

The net result in West Germany, as in other Western countries, was a resurgence of Marxism, coupled with a strong and sincere denial of traditional German national patriotism amongst a great part of the intellectual elites, including future teachers, Protestant churchmen, lawyers, actors, artists and writers. After the elections of 1969, which made possible a coalition of the SPD and the liberal FDP on a very narrow margin indeed, that new left-wing movement gave a powerful tailwind to the new Social–Liberal *Ostpolitik* with a curious mixture of left-wing sentimentalism and a moralizing *Realpolitik* that was in accordance, for about a decade, with the general trend in the Western world. In the end, the Moscow and Warsaw Treaties with the USSR and

Poland of 1970 found a new *modus vivendi* blunting the rigours of the Cold War.

Both practical recognition of the GDR, though with some formal reservations, and the Oder–Neisse frontier found an almost crusading support in public opinion, which made most of even the CDU/CSU opposition abstain in the decisive parliamentary vote. But since the slim majority of the Social–Liberal coalition dwindled, because members from both government parties crossed the floor to the opposition over that issue of foreign policy, the *Bundestag* slipped into stalemate and had to be dissolved. The great victory of Willy Brandt's SPD in November 1972 gave political ratification to the breakthrough of the new *Ostpolitik*. A *modus vivendi* with the GDR followed, even for West Berlin, surrounded as it was by the territory of the GDR.

The Federal Republic and the GDR became members of the United Nations in 1973. The establishment of the Conference on Security and Cooperation in Europe at Helsinki, and the Helsinki-institutionalized *détente* in Europe, had eroding effects on the communist systems after the conclusion of the Helsinki Charter in 1975, when the communist East had to barter human rights against economic aid from the West. But the more the Federal Republic, in line with its Western allies, genuinely sought peaceful co-existence with the GDR, the more the SED regime stressed the need for ideological struggle and differences (*Abgrenzung*). The Social–Liberal *Ostpolitik* represented so much long-overdue political common sense that the new Christian–Liberal government under Kohl and Genscher in 1982 carried on with it, not even changing its rhetoric.

Later, however, the ruling SPD gradually, at first almost imperceptibly, changed the very substance of its *Ostpolitik* with its success in the installation of the Helsinki process, i.e. after 1975. The *modus vivendi*, which was indispensable for preventing an ever-looming Third World War over a confrontation of the superpowers in divided Germany, became an end in itself and the party's last visible success after it began to falter spectacularly in its domestic policies. Finally, good relations with Moscow as a prime consideration of West German foreign policy acquired the quality of outright appeasement: no criticisms of the Soviet Union, over the Soviet invasion of Afghanistan in December 1979 or the chronic Polish crisis since the strikes in Gdansk in August 1980 or the state of war over Poland on 13 December 1981, were uttered. Schumacher with his socialist nationalism and anti-communism was definitely out; his anti-communist *Ostbüro* was quietly wound up. Willy Brandt openly condemned 'Solidarnosc', the Polish independent trade-union movement, for threatening stability by strikes against the Polish regime in September 1981. After the coup of 13 December 1981, both Brandt and Chancellor Helmut Schmidt expressed their agreement with Erich Honecker, probably not knowing that Honecker, one year earlier, had pressed in Moscow for military intervention in Poland on the lines of Czechoslovakia 1968. The official Federal Republic, in fact, helped to isolate unruly Poland from the West, to squeeze her between Moscow and the GDR.

Although Chancellor Schmidt himself had initiated the NATO decision to put up middle-range rockets in Western Europe to answer Soviet SS-20 rockets, unless the Soviet Union entered into negotiations about its new stage of armaments, his own party, the SPD, quickly drifting even further to the left in its last years as a ruling party, disavowed Schmidt and eroded his position as Chancellor. After the SPD had to return to opposition in October 1982, the party quickly and openly withdrew from the NATO line and made more or less common cause, at least indirectly through some of its leading figures (Brandt, Erhard Eppler), with the 'Peace Movement' in the Federal Republic, although the latter's leadership was clearly dominated by communists. The SPD also supported the political demands of the SED regime: they wanted international recognition of GDR citizenship, and the common frontier on the River Elbe between the two states to be shifted to the middle of the river. During the eighties, there was practically no political and ideological struggle against communism from the SPD: any criticism of the Soviet Union and ruling communism was branded as 'anti-communism' – in line with communist propaganda itself.

A shrill climax to this new kind of social-democratic appeasement was reached with the *Historikerstreit* in June 1986, when left-wing intellectuals, writers and historians, led by Jürgen Habermas, who were members of or close to the SPD, charged four 'conservative' historians with belittling or even defending in an apologetic way the crimes of Nazism, culminating in Auschwitz.[17] This charge, based on falsified quotations torn out of context and sometimes twisted to the opposite of what had been originally intended,[18] was a powerful propaganda campaign which the SED could not have staged better, although it was executed by Western intellectuals free of charge. They have refused any fair debate ever since, after being confronted with their ideological distortions, even after the collapse of the Soviet Union.

17. See *'Historikerstreit'. Die Dokumentation der Kontroverse um die Einzigartigkeit der nationalsozialistischen Judenvernichtung* (Munich, 1987); an English version has recently appeared under the title *Forever in the Shadow of Hitler* (Atlantic Highlands, NJ, 1993).

18. I. Geiss, *Die Habermas-Kontroverse. Ein deutscher Streit* (Berlin, 1988); idem, *Der Hysterikerstreit. Ein unpolemischer Essay* (Bonn, 1992).

'Anti-fascist', anti-anti-communism became a progressive virtue for its own sake, as demonstrated by the curious SPD–SED platform proudly presented in 1987 by Erhard Eppler as a 'historical' step towards ending the Cold War.[19] A new 'culture of controversy' (*Streitkultur*) was generously accorded to the SED, which was considered as a partner for peace, though not by internal critics of such appeasement in the SPD. In the same vein, SED and SPD historians met in Bonn under the auspices of the SPD, welcomed by Willy Brandt himself.[20] The 'discussion' about the Weimar Republic was an exchange of soft niceties, without any political or ideological drive, and the sub-title of the quasi-official proceedings even adopted the communist nomenclature for the Federal Republic – 'BRD': 'change through rapprochement' (Egon Bahr, *Wandel durch Annäherung*) was clearly telling on the SPD.

The historical value of the *Historikerstreit*, the SPD–SED paper and the fraternization of historians of both 'workers' parties', as they saw themselves in 1986–87, lies in the way they demonstrate the ideological selective blindness of a large sector of public opinion in the old Federal Republic, blindness which even affected parts of the CDU governing party, who meekly submitted to the ideological verdict of the Habermas faction. This ideological bias made the political class in the Federal Republic especially blind to the decline and agony of the Soviet Union and of Soviet communism since the Afghanistan War and the Polish crisis, perhaps more so than any other Western country. Subservience to Soviet communism as compensation for the crimes of Nazism against the peoples of Eastern Europe in the Second World War, including Jews, became a hallmark of West German progressivism, writ large. In particular, any reference to the 'totalitarian' paradigm was condemned as sheer anti-communism in a high-pitched, moralizing tone.[21]

Parallel with this ran the furious denial of any kind of national identity of and for the Germans, which Heinemann still had circumscribed as the 'difficult Fatherland' (*schwieriges Vaterland*) – difficult or problematic but, nevertheless, a *'Vaterland'* or nation. Instead, even using the word 'identity' in the context of Germans was denounced, again on the basis of distorted and falsified evidence, by Habermas, projecting something like a monolithic Wilhelmine historical ideology.[22] The declamatory

19. *Aktion Sühnezeichen/Friedensdienste: Das SPD:SED-Papier. Der Streit der Ideologien und die gemeinsame Sicherheit*, ed. by Wolfgang Brinkel and Jo Rodejohann (Freiburg im Breisgau, 1988).

20. Susanne Miller and Malte Ristau, eds, *Erben deutscher Geschichte. DDR–BRD: Protokolle einer historischen Begegnung* (Reinbek, 1988).

21. See Erhard Eppler, *Wie Feuer und Wasser. Sind Ost und West friedensfähig?* (Rowohlt, 1988), pp. 57–72.

22. *'Historikerstreit'*, pp. 62f.

exhortation to join the West and avoid a German *Sonderweg* became obtuse, since Habermas and his adherents never defined one or the other in a rational way.[23] The net result was a kind of national vacuum in the minds of many Germans, mostly in the younger generation, but extending by 1989 to those of about 50 years of age. Unification was no longer thought possible or desirable, except for a few politicians who adhered to the ideal in their 'Sunday speeches' (*Sonntagsreden*), as the saying goes in German. Progressive anti-nationalism was, however, bound to provoke new chauvinism – after unification.

THE DILEMMAS OF NEW GERMANY SINCE UNIFICATION, 1989/90

The complete lack of any kind of preparation, mentally, politically and infrastructurally, for X-day is one of the most curious aspects of German unification. It came about as a by-product of the collapse of communism and the Soviet Union. Very quickly, unification turned into the greatest crisis Germany had faced since 1945, with ominous consequences for the present and the future, both internally and externally. Germans were plunged into various dilemmas, which they never honestly analysed for themselves in a rational way. The German reaction to unification remained confused and is becoming more and more self-destructive, because of the absence of historical clear thinking.

Unification through the Collapse of Communism

Unification came about by default, through no particular action or merit on the part of the West Germans. After Afghans, Poles and Hungarians had eroded Soviet power, each in their particular way, through the previous decade, it was the East Germans who dealt the decisive final blow. West Germans only looked on in stunned amazement, not believing what most no longer wished to come true. The possibility of German unification – chances and dangers, for both Germany and Europe – had been overlooked in blissful ignorance, because the downfall

23. For a constructive critique see I. Geiss, 'Der Holzweg des deutschen Sonderweg', *Kirchliche Zeitgeschichte* 7.2 (1994), 191–208.

of Soviet communism and of the Soviet Union had become unthinkable, on the left clearly also for ideological reasons.

After unification, Foreign Minister Klaus Kinkel confided to a selected group of foreign press correspondents in Bonn that, until the last moment, he had been taken completely by surprise by the events leading to German unification, although for years he had headed the Planning Division of the Auswärtiges Amt and for some years had been at the head of the Federal Intelligence Service (Bundesnachrichtendienst, BND). If Kinkel was ignorant of what was in the offing, one can imagine how ignorant less well-informed people in Germany must have been.

While the East German and East European nations of Latin culture tried to save themselves from the impending chaos in the Soviet empire by going west, Chancellor Kohl in a last-minute effort improvised means to make them land safely in the haven of German unity. He handled the business of liquidating the GDR with unusual adroitness, using the window opportunity of Gorbachev and the failure of his reform policy. While he coordinated activities with the USA, he kept the other Western powers only sparsely informed. But he had to fulfil basic conditions: substantial reduction of military power for united Germany, massive guarantees in the form of continued membership of NATO, recognition of the Oder–Neisse frontier, however belatedly, because of internal pressure within his own party.

Muddled Reactions in United Germany

When Germans stumbled into their national bonanza of unification, they fell into sweet national euphoria, well expressed by the *Bürgermeister* of West Berlin at the time, Walter Momper, as 'das glücklichste Volk der Erde' ('the happiest people on earth'). Meanwhile, the two Germanies had become more estranged than national sentimentalism had realized, as became painfully obvious after unification in 1989/90. Delusory enthusiasm quickly turned sour, once it was found out that unification would be much more costly than had been imagined and would create old problems in new form, both at home and abroad. Differences between West and East Germans had become far greater in 45 years than national indifference and ignorance of the real conditions in the GDR would have warranted. Obstacles to smooth unification even domestically were much more powerful than was seen in the first rush of sentimental emotions when the Berlin Wall fell. This author's realistic guess in early 1990 that at least ten years would be necessary to achieve some kind of internal cohesion was in contrast to Kohl's rash promises of early prosperity for East Germany.

Instead, a policy of brutal de-industrialization and the demolition of many academic and university structures in the ex-GDR caused widespread unemployment and resentment over the often fraudulent practices of white-collar criminals from both West and East. Very soon, many people in East and West wished the Berlin Wall back again, for different reasons – many Easterners in frustration over arrogant Westerners, many Westerners because of the high financial costs, which are throwing part of the Western infrastructure and cultural establishments into decay and serious crisis. On top, the *Stasi* syndrome is poisoning relations. Parts of the *nomenklatura* turned managers and industrialists by privatizing 'public property' into their own pockets, often with mafia-like methods and building up mafia-type substructures, as in other 'post-communist' countries, with consequences unforeseeable for the future. Also the role of *Stasi* informants in the past, about 100,000 of them, and their place in post-communist Germany is creating bad blood all around. Nostalgia for the GDR is swelling the electorate of the PDS, the successor party of the SED.

At the same time, there raged a strange debate within the political class. Both the CDU and the SPD claimed for themselves an overwhelming share in bringing about German unification. The CDU advanced the *Westbindung* and Adenauer's practised 'magnet theory', which had strengthened the Federal Republic, while the SPD pointed to its *Ostpolitik*, and even the SPD–SED paper, for having eroded the communist bloc from within. In fact, both sides had their valid points: Germany *was* united on the basis of integration with the West and the collapse of Soviet communism. But the process had taken much longer than Adenauer had expected. Without *Ostpolitik*, the *Westbindung* would have become sterile and petrified, but without the solid foundation of *Westbindung*, the *Ostpolitik* would have become a political adventure, while with *Westbindung* it did erode the Soviet Bloc from within. Yet this had never been the intention of its inventors and executors, as borne out by the SPD–SED paper, when the SPD had given a kind of moral guarantee for the indefinite existence of Soviet communism, including the GDR. The collapse of communism was the last thing the SPD since about 1979 had thought possible or would have wished for. If the SPD now claims credit for effects which it never intended in the last decade before unity, it only widens its credibility gap.

In contrast, a realistic guess by this author, from the position of an independent left within the SPD, suggested in 1965 that if there ever were German unification, it would take at least as many years to arrive as the country had then been divided.[24] In 1965 the division of Germany had lasted, in fact, for 20 years. Another 20 years into the then unknown future came to 1985, and even that four-year difference was covered by the cautious rider 'at least'. But even then, conditions for any future unification were already spelled out: recognition of the Oder–Neisse frontier; reduction of German military power; international controls or massive German guarantees,[25] which no relevant political force was then really prepared to concede, not even the SPD.[26]

On the other hand, the radical change – in that respect – can be measured between 1965 and 1990, because by now most of the German political nation welcomed the conditions outlined in the abstract in 1965, and this was certainly one positive result of political education both in the former GDR in the East and of the '68 Movement in the West. But while traditional German nationalism was largely burned out, a rigorous and excessive political anationalism created the kind of political vacuum from which Germans are suffering today, because the great danger is that it will be filled by a new right-wing extremism.

Convergence of European Problems in Germany

The muddled reactions of German society since the fall of the Berlin Wall reflect in a dialectical way the character of West German political existence before 1989/90 – the old Federal Republic had been smugly enjoying an increasingly opulent existence, largely sheltered from the storms of an ugly world, while its 'brothers and sisters' had been safely tucked away, provoking only sentimental sighs and charitable parcels to poor and happily distant relatives. Whereas Germans as a whole had continued to look vaguely towards a mystified Europe, they refused even to think rationally about their collective identity as a nation, however problematic and torn between conflicting political forces they were and still are.

24. I. Geiss, 'Tradition und Kontinuität der deutschen Frage', *Atomzeitalter* 4 (1965), 110–15; the relevant quotation is on p. 110: 'Heute wäre die Wiedervereinigung nur als langwieriger und komplexer Prozess denkbar, der wohl mindestens so lange dauern würde, wie der bisherige Prozess des Auseinanderlebens.'

25. Ibid., p. 110: 'Ausserdem wäre die Wiedervereinigung ohne deutschen Machtverzicht unmöglich – was in der historischen Situation bedeuten würde – Verzicht auf eine starke militärische Macht für das wiedervereinigte Deutschland; internationale Kontrollen oder massive deutsche Garantien, Anerkennung der Oder–Neisse–Grenze.' See also p. 114.

26. Ibid., p. 110: 'Zu allem wäre, von kleinen Minderheiten abgesehen, heute keine organisierte politische Kraft in der Bundesrepublik bereit.'

Pampered materially and politically for 40 years, West Germans had become ideologically obsessed with only bemoaning the (truly disastrous) history of Germany since Bismarck and the First World War, leading to Hitler and Auschwitz. Their left-wing historians claimed to be rational in their approach, but just offered a left-wing variation of the traditional right-wing hysterical German *Weltanschauung*. The cool historical analysis necessary to draw peaceful and humane consequences from Germany's potential new power is still largely missing.

Brought about by the downfall of Soviet communism, unification abruptly ended that post-war, Cold War idyll. By catching Germans completely unprepared for the challenges and risks of the new situation, it raised a host of awkward new questions, which Germans can no longer afford to shun as they once did. What is the collective (national) identity of the (now united) Germans? What is their place in Europe, into which they want to integrate themselves? How can they and will they square the circle between their quantitative and qualitative weight, which inexorably throws on them the terrible burden of leadership or even hegemonic status on many accounts, on the one hand, and the aversion built into the European system against any such leader or would-be overlord, on the other?

On paper, united Germany crashed back into its normal position in Europe – whenever it has been united, it has been the strongest power. Now, the threat of new Great Power status is looming again over Europe, and most Germans do not even understand why that is so. They see neither the tension between German national unity and potential hegemonic status, nor how justified fears of German neighbours are in reality, in particular to the West.

With the fall of the Berlin Wall and of Soviet communism, Germany was also propelled back to its traditional position in Europe, between East and West. Many of the problems of post-communist Europe – unemployment, the breaking-up of families, drugs, Aids, mafias of all kinds and nationalities, the massive influx of foreigners provoking xenophobic violence, usual in similar situations of strain – are converging on Germany and in particular on Berlin, although they are still softened by a high average standard of living. Ideological bewilderment is compounded with real economic and social hardships, in particular long-term youth unemployment. Unification and the attainment of full sovereignty released many a restraint under the conditions of incomplete sovereignty. Yet despite the shocking burning of homes of unwanted foreigners, usually by socially deprived youngsters who feel the real losses compared with foreign asylum-seekers, the majority of the population are just as tolerant and non-xenophobic as other West Europeans who have closed their frontiers against the influx of unwanted immigrants much earlier.

In addition, Germany also suffers from the universal dislike of the ruling political classes. Their almost unbridled greed, selfishness and incompetence in tackling the great problems of our time in an appropriate spirit of public service are provoking anger, resignation and cynicism almost everywhere. The German variation, *Politikverdrossenheit*, is real and well-founded enough, but only worsens the crisis because, apart from a few remarkable public figures, no alternatives are in sight.

On the other hand, Germans see themselves as charged with historical burdens, even if they were quite innocent, for a change, in particular over the conflict in former Yugoslavia, which is of course overwhelmingly a product of internal tensions and traditional conflicts.[27] But old rivalries and suspicions, lurking just below the surface of European communities, are reappearing and threatening relations.

The Dilemmas of New Germany in a New Europe

Unification is inevitably shifting Germany's point of gravity away from the Rhine and further to the east. The hidden rivalry and tension between Bonn and Berlin, between the 'provisional', but materially real, and the rhetorical-but-never-believed-to-become-true capital in the faraway east, broke out in all bitterness in 1991 when the newly elected *Bundestag*, including members of parliament from the east for the first time, had to decide. The battle had been raised to ideological dimensions, because the decision between Bonn and Berlin was made out to be between *Westbindung* and neo-imperial militarism. There was much exaggeration in demagogic slogans on both sides, both for and against Bonn or Berlin. But the shift is real and possibly of far-reaching consequences. Since both capitals had their valid points, a sensible compromise was struck, befitting the traditions of German federalism. Berlin was made the *political*, Bonn the *administrative* capital of the united Germany. While in practice this might be clumsy and financially costly in the future, the unilateral choice of Bonn, preserving the *status quo*, would have had disastrous psychological effects in East Germany, as another symptom of the quasi-colonial take-over which the East Germans feel they have been subjected to. Berlin as the political capital will make parliament and government more susceptible to the massive problems

27. This is explained in greater detail by idem, *Der Jugoslawienkrieg* (Frankfurt am Main, 1993, 2nd expanded edn with Gabriele Jufemann, 1995).

of East Germans and of Eastern Europe as a whole, while Bonn as the administrative capital may help to preserve the necessary and constructive links to the West. Thus, both capitals may have their useful functions in a delicate but unavoidable compromise.

On the whole, united Germans have to execute a hair-raising balancing act between two possibilities, threatening enough in themselves – instability and new hegemonic aspirations. Irritations in united Germany, largely between east and west, may escalate under the strains of economic crisis to serious trouble, even to a vague kind of civil war, fused by violence against unwanted foreigners. The wave of New Right extremism is using foreigners mainly as lightning-rods to ease internal tensions in the national society. The realistic guess that 'internal' German unification may take about as long as German division lasted – about 40 years or another 35 years from now[28] – is about to come true.

Because it was one of those great changes which are normally connected with the use of violence, peaceful unification really was a political miracle. But historical experience shows that in such rare cases of non-violent major changes, violence comes later, one way or another. Thus, violent conflicts in and between post-communist successor states on the soil of the former Soviet Union and Yugoslavia may yet spread to Western Europe and united Germany, if only ignited by the influx of refugees from regions where civil and international wars, ethnic conflicts and hunger are raging, presumably already between Kurds and Turks.

On the other hand, if Germans were to overcome the greatest of their economic and social problems after the shock of unification has disturbed their peace of mind behind the Wall, a truly united Germany would be again the giant that Europe fears just as much as it fears new German instability. Any return to the grandeur and mystique of the Reich, so far foreshadowed only by a small intellectual ginger group of a New Right calling for a renewed nationalism, would be an alarm signal to the rest of Europe and to many Germans themselves. Disquieting enough is their plea for an 'ethnically homogeneous' (German) nation, because it would lead to more burnings and the kind of ethnic cleansing that ex-Yugoslavia has already practised with self-destructive brutality. Perhaps more disquieting is that German intellectuals are apparently not aware of the sinister consequences of such new nationalism, which does not distinguish between 'nation' and 'empire'.

Again on the other hand, old resentments against united Germany,

28. For a realistic warning after several earlier and shorter articles, see idem, 'The Trouble with German Unity', *Journal of Australian Politics and History* 37 (1991), 236–45.

objectively unfounded in the case of the conflict in former Yugoslavia, were blowing up again in the West, in particular in Britain, the Netherlands and France, while orthodox Greece was almost openly taking sides with the arguments of orthodox Serbia and Russia. If old alliances of two world wars are again resurging (Serbia–Yugoslavia as counterweights against a united Germany), the dialectics of the Machiavelli dictum ('The neighbour is the enemy; the neighbour's neighbour the natural ally') threaten to destroy all European structures or fine verbiage, because New Germany would emerge as the old–new enemy.

Options for the Future – Between Federal Republic and Reich

For the first time since 1945, Germany, now united, has to develop a genuine foreign policy of its own, has to formulate and pursue legitimate national interests. So far, it has done this with a remarkable mixture of diffidence and overbearing, which betrays the difficulties of finding a proper balance in its new role. Much depends on how Germans see themselves, Europe and the 'West', which they have never defined rationally so far.[29] If Germans see themselves as a part of Latin Europe and partners in democracy on the basis of real equality for all the nations of Europe, there is a chance that united Germany will succeed in evading the hegemonic trap, which quantitative and qualitative factors have prepared for Germans whenever they are united politically, with such devastating effect in two world wars. If Germany cultivates new dreams of going it alone and lording it over the rest of Europe again, possibly with pliant clients of Latin culture in the post-communist East and South-East, Europe would be right to be worried.

It would be only an outward symptom or symbol if the Germans were ever to return to Reich for the official name of their united national state, abolishing the Federal Republic as such, even the new one. Even if most Germans now do not want such a central and leading position for their united Germany, what about the young generation, almost devoid of historical knowledge and perspectives? In the dialectical tensions between economic power through prosperity and political weakness in times of serious economic crisis they might again choose the short cut to transforming economic potential into political power, and from there to hegemonic or even imperial power politics, as their extreme right wing on the lunatic fringe is already trying to do, so far mainly against unwanted foreigners. But their brutal intimidations might

29. For a first recent attempt see idem, *Die deutsche Frage* and *Europa*.

spread to other sectors of German society, and then there would be trouble ahead again for and through a united Germany, once more too powerful to be contained by European structures.

Federal and democratic structures plus a lasting commitment to Europe must provide some constitutional containment for the 'fast breeder' which Germany has been for so long, to its own and Europe's detriment in two world wars. For this, it will also need a helping hand from its European partners, which will have to understand Germany's complicated position in the centre of Europe.

PART TWO

Politics, Society and Economy in the Federal Republic: Key Themes

CHAPTER SIX

State Intervention in the Post-war German Economy

Graham Hallett

Everyman's Dictionary of Economics defines 'state intervention' as 'the positive action of governments to affect economic activity. State intervention can take the form of regulation, participation, control and direct operation and ownership.'[1] However, the term has different connotations in 'Germany', or, rather, in the two Germanies, than it has in Britain. Before 1990, there was no 'Germany'; there were only two German states with fundamentally different economic systems. The Federal Republic of Germany (FRG) has now absorbed the former German Democratic Republic (GDR). The 'new' FRG is still, however, 'two nations', and likely to remain so for some time. In dealing with unified Germany, I shall therefore follow the *Bundesbank* in referring to 'western Germany' and 'eastern Germany', omitting capital letters to indicate that the references have no political connotation.

On 3 October 1990, under the terms of the Unification Treaty, the law and institutions of the FRG became applicable – with only a few exceptions for a limited transitional period – in the territory comprising the former GDR. It now looks as though nothing will be allowed to remain of the economic and administrative system of the GDR – apart from the useful traffic rule that a right turn can be made on a red light. Nevertheless, something must be said about the GDR, to explain the present situation.

There is no historical precedent for what has happened in eastern Germany. In the past, national boundaries have changed and governments have fallen, but there has been no previous case where a state with 15 million people has, virtually overnight, been absorbed into a state with a completely different economic and political system, followed by the collapse of its main industries, with unemployment rising to unprecedented levels. The collapse of employment, and of social life organized around employment, came, moreover, after half a century of

1. A. Seldon and F. G. Pennance, *Everyman's Dictionary of Economics* (London, 1965).

full employment. Many people are still in a state of shock. One of the most telling statistics from eastern Germany is that the birth rate – which under the GDR was only slightly higher than that in the FRG, and hence among the lowest in the world – has halved. In the aftermath of unification, fears were expressed that there would be a violent political backlash, or that eastern Germany would remain an economically depressed *Mezzogiorno*. There are now, however, clear indications that there is likely to be a steady but patchy economic recovery, so that, by 2005 or 2010, eastern Germany will be comparable with parts of western Germany.

THE GERMAN DEMOCRATIC REPUBLIC

In the 'peasants' and workers' state', state intervention in the form of direct operation and ownership was dominant. Virtually all industry was nationalized, in large *Kombinate* (trusts), and operated on the basis of a 'centrally planned economy' rather than a market economy. Agriculture was organized in 'collective farms'. Ninety per cent of new housing was state-owned. Most pre-1939 tenanted housing remained in the hands of private landlords, but at rents at 1936 levels, and with tenants selected by the state. Rents, and charges for public services, were kept at extremely low levels by massive subsidies.

Although sometimes called 'red Prussia', the GDR did not (as we now know) have an efficient public administration like that of Prussia or the FRG. Administration was highly centralized, but also fragmented, remote and chaotic. The various national agencies operated without co-ordination; they even had separate telephone networks. The predominantly 'vertical' nature of the command structure was inimical to efficient industrial management; directives were sent down to firms from above, but industrially related firms had little contact with each other.

It also has become known that the supposed achievements of the GDR were based on fabricated official figures. Productivity was low, and the economy was consuming its capital stock. Industrial equipment was antiquated; road, rail and telephone networks were crumbling; pollution was often horrendous; a large amount of housing was in a serious, and often catastrophic, state of disrepair.[2] Nevertheless, the

2. Otto Dienemann, 'Housing Problems in the German Democratic Republic and "the New German States" ', in Graham Hallett, ed., *The New Housing Shortage: Housing Affordability in Europe and the USA* (London, 1993), p. 128.

system had some virtues. There was no unemployment, although there was considerable disguised unemployment. There was hardly any street crime or vandalism, thanks to the rough justice of the 'People's police' and the unseen but ubiquitous eyes and ears of the *Stasi*. There was no homelessness and, in the tower-blocks, there was a social mix of street sweepers and professors. Food and consumer goods, although lacking in variety, were adequate. In some ways, the population of the GDR enjoyed good living conditions, like the animals in a well-kept zoo. When the animals eventually rebelled, they found that freedom was not an unmixed blessing.

THE 'OLD' FEDERAL REPUBLIC OF GERMANY

On the other side of the 'socialism-protecting' barbed wire and minefields, the relations between the state and the economy were very different. The West German view of the state has roots in nineteenth-century German history which can only be listed: the late unification; the way in which reformers had to seek 'the rule of law' before democracy; the survival of a 'guild' tradition; industrialization in the 1870s, when sophisticated industry needed supporting financial and research services.[3] National Socialism and its catastrophic aftermath led to the rejection of a 'centrally planned economy' and a return to older traditions which stressed the need for executive power to be decentralized and subject to checks and balances. There was a wide acceptance of the need for the state to maintain 'the public interest' but, at the same time, the powers of the state were both limited by the Basic Law and extensively devolved to regional or local government, or even to non-state bodies. The organization of industrial training, for example, is the responsibility of 'chambers of industry and commerce', in which membership by firms is compulsory, although training is carried out mainly by the firms themselves.

Soziale Marktwirtschaft

The FRG has, since its origins, been characterized by considerable continuity in policy. In the western zones after 1945, there was a debate

3. K. Dyson, *The State Tradition in Western Europe* (Oxford, 1980).

between the 'neo-liberals' and the advocates of *soziale Marktwirtschaft*, 'socially responsible market economy', a phrase coined by the economist and civil servant Müller-Armack.[4] The neo-liberals advocated an individualistic market economy, and wished to confine the role of the state virtually to the maintenance of 'law and order' and competition. Müller-Armack, although he defended market mechanisms and private ownership as the norm, argued that the kinds of state (or state-supported) activities which had developed under the Empire and the Weimar Republic – social security, industrial training, social housing – as well as a full employment policy, were necessary to provide both a framework for market processes and a safety net for its casualties; his views largely prevailed.

'*Soziale Marktwirtschaft*' became the slogan of the Christian Democrats (CDU), who were the major party in the first Federal governments, and was – most historians would say – subsequently adopted and developed by the Social Democrats (SPD), who participated in the Federal governments from 1966 to 1982. Some CDU politicians speak of *soziale Marktwirtschaft* being suspended during these years of 'central planning', and of damage to the economy, but most foreign observers find it hard to find much evidence of either. Even in the SPD-led coalitions of 1969–82 there was (virtually) no nationalization, no prohibitive taxation, no price or wage control. The only 'central planning' was '*konzertierte Aktion*' – a 'round table' representing the Federal government, the employers' federation and the trade union congress (DGB) at which the government outlined its macro-economic strategy and sought a consensus on wage rises and other matters of common interest. The employers' federation later departed from the *konzertierte Aktion*, after a dispute about an extension of worker representation on company 'supervisory boards' (which the federation later accepted). The end of *konzertierte Aktion* made little difference, as there have always been close informal contacts between the three participants. Moreover, the main macro-economic mechanism has always been the reaction of 'the social partners' to the monetary policies of the *Bundesbank*.

The distinctive features of the 'FRG model' have thus been a federal, decentralized state, characterized by checks and balances; public backing for industry by means of basic research and credit facilities; an independent central bank; and a legally enforced (although

4. A. Müller-Armack, 'Wirtschaftslenkung und Wirtschaftspolitik', in *Wirtschaftsordnung und Wirtschaftspolitik* (Freiburg im Breisgau, 1967), p. 19.

independently operated) system of industrial democracy and industrial training.

Criticisms of the West German Model

The 'West German model' has often been criticized, both from inside and outside the country, most vehemently by British writers – from contradictory points of view. Most earlier British criticism came from the 'Fabian Left', which criticized the absence of central planning and nationalization, the constraints on 'parliamentary sovereignty', federalism and the *Bundesbank*'s 'obsession' with price stability.[5] Some Marxist commentators still portray the GDR as a legitimate state with social achievements which fell victim to West German aggression.[6] In recent years, however, most of the running – especially in the press – has been made by the 'radical conservatives', who, like the socialists, criticize consensus, constitutionalism and federalism but, unlike them, advocate 'neo-liberal' micro-economic policies.

In Germany, as well as in Britain, 'radical conservatives' (as represented by the Free Democrats) argue that national wage-bargaining should be abolished; that managers should be free to hire and fire; that 'bureaucratic' regulations on town planning, shop opening hours, pollution, etc., should be scrapped; that the transport and energy sectors should be privatized and deregulated; that state provisions for health, pensions and social security should be abolished or cut back. The USA and Britain are held up as models. Some German political scientists also criticize the federal and consensual nature of the FRG. The need to obtain widespread agreement means, they argue, that decisions are never made; the system is characterized by 'immobilism'.[7] Other commentators argue that the social consensus which underlay the post-war achievements has broken down under the impact of affluence, unemployment, the fragmentation of lifestyles and a self-seeking philosophy. There is undoubtedly some truth in this view, but recent cross-party agreements suggest that consensus is not dead; it might be added that the 1950s were not periods of unrelieved harmony.

It is widely accepted, even among 'centrist' opinion, that some

5. T. Balogh, *Germany, an Example of 'Planning' by the 'Free' Price Mechanism* (Oxford, 1950); A. Shonfield, *Modern Capitalism* (Oxford, 1965); J. Leaman, *The Political Economy of West Germany 1945–85* (Oxford, 1965).

6. J. Osmond, ed., *German Reunification. Reference Guide and Commentary* (Harlow, 1992).

7. F. Scharpf, *The Joint-Decision Trap: Lessons from German Federalism and European Integration* (Berlin, 1985), Discussion Paper IIM/LMP 85–1, Wissenschaftszentrum.

changes in 'the German model' are needed. Helmut Schmidt, the former SPD Chancellor, criticizes the excessive complexity of West German regulations, and makes an unfavourable comparison with Austria.[8] However, if the more sweeping criticisms were valid, the FRG would show up badly in internatiornal comparisons. In fact, the 'old' FRG was always near the top of international league tables, of both 'economic performance' and 'quality of life' – even though the FRG has not escaped an international decline in some aspects of 'quality of life', such as the rise in crime and increased stress in work (or out of work).

In terms of narrowly defined 'economic performance', the FRG scored relatively well in the 1970s and 1980s, although less well than in the preceding 'miracle' years. In the period of the 'first oil shock', 1973–79, under an SPD–FDP Federal government, the FRG did considerably better than the OECD average on economic growth, inflation and unemployment.[9] The public sector deficit at first rose from under 1 per cent of GNP to 3.7 per cent, but then fell to 2.5 per cent in 1979, not far above what the *Bundesbank* regarded as 'normal'. In the period 1979 to 1989, which began with the 'second oil shock', the FRG (mainly under a CDU/FDP Federal government) acquired a serious unemployment problem – although at levels below those for the OECD as a whole, or for Britain and the USA. On the other hand, it recovered remarkably well from the current account deficits of 1979–82, and eliminated both inflation and the public sector deficit. The FRG was thus in a good condition in 1989 to withstand the enormous shock of reunification.

UNIFICATION

The fall of the Berlin Wall on 9 November 1989 presented the FRG with the greatest challenge of its history, and one for which it was totally unprepared. In spite of the continuing official commitment to unification, no-one in the Federal government believed that it would occur in the foreseeable future. No-one was charged with keeping up to date with the problems which would arise following unification, and

8. Helmut Schmidt, *Handeln für Deutschland* (Berlin, 1993), p. 122.

9. Graham Hallett, 'West Germany', in A. Graham and A. Seldon, eds, *Government and Economies in the Postwar World: Economic Policies and Comparative Performance 1945–85* (London, 1990), p. 93.

no attempt had been made by West German TV and radio (which had a strong influence in the GDR) to prepare the population of the GDR for the changes which the introduction of a market economy would bring. In the SPD the accepted policy was to work for a gradual rapprochement of 'the two German states'; the SPD leaders were unable to adapt their thinking to the sudden collapse of the GDR. Many neo-liberals were equally mistaken in their diagnosis, in that they denied the need for any tax rises.

The members of the citizens' committees which led the revolution in the GDR wanted, for the most part, to retain a separate East German state, and to build 'socialism with a human face'. In the FRG, many economists favoured a step-by-step approach in eastern Germany, with the gradual creation of market conditions before the introduction of an economic union. There were also two possible legal routes to unification. One was under Article 146 of the West German Basic Law, which provided for the framing of a new constitution for a reunited Germany, and its submission to popular vote. The other was under Article 23, by which 'German *Länder*' could simply join the FRG. In February 1990, the Federal government took the crucial decision to seek rapid unification under Article 23, preceded by a currency union (which took place on 1 July 1990).

Was this decision correct? A strong case can be made that it was. The whole administrative basis of the GDR had collapsed, and there was no prospect of a 'reformed GDR' enjoying popular support; the elections of March 1990 were a crushing defeat for its (idealistic and personally attractive) advocates. Given the inevitability of unification, was it right to use the 'take-over' route of Article 23? Under Article 146, all aspects of the West German constitution could have been examined, with a view to their appropriateness for eastern Germany, and even western Germany. Such a review would, as such, have been highly desirable, but it would have taken years, during which time there would have been a political and economic vacuum in eastern Germany. It is very doubtful whether such a policy would have been feasible. There was the prospect of massive emigration to the FRG if an attempt had been made to retain the GDR system in any form, with a material standard of living so much lower than in the FRG. In the demonstrations in Leipzig in 1989, one of the banners read, 'If the D-Mark comes to us, we'll stay; if it doesn't, we'll go to it.' The citizens of the GDR had unrealistic expectations about unification (encouraged by the Kohl government), but anyone who saw serviceable but dowdy GDR goods being remaindered in East Berlin in February 1990, while shoppers clamoured for West

German goods, must doubt whether consumers would have stood for the maintenance, even with reforms, of the GDR economic system.

Moreover, the GDR would have needed massive aid from the FRG, which might well not have been forthcoming for an independent state. Given the bankruptcy of the GDR in 1989, there was – with the benefit of hindsight – no realistic alternative to rapid political and currency union. Nevertheless, the Federal government's decision to go for rapid unification was not an easy one. A currency union was strongly opposed by the *Bundesbank*, while abroad, the French government was doubtful about German unification, and the British government was openly hostile. To resolve all the complex issues involved, and achieve unification in six months, showed not 'immobilism' but a remarkable degree of decisiveness, resolution and diplomatic nimbleness.

Seven Cardinal Errors of Unification?

But were mistakes made in the rush to unification? In the sour economic aftermath, it has often been argued that unification was botched. Helmut Schmidt lists 'seven cardinal errors': the failure to foresee the consequent economic difficulties, and to prepare the citizens of the 'old' FRG for sacrifices; the belief that the introduction of a market economy in eastern Germany would rapidly produce a flourishing economy; the conversion of Ostmarks into Deutschmarks at one-to-one; the failure to introduce a general 'financial equalization' to assist the new *Länder* at the expense of the old; the setting up of the *Treuhand*; the treatment of real estate; and the rapid equalization of wages in western and eastern Germany.[10]

Schmidt's first two criticisms are widely accepted. It can hardly be denied that the Federal government initially shut its eyes to the impending 'economic catastrophe' in eastern Germany. Most informed observers knew in 1990 that the collapse of the centrally planned economy would bring economic disruption (although few foresaw how much), and that there would be no 'economic miracle' similar to that in West Germany after the currency reform of 1948. The conditions were too different. The National Socialist regime lasted only 12 years, and by no means destroyed the institutions of a market economy. Moreover, in 1948 the world was crying out for the products of German industry; today Germany faces intense competition from low-wage countries using the latest technology.

If Chancellor Kohl had appealed to the West Germans to make

10. Schmidt, *Handeln für Deutschland*, p. 29.

sacrifices for the sake of their compatriots in the former GDR, and introduced in 1990 the tax-raising/expenditure-cutting measures which he introduced in 1993, several harmful consequences for the economy of western Germany, and its neighbours, would have been avoided. The immediate impact of the demand for goods from eastern Germany was to produce an inflationary boom in western Germany and raise the external value of the Deutschmark. High interest rates were introduced to curb the boom, which aggravated the depression in other countries of western Europe and contributed to the partial breakdown of the exchange rate mechanism (ERM) in 1992.

In the 'unification boom' of 1990–92, employment in western Germany rose by 1.4 million, while employment in eastern Germany fell by 3 million, from 9.2 million to 6.2 million. The 'unification boom' in western Germany induced an unfortunate complacency with regard to the growing international threats to German competitiveness. Whereas Germany's competitors had, by 1990, absorbed the worst of the depression, and had undertaken extensive 'restructuring', West German firms were still hiring more workers and paying large wage increases. When boom turned to depression in 1993, the high cost level of German business was exposed. Firms began cutting their workforce, and planning to move production to cheaper countries, especially in eastern Europe. Employment in manufacturing in western Germany fell by 14 per cent in 1993/94.

Schmidt's third criticism is that east German industry was made uncompetitive by the exchange of Ostmarks into Deutschmarks on a (partly) one-to-one basis. The suggestion is that the exchange should have been on a one-to-three basis, which corresponded to productivity levels. But it is questionable whether such a rate would have been politically or economically feasible. The East Germans felt very strongly that anything other than a one-to-one exchange would defraud them of their savings. Moreover, a one-to-three exchange would have produced a comparable difference in wage levels within Germany. Given freedom of movement of population, it is doubtful whether such a difference could have been maintained – a view which is even beginning to be accepted in the *Bundesbank*.

Schmidt's fourth criticism is the failure to revise the system of 'financial equalization', whereby the richer *Länder* help the poorer. Revisions to the system were under discussion in the FRG before unification. Schmidt argues that a new system should have been introduced on unification, so that the western *Länder* contributed directly to the support of their eastern counterparts. Instead, the cost of supporting eastern Germany fell mainly on the Federal government, thus weakening the federal nature of the FRG. It would, however, almost certainly have been impossible to have devised a new system before unification. After unification, discussions began between the Federal government and all the *Länder*; a new – although not radically reformed – system was agreed in 1993, to begin in 1995. It is clear that such a complicated change could not have been devised and agreed in a few months.

Schmidt fifthly regards it as undesirable that crucial decisions on the sale of state-owned enterprises should have been taken by the *Treuhand* agency – an unelected, centralized body – rather than by the new *Länder.* There were undoubtedly devious political ramifications; the Kohl government was only too happy to leave the 'dirty work' of dealing with the ex-state enterprises to the *Treuhand*, so that the government would not be blamed. On the other hand, it is clear (from their subsequent history) that the newly created *Länder* governments would not have been capable of undertaking the work of the *Treuhand*; being administratively weak, unproven and scandal-ridden, they would have been remorsely lobbied – or bribed. The kernel of truth in Schmidt's criticism is that the *Treuhand* suffered from centralization and remoteness; more contacts with the *Länder* and the communes would have been desirable.

With his sixth 'error', Schmidt is on much surer ground. The negotiators of the Unification Treaty had to decide what was to be done about real estate which had been nationalized by the GDR. For housing, the last (democratic) government of the GDR wished to rely mainly on monetary compensation for previous owners (or their heirs), with exceptions such as when an original owner wished to return to his/her old home. The Federal government, however, insisted that, as a general rule, the property should be returned – 'restitution in preference to compensation'. This principle was, at the time, criticized on two grounds: firstly, that the inevitable legal complexities (given the almost non-existent state of land registration in the GDR) would last for years, with prejudicial effects on investment and management; secondly, that tenants who had lived in a dwelling for many years (sometimes as many as 30) should also be considered to have acquired rights.

These criticisms have been only too clearly borne out. Unclear property ownership has hampered investment in housing and created inequities. Over one million claims for the return of housing have been made by former owners (or their heirs); around a half had been settled by the summer of 1994, but many will not be settled for years. Even when housing has been handed back, the new landlords often lack either the inclination or the means to renovate their dilapidated property. There have been cases of elderly people, threatened with the loss of their home, who have committed suicide. Nothing has done more to alienate '*Ossis*' from '*Wessis*' than disputes over the return of housing. In the unification negotiations, the Federal government appears to have been obsessed with righting the wrongs done to expropriated owners, without regard to the rights of subsequent occupiers. More justifiably, it was concerned about the financial costs of compensation. It is clear, however, that a more satisfactory formula could have been devised. Since unification, the Federal government has done a great deal to remedy those consequences of the Unification Treaty that could be remedied – notably by writing off the debts of the formerly state housing enterprises – but it was impossible to alter the main provisions of the treaty.

Schmidt's seventh 'error' is the agreement between West German trade unions and employers' organizations in 1990 that wages in eastern Germany would be raised to equality with western Germany by 1994 (subsequently put back to 1996). The criticism is that this rise far exceeded the rise in productivity, and thus caused, or contributed to, the sharp fall in employment in eastern Germany. Schmidt argues that the Federal government should have intervened in the agreement between the two parties (both of which may have covertly wished to eliminate east German competition) and pressed for lower wage levels.

There is no doubt that east German wages have been 'too high' in relation to productivity. In 1993 gross wages per employee were 85 per cent of the west German level, while productivity was around 50 per cent. The fact that unit wages costs were thus some 50 per cent higher than in western Germany must have had some effect in increasing unemployment. However, there was strong political pressure in eastern Germany for an equalization of wages, and the open border imposed limits on differences in wage levels. Moreover, no feasible wage level would have had more than a small effect on the collapse of employment in 1990/91. Many industries were grossly over-manned, and most of the GDR's markets for heavy equipment in the Soviet Union and eastern Europe would have been lost in any event, following the break-up of COMECON. Thus Schmidt may be right in criticizing the Federal government for not putting pressure on the 'social partners' for lower wage levels (it had no legal power to do more), but he is wrong to suggest that such a policy could have saved 'millions' of jobs. The loss of most of these three million jobs in eastern Germany was, sadly, inevitable.

In short, Helmut Schmidt's seven 'cardinal errors' are too many and too clear-cut. Mistakes were undoubtedly made. Firstly, Chancellor Kohl, instead of making 'feel good' speeches, should have appealed more strongly to West Germans to accept some belt-tightening, and to show respect and understanding for their new compatriots. Secondly, grave mistakes were made in the treatment of real estate. Thirdly, the Federal government could at least have pressed for a slower equalization of wage rates. More generally, it can be argued (as many former dissidents in the GDR have done) that the West Germans were too 'neo-colonialist', and assumed too readily that all problems could be solved simply by pumping in money. In spite of the mistakes that were made, it is increasingly being recognized, however, that at a time (the early months of 1990) of great confusion and conflicting pressures, the Kohl government took the right decisions on the big issues.

THE ECONOMIC RESTRUCTURING OF EASTERN GERMANY

The Federal government's original policy for east German industry was rapid privatization, and this remained the dominant policy, even though some slowing down, designed to preserve employment, was introduced after the assassination of the first Director of the *Treuhand*, Herr Rohwedder, in 1991. The original, over-optimistic theory was that new management would transform the firms, enabling output to rise and employment to be maintained. Most privatizations were by tender, and many firms were disposed of for nominal sums, or even with 'sweeteners'; 85 per cent of disposals were to west German firms.

The scale of the disposals is breathtaking. Of 12,246 original companies, by 1 January 1994, 7,838 had been sold, 3,196 had been liquidated, 266 were still for sale, 685 were not for sale and 261 had been returned to public ownership. At the end of 1994, the *Treuhand* was wound up and replaced by three successor companies. Of the original jobs in the companies, only 37 per cent had, in 1994, been saved. The financial results are even more breathtaking. The state enterprises were valued at DM1000 billion by Modrow, and at DM600 billion by Rohwedder; the *Treuhand*, however, closed with *debts* of around DM275 billion!

There are several possible reasons for this astonishingly poor financial return. There was widespread fraud, but that can account for only tens, rather than hundreds of billions of Deutschmarks. The assets were initially overvalued. Given antiquated plant, collapsed markets and high costs for environmental cleaning-up, some of the firms were indeed worth less than nothing. On the other hand, 'fire sales' inevitably depressed prices, and there is anecdotal evidence that some West German firms bought up firms for their real estate and then closed them down to suppress competition.

There has been considerable criticism of the *Treuhand*'s breakneck rate of disposals, and discussion of possible alternatives.[11] One proposal was to retain majority ownership, but to allow minority shareholders to carry out restructuring, before increasing their shareholding. The SPD proposed a more interventionist industrial policy, involving heavy subsidization and more gradual restructuring. On the limited information available, it is impossible to reach firm conclusions but the suspicion must remain that more could have been saved from the wreck of East German industry. One would have more confidence that alternative policies had been considered, and rejected for defensible reasons, if Ms Birgit Breuel, the Director of the *Treuhand*, had not merely asserted, 'There is no alternative.'

In fact, political pressure has forced the *Treuhand* to modify its policy in some cases. In the old 'industrial cores' (shipbuilding, chemicals, steel, heavy engineering), which actually have rather poor prospects, the *Treuhand* has effectively retained ownership and is keeping the business going for social reasons, trying to provide retraining for some of the workers.

There has been a wider debate on the role of wage policy in the collapse of east German industry. In addition to the arguments for a more gradual equalization of wages, there have been proposals for wage subsidies. Unfortunately, this superficially attractive idea has disadvantages, including a tendency to force up wage levels. The alternative is capital subsidies, and these have been provided in the form of tax concessions for investment in eastern Germany. However, the phrase 'tax free' seems to drive all commercial considerations out of investors' minds. Tax concessions have encouraged the construction of huge out-of-town shopping and office developments. Almost certainly, too much such property is being built, and it is already impoverishing the city centres.

In 1993, output in eastern Germany was only 51 per cent of consumption plus investment. In other words, about half was transferred from western Germany, of which three-quarters was for consumption. The Federal government has financed nearly all social insurance payments. Infrastructure investment is being undertaken by the German Unity Fund, as well as by the *Deutsche Bahn* (railways) and *Deutsche Telekom*

11. G. and H.-W. Sinn, *Jumpstart: The Economic Unification of Germany* (Cambridge, Mass., 1992).

(telecommunications). The costs of short-time working, retraining and job creation are met by the Federal Labour Office. Other payments included regional assistance and subsidies to cover the losses of the firms still owned by the successors to the *Treuhand*. Total financial transfers in 1994 were DM180 billion a year, over three times the original estimate.

These transfers have been partly financed by a sharp rise in the indebtedness of the Federal government, its agencies and the new *Länder*. However total government debt began to level off in 1994 and is likely to stabilize in 1995 and 1996 at slightly below the 'Maastricht' level of 60 per cent of GDP.

The Prospects for Eastern Germany

The huge investment in the infrastructure of eastern Germany – roads, railways and telecommunications – and in new plant is already showing visible results. Since mid-1993, there has been a clear upward trend in output, not only in construction, but also in industrial production and in services. Some new manufacturing plants are fully competitive with western Germany. There is thus an upturn, but from a low base, and often of a 'jobless' kind; the new, competitive manufacturing plants are capital-intensive and do not employ many workers. Moreover, eastern Germany is no 'sun belt', and has few natural advantages – apart, perhaps, from its position as a bridge to eastern Europe. Unemployment has stabilized, and may be falling, but the official level (in March 1995) was 14.2 per cent – and the actual level was over 20 per cent. Two-thirds of the unemployed are women, as are undoubtedly most of the 'discouraged workers'; in a variety of ways, women have been the main sufferers in eastern Germany. The prospect is thus of an uneven pattern of development, and a high level of unemployment throughout the 1990s.

RESHAPING THE 'WEST GERMAN MODEL'

In the 1980s, a debate began in the FRG on three economic issues: unemployment, industrial competitiveness and the future of the welfare state, particularly pensions and health care. These issues were shelved when unification was the centre of attention, but they have been taken up since 1992.

Unemployment

It became clear in the mid-1980s that the rise in unemployment which took place after 1982 was not being eliminated by 'recovery' (and it is equally unlikely that 'full employment' will be restored by the recovery which began in 1994). The response by the Federal government in the 1980s was to encourage early retirement (which is now recognized as a misguided long-term policy) and to set up *Arbeitsbeschaffungsmassnahmen* (community programmes), which have since been used extensively in eastern Germany.[12] These programmes at first paid the 'going wage', but there were criticisms that this was deterring participants from seeking 'normal' work, and recent legislation has reduced the rate to 80 per cent.

The neo-liberal prescription for solving unemployment is to deregulate the labour market, so as to achieve lower and more unequal wages. It seems unlikely, however, that Germany will abandon its system of national wage bargaining, which has served it well; between 1979 and 1994, unit labour costs rose by 40 per cent, compared with virtually the same rise in the USA and a doubling in the UK. The trade unions have, however, reached an agreement that specific firms, which could not afford nationally agreed wages, may be given permission to pay lower wages.[13] This is, in principle, an important concession, even though very few firms have so far been given such permission.

Since 1993, the Federal government has led a drive for increased part-time work as a means of reducing unemployment. It has laid down that all civil service posts must be available on a part-time basis, and has improved the tax/social security position of part-time workers. The government rejects any suggestion of *Arbeitsdienst* (civilian conscription), which acquired a bad name under the Nazis. In fact, however, it already exists. The number of young men undertaking *Zivildienst* (community service, often as badly needed 'carers') as an alternative to National Service in the armed forces has steadily risen, and in 1993 almost equalled the number undertaking National Service (135,000 against 154,000).

12. Graham Hallett, 'Unemployment and Labour Market Policies: Some Lessons from West Germany', *Social Policy and Administration* 19.3 (1985), 180–90.

13. Karl Koch, 'Regulatory Reform and German Industrial Relations', in K. Dyson, ed., *The Politics of German Regulation* (Aldershot, 1992), p. 235.

The 'old FRG, although it acquired an unemployment problem in the 1980s, had a lower unemployment rate than other major economies (apart from Japan). In 1995, united Germany had an unemployment rate near the (appallingly high) EU average, and a serious 'regional problem'. The debate on whether these problems should be tackled by moving to an Anglo-American-style deregulated labour market, by schemes for 'pricing the unemployed into work', by direct state action, or by some combination of methods seems set to continue.

Standort Deutschland

In the 1980s, a debate began in the FRG as to how the country could maintain its position as a trading nation in the face of new competition, and how it could continue to pay for the welfare state as the population aged over the coming decades. These issues were taken up by the Federal government in 1993, when it initiated a debate on *Standort Deutschland*. This term literally means 'Germany as an industrial location', but has been used as a shorthand for a range of issues concerning international competitiveness and the proper division between government and private individuals in the provision of medical services, pensions and education. The Federal government began to strike a note of urgency. As Chancellor Kohl put it:

> Just a few kilometres east of Berlin and Munich, serious new competitors are growing up, with great cost advantages and increasingly attractive products. Yet we allow ourselves the luxury of being a country with ever younger pensioners and ever older students. . . . With ever shorter working hours, rising wage costs, and ever longer holidays, our competitiveness is in danger. . . . The simple fact is that a successful industrial country cannot allow itself to be organised like a collective leisure park.[14]

In Septemer 1993, the government published a report by Günter Rexrodt, the Economics Minister, on *Zukunftssicherung des Standortes Deutschland* (Safeguarding Germany's Future as an Industrial Location).[15] The report begins with a relentlessly, perhaps excessively gloomy review of the current situation. It gives a series of charts showing that the number of people over 60 will rise from 20 per cent of the population to 33 per cent by the year 2030; that Germany has the shortest working

14. 'Germany', *Financial Times Survey*, 25/10/1993.

15. Press and Information Office of the Federal Government, *Bericht der Bundesregierung zur Zukunftssicherung des Standortes Deutschland* (Bonn, 1993). Abridged version: *Report of the Federal Government on the Safeguarding of Germany's Future as an Industrial Location.*

week and the shortest machinery running time of the major industrial countries; that the 'ancillary costs' (taxes and social security charges) paid by employers now add 84 per cent to labour costs, making German labour the most expensive in the world. German companies are criticized for a lack of innovation.

The *Standort* debate has been criticized by a group of social scientists as being too narrowly concerned with international competition and economic growth, and ignoring the need to adapt the German 'social state' (welfare state) to deal with the new problems of insecure employment and poverty.[16] However, the Rexrodt report does contain references to social and moral issues – in a way which would be inconceivable in a government publication in Britain in recent years. It calls for a return to 'older values', not only of thrift and initiative but also of 'solidarity, tolerance and humanity'.

> The right to self-fulfilment is too often confused with inconsiderate egoism, instead of being combined with the necessary feeling of responsibility towards others. . . . Market efficiency and social equalization are intertwined. Social peace and social consensus are the indispensable prerequisites of economic stability and prosperity. . . . Loneliness and isolation can be combated only by the strengthening of small networks of social support. . . . The preservation of the natural basis of life for future generations is an ever more important duty. (Author's translations)

All of which would seem to show that the 'social' aspects of *soziale Marktwirtschaft* are still influential enough to be mentioned, even in a report by a Free Democrat minister.

The Rexrodt report, and other statements by the Federal government, have spelled out, in general terms, a programme for dealing with the economic challenges facing Germany. One short-term aim is to reduce the general government deficit from around 4.5 per cent of GDP in 1993 to 3 per cent by 1996; in the event this level was achieved in 1994, and will almost certainly be maintained in 1995–6. After unification, there were fears (or hopes) that Germany would become a country with chronic budget deficits and persistent inflation. It now seems set to be the only *EU* country (apart from Luxemburg) which will meet the 'Maastricht' criteria for budget deficits and public debt in 1996; it is also likely to have achieved the *Bundesbank*'s inflation target of under 2 per cent. The longer-term aim is to reduce government expenditure as a percentage of GDP from around 51 per cent to the pre-unification level of 45 per cent; this will be difficult to achieve as long as financial

16. 'Solidarity with "Standort" Germany', *Debatte* 2.1, 1994 (Carfax Publishing Co., Oxford).

transfers to eastern Germany continue. There are various proposals to shift responsibility from the public to the private sector wherever possible, and to concentrate government spending on fields which promote investment, innovation and employment. Regulations will be reviewed so as to 'cut red tape'. 'Value for money' will be sought in publicly financed social and health services. Business taxation will, if possible, be reduced.

Some of the proposals in the Rexrodt report are within the competence of the Federal government, and were the basis for the *Standortsicherungsgesetz* in 1993; this act included provisions for a reduction of business taxation, for part-time working in the civil service, and for some simplification of business regulation. Other proposals, such as privatization, are more long-term, and others attempt to give a lead to action by the 'social partners'.

Privatization

A steady process of privatization is under way. *Deutsche Telekom*, the nationalized telecommunications body, has been privatized, and had its monopoly relaxed. Similarly, *Deutsche Bahn*, the organization formed from the merger of the railways in western and eastern Germany, had its debts written off and has been privatized. There is no intention, however, of stopping the large publicly supported investment in railways. The west German railway system (which is rapidly being extended to eastern Germany) provides an excellent ordinary train service and a network of high-speed ICE trains. An innovative, although controversial, ultra-high-speed magnetic levitation line will be built from Berlin to Hamburg. There is no intention of fragmenting the *Deutsche Bahn*, or the excellent municipally owned urban transport systems, on which a single ticket can be used for any combination of bus, tram, underground or local trains. The Germans love their cars, but they possess – in marked contrast to the 'Anglo-American model' – an excellent system of public transport. There are, however, increasing reports that it is dangerous to use it late at night.

The airline *Lufthansa*, and various miscellaneous industrial holdings by the Federal government, are to be privatized in stages. It seems unlikely that gas, electricity and water will be fully privatized, although the Federal government is undertaking a study of the 'English model' for the electricity industry. The utility sector is dominated by a number of large companies in which local authorities are the main shareholders, and this system is likely to remain.

Attempts have also been made to contain the cost of the health system. The German health system is based on a large number of occupational funds, which negotiate contracts with independent hospitals and doctors. It provides high-quality cover for all citizens, but there has been concern over escalating costs. The Federal government has recently imposed 'cash limits' on hospitals. This has succeeded in controlling costs, but there are criticisms that hospitals are now discriminating against 'unprofitable' patients. The basic dilemma is one familiar to all collective health schemes. As there is now virtually no limit to possible medical treatment, some 'rationing' is unavoidable. The only way of combining comprehensive coverage with a limit on costs is (as the Council of Economic Advisers has urged) for the public authorities to lay down a list of treatments which are available free of charge, leaving other treatments to patients who are able and willing to pay for them. However, no country has yet implemented such a system.

Moves are also afoot to give more flexibility in the apprenticeship system and in the *Handwerksordnungen* (regulations governing the setting up of craft businesses). In Germany, no-one can set up as a plumber or carpenter without having served an apprenticeship. The system has worked well in the past but tends to be based on a system in which a skill, once learned, lasts a lifetime. It is widely accepted that a shorter and more general basic training, with periodic updating, is needed. Is it sensible, critics ask, that someone who wishes to set up a bicycle repair business in the 'new *Länder*' must have served a three-year apprenticeship and worked in the trade for seven years?

The Greying of Germany

A subject which has attracted a great deal of attention in recent years is the economic effect of the very low birth rate and the 'greying' of the population. Should Germany be more 'children friendly'? Should changes be made in the pensions system? What should be done about care for the elderly? But although Germany will undoubtedly face serious demographic problems over the next half-century, it is generally agreed – even by the authors of a recent book which begins in an apocalyptic vein[17] – that the 'burden' of old people is likely to be tolerable, given changes which seem feasible in the time available: an emphasis on 'lifetime learning'; the adaptation of work to the needs of

17. Meinhard Miegel and Stephanie Wahl, *Das Ende des Individualismus* (Munich, 1993).

older people; the replacement of the 'earnings-related', state-supported pension schemes by a flat-rate pension, supplemented by private pensions.

On pensions, the FRG has yet to take any decisive steps. Recent discussion has been dominated by a new insurance scheme for care for the elderly, the legislation for which was passed with all-party support in 1993. Contributions will be paid in the traditional way by employers and employees, and contributors will be entitled to a fixed sum of money if they go into a home. If the money is insufficient, children will (as before) be required to make a contribution according to their means, and there will continue to be a means-tested 'safety net'. The political debate on this scheme was factual and reasonable, but seemed to ignore the recent calls for public belt-tightening. It can be questioned whether it was wise to load further burdens on to employers, and to encourage an increased reliance on old people's homes, rather than promoting the provision of 'home help', while retaining a 'safety net' for people for whom institutional care is unavoidable (with the financial burden shifted away from local authorities, who are at present responsible for all 'social help').

Subsidies

Another field in which the Rexrodt report calls for action – and for which the FRG has often been criticized – is subsidies. This question needs to be put into perspective. In western Germany, the cost of industrial subsidies has, for several years, been falling; the sharp rise in united Germany after 1991 was *solely* the result of payments to eastern Germany. In 1993, total subsidies from the Federal government amounted to 1.2 per cent of GNP; the main recipients were regional economic developments, housing and agriculture. In addition, subsidies to public transport were paid by *Länder* and communes. Many of these subsidies can be defended on economic grounds; they need to be critically examined, but are not *ipso facto* unjustified.

Reshaping the 'West German Model': Conclusions

The Federal government has done more to initiate a programme for the modernization of the German economy than it is often given credit for. The programme can, of course – according to one's viewpoint – be described as judicious and well thought-out, or hesitant and inadequate.

There has also, under the terms of the Unification Treaty, been a wide-reaching review of the Basic Law by the *Bundestag* and *Bundesrat*. The representatives of the 'new *Länder*' have taken part in this review, most effectively in the *Bundesrat*, where the *Länder* are represented as such. However, the joint commission of *Bundestag* and *Bundesrat* did not recommend any radical changes when it completed the review in 1994. For example, proposals for incorporating a 'right to employment' and a 'right to housing' into the constitution were not accepted. Moreover, united Germany's constitution will continue to be called the 'Basic Law'.

PROSPECTS FOR THE FUTURE

One (comparatively favourable) assessment of the West German economy, written in 1987, concluded that: 'The Federal Republic has its period of rapid youthful growth behind it, but it has entered its middle-age without inflationary problems, balance of payments constraints, or skill shortages, and with a modern and well-maintained infrastructure.'[18] This comfortable life has been disrupted by the arrival of the 'new *Länder*'. It is hazardous to make predictions, but the indications are that the 'socially responsible market economy' will bend but not break. The economy of western Germany is undergoing a degree of deregulation and privatization, which was being discussed before unification, while retaining – albeit in a somewhat attenuated form – a role for the decentralized state in the attainment of 'public goods', a safety net for the casualties of the economic system, and the organized representation of employees' interests. German firms, encouraged by the state, are taking major steps to increase productivity so as to maintain internatational competitiveness, but are also tending to move some of their manufacturing operations to low-wage countries. This 'restructuring' is likely to mean that unemployment will remain a problem affecting all levels of society during the rest of the 1990s. In eastern Germany, unemployment is likely to remain at even higher levels, although a process of convergence with western Germany is clearly under way.

Narrowly defined economic problems, however, are not the only, or perhaps the most serious, problems facing the new Germany. Although the FRG has created one of the more civilized of industrial societies,

18. Hallett, 'West Germany', p. 101.

both western Germany and (more suddenly and dramatically) eastern Germany are experiencing many of the negative socioeconomic developments of our age: crime, violence and anti-social behaviour; the breakdown of family life; job insecurity; a growing gap between 'haves' and 'have nots'; technological marvels in communication, and a trivialization of what is communicated. If the rejection of 'inconsiderate egoism' in the Rexrodt report heralds a move away from the excessive individualism which underlies these social ills, perhaps *soziale Marktwirtschaft* will eventually enter its second phase, envisaged by Müller-Armack, in which the prime objective will be the creation of a humane society.[19]

FURTHER READING

David Goodhart, *The Reshaping of the German Social Market*, IPPR (London, 1994).

Graham Hallett, *Housing Needs in Western and Eastern Germany* (Anglo-German Foundation, London, 1994).

Gordon Smith, 'Structures of Government', in Smith *et al.*, eds, *Developments in West German Politics* (London, 1989), p. 24.

W. R. Smyser, *The Economy of United Germany* (London, 1992).

19. A. Müller-Armack, 'Die zweite Phase der Sozialen Marktwirtschaft', in *Wirtschaftsordnung und Wirtschaftspolitik* (Bern, 1976), p. 267.

CHAPTER SEVEN

Race in the Federal Republic of Germany: Immigration, Ethnicity and Racism since the Second World War[1]

Panikos Panayi

INTRODUCTION

The growth of nationalism since the eighteenth century and the resulting creation of the nation-state has meant that all countries which have come into existence have operated on the basis of in-groups and out-groups, whether the form of government consists of autocracy, liberal democracy or dictatorship. Germany offers a good example of a state which has passed through all three types of rule in the past century, and one in which immigration, ethnicity and racism have been fundamental in the economic, social and political development of the country since 1871. In short, since the creation of the first German state, race – in its various manifestations – has been central in the country's development, from the *Kaiserreich* through the Weimar Republic and the Nazi period to the Federal Republic both before and after unification. This has shown itself both in the existence of indigenous minorities, significant immigration into the country and, perhaps above all, in the constant preoccupation, or obsession in some periods, with the concept of race amongst policy-makers.

Immigration has played a fundamental role in the development of the German economy since the late nineteenth century, so that successive waves of newcomers have entered Germany from eastern, southern and even western Europe and, in the modern period, from further afield.

1. I am grateful to the following for financing the research for this article: the Alexander von Humboldt Foundation, the Nuffield Foundation and the Department of Historical and International Studies at De Montfort University.

These newcomers have usually moved to the country to fill labour shortages but, on some occasions, they have arrived 'uninvited' as refugees.

In all periods of German history minorities have remained very much outside German society, economically, socially and legally. The fact that foreign workers have usually been imported has made their isolation easier. They have often faced physical separation from the rest of society, living in specially constructed barracks or sub-standard housing. As in other countries, both indigenous minorities and newcomers to German society have developed their own ethnicity, although this has been easier in some periods than in others and the extent of the development of ethnicity has varied from one group to another. Legally, all German governments have made much effort to exclude newcomers from citizenship.

Finally, from the *Kaiserreich* to the Federal Republic, racism has existed throughout German history, usually led by the state. Perhaps no government in history has perfected racial persecution in a similar fashion to Nazi Germany. The events of 1933–45 should be viewed as an earthquake, which had both pre-shocks and after-shocks. The persecution of these years was both preceded and succeeded by milder forms of racial intolerance.

The purpose of this essay is to examine race in the Federal Republic of Germany by dealing with the concepts of immigration, ethnicity and racism. It will place these questions into a historical perspective, and will therefore open with an outline of their development from German unification in 1871 until the fall of Nazism. The core of the article will examine the years 1945–90, and it will then conclude with the changes which have taken place since unification in 1990. The essay will ask whether national traditions or the system of government has been the main factor in determining the role of race in the Federal Republic.

HISTORICAL BACKGROUND

The history of population movement in nineteenth-century Germany is essentially a transformation from mass emigration to immigration. Until the 1890s, when the country was not developed enough industrially, the main population flow was outward, so that approximately four million Germans emigrated during the nineteenth century. However, with the completion of the industrialization process in Germany by about 1900, the country's population growth could be absorbed by the opportunities provided by its own economy.[2]

In fact, industrialization led to several new developments. First, there was a general move in population from the less advanced eastern provinces of Prussia to the industrialized western areas. Second, within this migration were also Poles who had lived in Prussia since the disappearance of their homeland through partition in the late eighteenth century. Finally, especially after the turn of the century, an importation of both agricultural and industrial workers from other parts of Europe took place.

The migration from east to west, which really took off from the 1890s, involved as many as two million people, and those within it can be divided into three groups consisting of the German rural lower classes, Masurians and Poles. The second of these spoke a Polish dialect, but were Protestants and supported the Prussian monarchy. Just before the outbreak of the First World War there were about 150,000 of them living in the Ruhr. The figure for Poles, meanwhile, had reached approximately 300,000. The two groups were involved in similar occupations. In 1905 as many as 80 per cent of Poles were employed as miners or iron and steel workers, while by 1926 about 75 per cent may have been miners and 25 per cent factory workers. Although initially the Polish population in the Ruhr consisted overwhelmingly of males, women, often wives, followed. A marked ethnicity developed in the area revolving around religion, newspapers, trade unions, politics and culture, although throughout the early twentieth century the processes of integration and assimilation were proceeding, partly accelerated by local and national hostility towards the Poles.[3]

The movement of population from east to west created an agricultural labour shortage which Prussian landowners solved by importing workers from further east. In 1907 there were 294,893 foreigners involved in agriculture, the overwhelming majority in Prussia, with the largest proportion consisting of Russian Poles. Industrial recruitment also took place. While Prussia was an important destination, a significant percentage of the foreign workforce was employed in other areas, notably the Ruhr. They came from (in order of importance) Austria (both German

2. This argument is put forward by Klaus J. Bade, *Vom Auswanderungsland zum Einwanderungsland? Deutschland 1880–1980* (Berlin, 1983).

3. Christoph Klessmann, *Polnische Bergarbeiter im Ruhrgebeit 1870–1945* (Göttingen, 1978); Hans-Ulrich Wehler, 'Die Polen im Ruhrgebeit bis 1918', in idem, ed., *Moderne Deutsche Sozialgeschichte* (Cologne, 1966), pp. 437–55; Wojciech Wrzesinski, 'The Union of Poles in Germany (1922–1939)', *Polish Western Affairs* 9 (1968), 19–43.

speakers and various minorities), Italy, Russia and the Netherlands. Their most important occupations within the industrial sector were in mining, iron and steel manufacture, construction and brickmaking. Living and working conditions were very poor, and short-term and seasonal contracts were used. In total, 882,315 foreigners worked in the German Empire in 1907, making up 3.58 per cent of the workforce. With the coming of the First World War the situation for foreign workers deteriorated as the German state turned to using forced labourers, from both eastern and western Europe, as well as prisoners of war.[4]

Jews represented the most important indigenous minority until the late nineteenth and early twentieth centuries. By the early years of the *Kaiserreich* their emancipation had been completed, although the years leading up to the First World War represented a period of growth in unofficial antisemitism, partly as a reaction against emancipation and partly as a product of growing racial nationalism. This hostility towards Jews manifested itself especially in the development of extremist organizations. The growth of antisemitism received a further boost from the reaction against Jews fleeing Tsarist Russia, nearly 80,000 of whom made their way to Germany. By 1910 the size of German Jewry had reached 615,000, most of whom were primarily involved in industry and commerce. While Jewish ethnicity, revolving primarily around religion and politics, developed during the late nineteenth and early twentieth centuries, a loss in the Jewish population also occurred due to marriage and conversion. The First World War resulted in a further upsurge of antisemitism as Jews were associated with the enemy and with the defeat of the country.[5]

4. Ulrich Herbert, *A History of Foreign Labour in Germany, 1880–1980: Seasonal Workers/Forced Workers/Guest Workers* (Ann Arbor, 1990), pp. 9–119; Lothar Elsner, 'Ausländerbeschäftigung und Zwangsarbeiterpolitik in Deutschland während des Ersten Weltkrieges', in Klaus J. Bade, ed., *Auswanderer – Wanderarbeiter – Gastarbeiter: Bevölkerung, Arbeitsmarkt und Wanderung in Deutschland seit der Mitte des 19. Jahrhunderts* (Ostfildern, 1984), pp. 527–57; Volker Merx, 'Ausländische Arbeitskräfte im Deutschen Reich und in der Bundesrepublik', *Wirtschaftspolitische Chronik* 1 (1967), 65–91.

5. Paul Kennedy and Anthony Nicholls, *Nationalist and Racialist Movements in Britain and Germany Before 1914* (London, 1981); Lucy S. Dawidowicz, *The War Against the Jews, 1933–45* (Harmondsworth, 1988 reprint), pp. 62–75; Peter Pulzer, *The Rise of Political Anti-Semitism in Germany and Austria* (London, 1964); H. G. Adler, *The Jews in Germany: From the Enlightenment to National Socialism* (Notre Dame, Ind., 1969), pp. 73–104; Ismar Elbogen and Eleonore Sterling, *Die Geschichte der Juden in Deutschland* (Frankfurt, 1988); Jack Wertheimer, *Unwelcome Strangers: East European Jews in Imperial Germany* (Oxford, 1987); Marjorie Lamberti, *Jewish Activism in Imperial Germany* (London, 1978); Jonathan Steinberg, *All or Nothing: the Axis and the Holocaust, 1941–43* (London, 1990), pp. 236–8.

These stereotypes remained in existence during the Weimar Republic[6] and formed part of the antisemitism of Adolf Hitler and the Nazis, who, however, were mainly driven by *völkisch* racial ideas. The consequences of their rise to power during the pre-war years were the disenfranchisement and dehumanization of the Jewish population, with regular violent outbreaks, culminating in the *Kristallnacht* pogrom of November 1938.[7] The legalistic antisemitism of the years 1933–39 prepared the way for the destruction of European Jewry during the Second World War.[8]

However, Jews were not the only victims of Nazi persecution, as racial policy during the Second World War dictated not just the extermination of Jews and Gypsies,[9] but also the use of slave labour from all parts of occupied Europe as fuel for the German economy. The low numbers of foreign workers during the Weimar period, which reached a peak of just 236,000 in 1928, had only recovered to 301,000 by the outbreak of the Second World War. However, the years 1939–45 saw an enormous increase in the number of foreign workers, who totalled more than five million for much of the conflict. By the end of 1944 one in every five workers employed in the Reich was a foreigner. By this time, including prisoners of war, 7,615,970 non-Germans worked for the Nazis. The areas of employment included both the armaments industry and agriculture. The main countries of origin were (in order of numerical importance) the Soviet Union, Poland and France. The condition of foreigners in the history of Germany, like much else, reached its nadir under the Nazis, in accordance with racial ideology, people from Eastern Europe suffering worst of all. The degradation of foreign workers manifested itself clearly in working and living conditions, food provision and the penalties for coming into contact with Germans.[10]

6. Peter Pulzer, *Jews and the German State: The Political History of a Minority, 1848–1933* (Oxford, 1992), pp. 207–85; Adler, *Jews in Germany*, pp. 121–8; Steinberg, *All or Nothing*, pp. 238–9.

7. Dawidowicz, *War Against the Jews*, pp. 215–46; Michael Burleigh and Wolfgang Wipperman, *The Racial State: Germany 1933–1945* (Cambridge, 1991); Anthony Read and David Fisher, *Kristallnacht: Unleashing the Holocaust* (London, 1991); Walter H. Pehle, *November 1938: From 'Kristallnacht' to Genocide* (Oxford, 1991).

8. The best recent books on this subject include: Michael R. Marrus, *The Holocaust in History* (Harmondsworth, 1987); and Arno J. Meyer, *Why Did the Heavens Not Darken? The Final Solution in History* (London, 1988).

9. For gypsies see, for instance, Burleigh and Wipperman, *Racial State*, pp. 113–35; Michael Berenbaum, ed., *A Mosaic of Victims: Non-Jews Persecuted and Murdered by the Nazis* (London, 1990).

10. Herbert, *History of Foreign Labour*, pp. 127–92; Edward L. Homze, *Foreign Labor in Nazi Germany* (Princeton, 1967); Hans Pfahlmann, *Fremdarbeiter und Kriegsgefangene in der deutschen Kriegswirtschaft, 1939–1945* (Darmstadt, 1968); Eva Seeber, *Zwangsarbeiter in der faschistischen Kriegswirtschaft* (Berlin, 1964).

RACE IN THE 'OLD' FEDERAL REPUBLIC

For the purposes of this essay the movement of people into Germany in the post-war period can be divided into four periods. The first consists of the years immediately after the cessation of hostilities, when Germany resembled a vast refugee camp, in common with much of Central Europe. The Second World War may have resulted in as many as 30 million refugees on the continent. At the end of the conflict between seven and ten million displaced persons found themselves in Germany, consisting primarily of forced labourers of 20 different nationalities, speaking 35 different languages. In addition, the western occupation zones also contained as many as 300,000 Jews, both those of German nationality who had survived the conflict and former concentration camp inmates. The reaction of the Allies to the presence of millions of displaced persons who had worked as forced labourers was straightforward repatriation to their countries of origin, and between May and September 1945 over five million people were dealt with in this way, some of them being forced to return to the Soviet Union to face the consequences of having aided the enemy. However, at the end of 1945 approximately 1.7 million displaced persons still remained in the western occupation zones of Germany. By this time the United States had stopped forceable repatriation of all Soviet citizens. The majority of displaced persons who left Germany after this date did so as part of United Nations-sponsored schemes which involved the transportation of over a million refugees from throughout Europe to a variety of destinations, mostly as workers to assist in post-war reconstruction. The main destinations included the USA, Canada, Australia and Britain. The Jewish refugee problem was eventually solved by the creation of Israel, which took in the survivors of the Holocaust. By 1950 only about 150,000 displaced persons remained in Germany and Austria.[11]

At the same time as this refugee movement was progressing out of Germany, another of equally large proportions brought millions of ethnic Germans into the country, until the construction of the Berlin Wall in 1961. This group consisted of a variety of people. First, there were refugees fleeing the Russian advance through Eastern Europe and eastern Germany at the end of the war. To these we must add Germans affected

11. Michael R. Marrus, *The Unwanted: European Refugees in the Twentieth Century* (Oxford, 1985), pp. 296–346; Wolfgang Jacobmeyer, *Vom Zwangsarbeiter zum heimatlosen Ausländer* (Göttingen, 1985); Yury Boshyk, 'Repatriation and Resistance: Ukranian Refugees and Displaced Persons in Occupied Germany and Austria, 1945–1948', in Anna C. Bramwell, ed., *Refugees in the Age of Total War* (London, 1988), pp. 198–218.

by the redrawing of German boundaries in the east as part of the post-war settlement and the movement of the German population from the Baltic states, Czechoslovakia, Poland, Hungary, Yugoslavia and Romania. Over 12 million people made their way to Germany in this way, with the result that by 1960 they constituted 20 per cent of the population of the Federal Republic. The legal basis of their movement into Germany lay in Article 116 of the Federal Constitution, which recognized as Germans all people who could claim German origin. More practically, the newcomers were welcomed into the Federal Republic because of the need for labour to reconstruct the destroyed German economy, and here they played a fundamental part.[12]

The drying up of this source of labour, which began during the 1950s, had serious consequences for the Federal Republic, which began to recruit employees from the European periphery during the 1950s as the country still needed more labour assistance with reconstruction. The first of these workers came from Italy as a result of an agreement signed by that country and the Federal Republic in 1955, followed by further treaties with Spain and Greece in 1960, Turkey in 1961, Portugal in 1964 and Yugoslavia in 1968. The results of these policies were a non-German population of over four million by 1974, totalling over 5 per cent of the population of Germany as a whole. If we focus simply upon the working population, immigrants made up 10.8 per cent of it by 1972, having risen from just 0.47 per cent in 1956.[13]

We can examine the above bare facts in more detail. As mentioned, the reasons for immigration lay in the need of the West German economy for labour to help in the reconstruction process, a need which continued after the bulk of this task had been completed into the 1960s, when the Federal Republic had an annual economic growth rate of between 2.9 and 9 per cent between 1960 and 1966, which fell back in 1967. This actually resulted in a temporary halt to the influx of foreign workers, which recommenced the German economy grew again at between 3

12. Albrecht Lehmann, *Im Fremden ungewollt Zuhaus: Flüchtlinge und Vertriebene in Westdeutschland, 1945–1990* (Munich, 1990); Siegfried Bethlehem, *Heimatvertreibung, DDR-Flucht, Gastarbeiterzuwanderung: Wanderungsströme und Wanderungspolitik in der Bundesrepublik* (Stuttgart, 1982); Rogers Brubaker, *Citizenship and Nationhood in France and Germany* (London, 1992), pp. 169–70. See also Chapter 2 in the present volume.

13. Klaus J. Bade, 'Einheimische Ausländer: "Gastarbeiter" – Dauergäste – Einwanderer', in idem, ed., *Deutsche im Ausland, Fremde in Deutschland* (Munich, 1992), p. 395; Herbert, *History of Foreign Labor*, p. 210; Stephen Castles with Heather Booth and Tina Wallace, *Here for Good: Western Europe's New Ethnic Minorities* 2nd impression (London, 1987), p. 76: G. E. Völker, 'Labor Migration: Aid to the West German Economy?', in Ronald E. Krause, ed., *Mobility Across Cultural Boundaries* (Leiden, 1975), p. 8; Hans Stirn, 'Ausländer-Beschäftigung in Deutschland in den letzten 100 Jahren', in idem, ed., *Ausländische Arbeiter im Betrieb* (Cologne, 1964), p. 11.

and 8 per cent between 1968 and 1973. The demand for labour in West Germany was further heightened during the 1960s by a combination of demographic factors which resulted in a decline in the number of natives entering the labour market. These included the consequences of the birth rate falling as a result of the war, a lower retirement age, a lengthening of the education period and a fall in the working week.[14]

The turning-point in the history of labour recruitment into post-war Germany came with the economic recession of 1973–75, consequent upon the oil crisis, when the government of Willy Brandt put a stop to the importation of workers from the European periphery. During the preceding two decades the mechanics of the recruiting process had involved applications by German firms, who payed a fee, to the Federal Labour Office, which had established offices in Mediterranean countries. The contracts issued were temporary, so that there was also a regular return movement throughout the 1960s.[15]

This situation changed from the mid-1970s when, although the number of foreign workers declined, they now sent for their families, which meant an increase in the overall number of non-Germans within the Federal Republic. Consequently, the number of foreign workers fell from 2.6 million in 1973 to 1.9 million in 1989, while the foreign population generally rose from 3.98 million to 4.9 million during the same period. By this time nearly 60 per cent of non-Germans in the Federal Republic had been resident in the country for more than ten years.[16]

At this stage another new foreign element, and the final one of the pre-unification period, had begun to increase in numbers: asylum-seekers. A feeling of remorse generated by Germany's Nazi past and the persecution of non-Germans carried out during that period meant that Article 16 of the Federal Constitution of 1949 provided a particularly generous right of asylum for refugees compared with other European states. Until the early 1980s the number of people entering Germany in this way remained relatively low, but, during this decade, the annual figure of applicants for asylum never fell below 20,000 and totalled over 100,000 on three occasions. This situation reflected a general growth in

14. Jürgen Fijalkowski, 'Gastarbeiter als industrielle Reservearmee: Zur Bedeutung der Arbeitsimmigration für die wirtschaftliche und gesellschaftliche Entwicklung der Bundesrepublik Deutschland', *Archiv für Sozialgeschichte* 24 (1984), 413; Herbert, *History of Foreign Labor*, pp. 209–10.

15. Castles *et al., Here for Good*, pp. 71–2; Herbert, *History of Foreign Labor*, p. 234; H. Dreyer, 'Immigration of Foreign Workers into the Federal Republic of Germany', *International Labour Review* 84 (1961), 1–25.

16. Bade, 'Einheimische Ausländer', p. 396; idem, ed., *Ausländer, Aussiedler, Asyl in der Bundesrepublik Deutschland* 2nd edn (Hanover, 1992), p. 198.

the number of refugees making their way to Europe because of international crises during the 1980s, especially in the Middle East and Eastern Europe. The latter area also began to release ethnic Germans who had not resettled in Germany at the end of the Second World War, but could still do so under Article 116 of the Federal Constitution. During the 1980s almost one million such *Aussiedler* made their way to the Federal Republic.[17]

Any assessment of immigration into the pre-1990 Federal Republic would point to the variety and number of newcomers who entered the country. As regards variety, they included not only Germans by origin, whose entry was based upon clearly racial grounds, but also foreign workers from the European periphery, whose presence was also determined by racial considerations, as they entered the country simply for the purpose of helping the German economy. Their importation clearly continued historical traditions in the use of foreign workers dating back to the late nineteenth century and through the Nazi period. It is difficult to dispute Marxist interpretations of their role as a reserve army of labour, called in by the capitalist economies during times of economic boom.[18] Nevertheless, the overall picture of migration is more complicated because of the continued entry of a variety of groups during the 1980s. As far as numbers are concerned, Germany has become a 'country of immigration *par excellence*', surpassing even the USA in the total number of newcomers attracted since 1945, so that the 1989 West German population of 61 million contained 18 million people, or one-third of the total, obtained through immigration since the end of the Second World War.[19]

An examination of the structure and socioeconomic position of newcomers in post-war Germany reveals a complex picture, and we can confine our examination to those of non-German origin. Beginning simply with the countries of birth of the newcomers, Table 7.1 indicates the situation in 1989.

If we move on to geographical distribution and residence patterns, we find some aspects of the classic picture common to all minorities in industrial societies, namely concentration in urban areas. However, before moving to this situation, virtually all groups of newcomers to

17. Jürgen Nielsen, *Muslims in Western Europe* (Edinburgh, 1992), pp. 25–6; Franz-Josef Kemper, 'New Trends in Mass Migration in Germany', in Russel King, ed., *Mass Migration in Europe: The Legacy and the Future* (London, 1993), pp. 265–6; Victor Pfaff, 'Asylrecht in der BRD', *Links* 14 (July/August 1982), 12–13; Bade, *Ausländer, Aussiedler, Asyl*, pp. 198, 199.

18. See, for example, Castles *et al.*, *Here for Good*.

19. Lutz Hoffmann, *Die Unvollendete Republik: Zwischen Einwanderungsland und Deutschem Nationalstaat* 2nd edn (Cologne, 1992), pp. 28–9.

Table 7.1: Non-German population in the Federal Republic, 1989

Country of origin	Total	Percentage of total foreign population
EC states	1,325,400	27.4
Greece	293,649	6.1
Italy	519,548	10.7
Yugoslavia	610,499	12.5
Morocco	61,848	1.3
Portugal	74,890	1.5
Spain	126,963	2.6
Turkey	1,612,623	33.2
Tunisia	24,292	0.5
Others	1,211,220	25.0
Total	4,845,882	

Source: Klaus J. Bade, ed., *Ausländer, Aussiedler, Asyl in der Bundesrepublik Deutschland* 2nd edn (Hanover, 1992), p. 198.

German society had initially to spend some time in camps. This applies not simply to ethnic Germans and asylum-seekers, but also to foreign workers who entered Germany from the 1950s onwards. A large percentage of people falling within this last group lived initially in 'plant accommodation' provided by their employers, where conditions were 'spartan' and very few people had a room to themselves. After spending some time in such accommodation, the newcomers would move into private apartments, although here also they tended to find themselves in sub-standard housing.[20]

Residential concentration of non-Germans has taken place on both a macro and a micro level. In view of the fact that foreign workers were important for the purpose of reconstruction, their main areas of residence within the country as a whole have been concentrated in the 'urban-industrial agglomerations', particularly Baden-Württemberg, North-rhine-Westphalia, Hessen and West Berlin. Within these Federal states, they are particularly heavily concentrated in certain cities, namely Stuttgart, Cologne and Frankfurt, the last of which has had the highest percentage of non-Germans. Within individual cities newcomers have tended to focus upon particular quarters, because, as with other immigrant settlers in the industrialized world during the last two centuries, this concentration has provided both security and the opportunity to

20. Clemens Amelunxen, 'Foreign Workers in Germany', in William A. Veenhoven, ed., *Case Studies in Human Rights and Fundamental Freedoms* (The Hague, 1975), pp. 122–3; Gerhard Kühlewind, 'The Employment of Foreign Workers in the Federal Republic of Germany and Their Family and Living Conditions', *German Economic Review* 12 (1974), 363–4; Dreyer, 'Immigration of Foreign Workers', 17.

maintain ethnicity. Also as in other cases, non-Germans have tended to settle in the more deprived areas in the city centres, often near their place of employment. However, concentration has not been as heavy as in the USA, and has not resulted in the type of 'ghettos' which exist in that country.[21]

The age and gender distribution of foreign workers has differed from that of the native population. In view of the reasons for the importation of non-Germans into the economy from the late 1950s, a substantial percentage of the newcomers were initially male and young. In the early 1960s the majority of migrant workers were males between the ages of 20 and 40, while in 1960 the male-female ratio stood at an extraordinarily unequal 84.5 per cent to 15.5 per cent. This statistic changed during the following decade, reaching 63:37 in 1970. During the 1970s, as a consequence of the recruitment of foreign workers, over a million family members migrated to Germany, which meant a gender ratio of 56:44 in 1982, 'thus approaching the ratio of a nonmigrant population'. With regard to the age-composition of the migrant populations, the main changes from the 1960s to the 1990s have been the expansion of the upper and the lower ends due to the aging of the original immigrants and the entry into the country of their children, although the foreign populations still remained 'markedly different from a nonmigrant population'.[22]

Much attention has focused upon the economic position of non-Germans in the post-war period and their role in economic growth. With regard to the former, both government and academic research has demonstrated that the overwhelming percentage of migrant workers have been largely involved in unskilled and low-skilled jobs, involving heavy, dirty and dangerous work. The major industries have consisted of iron and other metallurgical production and construction. In 1972 about 80 per cent of foreigners in the Federal Republic were employed in the secondary sector, while most of the rest played a role in the tertiary area. Only 1 per cent had jobs in agriculture. The main change in the above pattern by the start of the 1980s was a growth in the

21. Horst and Helga Reimann, 'Federal Republic of Germany', in Ronald E. Krane, ed., *International Labor Migration in Europe* (New York, 1979), pp. 80–3; Hans Heinrich Blotvogel, Ursula Mueller-ter Jung and Gerald Wood, 'From Itinerant Worker to Immigrant? The Geography of Guestworkers in Germany', in King, ed., *Mass Migration in Europe*, pp. 89–96; Bethlehem, *Heimatvertreibung*, p. 121.

22. Friedrich Heckmann, 'Temporary Labour Migration or Immigration? "Guestworkers" in the Federal Republic of Germany', in Rosemarie Rogers, ed., *Guests Come to Stay: The Effects of European Labor Migration on Sending and Receiving Countries* (London, 1985), pp. 70–1; Ray C. Rist, *Guestworkers in Germany: The Prospects for Pluralism* (New York, 1978), p. 115.

number of people involved in service industries to 30 per cent, at the expense of the secondary sector. In terms of class position, the majority of foreigners has clearly remained at the lower end of the social scale, consequently helping in the social mobility of Germans, whom they continue to push upwards. Two further but contradictory developments have been an increase in unemployment, especially amongst the children of the original migrant workers, and a growth in ethnic businesses, especially restaurants.[23]

Although there is little doubt about the positive economic effects of immigration into post-war Germany, a counter-argument exists which suggests that the importation of labour in the 1960s prevented an increase in efficiency which would have taken place by investment in new machinery. However, against this we have to place the positive effects of newcomers into the German economy. In simple terms, they have helped to increase the Gross National Product. The fact that they have worked in industrial production meant that they have contributed more than proportionately to the growth of the German economy from the time of their arrival. Furthermore, because of the age of the newcomers, the German state has not had to pay for their child-rearing and educational costs.[24]

All groups who have made their way to the Federal Republic have attempted to create an ethnicity, although, at the same time, the process towards integration and assimilation begins at an early stage. However, German nationality laws, based as they are upon origin, have hampered the latter to a greater extent than within countries where the children of immigrants automatically take citizenship in the place where they were born, because, for instance, second-generation immigrants in Germany, along with their parents, are deprived of basic rights such as voting and employment by the state.[25]

This situation may have encouraged the creation of ethnic organizations, which are, however, fundamental for all immigrant minorities in industrial societies, irrespective of nationality laws. Thus, for instance,

23. Herbert, *History of Foreign Labour*, p. 250; Kühlewind, 'Employment of Foreign Workers', 365; Friedrich Heckmann, *Die Bundesrepublik: Ein Einwanderungsland* (Stuttgart, 1981), p. 156; Stephen Castles and Godula Kosack, *Immigrant Workers and the Class Structure in Western Europe* (London, 1973), pp. 71–3, 82–3; Castles *et al., Here for Good*, pp. 127–38, 159–89.

24. For an introduction to these arguments see, for instance: Rudolph C. Blitz, 'A Benefit Cost Analysis of Foreign Workers in Germany', *Kyklos* 30 (1977), 479–502; Völker, 'Labor Migration', pp. 7–45; Herman Korte, 'Labor Migration and the Employment of Foreigners in the Federal Republic of Germany Since 1950', in Rogers, ed., *Guests Come to Stay*, pp. 44–6.

25. See, for instance, Hoffman, *Unvollendete Republik*; and Rist, *Guestworkers in Germany*, pp. 133–48.

religion has played an important role in the life of all minorities. For example, by the end of the 1980s there were over 65 Jewish communities in the Federal Republic, created mostly by immigration.[26] Mosques, meanwhile, were established in the Federal Republic from the 1950s, although those connected with the foreign worker influx only began in the late 1960s, often in flats, although since then minarets have been constructed. A city like Duisburg had 30 mosques by 1987. By this time mosques divided along national and religious lines throughout the country. In addition, cultural organizations have been created on both a local and a national basis amongst most groups. Similarly, countless newspapers for the newcomers have appeared in post-war Germany, while, with the increase in religious refugees, political activity has become important, a good example being the Kurds.[27]

Some integration has also taken place, however. This has partly occurred through the education of second-generation immigrants in German schools, although this has had limited success partly because children, especially those not born in Germany, have had problems in adapting to the use of two languages, while prejudice amongst the teaching profession meant that migrant children received only limited attention compared with the offspring of natives. The children of immigrants have had a lower success rate at school than the children of Germans.[28] However, integration is more clearly indicated in the incidence of marriages between Germans and non-Germans, which in 1990 made up 9.6 per cent of all such unions in the country.[29]

Nevertheless, despite moves towards integration, the existence of official and unofficial hostility towards immigrants and refugees has fundamentally slowed down this process. With regard to governmental attitudes, the preceding discussion has covered the two fundamental indications of the unwillingness to recognize newcomers to the Federal

26. Monika Richarz, 'Jews in Today's Germany', *Leo Baeck Yearbook* 30 (1985), pp. 265–74; Lynn Rapaport, 'The Cultural and Material Reconstruction of the Jewish Communities in the Federal Republic of Germany', *Jewish Social Studies* 49 (1987), 137–54.

27. Nielsen, *Muslims in Western Europe*, pp. 29–33; Winifred Schlaffke and Rüdiger von Voss, eds, *Vom Gastarbeiter zum Mitarbeiter: Ursachen, Folgen und Konsequenzen der Ausländer-Beschäftigung in Deutschland* (Cologne, 1982), pp. 98–9, 159–64; Barbara von Breitenbach, *Italiener und Spanier als Arbeitnehmer in der Bundesrepublik Deutschland* (Munich, 1982), pp. 111–26.

28. Thomas Faist, 'From School to Work: Public Policy and Underclass Formation Among Young Turks in Germany during the 1980s', *International Migration Review* 27 (1993), 306–31; Amelunxen, 'Foreign Workers in West Germany', pp. 125–7; von Breitenbach, *Italiener und Spanier*, pp. 101–8.

29. Harold Schumacher, *Einwanderungsland BRD: Warum die Deutsche Wirtschaft weiter Ausländer braucht* (Düsseldorf, 1992), p. 144.

Republic as equal citizens with 'Germans'. First, the way in which immigrants were imported as labour for the second industrial revolution, working in occupations which were not desired by Germans, meant that economically they initially fell into the working classes, perhaps even forming a sub-class. Even more important is the legal status of newcomers and their children in the Federal Republic. As mentioned above, Germany is an ethnic state. It has granted citizenship to individuals who have lived outside the country if they can prove German origin, yet denies it to people born within its borders of non-German parents, who have to proceed through a lengthy process of naturalization and sacrifice their original nationality. Consequently, immigrants and their children in Germany have been deprived of fundamental civil rights.

Against this background, overt unofficial hostility towards non-Germans has been rife and has manifested itself in countless ways. On a basic level, for instance, we can point to social prejudice, which has been recognized by numerous surveys carried out on the subject and which indicate a high level of negative attitudes towards both Jews and foreign workers in the Federal Republic.[30] These views have manifested themselves in everyday discrimination in various ways. For instance, in the workplace animosity has manifested itself in the fact that foreign workers have tended to obtain the most difficult jobs and in the lack of social mixing between Germans and non-Germans. The latter has also existed outside employment, so that signs forbidding entry to newcomers have not been unusual.[31] The above manifestations of racism have developed against the background of negative images towards immigrants in the mass media, to be found in the mainstream press, radio and television and, more crudely, in newspapers of a more extreme nature.[32]

But the most potent manifestations of racism in the Federal Republic have been the growth of extremist parties and, less obviously, racial attacks. From the end of the Second World War overtly racist political parties have always had a role to play in the political system, while racial violence began to take off during the 1970s and 1980s. Beginning with the first of these assertions, these organizations developed almost

30. See, for instance, the bulky academic study by Badi Panahi, *Vorurteile: Rassismus, Antisemitismus, Nationalismus in der Bundesrepublik Deutschland Heute* (Frankfurt, 1980).

31. Knuth Dohse, 'Ausländerpolitik und betriebliche Ausländerdiskriminierung', *Leviathan* 9 (1981), 499–526; E. Gaugler *et al.*, *Ausländerintegration in deutschen Industriebetrieben* (Königstein in Taunus, 1985); Georgios Tsiaklos, *Ausländerfeindlichkeit: Tatsachen und Erklärungsversuche* (Munich, 1983).

32. See, for instance, Horst Reimann, 'Ausländische Arbeitnehmer und Massenmedien', in Horst and Helga Reimann, eds, *Gastarbeiter* (Munich, 1976), pp. 111–29.

immediately after the end of the Second World War. The development of the most important of these parties can be divided into three stages. In the late 1940s and early 1950s the two major groupings consisted of the Socialist Reich Party and the German Reich Party, the former of which obtained 11 per cent of the vote in the Lower Saxony *Landtag* elections in 1951 but was banned in 1952. The German Reich Party had less support and in 1964 reconstituted itself into the National Democratic Party (NPD), the major right-wing force during the 1960s and 1970s. This reached a high point in 1969 when it secured 4.3 per cent of the vote in the Federal elections and its peak membership of 28,000. The 1970s 'were a dismal period for the far right in Germany', a situation which continued into much of the 1980s.[33] However, apart from the major groupings mentioned above, we also need to point to the countless smaller organizations which have always existed,[34] as well as to right-wing violence. The latter reached a peak in the late 1950s and early 1960s, focusing upon Jewish targets.[35]

The second half of the 1980s saw major growth in the support for extremist parties in both West Germany and the former German Democratic Republic. With regard to the former, we can point both to the development of militant neo-Nazi groupings and the violence associated with them, and the formation of the third major grouping in West Germany, the Republican Party, which was founded in 1983 and arrived on the political scene in the European elections of 1989, when it secured 7.1 per cent of the vote.[36]

33. David Childs, 'The Far Right in Germany since 1945', in Luciano Cheles, Ronnie Ferguson and Michalina Vaughan, eds, *Neo-Fascism in Europe* (London, 1991), pp. 62–75; Eva Kolinsky, 'A Future for Right Extremism in Germany?', in Paul Hainsworth, ed., *The Extreme Right in Europe and the USA* (London, 1992), pp. 61–7; Peter Dudek and Hans-Gerd Jaschke, *Entstehung und Entwicklung des Rechtsextremismus in der Bundesrepublik* (Opladen, 1984), pp. 272–85.

34. Those which existed from 1945 to 1989 are listed in Kurt Hirsch, *Rechts von der Union: Personen, Organisationen, Parteien seit 1945* (Munich, 1989), pp. 314–39.

35. Dudek and Jaschke, *Entstehung und Entwicklung des Rechtsextremismus*, pp. 266–9; Wolfgang Benz, 'Die Opfer und die Täter: Rechtsextremismus in der Bundesrepublik', in idem, ed., *Rechtsextremismus in der Bundesrepublik: Voraussetzungen Zusammenhänge, Wirkungen* (Frankfurt, 1984), pp. 28–31.

36. Christopher T. Husbands, 'Militant Neo-Nazism in the Federal Republic of Germany in the 1980s', in Cheles *et al.*, eds, *Neo-Fascism in Europe*, pp. 86–113; Richard Stöss, *Politics Against Democracy: Right-Wing Extremism in West Germany* (Oxford, 1991); Gerhard Paul, 'Republik und "Republikaner": Vergangenheit, die nicht vergehen will?', in idem, ed., *Hitlers Schatten verblasst: Die Normalisierung der Rechtsextremisten* (Bonn, 1989), pp. 134–63.

THE IMPACT OF UNIFICATION

Immediately after German unification, two fundamental developments occurred in the area of race in Germany, consisting of an increase in immigration and a significant growth in potent manifestations of racism, although both of these changes built upon developments which had occurred during the 1980s, as mentioned above. The first of these processes can actually be described as mass migration into Germany since the end of the Cold War, a movement helped by the factors indicated above in the form of Articles 16 and 116 of the Federal Constitution and by Germany's geographical proximity to Eastern Europe. Thus, between 1990 and 1992, 887,366 asylum-seekers and 849,606 ethnic Germans made their way to the new Federal Republic, averaging out at over half a million newcomers per year.[37] These figures are even more striking when we consider that in 1992 Germany received 79 per cent of all applications for asylum to EC countries.[38] However, if we put the above figures into the perspective of the history of migration into the Federal Republic, annual increases of the scale indicated above have not been uncommon.

However, in contrast with the earlier history of West Germany, the immigration of the early 1990s took place at a time when the German economy was not crying out for labour, as it had been during the first few decades after the Second World War. This serves as one explanation for the increase in racial violence at the start of the 1990s, which took off dramatically and, in its scale, represented a new phenomenon in the history of the Federal Republic. Patterns of racial violence in the new Germany have been complicated, and we can point to three different varieties: first, isolated attacks upon individuals involving small groups of youths, which have taken place throughout the country and have sometimes been murderous; second, large-scale riots against refugees, in which the local population have played a role, though these have been relatively few and far between and confined to eastern Germany; third, violence in which members of minority groups have been the perpetrators. Official statistics for attacks carried out by people with right-wing leanings indicate that in 1991 they totalled 1,483, and then peaked at 2,584 in the following year.[39]

37. Cornelia Schmalz-Jacobsen *et al.*, *Einwanderung und Dann? Perspektiven einer Neuen Ausländerpolitik* (Munich, 1993), p. 314.

38. The *Guardian*, 1/6/1993.

39. For details of attacks between 1990 and 1993 see Panikos Panayi, 'Racial Violence in the New Germany (1990–3)', *Contemporary European History* 3 (1994).

As well as the increase in racial attacks, parties of the right have also grown in the early 1990s, both neo-Nazi and quasi-democratic. The Amt für Verfassungsschutz estimated that by 1992 there were 43,100 members of right-wing groups, an increase from 33,600 in 1990. Just as significant is the increase in support for groups such as the Deutsche Volksunion and *Republikans* in German elections, so that such parties obtained between 7 and 13 per cent of the votes cast in elections in Bremen, Baden-Württemberg, Schleswig-Holstein and Hessen between 1991 and 1993.[40]

The explanation for the increase in potent manifestations of racism is extremely complex and would have to take into account a variety of factors. Apart from the perceived threat of mass immigration, these include historical traditions, as the end of the Cold War meant a partial release of the racism repressed since the end of the Second World War. In addition, we can also mention the economic crisis consequent upon unification, which meant the collapse of the east German economy and the experience of mass unemployment by its citizens for the first time, as well as a milder economic downturn in the west. Furthermore, the euphoria of unification led to an intense nationalism which had its 'dark side' in the form of potent racism.

Nevertheless, from late 1993 something of a downturn occurred in the manifestations of racism, so that electoral support for the *Republikans* collapsed to less than 2 per cent in the Federal election of October 1994.[41] Therefore, it seems that the traditions established during the 40 years of the existence of the Federal Republic have held it in good stead. At no time during its history has it approached the racial obsession of the Nazi period and, seemingly contradictorily, at no time has it escaped it. In terms of race, the Federal Republic functions as a liberal democracy. Like all liberal democracies, it has imported labour at times of economic growth and has marginalized its minorities once they have entered the country. This exclusion from power fits in neatly to the pattern of the German past, so that nationality laws draw strong links with the pre-1945 period, meaning that Germany remains a country in which race, as much as merit, determines who holds power.

Certainly, moves are afoot to remedy this situation and it seems inevitable that nationality laws will change, although how drastically they will alter is open to question. However, it is equally inevitable that manifestations of racism will not disappear. Perhaps Germany will make its way to a US-style post-modern society in which conflicting groups

40. *Verfassungsschutzbericht, 1992* (Bonn, 1993), pp. 66–7; Claus Leggewie, *Druck von Rechts: Wohin Treibt die Bundesrepublik?* (Munich, 1993), pp. 167–8; *Die Zeit*, 12/3/1993.
41. *Die Zeit*, 21/10/1994.

have their own power bases. This appears to be the only way open as one can imagine neither the extreme right seizing power nor minorities continuing to be deprived of their rights.

CHAPTER EIGHT

The Nationalist and Neo-Nazi Scene since 1945

David Childs

POTSDAM: 'ELIMINATE NAZISM'

Partly because they had greatly overestimated the strength of National Socialism, the Allies expected a surge of right-wing activity in their zones of Germany, after the initial impact of defeat in May 1945 had softened. This, by and large, did not happen. There were several reasons why it did not occur.

The leading Nazis were no longer available to continue their destructive work. Hitler, Goebbels (Propaganda Minister), Goering (Air Force Chief), Himmler (SS/Gestapo/Police Chief) and Ley (Labour Minister) all killed themselves. Others, lower down, followed their example. Some of their confederates – Flick (Minister of the Interior), Keitel (Army Chief), von Ribbentrop (Foreign Minister) and Seyss-Inquart (Commissar for Holland) among them – faced the gallows or, like Doenitz (Naval Commander), Hess (Deputy to Hitler), von Schirach (Hitler Youth Leader) and Speer (Armaments Minister), were to spend long years in Spandau Jail. Altogether, 22 Germans were tried by the International Military Court at Nuremberg in October 1945, and only three were acquitted of the charges. Many more Germans of lesser importance were interned, and thousands fled Germany or were in hiding. According to one estimate, by January 1947 some 245,000 persons had been arrested in the four zones of occupation.[1] This seems an underestimate. However, not all of those arrested and interned were Nazis, let alone dangerous Nazis.[2] But the fact is that the cadre for an organized opposition to the Allies did not exist. Even if it had, the occupying powers were in no mood to tolerate it.

1. Richard F. Nyrop, ed., *Federal Republic of Germany: A Country Study* (Washington, DC, 1983), p. 41.
2. Wolfgang Eisert, *Die Waldheimer Prozesse. Der stalinistische Terror 1950* (Munich, 1993), pp. 29–34.

At their meeting in Potsdam in August 1945 the United States, the Soviet Union and Britain had agreed to eliminate Nazism and militarism root and branch. Appropriate decrees were announced banning all bodies considered to be tainted with Nazism and militarism. All political and other organizations had to be licensed by the relevant Allied military authority.

Equally important was the fact that the Germans had suffered a psychological blow far greater than the defeat of 1918. This time, Germany was totally occupied and under military government. In 1918 it had been only partially occupied and Germany had had a democratic government. Moreover, the crimes and atrocities committed by the Nazis shocked the Germans, most of whom had not known the full hideousness of Himmler's SS state. The mass media were used by the occupiers to 're-educate' them. They knew too that they were regarded as lepers throughout Europe.

Moreover, the physical destruction of Germany, the chaos and the conditions of near-starvation conditions, also reduced the potential for resistance. For most, the best they could hope for was personal survival.

RESTORATION

When Ivone Kirkpatrick arrived in Germany in June 1950 to take over as the British High Commissioner with, in theory, ultimate control of the British Zone with its 24 million inhabitants, he saw as his job the elimination of all causes of Anglo-German friction. This included 'the continuance of war crime trials five years after the war' and 'the extradition of war criminals'.[3] The Germans were to be the allies of the three Western powers as soon as possible. The gathering Cold War between the Soviet Union and the three Western powers after 1945/46 had led to an improvement for the Germans and greater tolerance of them. Soon they would be sought as allies. Some former Nazis were even getting jobs with the occupying powers. Many convicted war criminals had their death sentences commuted, many more were released from prison. SS officer Joachim Peiper, sentenced to death by the Americans in 1945 for the murder of 71 unarmed US prisoners of war, had his sentence commuted to 25 years' imprisonment. He was released

3. Ivone Kirkpatrick, *The Inner Circle* (London, 1959), p. 220.

in 1956. Alfred Krupp, convicted of exploiting slave labour, was freed in 1951; so were other industrialists. General Gehlen, former head of German Army intelligence on the Eastern front, was engaged, as were his staff, by the Americans. Former members of the NSDAP appeared in all of Germany's political parties. Among the better known cases were Karl Carstens (CDU), later Federal President, the future Federal Chancellor, Kurt Georg Kiesinger, Professor Karl Schiller, the Social Democrat Economics Minister, Waldemar Kraft, the leader of the refugee party (BHE, see below) and a minister in Adenauer's governments, and Theodor Oberlander (BHE), also a minister under Adenauer. There was the disturbing case of Hans Globke, who served as Adenauer's chief aide in his office from 1950 to 1963. He had held a high position in Hitler's Ministry of the Interior. The integration of former members of the NSDAP and SS into the armed services, democratic parties, diplomatic service, judiciary, police, public administration and universities was another important reason why a mass movement of the far right failed to emerge in the early years of the Federal Republic. Thousands of former Nazi Party members had found status and prosperity in the new state, and saw no sense in putting them at risk.

THE DREP, THE BHE AND THE SRP

Nevertheless, in this changing atmosphere the far right regained its composure and started regrouping. There was the German Rights Party (Deutsche Rechtspartei, DRep) and the German Conservative Party (Deutsche Konservative Partei, DKP). They appeared in Schleswig-Holstein and Hamburg. Allied together, they gained five seats in the first *Bundestag* elected in 1949. The Economic Construction Association (Wirtschaftliche Aufbauvereinigung, WAV), which existed only in Bavaria, succeeded in getting 12 of its candidates into the *Bundestag*. It aimed its demagogic appeals largely at refugees. In Lower Saxony it was the German Party (Deutsche Partei, DP) that played a similar role. It attracted nearly a million votes and gained 17 seats in 1949. With the possible exception of the DRep, these parties did not identify themselves with the 'achievements' of the Third Reich, but tended to play on the idea of the Germans as victims, called for equality for Germany with other states and preached anti-Marxism.

By 1950 about 12 million 'expellees' lived in the Federal Republic.

In many cases they had been expelled from their homes in what before 1945 had been eastern Germany and had been annexed by Poland and the Soviet Union. Others were ethnic Germans who had been forced to leave their homes in eastern or central Europe or the Soviet Union. 'It was as though all the people from Scotland, Wales and Northern England had been expelled and accommodated into a Southern English rump state, itself badly damaged by the war.'[4] It was a dangerous situation. They could have formed the basis for a serious revanchist movement. In the regional election of 1950 in Schleswig-Holstein their potential was demonstrated. The Bloc of Expellees and Disenfranchised (Bund der Heimatvertriebenen und Entrechteten, BHE), formed only months before, gained 23.4 per cent of the vote, coming second only to the SPD with 27.5 per cent. The BHE's three main leaders had all been members of the NSDAP. The new Minister-President, Dr Walter Bartram of the CDU, himself a former Nazi, was elected with BHE support.[5] In 1951 the BHE became a national party organized throughout the Federal Republic. In the Federal election of 1953 it gained 5.9 per cent of the vote, giving it 27 seats (out of 509) in the *Bundestag*. Two of its members joined Adenauer's second coalition government. With so much poverty and unemployment in the country, the expellees and refugees from the Soviet Zone/GDR could have been a threat to German democracy. Instead, most of them were integrated into the democratic framework. This was achieved by the 1950s economic 'miracle' and by the Equalization of Burdens Act of 1952. Many expellees and refugees benefited from compensation under the Act. Most of the BHE were eventually absorbed into the CDU. In 1961 the remnants joined elements of the DP to form the All-German Party (Gesamtdeutsche Partei, GDP). The GDP had little success, and many of its supporters soon left it for other parties.

The first significant far-right party which openly sympathized with Hitler's Reich was the Socialist Reich Party (SRP). It was founded in 1949 by Otto-Ernst Remer and Dr Fritz Dorls. Its members were drawn from the DRep, DP, DKP and other splinter groups. Remer had helped to crush the July plot against Hitler in 1944. Dorls served in the first *Bundestag* (1949–53) as an independent. The success of the SRP climaxed in 1951 when it gained 11 per cent and 7.7 per cent of the votes respectively in the Lower Saxony and Bremen regional elections. After it was declared unconstitutional by the Federal Constitutional Court in 1952, many of its members joined the DRep, which then continued as

4. Dennis, L. Bark and David R. Gress, *A History of West Germany, Vol. 1: From Shadow to Substance 1945–1963* (Oxford, 1989), p. 305.
5. Ibid., p. 308.

the main standard-bearer of the far right until it dissolved itself in 1965. It had changed its name to the German Reich Party (Deutsche Reichspartei, DRP) in January 1950. Its chairman from 1953 to 1960 was Wilhelm Meinberg, a former *Gruppenführer* (major general) in the SS. It called for a neutral Germany in the boundaries of 1937 and changes within the Federal Republic which would have turned it into a corporatist state. Nevertheless, it claimed, 'the DRP does not seek the restoration of obsolete forms. It takes its stand on the Basic Law and decisively rejects totalitarian tendencies. It acknowledges an honest and free democracy.'[6] In the 1957 election it made a great effort but only secured 300,000 votes in the whole of the Federal Republic, only 12,000 more than in 1953. It campaigned hard for the rights of former members of the Waffen-SS.

RISE OF THE NPD

The massive economic, political and diplomatic success of the Federal Republic in the 1950s and early 1960s was reason enough to keep the attractiveness of the far right to a minimum. According to the 1968 annual report of the Federal Republic's internal security organ, the *Verfassungsschutz*, in terms of membership the far right had been disappearing: 42,000 members in 1960; 32,400 in 1961; 25,300 in 1962; 22,600 in 1963; 20,700 in 1964. However, a considerable reversal occurred in the second half of the decade: 26,300 in 1965; 34,700 in 1966; 38,700 in 1967; 37,000 in 1968. In November 1964 the National Democratic Party of Germany (Nationaldemokratische Partei Deutschlands, NPD) was founded in Hanover. The main elements of the new party were drawn from the DRP, but some of its members had formerly been in the BHE or the DP. Shortly after its foundation, some 4,000 people left over 70 splinter groups to join it.[7] Friedrich Thielen (DP) was elected chairman, and Wilhelm Gutmann (BHE), Adolf von Thadden (DRP) and Heinrich Fassbender (DRP) deputy chairmen. Von Thadden and Gutmann had been members of the NSDAP and von Thadden had been chairman of the DRP since 1961. He had been a

6. Uwe Kitzinger, *German Electoral Politics. A Study of the 1957 Campaign* (Oxford, 1960), pp. 185–7.

7. Alf Mintzel and Heinrich Oberreuter, eds, *Parteien in der Bundesrepublik Deutschland* (Bonn, 1990), p. 321.

Table 8.1: Percentage of votes gained by the NPD at Federal and regional elections, 1965–71

Land	*Bundestag* elections % of vote		Regional elections			
	1965	1969	Year	% of vote	Year	% of vote
Saar	1.8	5.7	1965	—	1970	3.4
Northrhine-Westphalia	1.1	3.1	1966	—	1970	1.1
Hamburg	1.8	3.5	1966	3.9	1970	2.7
Hesse	2.5	5.1	1966	7.9	1970	3.0
Bavaria	2.7	5.3	1966	7.4	1970	2.9
Rhineland-Palatinate	2.5	5.2	1967	6.9	1971	2.7
Schleswig-Holstein	2.4	4.3	1967	5.8	1971	1.3
Lower Saxony	2.5	4.6	1967	7.0	1970	3.2
Bremen	2.7	4.4	1967	8.8	1971	2.8
Baden-Württemberg	2.2	4.5	1968	9.8	1972	—

DRP member of the *Bundestag* from 1949 to 1953. Thielen had left the CDU in 1958 while Fassbender had left the Free Democratic Party (Freie Demokratische Partei, FDP) because it was 'too left' for him. As the NPD was a new attempt to fuse the disparate groups of extreme conservatives, nationalists and neo-Nazis, former Nazis and those too young to have been in Hitler's party, it attracted some fringe attention and therefore a few more members. Nineteen sixty-five was an election year, and this focused more attention on the new party. In the Federal election of that year it received 2 per cent of the vote or about 600,000. This could be regarded with some satisfaction by the NPD leaders given its relative lack of resources and time to organize.

In the years between the 1965 and 1969 Federal elections the NPD made the headlines again and again in the German and world press as it got its candidates elected into one regional parliament after another.

Where the NPD managed to gain 5 per cent of the vote it got representation in the *Land* parliaments, that is, in Hesse, Bavaria, Rhineland-Palatinate, Schleswig-Holstein, Lower Saxony, Bremen and Baden-Württemberg (Table 8.1). In no case did it come anywhere near getting a majority or even becoming the biggest single party, but the psychological impact of its breakthrough was great. It came at a time when there were a number of Nazi scandals in West Germany. The newly elected Chancellor in 1966, Kurt Georg Kiesinger, was a former member of the NSDAP. Some thought his election helped to make the NPD more acceptable. A number of other factors were, however, more important for the relative success of the NPD. West Germany had suffered a minirecession which hit coal-mining, steel and agriculture particularly hard. The resulting job loses inevitably led to some ill-feeling towards foreign 'guestworkers', many of them from Turkey. They had been recruited in increasing numbers after the supply of labour from the GDR was cut off with the building of the Berlin Wall in 1961. There was also the feeling among some right-of-centre voters that the Christian Democrats had 'gone off the rails' by joining the Social Democrats in a grand coalition which lasted from 1966 to 1969. Others thought that both big parties had ganged up in an attempt to monopolize political power. The increasing visibility of the student left wing in the late 1960s also encouraged the development of a counter-attraction on the far right. Another factor was the twentieth anniversary of Germany's defeat. Inevitably, some thought Germany was being unfairly treated, being still divided after so many years of peace and good behaviour. President Charles de Gaulle's robust patriotism in France acted as an example to Germans who thought the Federal Republic was too subservient to the USA and was in danger of losing its identity. To some extent the NPD was able to exploit such feelings, which also included a degree of anti-Americanism.

THE NPD PROGRAMME

The programme of the NPD claimed that a divided Germany in a divided Europe was suffering under the burden of foreign power. Germany was still bending to the will of the victors who had divided it and Europe. It rejected the claim that Germany alone was responsible for the two world wars. 'Research about the origins of the wars must serve historical truth, not propaganda against our people and its honour.'[8] It called for German unity, the end of foreign occupation of Germany and Europe, and the creation of a League of European States. There was to be no relinquishing of Germany's claim to unity, Germany's claim to the Sudetenland and Germany's claim to the territories beyond the Oder–Neisse line. The NPD demanded that laws promulgated by the war victors should be rescinded by revising the appropriate treaties. It wanted a general amnesty for all those facing prosecution because of the part they had played in the Second World War. Nowhere in the programme

8. *Programm Der NPD* (Hanover, 1967).

did one find any expression of remorse or regret, let alone shame for any German actions before or during the war.

In its domestic policy the NPD claimed to support the basic democratic order of the Federal Republic and the division of power within it. However, it wanted an end to the financing of political parties from taxation (something it benefited from). It also called for referenda on important issues and wanted to return to the Weimar system under which the President of the Federal Republic was elected directly. The *Länder* should be reformed so that they would be roughly equal in economic and financial terms. The duties and responsibilities of the Federation, *Länder* and local authorities should be clarified. The NPD wanted to see better qualified and politically independent judges. The programme called for a reform of the education system, to replace the regionally based system with a uniform, national school system. The whole trend harked back to the Weimar constitution, to de Gaulle's Fifth Republic and to earlier European authoritarian, plebiscitary democracies. The first point in the section, 'The Human Being and Work', demanded that the German worker must have priority over foreign labour in securing his job. In the same section there was a clause demanding the removal of outside trade union officials from the supervisory boards of firms. The NPD wanted to see old-fashioned class struggle finally overcome and replaced by a community of all (wealth) creators. Although it stressed that industrial peace should be achieved, this was preaching to the converted in a country which had very few strikes. The programme devoted a whole section containing 16 theses to demands related to compensation for those who had suffered as a result of the war. Basically, the NPD aimed to boost further the compensation the Federal Republic was already giving. The objects of NPD concern were soldiers, former SS men, expellees and refugees. The victims of National Socialism were not mentioned. Among the demands included in the section 'Family and the Health of the People' was compulsory service for young women in the same way as young men were compelled to do military service. This service would be completed in the health service or the welfare services. The party demanded that the Minister of Health should have appropriate expertise. Interestingly, this section contained several paragraphs demanding environmental protection.

In its defence policy, the NPD wanted to reverse the military reforms of the post-war period. 'An army cannot be administered, it must be led', asserted the NPD. It wanted, therefore, to end civilian control over the armed forces and restore military control. The introduction of pseudo-democracy into the barracks which undermined discipline would be reversed. Military courts should be reintroduced and trade unions and similar organizations would be banned in the armed forces. Former members of the Waffen-SS would be treated in the same way as other former soldiers. Soldiers should once again be given their proper status in society. Finally, the NPD wanted to re-establish a German General Staff.

NPD MEMBERS AND VOTERS

In 1966 20 per cent of NPD members had been members of the NSDAP, and out of the 18 members of the Executive Committee, 12 had been active Nazis.[9] Others too young to have been in the Hitler movement had been in post-war far-right bodies like the SRP or DRP. Worse still, according to the 1968 annual report of the West German internal security organ *Verfassungsschutz*, the former NSDAP members were old Nazis who had joined Hitler *before* he gained power. Geographically speaking, the NPD was over-represented, in terms of number of members per 10,000 of population, in Bavaria, Lower Saxony and Schleswig-Holstein. Thus the NPD was most successful in recruiting where the NSDAP had previously been strong. It tended to attract men rather than women, Protestants rather than Catholics, older age groups rather than younger ones, those whose political views had taken shape before 1945, those who lived in small towns rather than those who lived in cities, and those who had previously not voted. In terms of occupational background, peasants were over-represented among NPD voters in 1968, as were the self-employed. Industrial workers had average representation while white-collar employees and civil servants were under-represented.

A survey of voters in the Baden-Württemberg regional election of 28 April 1968 revealed that out of 9.8 per cent who voted for the NPD, 2.2 per cent were regular NPD supporters, 1.8 per cent were former non-voters and 5.8 per cent had previously been supporters of the main democratic parties (3 per cent SPD, 2.5 per cent CDU and 0.3 per cent

9. Reinhard Kühnl, Rainer Rilling and Christine Sager, *Die NPD. Struktur, Ideologie und Funktion einer neofaschistischen Partei* (Frankfurt am Main, 1969), p. 226.

Table 8.2: Age and sex distribution of NPD voters in Baden-Württemberg, 28 April 1968

	% voting for NPD		
Age group	Total	Men	Women
21–29	8.1	10.9	5.3
30–44	10.9	13.6	8.0
45–59	12.0	17.1	8.1
60 and above	7.7	11.2	4.9
Total	9.8	13.4	6.8

Source: Bundesinnenministerium, *Zum Thema Hier: Verfassungsschutz 1968* (Bonn, 1969), p. 32.

FDP).[10] Table 8.2 shows the age and sex composition of those NPD voters.

THE NPD DEFEATED

In its report for 1968, the *Verfassungsschutz* noted a decline in the NPD. This was in part the result of dissension within the party. In some cases functionaries had left because they felt the party was undemocratic in its internal arrangements. The *Verfassungsschutz* regarded the NPD as a body which had taken up Nazi ideas. Two foreign models recommended to party members by the NPD publication *Deutsche Nachrichten* (*DN*) were Spain and Greece, both then right-wing dictatorships. This, and other, NPD publications claimed that the democratic parties had no legitimacy, having gained power by the bayonets of the victors. Such attacks went too far for the more moderate elements among the NPD voters and members. Undoubtedly the onslaught on the NPD from both within and outside the Federal Republic led waverers to abandon the party. The big test was the Federal election of September 1969. The world's media had descended on Germany and they reported widely on the activities of the NPD. Such reports influenced the German electorate. Some feared German prosperity could suffer if the NPD gained access to the *Bundestag*. Relief came when the NPD narrowly failed to do so, gaining only 4.2 per cent of the vote. As Table 8.1 above indicates, the party only gained more than 5 per cent in four out of ten *Länder*. With the CDU/CSU in opposition to the new government of Social

10. Bundesinnenministerium, *Zum Thema Hier: Verfassungsschutz 1968* (Bonn, 1969), pp. 32, 68.

Democrats and Free Democrats, some of those who had voted NPD switched back to the Christian Democrats. The NPD went into steep decline. The nightmare had passed.

NPD RIVALS

Right-wing activists believed that one of the reasons for the defeat of the NPD was the lack of unity in the 'National camp'. There were any number of far-right splinter groups, most of little significance. This could not be said of Dr Gerhard Frey's circle. Frey, a lawyer by training, published and edited *Die Deutsche National-Zeitung und Soldaten-Zeitung (DNZSZ)* and other publications. Frey took over the *DNZSZ* and its parent company in 1958 when it was on the verge of bankruptcy. It had been set up in 1950 by, among others, former SS-General Paul Steiner and originally received subsidies from the Federal Press Office and the Americans.[11] Frey's publications soon became the most widely read in the right-wing camp. Many of his readers were not organized in any extremist group, though one-third of the readers of his main publication were NPD supporters. In 1968 the *DNZSZ*'s name was changed to *Die Deutsche National-Zeitung (DNZ)*. Frey attacked the politicians in Bonn, communism and Israel. He took an extreme revisionist attitude to the Second World War, seeking to prove German innocence and other nations' guilt. He also attacked the leaders of the NPD. The *Verfassungsschutz* reported that Frey sold 44,900 copies of his publications in 1965, 70,000 in 1966, 82,200 in 1967 and 88,200 in 1968. The print run of NPD publications over the same period was lower, seeming to indicate a smaller readership. Frey had the advantage that his publications had a firmer base over a longer period, and he was not tied to a party line.

Whereas Frey expressed his anger in words, others gave physical expression to their frustrations and hatred of the 'Bonn system' or parts of it. During the 1960s there were hundreds of known cases of right-wing extremist violence and other forms of law-breaking. This included attempted murder, violence against the person, verbal abuse of Jews, arson, damage to Jewish cemeteries, damage to church property and

11. Thomas Assheuer and Hans Sarkowicz, *Rechtsradikale in Deutschland* (Munich, 1992), p. 30.

graffiti daubing. For whatever reason, the number of cases known to the authorities fell during the second half of the 1960s: 521 in 1965; 449 in 1966; 387 in 1967; 349 in 1968. In 71 per cent of cases the crimes were committed by those aged under 30. In 1968 53 per cent were 20 or younger.

DECLINE IN THE 1970s

The 1970s witnessed a decline in far-right/neo-Nazi activities. Membership of the NPD peaked in the 1969 election year at 28,000, and then declined year by year: to 21,000 in 1970; 19,300 in 1971; 14,500 in 1972; 12,000 in 1973; 11,500 in 1974; and 10,800 in 1975.[12] By the end of the decade its membership had fallen to under 7,000. The NPD was unsuccessful in regional elections, failing to get any of its candidates into *Länder* parliaments. At the local level, the number of NPD members on town councils fell from 426 in 1971 to 54 in 1975. It is difficult to be certain why this occurred, for, after all, the *Ostpolitik* pursued by the Social Democratic/Free Democratic government involved, in effect, the recognition of the East German regime. Moreover, Brandt's government appeared to be sanctifying the *status quo*, including Germany's post-war frontiers. The far right regarded this as treason. However, Christian Democrats appeared to be strong in their opposition to the Brandt, and later Schmidt, governments. In these circumstances, right-of-centre voters felt happy to vote for the Christian Democrats. In 1972 and 1976 the Christian Democrats fought hard campaigns against the Social/Liberal coalition, led by Brandt until 1974 and then by Helmut Schmidt. In 1972 the SPD achieved its best result since the end of the war. The election was hard fought over the government's *Ostpolitik*, with its members being denounced as 'renunciation politicians' because they were prepared to recognize Germany's *de facto* post-1945 frontiers. In 1976 the slogan of the CDU/CSU was *Freiheit statt Sozialismus* (freedom instead of socialism), which had a strong ideological appeal.

The anti-abortion campaign was also directed largely from the opposition camp. In 1980 the CDU/CSU campaign was spearheaded by the Bavarian conservative leader and former Defence Minister, Franz-Josef Strauss. His tough electioneering style was attractive to the far right,

12. Bundesinnenministerium, *Verfassungsschutz 1975* (Bonn, 1976), p. 26.

but it put off moderate voters, especially women, and the Christian Democratic breakthrough failed to materialize. Schmidt remained Social Democratic Chancellor. In this situation the far right could do little. Its share of the poll fell from 4.3 per cent in 1969 to 0.6 per cent in 1972; 0.3 per cent in 1976; and 0.2 per cent in 1980. In terms of actual votes it fell from 1,422,000 in 1969 to only 68,000 in 1980.

The NPD also suffered from new splits within its own camp. In 1971 the party lost some of its members because they were not happy with the election of Martin Mussgnug as Party Chairman. They joined the Aktion Neue Rechte (ANR) founded in 1972 by Siegfried Pöhlmann, who had stood unsuccessfully against Mussgnug for the NPD chairmanship. In 1975 von Thadden left the NPD as he opposed its alliance with Frey, previously a hard critic of von Thadden. Martin Mussgnug arranged for Frey to be elected to the Executive Committee of the NPD. Frey, however, found it difficult to cooperate with the NPD leadership.

EXPANSION IN THE 1980s

At the beginning of the 1980s the far right was organized in 73 groups with a membership of around 20,300.[13] The NPD, with only 6,500, had been overtaken by Frey's Deutsche Volksunion (German People's Union, DVU) with around 10,400 members. The DVU was originally established in 1971 to coincide with the 100th anniversary of the founding of the German Reich.[14] Its founder claimed he wanted to unite all those from the middle to the right in politics. The DVU was not seen as a political party to begin with. It only became one in 1987 when its name was amended to Deutsche Volksunion-Liste D. Its main aims were: (1) Germany for the Germans, putting a stop to the immigration of foreigners; (2) concentration on the aim of German reunification; (3) protection of life, fight against the misuse of abortion; (4) equality for the German people, putting an end to the continuous accusations; (5) protection of the honour of Germany's war dead and soldiers.[15] Leading members of the NPD took part in the founding of the DVU-Liste D in Munich in March 1987. It was agreed that the NPD and the DVU-

13. Idem, *Verfassungsschutz 1981* (Bonn, 1982), p. 20.
14. Assheuer and Sarkowicz, *Rechtradikale*, p. 34.
15. Ibid., p. 36.

Table 8.3: Membership of far-right organizations in the 1980s

1980	1981	1982	1983	1984	1985	1986	1987	1988	1989
19,800	20,300	19,000	20,300	22,100	22,100	22,100	25,200	28,300	35,900

Source: Bundesinnenministerium, *Verfassungsschutz 1989* (Bonn, 1990).

Liste D would not put up candidates against each other. By that time Frey and Mussgnug had other serious competitors for their constituency.

In 1981 the *Verfassungsschutz* classified 18 of the 73 organizations mentioned above as directly neo-Nazi. The NPD and the DVU did not fit into this category. Among those which did, most had very few members. To a degree, the fortunes of the far right improved in the 1980s, especially towards the end of the decade. Net membership developed as shown in Table 8.3.

Membership of neo-Nazi bodies, included in the figures in Table 8.3, varied between 1,200 in 1980, 2,100 in 1987 and 1,500 in 1989.

DIE REPUBLIKANER

Little was expected of the Republicans (*die Republikaner*, REP) when the party was founded in November 1983. It appeared to be an unlikely alliance of disgruntled ex-CSU members. Two former CSU members of the *Bundestag*, Franz Handlos and Ekkehard Voigt, joined former deputy chief editor of the Bavaria broadcasting service, Franz Schönhuber, to lead the new party. The two MPs said they were protesting about Strauss's efforts to secure a loan for the ailing economy of Honecker's German Democratic Republic. The two seasoned politicians were soon put in the shade by the journalist and they left the party in 1985 and 1987 respectively. In 1989 Voigt returned to the REP. In political terms, Voigt stood to the right of Schönhuber, Handlos to the left. Schönhuber himself wanted to steer a course to the right of the CDU/CSU but to the left of the NPD. The fact that he had served in the Waffen-SS placed him (in the minds of many people at least) on a par with the NPD. But Schönhuber adamantly denied that he had sympathized with the Third Reich.[16] Frey at first saw him as an ally, and Schönhuber's book, *Ich war dabei*, in which he dealt with his war experience and which had cost him his television job, was warmly commended in Frey's

16. *Der Spiegel*, No. 6, 1989.

publications. Schönhuber, however, resisted the embrace of Frey and they became bitter opponents.[17] At first, Schönhuber was the winner. In the Bavarian regional elections of October 1986 the REP scored 3 per cent while the NPD received only 0.5 per cent of the vote. However, the NPD/DVU- Liste D went ahead of the REP in three later regional elections in Bremen, Baden-Württemberg and Schleswig-Holstein. In 1989 the world media were, however, paying more attention to the REP than to its right-wing rivals.

EURO-ELECTIONS 1989: SUCCESS

In January 1989 the REP attracted 7.5 per cent of the vote in the election to the West Berlin parliament. This secured them 11 seats. Their two main themes were law and order and stopping the influx of foreigners into Germany. They stood for a united, neutral Germany, opposing the transference of power to the European Community. In general, Schönhuber emphasized traditional values, for example the importance of the work of the housewife and the mother rather than the career woman. Although he came out strongly in support of the police, he claimed he rejected the reintroduction of the death penalty – unlike some of his supporters. One worrying aspect of the Berlin victory for the orthodox parties was the apparent support the REP enjoyed among the police, not only in West Berlin.[18] The NPD had not been allowed to compete in West Berlin, being banned there by the three Allied powers who still maintained their prerogatives in security matters. The election to the European Parliament on 18 June 1989 brought another shock both for the mainstream parties and for Dr Frey. With its slogan, 'Yes to Europe – no to this EC', the REP attracted 7.1 per cent of the votes, giving it six seats. Over two million Germans had voted for Schönhuber and his friends. Dr Frey's candidates could only garner 1.6 per cent. Once in the European Parliament the six Republicans soon split. Schönhuber and two others left the European Right group, which included the French National Front, and sat as independents. The other three, including ex-NPD functionary Harald Neubauer, remained.

The *Republikaner* were in turmoil outside the European Parliament as

17. Assheuer and Sarkowicz, *Rechtradikale*, pp. 42–3.
18. ARD television programme, *Panorama*, 16 May 1989.

well as inside. The sudden success of the party brought about an influx of members. Some of the new members were individuals who had previously not been politically active, others had been activists in the NPD and similar bodies. Schönhuber found it difficult to keep control of things and stop the party lurching to the right. Splits occurred, weakening the REP. But a far bigger blow was on the way. Once German unity became a real possibility in 1990, the Republicans started to fade. This had been their most fundamental demand. They had been the super-patriots who had accused Chancellor Kohl and the other mainstream politicians of giving in to the communists. The reality was, however, that Kohl, with careful diplomacy and a few well-chosen words to the East Germans who greeted him at rallies, was achieving German unification. At regional elections in the Saar, Northrhine-Westphalia and Lower Saxony, the Republicans were heavily defeated, polling 3.3 per cent, 1.8 per cent and 1.5 per cent of the vote respectively. Momentarily, Schönhuber lost the official leadership of the REP to Neubauer, regaining it on 7 July 1990 at the party congress in Ruhstorf.[19]

Republican voters in 1989 tended to be young, skilled workers, men rather than women, and pensioners of the war generation. They were likely to be nationalistic and anti-foreign.[20]

FOREIGNERS, ASYLUM-SEEKERS AND ETHNIC GERMANS

Many more people agreed with the Republicans on the issue of preventing foreigners from gaining residence in Germany than actually voted for the party. As for the foreigners themselves, they felt less secure in West Germany than they had done in the past. They felt hostility was growing. The problem was that, in addition to the millions of legal 'guestworkers' and their families living in West Germany, there were also many illegal immigrants, together with the growing number of those seeking political asylum and numbers of ethnic Germans from Eastern Europe. The German authorities estimated that at the end of 1992 there were over 6.5 million foreigners living in Germany, that is, 8 per cent of the population. The biggest single group were the 1.8

19. Assheuer and Sarkowicz, *Rechtradikale*, p. 51.
20. Ibid., pp. 48–9.

million Turks. About 47 per cent of the foreigners in Germany had lived there for more than ten years.[21]

It was estimated that at the same time 1.5 million foreign refugees lived in Germany. This included those seeking political asylum. Despite legislation being passed in 1993 which made it more difficult to seek asylum, thousands were still arriving. The collapse of communism had made it easier for ethnic Germans to leave the poor countries of the former Soviet Union and Eastern Europe. Large numbers did so: 202,000 in 1988; 377,000 in 1989; 397,000 in 1990; 222,000 in 1991; 231,000 in 1992.

Foreigners have played a considerable part in the German economy, often doing the jobs Germans did not want to do. In 1992 12 per cent of those employed in the building trade were foreigners, 11.3 per cent of those in industry and handicrafts, 10.9 per cent of those in agriculture, forestry and fisheries, 9.2 per cent of those in personal services, but only 2 per cent of those in insurance and banking. Nevertheless, the asylum-seekers and the ethnic Germans represented high costs for the German economy. Extra educational services were required and housing and welfare services were put under strain. In some areas the natives were afraid of losing their familiar environment.[22]

THE FAR RIGHT IN THE UNITED GERMANY

The coming of German unity on 3 October 1990 meant the former West Germany taking over responsibility for 16.3 million former East Germans living in an area which had been neglected since before the Second World War. The Federal Republic also had to make a contribution towards the costs of the Soviet/Russian armed forces on German soil, and towards their rehousing in the former Soviet Union. Inevitably, a minority on both sides of the old frontier were not happy with the new situation and having to make sacrifices for the greater good. This provided fresh opportunities for the far right. So did the admissions by the Russians that the Soviet Union under Stalin had committed countless crimes. The Katyn Wood massacre of Polish officers in 1940 and the early post-war executions by the Soviets in their zone of Germany

21. Presse und Informationsamt der Bundesregierung, *Almanach der Bundesregierung 1993/94* (Bonn, 1993), pp. 130–3, 146–7.

22. For further details see the the article by Hartmut Berghoff in Chapter 2.

were among them. Some young East Germans, indoctrinated by the communists, were shocked, disappointed and disorientated. If they had been lied to about the Soviets, perhaps they had been lied to about the Nazis too. Perhaps they had not been so bad after all. Maybe the Nazis had even been good for Germany – after all, they had built roads, created work, made the trains run faster and on time. Perhaps Germany had, in trying to gain its rights, been crushed by superior numbers, and then been made to feel guilty for 45 years. Moreover, many felt that the older generation had let them down, especially the teachers who had pumped them full of communist propaganda. In some cases they resented their parents, 2.3 million of whom had been members of the ruling SED, many others of whom had been members of satellite organizations. The relatively small number of foreigners who had lived in the GDR before 1990 were often associated with the SED regime, having been recruited by it. In some cases this made them the target of hatred and abuse. A poll of young people aged 14–25 in Saxony in 1992 showed that those who thought there were too many foreigners (54 per cent) had the advantage over those who thought there were not too many (46 per cent).[23]

This new 'ideological' situation helps to explain the frustration of East German youth which has resulted, in some cases, in young people being attracted to the far right. In addition, contrary to communist propaganda, East German youth experienced the same bored frustration that many young people living on similar anonymous housing estates in the West felt. There has also been growing youth unemployment since 1990. These conditions should be seen as the background to the skinhead violence of the 1990s. It should be pointed out that, although there was little reporting of crime in the GDR, racist violence was certainly not unknown under the communists. One typical example was an attack by young workers on two Africans in a train in May 1988. After verbally abusing the two foreigners they physically attacked them, throwing one of them from the train.[24] The general increase in right-wing violence in the early 1990s is shown in Table 8.4.

According to the *Verfassungsschutz*, the increase in violent activity was 74 per cent. In West Germany such acts had increased 22–fold over the ten years to 1992. The figures in Table 8.4 probably underestimate the acts of violence committed as some of them are likely to go

23. Harry Müller and Wilfried Schubarth, 'Rechtsextremismus und aktuelle Befindlichkeiten von Jugendlichen in den neuen Bundesländern', *APUZ: Beilage zur Wochenzeitung Das Parlament*, 11 September 1992.

24. Landeszentrale für politische Bildung Thüringen, *Rechtsextremismus in den neuen Bundesländern* (Erfurt, 1992), p. 7.

Table 8.4: Violence with far-right background

	1988	1989	1990	1991			1992		
				East	West	Total	East	West	Total
Homicides	0	1	2	1	2	3	7	8	15
Explosions, arson	12	12	47	123	260	383	222	487	709
Bodily harm	36	52	102	198	251	449	307	418	725
Damage to property with use of considerable force	25	38	119	171	477	648	329	793	1,122

Source: Various reports of Bundesinnenministerium, *Verfassungsschutz*..

unrecorded. Some victims, particularly illegal workers or asylum-seekers, are not likely to notify the police. The two East German regions of Mecklenburg-West Pommerania and Brandenburg revealed the largest number of violent acts relative to population size. They were followed by Schleswig-Holstein, the Saar, Saxon-Anhalt in the east and Northrhine-Westphalia in the west. Bremen had the honour of being the least troubled by right-wing violence, with Bavaria not far behind. As a result of 15 acts of homicide in 1992, 17 people died, seven of them foreigners. In the 14 cases in which the police held suspects, all those accused were men between 16 and 30 years old. Most were part of the skinhead culture. These acts of violence arose mainly from arguments or chance meetings with their victims. Often those involved were under the influence of alcohol. In one case in Buxtehude (Lower Saxony), two drunken neo-Nazi skinheads, aged 25 and 18, beat a man to death because he had spoken negatively about Hitler and the Third Reich. They were subsequently convicted of manslaughter and the older of the two was sentenced to eight-and-a-half years' imprisonment. His younger confederate received six years in a youth detention centre. Both had previous convictions. In another case, on 23 November 1992 in Mölln (Schleswig-Holstein), a 51-year-old Turkish woman and two children died in a deliberate act of arson. Several others suffered burns. Two skinheads, aged 25 and 19, were later arrested for the crime.

Equally serious have been attacks on political opponents. One case reported from Prenzlauer-Berg (Berlin) in 1992 involved three right-wingers throwing two Molotov cocktails at a house occupied by leftists. The one suspect arrested gave as his motive the help the leftists extended to foreigners. Other victims of right-wing attacks were the police, the homeless, homosexuals, the physically handicapped, prostitutes and, of course, foreigners. About 75 per cent of the attacks on the police took place in the former GDR. Because of their association with the communist regime, the police there enjoy less respect than their colleagues in the western regions of Germany. In cases of right-wing violence involving more than 20 culprits, over 76 per cent of them in 1992 took place in the former GDR. One example of this was the violence which erupted between 17 and 22 September 1991 in Hoyerswerda, Saxony, in the former GDR. Considerable numbers of skinheads attacked shelters for asylum-seekers. When the police intervened, they attacked the police. Worse still, several hundred onlookers expressed their solidarity with the skinheads. An almost identical incident took place in Rostock, focusing world-wide attention on the former GDR. The *Verfassungsschutz* concludes from these assaults that militant right-wing extremism is better organized in eastern Germany than in the western *Länder*. The *Verfassungsschutz* estimated in 1992 that there were 3,800 militant right-wing extremists in the former GDR and 2,600 in western Germany.

An analysis by the *Verfassungsschutz* of those involved in right-wing violence gave the occupational breakdown shown in Table 8.5. The figures related to 137 individuals in 1992 and 480 in 1988–91. These figures highlight youth and blue-collar workers. Job insecurity is thought to be one reason for this. However, right-wing violence cannot be simply explained by employment or social conditions. The fact is, many more people agree with aspects of far-right ideology than are revealed by far-right votes or membership of far-right bodies. It needs particular circumstances to exploit these views successfully and turn them into votes for right-wing extremist organizations. Many other individuals who would not consider themselves to be right-wing can be mobilized by 'respectable' extreme right-wing bodies in apparent emergencies. Recent developments in Italy prove this, as do events in Germany in 1933.

In 1994, the *Verfassungsschutz* reported that right-wing violence fell by 15 per cent in 1993 compared with 1992. A total of 2,232 violent

Table 8.5: Occupational breakdown of those involved in recent right-wing violence

Occupation	% of total perpetrators	
	1992	1988–91
Pupils, students and apprentices	43	36
Skilled workers, tradesmen	31	31
Unskilled workers	1	13
White-collar employees	9	7
Military personnel including conscripts	4	4
Unemployed	9	8
Others	4	1

Source: Bundesinnenministerium, *Verfassungsschutz 1992*, p. 83.

offences with suspected or actual right-wing motivation were registered in 1993 as against 2,839 in 1992. In the first quarter of 1994 this trend continued. However, the authorities knew they had no cause for complacency. In Solingen, western Germany, five Turks were killed in an arson attack in May 1993. Speaking on 16 June 1993, Chancellor Kohl said this crime, and also the many arson attacks which followed on the homes and businesses of Turkish fellow-citizens, revealed 'an incredible moral decay'. In the same speech, he claimed, 'not a few Germans today seem to find it difficult to show kindness to others that comes from the heart. Decency and dignity have become foreign words for some people.' He condemned the 'blatant egotism' of some Germans. He also felt that the media's negative reporting on Turkey had damaged German–Turkish relations. Riots in Magdeburg, in the former GDR, on 12 May 1994 – when foreigners were attacked and chased through the streets – confirmed that the potential for violence remained.

ELECTIONS OF 1994: FAILURE

The election to the European Parliament in June 1994 brought great relief in Bonn establishment circles and no joy for the far right. Taken together, the far-right parties received over 5 per cent of the vote. But once again the far right was divided. The REP was once again the most convincing, and the most moderate, representative of this tendency. Its vote fell from 7.1 per cent in 1989 to 3.9 per cent in 1994. In part this was because Conservative voters felt the German economy was showing signs of improvement. The 'feel good factor' worked in favour of Chancellor Kohl's governing Christian Democrats. In addition, Kohl had finely tuned his declarations in the period running up to the election in a way likely to appeal to potential right-wing defectors from the REP camp. In the former GDR, disillusioned CDU voters were more likely to have gone over to the former communists (the PDS) or to the Social Democrats. In western Germany the Greens gained many protest votes. The far right remained in a small ghetto. In the summer of 1994 Germany appeared to have gained greater immunity from the far-right bacterium than could be observed in the years immediately following unification. This was indeed confirmed in the Federal election of 16 October when the vote of the Republicans slumped to 1.9 per cent.

CHAPTER NINE

The SPD: the Decline of the Social Democratic Volkspartei[1]

Stephen Padgett

The post-war history of German social democracy can be analysed in three phases. In the early post-war years the SPD retained its pre-1933 identity: a class party, in which ideology, electorate and organization were rooted in what Lösche has called the working-class solidarity community.[2] Confined within this social ghetto, the SPD of Kurt Schumacher and Erich Ollenhauer remained in opposition throughout the early years of the Federal Republic. The second phase follows from the transformation which the party undertook in the late 1950s and early 1960s, marked by the adoption of the Bad Godesberg programme of 1959. The SPD of Willy Brandt and Helmut Schmidt conformed broadly to Kirchheimer's model of the *Volkspartei*: pluralist in the composition of its electorate and membership, social–liberal in ideology, and elite-orientated in its organizational structure. Electorally successful, the SPD exercised government responsibility, first as junior party in a Grand Coalition with the CDU/CSU (1966–69), then a dominant party in the Social–Liberal coalition with the FDP. The third phase follows the break-up of the Schmidt government in 1982, and is marked by the decline of the social democratic *Volkspartei*. In common with other large parties in Western Europe, the SPD struggled to come to terms with social change. The SPD of Oskar Lafontaine, Bjorn Engholm and Rudolf Scharping can be described as a post-modern social democratic party. Its predominant characteristics are electoral fragmentation, social decomposition and programmatic disorientation. All of these tendencies were exacerbated by unification, which wrong-footed the party, leading to a third electoral defeat in 1990. Although the party retained a hold on government in the *Länder*, the 1994 general election showed the weakness of the SPD at Federal level.

1. The author wishes to thank the Nuffield Foundation for an award supporting the research on the SPD in the east German *Länder*.

2. Peter Lösche, 'Ende der sozialdemokratischen Arbeiterbewegung?', *Die Neue Gesellschaft* 35 (1988), 453–63.

THE SPD AS A 'SOLIDARITY COMMUNITY': THE EARLY POST-WAR YEARS

The identity of the post-war SPD mirrored that of its leader. It has been said of Kurt Schumacher that 'he had forgotten nothing and had nothing left to learn'.[3] Guided by the unshakeable conviction that social democracy was the only force capable of undertaking the social and moral regeneration of Germany, Schumacher's main preoccupation was with building an apparatus to enable the party to fulfil this role. This meant reliance on pre-existing structures, with organization, ideology and electoral strategy rooted in the Weimar party.

This continuity with the past also reflected the composition of the party. Some two-thirds of the membership in 1946 had belonged to the party in 1933. Internal party life resembled the solidarity community of the classical mass party model, derived from the highly integrated party of Weimar days and the experience of repression under the Third Reich.[4] Cohesion derived also from the relative social homogeneity of the party's membership and electorate. Schumacher's SPD was a party of the working class. Whilst he was ready to widen his definition of the working class to embrace farmers, artisans, tradesmen and the intellectual professions in a *Partei aller Schaffenden* (party of all producers), he continued to emphasize the class character of the party. Thus he was not prepared to endorse a supra-class strategy in a *Partei aller Schichten* (party of all classes).

The organizational structures of the post-war SPD were those of the Weimar party, as was the composition of the party elite.[5] Schumacher's power base was the party executive, in particular the *Apparat* of salaried functionaries on the executive which symbolized the bureaucratic inertia of the SPD in the 1940s and well into the 1950s. Executive membership was extraordinarily stable between 1945 and 1958, with only two changes for reasons other than decease. Whilst reform elements gradually increased their representation of the wider executive, they were unable to penetrate its functionary core. Thus despite an undercurrent of reform, the leadership of the party remained in the hands of those who identified with the past.[6]

3. Joseph Rovan, *Geschichte der Deutschen Sozialdemokratie* (Frankfurt am Main, 1982), p. 179.

4. Lewis Edinger, *Kurt Schumacher: A Study in Personality and Political Behaviour* (London, 1965), p. 409.

5. Stephen A. Padgett and William E. Paterson, *A History of Social Democracy in Postwar Europe* (London, 1991), p. 71.

6. Douglas A. Chalmers, *The Social Democratic Party of Germany: From Working Class Movement to Modern Political Party* (New Haven, Conn., 1964), p. 63.

The reconstruction of the SPD took place in an ideological vacuum, occupied by default by the ossified neo-Marxism characteristic of the Weimar party. Under the iconoclastic Kurt Schumacher as party chairman, ideological renewal was discouraged as a distraction from the central tasks of organization-building.[7] Early policy programmes omitted statements of broad principle. Thus the Heidelberg programme of 1925 remained as the 'official' statement of basic values, although it had long since lost all relevance to practical party politics.[8]

Policy formulation was based on the three pillars of working-class socialist tradition: economic democracy (*Wirtschaftsdemokratie*), democratic planning and socialization.[9] Social democratic collectivism on these lines, however, progressively lost ground in the political struggle over reconstruction. With the renaissance of liberal capitalism after 1948, the SPD began to retreat from its programmatic commitment to collectivism. It was a silent retreat, however, unaccompanied by formal programmatic declaration.

The commitment to social democratic collectivism masked a progressive convergence in domestic policy with the Christian Democratic government. Increasingly, the SPD followed a strategy of 'constructive negotiation' in domestic policy, avoiding confrontation over principle in favour of persuasion.[10] Rapprochement between the SPD and the government in domestic economic policy was overshadowed, however, by Schumacher's rhetoric of intransigent opposition, his gladiatorial confrontations with Adenauer in the *Bundestag*, and his steadfast rejection of any openings the SPD may have had to participate in the institutions of the new state. Opposition centred mainly on foreign and European policy, where SPD positions reflected Schumacher's personal preoccupation with national unification, and his strategy of accommodating Soviet interests in a unification settlement. Integration with Western Europe conflicted with this strategy. In view of the success of the government's economic and foreign policies, Schumacher's opposition strategy left the SPD politically isolated and in an electoral ghetto.

7. Barbara Marshall, *The Origins of Post-War German Politics* (London, 1988), pp. 147–8.
8. R. Petry, 'Die SPD unter dem Sozialismus', in Ossip K. Flechtheim, ed., *Die Parteien in der Bundesrepublik Deutschland* (Berlin, 1973), pp. 78–9.
9. E.-U. Huster, *Die Politik der SPD, 1945–50* (Bonn, 1978), pp. 35–41.
10. Beatrix W. Bouvier, *Zwischen Godesberg und Grosser Koalition: der Weg der SPD in die Regierungsverantwortung* (Bonn, 1991), p. 34.

THE BAD GODESBERG TRANSFORMATION

The Godesberg course was set by the need to adapt to the socio-economic and political landscape of the Federal Republic. Firstly, the intensity of economic development meant that the effects of rising affluence and social homogeneity which weakened class identities in most West European countries were particularly pronounced. Secondly, the demographic upheaval brought about by the massive influx of refugees from the east inevitably disrupted social traditions and class ties, 'an important precondition for the development of catch-all parties in West Germany'.[11] Thirdly, the double trauma of the Third Reich, on the one hand, and the repressive, communist GDR regime, on the other, led to a recoil from radical ideology. Finally, the success of the CDU/CSU in re-establishing the cross-class tradition of political Catholicism, from Wilhelmine and Weimar days, and in forging a cross-confessional alliance with Protestant forces, created a powerful electoral force. The Christian Union parties became the prototype of Kirchheimer's[12] model of the *Volkspartei*, in which class politics and overt ideology were de-emphasized. The logic of the model was to force opposition parties to emulate their style.

The internal forces for change were unlocked by Schumacher's death in 1952, although the transformation of the SPD was not completed until the early 1960s. The intervening period can be characterized as 'the Erich Ollenhauer interregnum', during which critical changes took place in the composition of the leadership elite and its internal power balance. Firstly, Schumacher had been figurehead and patron of the bureaucrats in the party apparatus. Primarily concerned with maintaining the cohesion of the party organization, the functionaries were the bastions of tradition. Under Ollenhauer's leadership, their authority declined significantly. Secondly, the *Bundestagsfraktion* became more assertive. Increasingly critical of Ollenhauer's parliamentary leadership, the *Fraktion* sought to break up the ossified organizational structure of the SPD, and to present a more aggressive and modern form of leadership.[13] Thirdly, the new leadership signalled the rise of a nucleus of modernizers centred upon the so-called *Bürgermeisterflügel* (mayoral wing) of the SPD.

11. Eva Kolinsky, *Parties, Opposition and Society in West Germany* (London, 1984), p. 20.

12. O. Kirchheimer, 'The Transformation of the Western European Party Systems', in Joseph La Palombara and Myron Wiener, eds, *Political Parties and Political Development* (Princeton, NJ, 1966), pp. 177–200.

13. Harold Kent Schellenger Jr., *The SPD in the Bonn Republic: a Socialist Party Modernizes* (The Hague, 1968), p. 157; Alfred Grosser, *Die Bonner Demokratie* (Düsseldorf, 1960), p. 146.

Leaders of *Land* and city governments, they were attuned to pragmatic reform. The Ollenhauer interregnum was thus marked by a shift in the power balance within the SPD from professional bureaucrats to politicians orientated towards electoral success and modernizing change.

The SPD's new ideological orientation was formulated in a series of incremental programmatic revisions over almost a decade. Innovation, however, was unsystematic, new formulas appearing alongside the residue of the party's ideological tradition. The first move came with the Dortmund programme of 1952, drafted by Willi Eichler and Heinrich Deist, who were both to be central in the Godesberg programme review. Although socialization and planning still figured prominently, the shopping list of sectors earmarked for state ownership was curtailed. The emphasis was on increased production, full employment and a just distribution of the social product, to be accomplished by a 'combination of economic planning and competition'. This phrase was refined the following year by Karl Schiller, who was later to symbolize the party's new orientation in economics. 'Competition as far as possible, planning in so far as necessary' signalled the SPD's acceptance of the market economy in a formula which later became the centrepiece of the Godesberg programme. Reform was given further emphasis in the Berlin programme of 1954, which indicated a fundamental change in the party's self-perception from *Arbeiterpartei* to *Partei des Volkes*. 'Social Democracy has, from the party of the working class . . . become a party of the people.' The 'people's party' orientation was most clearly evident in the triad of principles – freedom, justice and solidarity – which formed the core of Godesberg social democracy.[14]

The Bad Godesberg programme of 1959 represented an ideological watershed of historic significance. It renounced the party's past in favour of a humanist ethos of social liberalism, embodied in the basic principles of freedom, justice and solidarity which represented the *Leitmotif* of the new programme. Disavowing the SPD's Marxist heritage, the programme emphasized the eclectic philosophical sources of democratic socialism and endorsed the liberal pluralism of the West German state. The Godesberg programme also marked the acceptance of the market economy, embracing the axioms of Keynesian social democracy – the political management of economic growth and full employment – and the extension of democratic principles into the social and economic sphere. It thus combined an acceptance of the post-war order with an

14. Kurt Klotzbach, *Der Weg zur Staatspartei: Programmatik, praktische Politik und Organisation der deutschen Sozialdemokratie 1945 bis 1965* (Berlin/Bonn, 1982), p. 321.

appeal for reform in a formula which was to typify European social democracy in the 1960s and early 1970s.

Ideological overhaul was accompanied by organizational streamlining and strategic change. The Stuttgart congress of 1958 abolished the bureau of salaried functionaries on the executive, replacing it with the praesidium elected within the executive. The praesidium signalled the end of the institutionalized dominance of professional bureaucrats at the apex of the party hierarchy. Composed largely of elected politicians, the new directorate emphasized the electoral orientation of the newly modernized SPD. Strategic reorientation came with the Hanover congress of 1960, which made the final break with Schumacher's strategy of opposition and established a new course towards accommodation with the government in a common front which was ultimately to lead to the Grand Coalition.[15] An important prerequisite for the realization of this strategy was the freedom of the leadership from encumbrance by the party decision-making process. The principle of leader autonomy was spelled out at Hanover, by the new chancellor candidate Willy Brandt. The transition from the principle (however loosely applied) of internal party democracy to that of leadership autonomy was part of a wider change in the SPD from solidarity community to *Volkspartei*.

THE SOCIAL DEMOCRATIC *VOLKSPARTEI*

The key characteristics of the *Volkspartei* are electoral diversity and a highly developed government vocation. In the decade following its transformation, the newly modernized SPD of Willy Brandt succeeded both in widening its electoral appeal and in entering government. Its vote increased steadily from 31.8 per cent in 1957 to 42.7 per cent in 1969 and 45.8 per cent in the election of 1972. Success was due to the party's ability to diversify its electorate; in particular, its ability to mobilize the so-called new middle class of salaried white-collar workers in the burgeoning tertiary sector. Support here compensated for the relative decline of the manual working class in the electorate. Thus the electoral foundation of the social democratic *Volkspartei* was a cross-class alliance of the working class and the *neue Mitte* (new middle class).

15. Bouvier, *Zwischen Godesberg und Grosser Koalition*, pp. 72, 79; Klotzbach, *Der Weg zur Staatspartei*, p. 502.

The electoral renaissance of the SPD provided a platform from which to enter government. In late 1966, the Free Democrats – the junior partner in a coalition with the Christian Democrats – walked out of the government, leaving it without a majority. Seizing the opportunity, the SPD leadership negotiated entry into a Grand Coalition with its Christian Democratic rival. Gaining electoral credibility from its control over the Ministry of Economics and the Foreign Ministry, it was sufficiently strong in 1969 to take over as dominant party in a Social–Liberal coalition with the FDP.

Initially, the Brandt government was very successful, especially in foreign policy. At the height of the Cold War, the SPD had always been at a disadvantage in this policy area, since it was unable to compete with the CDU–CSU in militant anti-communism and pro-American alignment. The onset of a measure of *détente*, however, created a more favourable climate for social democracy. Brandt used the international opening with great skill, in three years of dynamic *Ostpolitik* that brought treaties with the USSR and Poland, and a settlement of post-war borders and diplomatic relations with the GDR. These creative initiatives gave the government prestige abroad and popularity at home. An attempt by the CDU to overthrow it by a parliamentary coup in 1972 boomeranged in an electoral backlash that, for the only time in the history of the Federal Republic, gave the SPD a higher vote than the Union parties. Foreign policy initiatives, however, absorbed the energies of the government, at the expense of domestic reform. After a few initial welfare measures, all significant proposals for change – social, fiscal, educational or industrial – were blocked either by the FDP, or by the threat of veto by the CDU–CSU majority in the *Bundesrat* (upper house).

In 1974 the reformist Brandt was replaced as Chancellor by the pragmatist Helmut Schmidt. By now the economic conjuncture had deteriorated, as the Atlantic world entered recession. Stabilization now became the overriding priority in a strategy of crisis management. The growth of public expenditure was curbed, and monetary supply held tight. There was an occasional limited stimulus for employment – and electoral – purposes, but the general direction of policy was orthodox. The results were, in their own terms, quite successful. The strength of the West German economy withstood the downswing well. Export performance remained buoyant, and growth, although modest, was above the EC average. Schmidt's standing in the electorate was high – a firm leader in a time of crisis, guiding a state that set an example to the world. The SPD thus projected an image of *Modell Deutschland* to voters as proof of its competence.

With the second twist of the recession in the early 1980s, however, the Schmidt government faced harsher choices. In summer 1981, with a large budgetary deficit, rising inflation and unemployment over one million, the government decided to cut social spending and reduce taxes on business. Presenting the budget, Finance Minister Hans Matthöfer announced that the state could no longer underwrite full employment, and that its capacity to influence economic development had to be more modestly assessed.[16] Matthöfer's statement was an acknowledgement of the break-up of Keynesian economics, which in turn signalled the decline of Godesberg social democracy.

With the Godesberg model in decline, the SPD was increasingly subject to fissiparous internal forces, arising from changes in the social composition of the party's membership and electorate dating back to the beginning of the Social–Liberal era. Between 1969 and 1972, party membership had surged from 778,945 to 954,394, an increase of 22.5 per cent. In terms of social composition the new influx was significantly different from the traditional social democratic membership. The new middle class of white-collar employees and civil servants was much more heavily represented, whilst the proportion of manual workers was in steep decline. A similar shift was evident in the party's electorate, indicative of the SPD's success in transforming itself into a broadly based *Volkspartei*. However, it also meant that the party was less cohesive, since the new middle class contained a large new left enclave, posing a radical challenge to the pragmatism of the Godesberg model.

The initial influx of the new left into the SPD occurred through the Extra-Parliamentary Opposition movement (APO), the German variant of the trans-national student left of the late 1960s. After some hesitancy and mistrust, the SPD leadership adopted a strategy of opening up the party to the radical young of the APO movement.[17] The result was a radicalization of the party's youth wing, JUSO, which became the vanguard of a New Left opposition within the SPD. Whilst Brandt was somewhat tolerant of their dissent, Schmidt was contemptuous of what he regarded as Utopian dreaming. Assisted by the elite-dominated hierarchy of the party's organizational structure, he was initially successful in marginalizing the left opposition. By the end of the 1970s, however, two new causes served to catalyse the New Left opposition in the SPD.

16. Douglas Webber, *German Social Democracy in the Economic Crisis: Unemployment and the Politics of Labour Market Policy in the Federal Republic of Germany from 1974 to 1982*, PhD thesis (unpublished), University of Essex, 1984, pp. 99–100.

17. Steffen Gorol, 'Zwischen Integration und Abgrenzung: SPD und studentische Protestbewegung', *Die neue Gesellschaft/Frankfurter Hefte* 35 (1988), 597–615; Kurt J. Shell, 'Extra-Parliamentary Opposition in Post War Germany', *Comparative Politics* XXI (1970), 653–80.

The first of these was the Schmidt government's decision – in the face of the oil price shock – to expand the nuclear energy programme. The second explosive issue was Schmidt's advocacy of strengthening NATO's nuclear strike force with the stationing of Cruise and Pershing missiles in Germany. On both issues there was widespread opposition in the SPD; successive party congresses came close to renouncing government policy.

Faced with discontent within his own party, and with an increasingly hostile FDP seeking coalition openings on the right, the Chancellor's capacity to govern was now exhausted. On 17 September 1982 Schmidt dissolved the coalition. Two weeks later he was succeeded by Helmut Kohl as Chancellor of a Christian–Liberal coalition. Early the following year the *Wende* was consummated in an election in which the SPD vote slumped to 38.2 per cent, its lowest since 1961. The 1983 election saw the emergence of the Greens – a more serious challenge to German social democracy from the left than anything it had experienced since the war.

THE POST-MODERN SPD

Since the end of the Social–Liberal era the SPD has undergone a protracted crisis,[18] struggling to come to terms with social and political change. The social upheaval of the eighties and nineties has been seen by some in terms of a transition towards a new form of society.[19] Post-modern society is characterized by a multifaceted process of social fragmentation. In the primary economic sphere there has been a shift from standardized mass manufacturing towards high technology, specialist production employing a flexible and polyvalent workforce.[20] Alongside this is the continued growth and diversification of the tertiary sector. The diversification of production is reflected also in consumption, where

18. Jacobus Delwaide, 'Postmaterialism and Politics: The "Schmidt SPD" and the Greening of Germany', *German Politics* 2 (1993), 243–69.

19. Dieter Fuchs, *A Metatheory of the Democratic Process*, Wissenschaftszentrum für Sozialforschung, Publication Series, FS III 93; 203 (Berlin, 1993); Claus Offe, 'New Social Movements: Challenging the Boundaries of Institutional Politics', *Social Research* 52 (1989), 865–92.

20. Hans-Georg Betz, *Postmodern Politics in Germany: The Politics of Resentment* (Basingstoke, 1991), p. 11; M. Piore and C. Sabel, *The Second Industrial Divide* (New York, 1984).

new technologies of customization, information processing and marketing have led to market segmentation and cultural differentiation. The production-based class structures of industrial society have progressively given way to much more diffuse and differentiated social formations. Social differentiation – the dissolution of traditional social formations[21] – has undermined the structural foundations of social democracy.

The post-modern SPD retains some of the characteristics of the social democratic *Volkspartei*, but is increasingly subject to the forces of social differentiation. Its electorate is composed of diverse social and cultural milieux rather than the broad yet cohesive social groups of the *Volkspartei*. A pervasive social decomposition is evident in the Balkanization of internal party life, the individualism and egotism of the leadership elite, and the loosely coupled character of the party's organizational system. Social and organizational fragmentation is reflected in a 'department store catalogue' type of programme, with no unifying *Weltanschauung* (world view).

Since the end of the Social–Liberal coalition, the SPD has suffered a steady electoral decline. In the *Bundestag* election of 1983, the party suffered an electoral haemorrhage, losing 1.6 million votes to the CDU and 750,000 votes to the newly emerged Greens. At 38.2 per cent, the SPD share of the vote was the lowest since 1961. In 1987 it dipped still further to 37 per cent; although there was a slight reversal of losses to the CDU, a further 600,000 votes were lost to the Greens. In the unification election of 1990, the SPD vote fell again to 33.5 per cent (35.9 per cent west, 23.6 per cent east). Behind these setbacks lay deep-rooted structural faults in the party's electoral foundations.

The electorate of the post-modern SPD is deeply divided by social differences and value conflicts, in which two main cleavages stand out with particular clarity. The first runs between the traditional bulwark of social democracy in the old industrial working class and the outposts of a newly emergent post-materialist middle class. The 'post-materialist revolution' was first identified by Ronald Inglehart[22] and can be expressed as follows:

> As a society makes substantial progress in addressing traditional economic and security needs, a growing share of the public shifts their attention to

21. Betz, *Postmodern Politics*, p. 16; U. Beck, 'Beyond Status and Class: Will there be an Individualized Class Society?', in V. Mega, D. Misgeld and N. Stehr, eds, *Modern German Sociology* (New York, 1987), pp. 340–55.

22. Ronald Inglehart, *The Silent Revolution: Changing Values and Political Styles among Western Publics* (Princeton, NJ, 1977).

> post-material goals that are still in short supply, such as the quality of life, self expression and personal freedom.[23]

Inglehart initially saw this development as an opening of electoral opportunity for parties of the left, provided they were able to appeal to the new groups without alienating their traditional support. This assessment, however, greatly underestimated the difficulty of integrating the post-materialist New Left electorate with the traditional constituency of social democracy.

A second cleavage line runs between the affluent and upwardly mobile, orientated towards individual achievement and modernity, and the economically vulnerable, more inclined towards traditional values and social security. This cleavage presented a dilemma for the SPD. Whilst its old core values of social solidarity continued to appeal to the security orientation of the traditional milieux, they were antithetical to the achievement-orientated sections of the electorate.[24] Electoral strategy in the eighties and nineties revolved around largely unsuccessful attempts to reconcile the disparate interests and aspirations of these different constituencies.

The diversity of the SPD electorate is reflected also in internal party life. The relative stability of the Schmidt era had broken up by 1986, with a sharp increase in the representation of the 'affluence generation' from which the post-materialist New Left is drawn. This shift to the left was particularly pronounced in the *mittlere Basis* of intermediate-level party office holders. The 1986 party congress saw a sharp turnover in the party executive, with a number of prominent old-guard figures displaced in favour of the New Left. This group is marked by its tendency to adopt rigid Utopian positions, placing self-gratification before party objectives.[25] The result is a weakening of party cohesion which in turn gives freer play to policy differences.

This loss of cohesion is also evident in the party's top leadership elite. This is drawn mainly from the group known as the *Enkel* (grandchildren), after their close relationship with Willy Brandt. The most prominent of the circle were minister-presidents in the *Länder*: the charismatic and mercurial Oskar Lafontaine (Saarland), Bjorn Engholm (Schleswig-Holstein), Gerhard Schröder (Lower Saxony) and Rudolf Scharping (Rhineland-Palatinate). Broadly speaking, of the 1968 gener-

23. R. J. Dalton, 'The German Voter', in William E. Paterson, Gordon Smith and Peter Merkl, eds, *Developments in West German Politics* (London, 1989), p. 113.

24. SPD, *Parteivorstand, Analyse und Konsequenzen: Auswertung der Bundestagswahl 1987* (Bonn, 1987); Stephen A. Padgett, 'The German Social Democrats: A Redefinition of Social Democracy or Bad Godesberg Mark II?', *West European Politics* 16 (1993), 20–38.

25. *Der Spiegel*, 14/9/1992.

ation, a number had been leaders of the radical JUSO organization of the 1970s. However, their affinity with the New Left is tempered with a strong streak of pragmatism and strategic flexibility.[26]

It is from this group that the 1990s leadership elite was drawn: Lafontaine ran as chancellor candidate in 1990; Engholm was party chairman from 1991–93 and was succeeded by Scharping, who ran as chancellor candidate in 1994. Lafontaine became chairman in November 1995. The new leadership elite is less cohesive than the generation of Brandt and Schmidt. Thus decisions which were previously taken on the basis of informal mutual understanding among like-minded individuals are now subject to acrimonious public discussion.[27] According to one critical observer, the new generation is 'made of a quite different, less robust material; they are more spontaneous and independent; they confess their doubts more readily in public; they are bon viveurs, and enjoy cultural events; they prefer an evening at the opera to laborious reports and discussions at a regional party congress.'[28]

The formal organizational structures of the SPD are those of the post-Godesberg party: a hierarchical, centrally led, closed organizational system. In the last decade, however, these structures have degenerated into a 'loosely coupled system' – a 'complex, mixed organizational type'[29] which no longer corresponds to the statutory ordering of internal party life. Organizational degeneration stems from the social and cultural heterogeneity of the party, and fragmentation along the lines of generation, gender, social class and lifestyle. Internal party life is thus characterized by the formation of temporary and unstable coalitions and alliances amongst a disparate variety of cliques, factions, patronage groups and interest organizations.[30]

Prominent amongst these are the *Arbeitsgemeinschaft für Arbeitnehmerfragen* (AfA) (Working Group for Labour Affairs), formed as a defensive response of the SPD labour wing to the rise of the New Left; JUSOs (Young Socialists), with a very pronounced new left orientation; and

26. Tilman Fichter, 'Political Generations in the Federal Republic', *New Left Review* 186 (1991), 78–88.

27. S. J. Silvia, 'Loosely Coupled Anarchy: the Fragmentation of the Left', in Stephen A. Padgett, ed., *Parties and Party Systems in the New Germany* (Aldershot, 1993), pp. 171–89.

28. Peter Lösche and Franz Walter, *Die SPD: Klassenpartei, Volkspartei, Quotenpartei: Zur Entwicklung der Sozialdemokratie von Weimar bis zur deutsche Vereinigung* (Darmstadt, 1992), p. 383.

29. A. Mintzel and H. Oberreuter, 'Zukunftsperspektiven des Parteiensystems', in Alf Mintzel and Heinrich Oberreuter, eds, *Parteien in der Bundesrepublik* (Opladen, 1992), pp. 463–4.

30. Lösche and Walter, *Die SPD*, pp. 380–6.

the *Arbeitsgemeinschaft Sozialdemokratischer Frauen* (ASF) (Working Group for Social Democratic Women). Gender distinctions in the SPD have been formalized through the introduction of a quota system allocating 40 per cent of party posts and electoral mandates to women. Internal party groupings are not new to the SPD, but over the last decade they have become progressively institutionalized. Recent reforms allow the *Arbeitsgemeinschaften* to accept members from outside the party, and to submit congress resolutions. The decentralizing reforms proposed under the *SPD 2000* programme issued by the then party business manager Karlheinz Blessing may serve to strengthen auxiliary organizations still further.[31] The institutionalization of social and cultural milieux in the interests of openness and decentralization threatens to lead to a form of Balkanization or fragmentation in the internal life of the party.[32]

The organizational fragmentation of the SPD runs parallel to a process of *Tertiarisierung* – the transformation of the party (in common with other large parties) into a professionally and functionally specialized service sector organization for the provision of 'political services'.[33] With the 'commercialization' of politics, and the increasing exploitation of information and marketing technologies in electoral strategy and planning, the party apparatus has become a centre for technical expertise,[34] backed by the quasi-academic social science of the state-financed party foundation (the Friederich Ebert Stiftung). Technical sophistication is a prerequisite for the mobilization of the segmented post-modern electorate, but it has led to an increasing remoteness between apparatus on the one hand and membership and electorate on the other.

The disorientation of the post-modern SPD is also evident at the programmatic level. The programme review which the SPD undertook between 1984 and 1989[35] was designed to bridge the gulf between the old left and the new, and to reconcile the value conflict between social solidarity and individual achievement. Economics provoked a particularly sharp conflict between social democratic orthodoxy and New Left hostility towards market capitalism.[36] Ultimately, though, the Berlin programme did little more than reiterate the economic orthodoxies of Godesberg social democracy. Onto these were grafted the new political issues of environment, the humanization of the workplace, gender equal-

31. Karl-Heinz Blesing, *SPD 2000: die Modernisierung der SPD* (Marburg, 1993).
32. Silvia, 'Loosely Coupled Anarchy', pp. 185–6.
33. Mintzel and Oberreuter, 'Zukunftsperspektiven des Parteiensystems', pp. 493–4.
34. Elmar Wiesendahl, 'Volksparteien im Abstieg', *APUZ: Beilage zur Wochenzeitung Das Parlament* B 34–35 (1992), 12–3.
35. Gerard Braunthal, 'The 1989 Basic Programme of the German Social Democratic Party', *Polity* XXV (1993), 375–99; Padgett, 'The German Social Democrats', 20–38.
36. *Frankfurter Rundschau*, 6/1/1989.

ity and commitments to a 'critical dialogue between elected representatives and citizens'.[37] Rather than reconciling old and new politics, therefore, the new programme merely counterposed the two positions. Incorporating the conflicting concerns of diverse intra-party groups, the programme resembled a 'department store catalogue . . . contradictory in style and argumentation . . . more of an internal party scorecard than a statement of party policy'.[38]

Attempts to redefine the principles of social solidarity to give greater emphasis to individual achievement were led by Oskar Lafontaine and the *Enkel*. In an attack on party and labour movement orthodoxy, they argued for a more positive approach towards technological development, structural change and economic success. The centrepiece of their agenda was a new labour market order, combining a reduced working week with deregulation. It was presented in very ambitious terms as 'a concrete Utopia which can move millions . . . a human idea capable of binding together different strata in society'.[39] The attempt to modernize party policy in defiance of labour movement orthodoxy was met by a heterogeneous coalition of the SPD's labour wing, the conventional left and the right, which was largely successful in repulsing this attack upon tradition. In the new programme, Lafontaine's ideas were severely attenuated, and were hedged around with qualifications designed to make them more acceptable to the traditionalists.

THE SPD IN THE *WENDE*

As the drama of the collapse of communism and the GDR unfolded in the winter of 1989–90, it appeared that the 'wild card' of German unification might provide the SPD with a way out of the impasse it had reached. There were good historical reasons for thinking that eastern Germany would prove to be natural electoral terrain for the Social Democrats. Prussia and Saxony had been strongholds of the labour movement in the Weimar Republic. The overwhelming majority of the population was Protestant, and in West Germany, SPD regional strength had always been strongly correlated with Protestantism. Moreover, the social structure of the GDR was much more heavily dominated by

37. Padgett, 'The German Social Democrats', 33.

38. Silvia, 'Loosely Coupled Anarchy', p. 175; Peter Lösche, 'Zur Metamorphose der politischen Parteien in Deutschland', *Gewerkschaftliche Monatshefte* 43 (1992), 535.

39. *Wirtschaftswoche*, 29/4/1988.

the industrial working class than that of the Federal Republic. Political, social and confessional factors all seemed to point towards social democratic hegemony beyond the Elbe. These expectations were reinforced by opinion poll results which gave the SPD a substantial lead in the run-up to the GDR *Volkskammer* elections of March 1990.

The failure of the SPD to realize its full potential in the east resulted in part from the profound ambivalence of the left in the old Federal Republic towards unification. A number of factors have been adduced to account for this ambivalence. First, in its recoil from the Third Reich, the post-war left had consistently underestimated the potential of nationalism as an agent of collective identity. With its emphasis on internationalism, particularist or naturalistic forms of identification were alien to its vocabulary.[40] Second, the SPD's own approach to the national question, as it had developed in the 1970s, concentrated on efforts to persuade the GDR regime to improve human rights and freedom of movement for its people in exchange for recognition – a line extended into the 1980s with a second *Ostpolitik* of active engagement with the GDR in pursuit of *détente*. In its time, this approach had been innovative and popular in both East and West. Having led the way out of the impasse of the Cold War, however, the SPD was slow to adjust to the degeneration of communism in Eastern Europe, and the collapse of the GDR, whose acceptance it had pioneered.[41] Finally, on the margins of the party, some also felt misgivings about the imposition of the constitution of the Federal Republic on the east, under Article 23, as the blunt instrument of unification. Critics argued that a new constitution, drafted by a convention of representatives from both German states and ratified by a referendum, would be a more democratic procedure.

The Christian Democrats, on the other hand, were able to invoke their long-standing commitments to unification. The Bonn government, moreover, had complete freedom of manoeuvre, and Chancellor Kohl was able to command the political agenda, moving decisively to conclude a deal with Gorbachev, and prevailing on the *Bundesbank* to accept a form of currency union designed to consolidate CDU support in the east. The SPD was thus left behind, carping and critical of a unification

40. Andrei Markovits, 'The West German 68-ers Encounter the Events of 1989: More than a Numerical Reversal', *German Politics* 1 (1992), 13–30; Herbert Kitschelt, 'The 1990 German Federal Election and the National Unification', *West European Politics* 14 (1991), 121–48.

41. W. E. Paterson, 'Foreign and Security Policy', in Gordon Smith, William Paterson and Peter Merkl, eds, *Developments in German Politics* (Basingstoke, 1989), pp. 192–210.

policy which was both acceptable to the international community and legitimate in the east.

Ambivalence towards unification was expressed most emphatically by Oskar Lafontaine, the SPD's chancellor candidate for the 1990 election. This brought him into conflict not only with the newly formed east German SPD which favoured rapid unification, but also with other sections of the leadership of the party in the west. Brandt in particular wholeheartedly embraced German unity – 'Jetzt wächst zusammen, was zusammengehört' (that which belongs together is now growing together) – and pleaded with the party to do likewise. Although the Berlin Congress of December 1989 accepted the principle, the party's position in the election campaign was indelibly stamped by its chancellor candidate. Emphasizing the economic burden of unification for the west, and criticizing the terms of the economic and monetary union, Lafontaine urged the party to oppose the unification treaties in the *Bundestag*. This issue publicly divided the SPD, with party and parliamentary group chairman Vogel, along with the majority of the parliamentary party and most of the SPD minister-presidents in the *Länder*, combining to overrule Lafontaine. In view of the historic importance of unification, conflict between the main body of the party leadership and its chancellor candidate was electorally damaging, especially in the east.

Confounding the early poll predictions, the result of the GDR *Volkskammer* election was an endorsement of unification on the terms set by the Bonn government. The CDU-led 'Allianz für Deutschland' polled 48.1 per cent against 21.8 per cent for the SPD. For the Social Democrats, the results of the first all-German elections of December 1990 were similarly disastrous. In the east the SPD won a derisory 23.6 per cent against 43.4 per cent for the CDU. The unexpected success of the *Partei des Demokratischen Sozialismus* (PDS) – the democratized successor to the communist SED – added a new split to the already fragmented German left, further disadvantaging the SPD. In both elections, manual workers in the east confounded earlier expectations by voting overwhelming for the CDU.

THE SPD IN EASTERN GERMANY

Unlike the other major parties, the SPD did not exist in the GDR. Under Soviet coercion, the party had been absorbed into the communist

SED in 1946. The new party emerged in the early stages of the break-up of the Honecker regime in late summer 1989. Its roots were in the loosely formed citizens' movements surrounding the Protestant church, from which an appeal was launched (26 August 1989) by a four-man 'initiative group' consisting of three church pastors, Markus Meckel, Martin Gutzeit and Arndt Noack, and the historian Ibrahim Böhme.[42] After some hurried statute drafting in September, the formal establishment of the party took place at a conspiratorial meeting of around 40 founder members in Schwante, near Frankfurt an der Oder, on 7 October 1989. Its title, Social Democratic Party in the GDR (SDP), reflected a guarded attitude towards unification, and towards the SPD in Bonn. The founders of the SDP in the GDR were anxious to avoid subordination to the larger party, and averse to the hierarchical organization structures of the party in the west. For its part, the SPD in Bonn was slow to recognize the new party as a partner, its long-standing relationship with the SED discouraging it from official contact with the GDR opposition. It was not until after the fall of the Berlin Wall, as the unification movement gathered unstoppable momentum, that the two parties concluded a formal partnership agreement, with the GDR party adopting the title of its west German counterpart and electing Brandt as honorary president.

The relationship was consummated shortly before German unity, with a unification congress in Berlin on 26/27 September 1990. Given the organizational fragility of the infant party in the east, the merger was bound to be grossly unequal. Some attempt was made to redress the balance through the election of the emergent leader of the eastern SPD, Wolfgang Thierse, as a deputy chairman of the SPD. For a transitional period to 1993, the eastern *Länder* were allocated over-proportional representation in party congresses. Moreover, the federal structure of the party, and its strong institutional base at *Land* level, gave the SPD in the eastern *Länder* some sense of its own identity. Nevertheless, the 'merger' has to be seen in terms of institutional transfer, and the absorption of the new party within the western SPD.

The founders of the SDP in the GDR possessed a distinctive conception of the party they wanted to create, central to which was a preoccupation with internal democracy.[43] In a number of ways, the first Social

42. Peter Joachim Lapp, *Das Zusammenwachsen des deutschen Parteiengefüges*, Friedrich Ebert Stiftung, Forum deutsche Einheit Nr 13 (Bonn, 1993), p. 29.

43. K. Elmer, 'Vor- und Wirkungsgeschichte des Organisationsstatuts der SDP', in Dieter Dowe, ed., *Von der Bürgerbewegung zur Partei: die Gründung der Sozialdemokratie in der DDR*, Friedrich Ebert Stiftung, Reihe Gesprächskreis Geschichte, Heft 3 (Bonn, 1993), pp. 29–39.

Democrats in the east resembled the Greens in the Federal Republic in their early years. Their origins in loosely constituted citizens' movements, and their recoil from the experience of the GDR, engendered a mistrust of the centralized, hierarchical and bureaucratic structures of orthodox parties. The first statues of the SDP in the GDR sought to create 'a party of a new type'[44] characterized by *Basisdemokratie*: decentralization, openness, a collegial, group-orientated structure and a strict division between party office and electoral mandate.[45] After the merger, these aspirations were constrained by the organizational structures inherited from the west.

Incorporation in the larger party meant that it was difficult for the SPD in the new *Länder* to maintain an identity of its own. As in the west, the eastern *Land* party organizations exercise a certain degree of autonomy, but there is no formal party apparatus for the collective representation of eastern interests or perspectives. At the informal level, however, there are regular *Ostsprechertreffen* – meetings of the SPD *Landtag* group spokesmen for the specialist policy areas. The chairmen of the *Land* party organizations and *Landtag* group chairman also meet quite regularly. In the *Bundestag*, deputies from the east constitue a sort of *Unterfraktion*, meeting regularly on an informal basis.

In the absence of formal structures of its own, the SPD in the new *Länder* derives some 'eastern profile' from its leadership. In contrast to the CDU, the SPD resisted the 'parachuting' of westerners into top leadership positions. All SPD *Land* party chairmen and *Landtag* group chairmen are easterners. With very few exceptions, all members of the parliamentary groups are from the east. In Brandenburg (the only *Land* in which the SPD held power in the first post-unification state governments), Minister-President Manfred Stolpe and a substantial number of his government were easterners. All SPD business managers in the new *Länder* are westerners. The impact of the indigenous leadership, however, is reduced by its lack of experience and public profile. The only figures commanding wide public attention are Stolpe, Regine Hildebrandt (Brandenburg Minister for Labour and Social Affairs) and Wolfgang Thierse (SPD Vice-Chairman).

The social composition of the SPD in the east is difficult to ascertain with accuracy, due to the absence of reliable data in *Land* party offices. What data are available suggest that the membership is dominated by white-collar workers (c. 40 per cent), with manual workers (c. 20 per cent), pensioners (c. 10 per cent) and the unemployed (10 per cent) the

44. S. Reiche, 'Motivationen der Gründergeneration', in Dowe, ed., *Von der Bürgerbewegung zur Partei*, p. 20.
45. Elmer, 'Vor- und Wirkungsgeschichte des Organisationsstatuts', pp. 30–1.

other significant groups. Amongst white-collar workers, the so-called technical intelligentsia of teachers, engineers and doctors is heavily represented. These social groups made up the second wave of recruits, bringing a pragmatic, 'problem-solving' orientation to the new party. This was alien to many of its founders, many of whom either were pushed aside by the new elements, or withdrew disappointed from the local and regional leadership of the party they had created. Thus the *Pfarrerpartei* (party of the priests) has given way to the party of the technical intelligentsia.

The political profile of the party in the new *Länder* is less clearly defined than in the west. Ideological identities have not yet crystallized, at either the group or individual levels. Ideological identities based on left/right, old politics/new politics are not immediately recognizable in the eastern SPD. Thus, the western model of individuals and groups adopting consistent issue positions corresponding to a clearly defined *Weltanschauung* is not fully applicable in the east. With this caveat, however, it is possible to identify three broad ideological positions in the SPD in the east: a *Basisdemokratie*-orientated humanism associated with the founders of the party; the pragmatic, old politics perspective of the technical intelligentsia; and an enclave of traditional left-of-centre social democracy.

In common with the other parties in the east, the SPD faces severe organizational problems, stemming from an inability to recruit a mass membership. Early membership estimates of around 100,000 (February 1990) were based on attendance at inaugural meetings or signatures of support, and proved inauthentic. With the introduction of proper documentation based on formal membership, the figure fell sharply to just over 30,000. By 1993, membership had fallen further, stabilizing at around 27,000. The proportion of voters in the east who are SPD members is 1.2 per cent as against 6.9 per cent in the west.

Two explanations have been advanced to account for the low level of party membership in the east. First, the economic and social instability accompanying the transformation process created widespread insecurity, leading to an individualistic preoccupation with private affairs over participation in public life. The aversion to the public sphere has also been related to the legacy of state penetration of public life under the GDR regime. The second explanation centres on the poor penetration of the SPD in the manual working class, which it relates to the absence of supportive social and organizational infrastructures. In the west, SPD membership rests heavily upon bonds of identification engendered by the party's historic links to the labour movement. Although trade unions have recruited successfully in the new *Länder* (at the beginning of 1993 (trade union membership was 3.4 million), they are much less politicized than in the traditional model. The networks between the unions and the SPD are correspondingly weaker, particularly at grassroots level.

The low organizational density of the SPD in the east has a number of implications. Revenue (derived in large part from membership subscriptions) falls far short of the requirements of maintaining a western type of mass party organization. Hitherto the shortfall has been met by financial support from the party in Bonn, and from a special levy on membership subscriptions in the west. Of the 18 salaried party officials employed by the Brandenburg party (with the largest membership of all the new *Länder*), only two or three can be financed from *Land* party revenues. Human resources are also scarce, and in many areas the SPD is hardly able to sustain the functions associated with the mass party. In the mass party model, members serve a communication function as 'multipliers' in the wider social context. A low level of membership reduces the party's capacity for electoral mobilization.

The main electoral weakness of the SPD in the east is its inability to penetrate the working-class electorate. Under the Third Reich and GDR regimes, the connective tissue between working class, labour movement and social democracy appears to have withered irretrievably. In the *Volkskammer* election of March 1990, the SPD suffered some of its worst results in Saxony – the historic working-class heartland of pre-war social democracy.[46] In the industrial cities of Leipzig, Chemnitz and Dresden, it polled 21.5 per cent, 15.6 per cent and 9.7 per cent respectively. Across the five new *Länder* in the 1990 *Bundestag* election, the SPD polled only 24.6 per cent of the working-class vote, against 51.2 per cent attracted by the CDU. The SPD electorate was evenly spread between manual workers and the new middle class, where it polled 22.0 per cent.[47] The best electoral performance was in Brandenburg, which has the lowest density of manual workers of the five new *Länder*, and a high concentration of white-collar functionaries of the old regime. The organizational weakness of the party in the east, and its reliance on white-collar voters, has led some observers to characterize the SPD as little more than a *kleinbürgerlicher Wahlverein* (petty bourgeois electoral association).[48]

46. Franz Walter, 'Sachsen – ein Stammland der Sozialdemokratie?', *Politische Vierteljahresschrift* 32 (1991), 207–31.

47. R. J. Dalton and W. Bürklin, 'The German Party System and the Future', in Russell J. Dalton, ed., *The New Germany Votes* (Oxford, 1993), p. 244.

48. Rolf Schneider, 'Die SPD-Ost ist ein kleinbürgerlicher Wahlverein', *Die neue Gesellschaft/Frankfurter Hefte* 39 (1992), 517.

THE SPD SINCE UNIFICATION

The susceptibility of the SPD to conflict was graphically illustrated by its response to the contentious issues arising out of Germany's post-unification traumas. Indeed the inability of the SPD to exploit deepening economic recession and successive political crises in the governing coalition was due in large part to its own internal disunity. By 1993, unemployment had risen to 3.3 million (7.1 per cent in the west, 14.7 in the east), the economy was contracting by around 2 per cent and the budget deficit was spiralling out of control. Moreover, there was a growing perception that the downturn was neither a temporary effect of unification, nor part of the international economic cycle, but reflected the structural condition of the new German economy. Pessimism over economic prospects was compounded by disarray in the governing coalition and the perception of a power vacuum at the centre of government. Far from being able to capitalize on these uniquely favourable circumstances, however, the SPD was itself tainted by the syndrome of *Parteiverdrossenheit*, a profound disaffection towards the entire 'political class'.[49]

In addition to economic recession and government unpopularity, the Social Democrats might also have been expected to derive an advantage from their structural majority in the *Bundesrat* (upper house). This placed the SPD in a strategic position in the legislative process, especially in relation to constitutional amendments and financial legislation in which the *Bundesrat* has a key role. However, Kohl was able to counter the SPD's hold on the *Bundesrat* by offering incentives for social democratic *Länder* to break ranks and vote with the government. Thus in 1992, Brandenburg secured additional revenues by voting for government measures to increase VAT, undermining the SPD's *Steuerlüge* (tax-lie) campaign against the Chancellor.

The SPD's governing role in the *Länder* also meant that it was obliged to acquiesce in policy compromise, thereby shouldering responsibility in a quasi-coalition with the government.[50] This was particularly evident in the 'Solidarity Pact' for financial stabilization, negotiated between the governing parties, the Federal SPD and state governments in spring 1993.[51] For some Social Democrats the formalization of cooperation

49. Werner A. Perger, 'Ein Winter der Ohnmacht', *Die Zeit*, No. 6, 5/2/1993, p. 6.
50. R. Sturm, 'The Territorial Dimension of the New German Party System', in Padgett, ed., *Parties and Party Systems*, pp. 120–2.
51. Razeen Sally and Douglas Webber, 'The Solidarity Pact: a Case Study in the Politics of the Unified Germany', *German Politics* 3 (1994), 18–46.

through a Grand Coalition represented an attractive route towards government power. Signalling its readiness for coalition, the SPD adopted a *Schmusekurs* (soft-soap approach) towards Kohl, at the expense of effective opposition. Thus, despite his unpopularity, Kohl was consistently able to outmanoeuvre the SPD.

His ability to do so was greatly enhanced by the internal schisms in the SPD over the contentious issues arising out of Germany's post-unification traumas. The Chancellor was able to turn his reliance on opposition consent to his own advantage by deflecting attention away from the divisions in the government and towards the disunity and indiscipline in the SPD. This was graphically illustrated by the party's response to the emotionally charged issue of immigration following the explosion of racially inspired violence in a number of German cities in 1992. The debate over a constitutional amendment restricting legal rights to political asylum precipitated a bitter and debilitating conflict in the SPD. As party chairman, Engholm initially remained somewhat detached from the debate, reluctant to commit himself to measures for which he was uncertain of winning majority party support. With his leadership under critical scrutiny, however, and with the SPD driven into an untenable corner, he reversed his personal position, urging the party to accept the need for more restrictive asylum laws. At a special congress in November 1992 the SPD endorsed the principle of constitutional change, subject to a number of qualifications. The obscurity of the resolution, however, was indicative of the continuing ambivalence and disunity of the party on this issue. A similar disarray was also exposed in the debate over Germany's new security role, and constitutional amendments to enable German forces to participate in UN operations.

Disunity in the SPD almost certainly contributed to Engholm's decision to resign as party chairman and chancellor candidate in May 1993, following revelations of a relatively trivial impropriety in his conduct before a parliamentary commission of inquiry into the scandal surrounding his opponent in the Schleswig-Holstein election of 1987. Frustrated in his attempts to lead the SPD towards the political centre, and undermined by the fractiousness of the party, Engholm lacked the will to withstand the affair.

In the contest for his succession, the two main candidates represented the conflicting tendencies in the SPD. Identified with the New Left, Gerhard Schröder, state premier of Lower Saxony, stood for a strategy of coalition with the Greens. Rudolf Scharping, his counterpart in Rhineland-Palatinate, was more centrist, and indicated a preference for coalition with the centre-right parties. For the first time, the choice was put to a membership election. The result of the poll was a convincing win for Scharping, whose low-key style and moderate outlook seemed a safer option to a rattled party. In advance of the Federal election of October 1994, Scharping rallied the SPD, reasserting some of its lost discipline, but with disunity never far beneath the surface, this was not enough to save the party from a fourth successive defeat.

CONCLUSION

It is clear from the foregoing analysis that the contemporary SPD can no longer be described as a social democratic *Volkspartei*. Its capacity for electoral integration is now greatly reduced. From a plateau of around 42 per cent between 1969 and 1980, its share of the vote fell steeply, stabilizing at around one-third of the electorate. The cross-class alliance of manual workers and the new middle class which sustained the social democratic *Volkspartei* has been undermined by the forces of social change. Electoral decomposition is the outcome of the break-up of customary social formations in an increasingly post-industrial society which creates new opportunities for some strata whilst marginalizing and disorientating others, and which divides traditional from post-modern milieux along generational and cultural lines.

Social fragmentation is evident also in the Balkanization of internal party life, in the individualism and egotism within the leadership elite, and in the loosely coupled character of the party's organizational system. The intra-party distribution of power is now much more diffuse, and the SPD is no longer the tightly structured, elite-dominated party of Brandt and Schmidt. Reduced organizational discipline is reflected in programmatic and policy conflict between the old left and the new, and between the traditional ethos of social solidarity and the modernizers' orientation towards individual achievement and economic success. These conflicts were evident in the 1980s' programme review, and in the contentious issues accompanying unification and Germany's post-unification trauma.

In the eastern *Länder*, the party's capacity for electoral mobilization and organizational penetration is very restricted. The SPD is very much a party of the old Federal Republic, its roots in the residual structures of a traditional industrial society, entwined with the outgrowth of the New Left of the 'affluence generation'. The uneasy blend of labour movement orthodoxy and new left politics has a very limited appeal in the east. The SPD in the new *Länder* cannot be expected to evolve towards a model with its roots in the historical experience of the west.

Whilst the SPD no longer corresponds to the model of the social democratic *Volkspartei*, it is not yet clear how to conceptualize its new form, or to predict its future. The term 'post-modern social democratic party' has been used above to indicate the social, organizational and ideological decomposition of the SPD in the 1990s, and its increasing remoteness from society. Its future seems to lie either in the continuation of the current tendency towards fragmentation, or in a progressive reconstitution in the form of a broadly based *Wahlverein* on the American model – a road on which the more electorally successful parties of the European left have already embarked, but which the SPD at present seems unwilling to contemplate.

CHAPTER TEN

The Soviet Union's Policy Towards West Germany, 1945–90[1]

Terry McNeill

The USSR's policy towards West Germany during the period from 1945 to 1990 cannot be viewed in isolation, but must be seen in the context of Moscow's policy towards the West as a whole, in which its relations with Washington figure most prominently.[2] However, the Federal Republic of Germany's (FRG) special significance for the Soviet Union has to be understood in terms of specific historical and geographical factors, in addition to the sensitivity associated with partitioning and its symbolic importance as a consequence of war. These factors include Germany's invasions of Russia, of which the last one, in 1941, almost brought about the destruction of the Soviet Union, and led to some 20 million Soviet casualties; and, secondly, the FRG's pivotal location on the divide between East and West during the Cold War, bordering directly on the territory of the Warsaw Treaty Organization (WTO). Thus the FRG had unique features which determined the character of its relationship with the Soviet Union across the years, and placed it on a different footing from those relations that existed between Moscow and other states of the Western Alliance that bordered on the former Soviet empire, such as Turkey, Norway and Greece.[3]

Soviet policy towards West Germany since 1945 may be divided roughly into five phases. In the first period, from 1945 to 1955, Moscow attempted variously to bring West Germany under its influence, to prevent it from becoming rearmed, and from being integrated into the Western Alliance. When this failed, the Soviet Union established diplomatic ties with the FRG in 1955. This ushered in the second phase, in which the policy adopted was one of co-existence coupled

1. I am deeply indebted to Dr Sally Harris of Hull University for her invaluable research support in preparing this analysis.

2. Angela Stent, 'The USSR and Western Europe', in Robbin F. Laird and Erik P. Hoffmann, eds, *Soviet Foreign Policy in a Changing World* (New York, 1986), p. 443.

3. Roland Smith, 'Soviet Policy Towards West Germany', *Adelphi Papers No. 203* (Winter 1985), 4.

with containment which was rigorously applied, on all fronts, in a determined Soviet bid to attain legitimization of the new *status quo* in Europe. For Moscow, Germany now had to remain divided, for a united neutral Germany would have meant East Berlin relinquishing its form of government, which would in turn have entailed dangers for the cohesion of the Eastern Bloc.[4]

In the late 1960s, in response to external political factors and Bonn's new *Ostpolitik*, the third phase of Moscow's policy began, which revealed itself in a softer approach towards the FRG. The policy was still one of containment and co-existence, but was more flexible and accompanied by a substantially increased level of dialogue and exchanges. The fourth phase began in 1979 when it became clear that, not least due to the Soviet invasion of Afghanistan and the divisive debate about Intermediate-Range Nuclear Forces (INF) and their implications for European security, a rejuvenation of East–West *détente* was impossible. Moscow did its utmost to exploit NATO differences and concerns, while Bonn devoted its efforts to trying to preserve the fruits of its *détente* with Moscow and East Berlin. The final phase commenced in 1987 with Gorbachev's new initiatives towards Bonn, as part of the radical 'new thinking' in Soviet foreign policy that helped to restore their bilateral relations to what they were in the early 1970s. This period ended with the German revolution, the breaching of the Berlin Wall in November 1989 and the subsequent unification of Germany in 1990. These five phases will be discussed in depth in what follows.

SOVIET ATTITUDES TOWARDS WEST GERMANY, 1945–55

The four-power policy on the future of Germany, agreed at Potsdam in 1945, was one which led to Germany being demilitarized with its military formations disbanded, and the country divided into four Occupation Zones. At the same time, it left open the possibility of a united Germany and a central government. It was also agreed at Potsdam, on the issue of reparations, that German industries should be dismantled, and that Russia would receive a share of the industrial equipment from

4. Herbert Ammon and Peter Brandt, 'The Relevance of the German Question for Peace in Europe', in Rudolf Steinke and Michel Vale, eds, *Germany Debates Defense: The NATO Alliance at the Crossroads* (New York, 1983), pp. 89–90.

the western zone, in addition to receiving assets from its own zone of occupation.[5] It soon became clear, however, that this basic agreement needed to be extended and adjusted in response to changing political requirements. It also gradually became apparent that the four-power solidarity on German policy could not be maintained. Centralization and reparations proved to be the divisive issues.[6] By the end of 1946, any possibility of achieving Soviet cooperation on the administration of Germany, as on most other outstanding problems, was effectively ruled out. George Kennan perceived the situation thus: 'Russian rulers sought security . . . only in the patient but deadly struggle for total destruction of a rival power, never in compacts and compromises with it.'[7]

The principal underlying area of disagreement lay in the fact that Moscow's fundamental long-term strategy for Europe, including Germany, conflicted sharply with that of the three Western powers, both ideologically and politically. Soviet President Kalinin expounded his country's policy in unequivocal terms in August 1945; it was to deepen 'cooperation between the peace-loving Socialist powers' and to 'overtake and surpass the most developed countries of Europe and the United States'.[8] The potential Soviet threat to Western Europe in its demobilized and impoverished economic state, posed by Stalin's advancing 'satellization' and Moscow's retention of some 4.5 million men under arms, had been recognized by Churchill as early as May 1945.[9]

By 1947, Moscow's hegemonic aspirations towards Germany seemed to be patently clear. At the four-power Moscow Conference on the future of that country, which opened on 1 March 1947, the Soviet Union was determined to accept nothing less than a unitary solution for Germany, in order to build a socialist state based on 'democratic centralism'. Moscow saw a socialist system as being the only means of securing control by a central German government. A federal solution, the Soviet leaders believed, would only enable reactionary forces to remain entrenched in individual states, as happened after 1919.[10] The conference closed with no agreement, as did the later Four-Power London Conference of 25 November–15 December 1947, which was

5. Edward Fursdon, *The European Defence Community: A History* (London, 1980), pp. 42–3.

6. Timothy P. Ireland, *Creating the Entangling Alliance: The Origins of the North Atlantic Treaty Organisation* (London, 1981), pp. 18–19.

7. Quoted in *Foreign Relations of the United States* (hereafter: *FRUS*), 1946, Vol. 6, p. 699.

8. Quoted in Anthony Nutting, *Europe Will Not Wait* (London, 1960), p. 8.

9. Lord Ismay, *NATO, The First Five Years 1949–1954* (Paris, 1954), pp. 3–4.

10. *Germany and the Moscow Conference, March 1 1949*, UDC Publications (London, 1947), p. 17.

characterized by hostile exchanges, not least in relation to the Soviets' insistent call for $10 billion in reparations, and for the subjugation of much of German industry to Moscow's control.[11] The Western Allies dismissed this out of hand, not least because they realized that an economically crippled entity in the centre of Europe would be an unstable and perhaps a dangerously contagious presence.[12] It would also have prevented the revival of a Germany able to boost Western European recovery.[13] The failure of this conference marked the end of serious East–West attempts to reach agreement on Germany's future. The American leadership suspected that the Soviets' aim was to deploy a variety of devices to remove the Western powers from Germany, and then set up a communist state. They therefore resolved to take the lead in encouraging Western states to pursue their own security arrangements in western Germany, and to strengthen their position there.[14]

The impasse reached at the London Conference of December 1947 did much to ensure America's subsequent commitment to Western Europe's security. Its failure, combined with the Soviet offensives involving the Prague coup in February 1948, the Berlin blockade in June 1948 and Stalin's efforts to draw Norway into Moscow's sphere of influence,[15] provided the impetus for the consolidation of the western occupation zones of Germany, and the inclusion of western Germany into a new integrated Europe.[16] At the Council of Foreign Ministers' meeting in Paris in May 1949, Russia once more reiterated its previous plan for Germany: a four-power administration of the Ruhr, restoration of the Allied Control Council and the creation of an All-German State Council from existing economic bodies in both the eastern and western zones.[17] The Western powers regarded this as an empty and retrograde scheme, a ploy to increase Soviet influence over a united Germany, and decided to press on with their own plans.[18] Thus, on 23 May 1949 the Constitution of the Federal Republic of Germany was established, and the FRG came into being on 20 September 1949.[19]

The foregoing is illustrative of the duality evident in Moscow's approach towards Germany after 1945, which was, on the one hand,

11. Michael Freund, *From Cold War to Ostpolitik: Germany and the New Europe* (London, 1971), p. 23.
12. Ibid., p. 20.
13. Ireland, *Creating the Entangling Alliance*, p. 55.
14. Daniel Yergin, *Shattered Peace* (Boston, 1977), p. 330.
15. Nicholas Henderson, *The Birth of NATO* (London, 1982), pp. 11–12.
16. Ireland, *Creating the Entangling Alliance*, p. 68.
17. *Kessing's Contemporary Archives*, Vol. VI, 3–10/5/1947, pp. 8581–2 (London, 1948).
18. *FRUS*, 1949, Vol. 3, p. 924.
19. Fursdon, *The European Defence Community*, p. 44.

defensive, and directed towards preventing a resurgence of German militarism, and, on the other hand, offensive, and aimed at extending Soviet influence over the whole of Germany.[20] It was the conflicting nature of the priorities in this approach, coupled with Stalin's confused long-term objectives and strategy for Germany, that were probably most responsible for what Michael Howard has described as the clumsiness and 'stupidity' of Moscow's policy in the early years after the war. According to him, 'all the cards were in Soviet hands' in terms of achieving their own objectives for Germany, for there was a fund of goodwill towards Moscow in the Western states linked with deep enmity and suspicion towards Germany. But Moscow, by its antagonistic behaviour, 'dissipated' this goodwill 'with astonishing speed' and thereby lost the opportunity to influence events in its favour.[21]

Having failed in its bid to achieve a united Germany under the political aegis of Moscow, the Soviet leadership had to be content with consolidating its hold over its own zone. In October 1949, the German Democratic Republic (GDR) was created. But Germany still remained *the* unsolved issue in Europe, and for the Soviet Union it presented from thenceforth a particularly intractable problem,[22] not least as a result of Moscow's own policies, which frequently had the opposite effect to that intended. For example, in the aftermath of the FRG's formation, Soviet policy was aimed predominantly at preventing its rearmament and inclusion in the Western Alliance. However, Moscow's atomic bomb explosion in the autumn of 1949, together with the outbreak of the Korean War in 1950, only served to hasten this process.[23] These events were interpreted by the West as evidence that the Soviet Union might well be prepared to achieve its expansionist aims in Europe via conventional military, or even nuclear, means.[24] They also led to highly unfavourable estimates of Western military strength *vis-à-vis* that of the Soviet empire.[25] In addition, there was evidence that Moscow was vigorously transforming units of the GDR's *Volkspolizei* into a well-equipped armed force.[26]

20. See, for instance, A. H. Gromyko and B. N. Ponomarev, *Soviet Foreign Policy 1945–1980* (Moscow, 1981), p. 65.

21. Michael Howard, 'Introduction', in Olav Riste, ed., *Western Security: The Formative Years. European and Atlantic Defense 1947–1953* (New York, 1985), pp. 14–15.

22. Fursdon, *The European Defence Community*, p. 47.

23. Gregory F. Treverton, *America, Germany and the Future of Europe* (Princeton, NJ, 1992), pp. 65–8.

24. US Congress, House of Representatives, Defense Subcommittee of the Committee on Appropriations, Hearings, *Supplemental Appropriations Bill for 1951*, 25/7/1950 (81st Congress, 2nd Session), p. 20.

25. William Park, *Defending the West: A History of NATO* (Brighton, 1986), pp. 21–2.

26. Treverton, *America*, p. 71.

These developments, particularly the Korean War, seemed to intensify the need for a sound West European defence. In this respect the FRG's iron ore, its soldiers and its territory came to be regarded as indispensable elements.[27] In 1952, in the midst of the heated debate in the West on proposals for a European Defence Community to tie a rearmed FRG into Western defence,[28] Moscow attempted to undermine the scheme by saying that this would only legalize German militarism, and then came up with a more far-reaching and dramatic plan of its own. Stalin, in his note of 10 March 1952, called for a four-power conference to agree a peace treaty with a neutralized Germany restored to unity, with the right to set up its own military forces, and to equip them through domestic manufacture.[29] In November 1954, Moscow again proposed a conference to discuss the German problem, this time directed against the FRG's entry into NATO.[30] Once the FRG was integrated into NATO in 1955, Adenauer was invited to Russia for talks which resulted in the implementation of diplomatic relations between the Soviet Union and Moscow.[31]

MOSCOW'S POLICY TOWARDS BONN, 1955–69

Throughout the remainder of the 1950s and most of the 1960s, the Soviet stance towards the FRG was based on co-existence and containment, for reasons that were economic, political and military, and each of these requires some elucidation in turn.

Firstly, the Russian policy of plundering the GDR's industry in its determination to exact reparations almost bled the zone to death for several years after the war.[32] Up until 1962, the depth of suffering and deprivation experienced by the GDR's populace was severe, and led to the uprising of June 1953, which was quelled by the Soviet army. It also

27. Ibid., pp. 109–10; see also Fursdon, *The European Defence Community*, p. 64.

28. See, for instance, *Guns for the Germans? The Arguments for and Against German Rearmament* (London, 1951); Basil Davidson, *Two Sides in Germany – Which is Yours?* (London, 1955).

29. *Current Digest of the Soviet Press*, V. 7 (1952), 7–8.

30. V. Khatuntsev, 'Demagogic Arguments: Manoeuvres of the Advocates of a Revival of the Wehrmacht', *Soviet News*, November 1954, No. 3048, pp. 23–4; Gromyko and Ponomarev, *Soviet Foreign Policy 1945–1980*, p. 186.

31. See Chapter 11 in this book.

32. Freund, *From Cold War to Ostpolitik*, p. 35.

contributed to the flood of refugees, year by year, to the FRG, where economic recovery was well under way.[33] By 1961, the exodus of people was so massive, and the depopulation of the zone so advanced, that the GDR's demise looked to be imminent. Moscow countered this by having the Berlin Wall erected in August 1961, which sliced the city in half and sealed off the sector boundary. From that time onwards, the GDR was left to attend to its own economic reconstruction, and regarded itself politically not as a transitional state, but as one in waiting for German unity under a communist regime.[34]

Secondly, the preamble to the Basic Law, which was the FRG's founding document, made clear West Germany's fundamental objective based upon the 'reunification imperative' which called upon all German people to 'achieve in free self-determination the unity and freedom of Germany'.[35] In view of this provision in the Basic Law, and the conferment of legitimacy on the FRG by virtue of its elected government, Bonn governments took it upon themselves to speak on behalf of all the German people. The Hallstein Doctrine (so-called after Adenauer's State Secretary Walter Hallstein whose brainchild it was) dictated that there should be no recognition of the GDR, and that, with the exception of the Soviet Union, relations with other states that recognized it would be ended. By contrast, the Soviet Union and the GDR pursued a 'two German states' policy, in deference to the existing situation.[36] The FRG thus presented something of a continuing political threat to Moscow with its aspirations, especially since it was the only Western state that sought a fundamental overturn of the *status quo* between East and West in Europe.

By the end of the 1950s, Moscow decided that the FRG would be denied any opportunity for influence in Eastern Europe until such time as it was prepared to accept the division of Germany. The second Berlin crisis, from 1958 to 1961, represented an unsuccessful Russian attempt to force a formal acceptance of this *status quo* on Bonn and the West.[37] Khrushchev threatened to annul the four-power control of Germany, and to convert Berlin into a 'free' city by signing a separate peace treaty

33. Industrial production grew by 60 per cent after the currency reform and attained pre-war levels by 1950. See Klaus Larres, 'Preserving Law and Order: Britain, the United States and the East German Uprising of 1953', *Twentieth Century British History* 5.3 (1994), 320–50.

34. Hermann Weber, *Die DDR 1945–1986* (Munich, 1988), pp. 56ff.

35. *Basic Law of the Federal Republic of Germany* (Bonn, 1979), p. 13.

36. Ernest D. Plock, *East German–West German Relations and the Fall of the GDR* (Boulder, Colo., 1993), pp. 9–10.

37. George D. Embree, ed., *The Soviet Union and the German Question: September 1958–June 1961* (The Hague, 1963).

with the GDR, thus ensuring that the Allies could only gain access to Berlin by negotiating with the GDR as a sovereign state.[38]

Thirdly, as a legacy of the war, deep and persistent Soviet fears of German revanchism throughout these years led to successive Soviet leaders making strenuous efforts to prevent the possibility of revived German aggression. There are numerous references to the dangers of FRG militarism in the Soviet press in this period.[39] In 1958, for instance, Moscow appealed desperately to the West not to allow the FRG to be armed with atomic and missile weapons.[40] Moscow even cited the military threat from West Germany as the reason for invading Czechoslovakia in 1968.[41] It is hard to view these fears as being real, or rational, bearing in mind the FRG's extreme vulnerability to attack from the Warsaw Treaty Organization with some 400,000 Soviet troops stationed in the GDR, and considering the difficulties involved in defending West German territory in view of its 1,700-kilometre boundary with the Warsaw Treaty Organization, and its relatively shallow depth.[42] Moreover, the Russians enjoyed reminding Bonn's leaders of this vulnerability. Khrushchev is quoted as saying:

> 'If a third word war is unleased', Adenauer often said, 'West Germany will be the first country to perish.' I was pleased to hear this, and Adenauer was absolutely right in what he said. For him to be making public statements was a great achievement on our part. Not only were we keeping our number one enemy in line, but Adenauer was helping to keep our other enemies in line too.[43]

It seems more likely that Soviet leaders pursued this tack of concern at possible German revanchism as a useful propaganda ploy, playing upon

38. Edwina Moreton, 'The German Factor', in Edwina Moreton and Gerald Segal, eds, *Soviet Strategy Towards Western Europe* (London, 1984), pp. 119–20.

39. See, for instance, 'Governments Approve Soviet Decision to End Nuclear Weapons' Tests', *Soviet News* No. 3846, 29/5/1958, p. 188; also Yuri Zhukov, 'Atlantic Pact, European Defence – Caution! Aggressor is Hiding Under Water', *Current Digest of the Soviet Press* XV.6 (6/3/1963), 26–7.

40. Resolution of the Supreme Soviet of the USSR commissioning the Chairmen of the Chambers to Address a Message to the Parliaments of Member States of the Anti-Hitler Coalition and the Countries which Suffered from Nazi Aggression During the Second World War. Adopted on 31 March 1958, *Gazette of the Supreme Soviet of the USSR* 7 (1958).

41. *Current Digest of the Soviet Press* XX.37 (2/10/1968), 12–13.

42. *Defence White Paper 1983: The Security of the Federal Republic of Germany* (Bonn), para. 268.

43. Quoted by Hannes Adomeit, 'The Political Rationale of Soviet Military Capabilities and Doctrine', in *Strengthening Conventional Deterrence in Europe: Proposals for the 1980s, Report of the European Security Study (ESECS)* (London, 1983).

the genuine concerns about German aggression harboured by many amongst its population.

A NEW PHASE IN SOVIET–FRG RELATIONS, 1969–79

Since it was primarily West German initiatives that were responsible for the FRG–Soviet *détente* which arose during this period,[44] it is helpful to provide a brief exploratory introduction to this change of policy at this point. By the end of the 1960s, the FRG's animosity towards the GDR, and its refusal to recognize it as a sovereign state, were becoming a manifestly counter-productive policy. This was firstly because of the increasing isolation of the FRG amongst Western states, which were by then keen to extend negotiations with the Eastern Bloc countries, not to isolate them; and secondly, in view of the increasing polarization of the two Germanies, as both consolidated their economic and political positions, but in diametrically opposite directions. Thus, the FRG's ultimate objective – of a reunified Germany – was becoming a more and more remote prospect.[45]

In 1967 and 1968, the FRG government engaged in a flurry of diplomatic moves to mend fences with the USSR, Czechoslovakia and Poland in a way that would lead to a peace treaty. Bonn did not want such a treaty with the GDR at this stage because it would have meant recognizing it as a sovereign state. Moscow was also vehemently opposed to this and made it clear in October 1967 that nothing other than a non-aggression pact between the FRG and GDR would be acceptable to the Soviets as a prerequisite to any agreements between Moscow and Bonn.[46] It also demanded that all links between West Berlin and the FRG be severed because they were a threat to the GDR's claim to absolute sovereignty over the whole city and violated Moscow's just entitlement as a prize of war. No progress was made in the ensuing months, and, following further setbacks caused by the Soviet invasion of Prague in August 1968, the Bonn government decided that new

44. Angela Stent Yergin, 'Soviet–West German Relations: Findlandization or Normalization?', in George Ginsburgs and Alvin Z. Rubinstein, eds, *Soviet Foreign Policy Toward Western Europe* (New York, 1978), pp. 110–11.

45. Plock, *East German–West German Relations*, pp. 11–13.

46. 'Bonn Continues to Follow Revanchism: Chancellor Kiesinger's Reply to GDR Proposal', *Soviet News* No. 5402, 10/10/1967, p. 28.

initiatives were required in its policy towards the GDR which would foster closer inter-German ties, and balance the interests of East and West.[47] It also understood plainly by this time that a reconciliation with Moscow was a necessary prelude to achieving this.

The Soviet leadership was by now also moving towards a desire for *détente* with the FRG and the West, for at least three reasons. First, with a marked deterioration in Sino-Soviet relations in 1969, Moscow was hoping for better East–West relations in the European arena. Secondly, it was still very interested in securing Western recognition of prevailing boundaries and governments within the Soviet sphere of influence. Thirdly, Moscow was particularly keen to gain FRG economic and technological assistance to counter its industrial and general economic backwardness.[48] For Moscow, the conditions were right as well. The outcome of the Prague invasion was a strengthening of the Soviets' grip over Eastern Europe, sufficient to give Moscow a breathing space in which to relax its attitude towards Bonn.

The advent of the SPD–FDP governing coalition in the FRG under the leadership of Chancellor Willy Brandt in 1969 resulted in Bonn's new policy being adopted and developed. It was in response to Willy Brandt's version of *Ostpolitik* that the Moscow government then launched its complementary brand of *Westpolitik*. This phase of Soviet policy towards the FRG has been described as 'containment through negotiation'.[49] The ensuing negotiations led to the conclusion of two bilateral treaties between the FRG with both the Soviet Union and Poland in 1970; the Quadripartite agreement on Berlin, in 1971; a Basic Treaty signed between the FRG and GDR (although reluctantly by the latter) in 1972; and the treaty between the FRG and Czechoslovakia in 1973.[50] The main provisions of these treaties were recognition by the FRG and the West of the GDR and its borders, though falling short of establishing full diplomatic ties between the two Germanies; a willingness on Bonn's part to accept the loss of the 1937 German boundaries and to recognize the legitimacy of the Oder–Neisse borderline; and the Soviet Union's acceptance of the links between West Berlin and West Germany, leading to a regularization of traffic with Berlin. The GDR's leader, Ulbricht, was opposed to any formal links between the GDR and the FRG until the latter left NATO and renounced

47. Freund, *From Cold War to Ostpolitik*, p. 71.

48. Plock, *East German–West German Relations*, pp. 13–14.

49. Smith, 'Soviet Policy', p. 13.

50. Department of State, *Documents on Germany, 1944–1985* (Washington DC: US Printing Office), pp. 1103–5, 1124–7, 1135–43.

imperialism.[51] His departure from office in May 1971 smoothed the path for Moscow to establish a 'limited special relationship' with the FRG.[52]

Attention has been drawn to the 'asymmetry in the compromises' made by Bonn and Moscow in this act of reconciliation, and also in the subsequent rewards, both to Russia's advantage.[53] From Moscow's point of view, it had achieved significant advances in its relations with Bonn without having to yield to any of the FRG's former demands over the national issue, and it maintained its four-power responsibilities over Berlin and Germany. The Soviet Union also retained its control over Eastern and Central Europe, and gained ratification of Europe's post-war boundaries at the CSCE accord at Helsinki in 1975. Moreover, because of the GDR's satellite status, Bonn's continuing aspirations towards reunification were at the mercy of Soviet whims.[54] Moscow, therefore, hoped it could exploit these unrealized goals of Bonn's in an effort to persuade the FRG to pursue a more neutral foreign policy.[55] Aside from the political benefits, the Soviet Union reaped handsome rewards on the economic and trading fronts in the years that followed, making the FRG the Soviet Union's leading Western trading partner every year from 1971.[56] In 1983, for instance, Soviet trade with the FRG represented 18.2 per cent of total trade with the West, and about 5.5 per cent of total overseas trade, and amounted to nearly 7,000 million roubles.[57] The significance of this trade for Moscow, in political terms, was, first, that it was said by Soviet leaders to assist in the consolidation of political ties[58] and, secondly, that the threat of withdrawal of trade could be used as a bargaining chip[59] should bilateral political relations deteriorate.[60]

The benefits for the FRG were more mixed. On the plus side, in spite of making very considerable concessions in terms of forgoing its basic objective of all-German legitimacy, Bonn achieved a measure of

51. Treverton, *America*, p. 144.

52. 'West Berlin Agreement is Success for Peace Policy', *Soviet News* No. 5605, 14/9/1971, p. 279.

53. Stent Yergin, 'Soviet–West German Relations', p. 111; Moreton, 'The German Factor', pp. 124–5.

54. Moreton, 'The German Factor', p. 125.

55. Stent Yergin, 'Soviet–West German Relations', p. 111.

56. Angela Stent, *From Embargo to Ostpolitik* (Cambridge, 1981), pp. 179–207.

57. *Tass*, 18/4/1984.

58. 'Andrei Gromyko's Talk with Hans-Jochen Vogel', *Soviet News* No. 6157, 26/1/1983, p. 27.

59. For instance, it was estimated in 1982 that 90,000 persons in the FRG were employed in relation to the Soviet export trade.

60. *Pravda*, 6/7/1983.

security for West Berlin, and the road to unification, although a distant prospect, was not firmly closed. At the same time, the *Ostpolitik* process conferred upon the FRG the status of the leading protagonist of East–West relations in Europe in view of the fact that Moscow regarded it not only as a significant trading partner, but as its key mediator and communication channel on all important East–West issues, from arms control to trade.[61] An indication of this development is that in the period 1970–83, more high-level talks took place between Moscow and Bonn than between the Soviet Union and any other Western country.[62] Less beneficially, Brandt had to weather extensive domestic opposition arising from the depth of the concessions made to Moscow and the East in securing agreement on the treaties.[63] Secondly, Brandt's initiatives provoked considerable concern in NATO regarding the strength of the FRG's commitment to the Alliance. It was also feared that Moscow might use its 'special' relationship with Bonn as a vehicle for exploiting NATO disagreements.[64] Thirdly, the FRG did not achieve the degree of East–West economic and political freedom that Brandt had envisaged in his 'change through rapprochement' goal, especially as the policy applied to the GDR.[65] This was principally because East Berlin responded defiantly with its rigidly enforced policy of *Abgrenzung*, which meant sharply dividing functions in the GDR's relations with the FRG. Economic and technological exchanges were actively encouraged, but the political, cultural and social variety were firmly opposed. This was endorsed by Moscow, which was concerned about the possible threats to the stability of the East which could arise from a relationship between the two Germanies that was too intimate. 'Détente, in Soviet eyes, should remain a limited and non-dynamic condition of international relations, particularly as it affected Eastern Europe.'[66]

61. Philip Windsor, 'Germany and the Western Alliance', *Adelphi Papers No. 170* (London, 1981), p. 5.

62. See, for instance, Smith, 'Soviet Policy', Table 1, p. 14.

63. See, for instance, *The Times*, 18/5/1972.

64. See Chapter 11 in this book.

65. Ibid.

66. Windsor, 'Germany and the Western Alliance', p. 6.

'OFFENSIVE *DÉTENTE*':[67] THE FOURTH PHASE IN SOVIET–WEST GERMAN POLITICS, 1979–86

The mid-1970s saw the most productive and amicable phase in East–West relations since 1945, during which Moscow dropped its opposition both to American participation in Western Europe's defence and to regarding security in Europe as a matter for negotiation rather than conflict. By the end of the 1970s, however, the NATO alliance was in deep crisis, and East–West relations reached a low ebb. This had potentially profound implications for Soviet–FRG relations. The reasons for this altered situation were security-related and were, broadly speaking, twofold. The first was that during the 1970s the Soviet Union reached strategic nuclear parity with the US. At the same time, the Soviet build-up of theatre nuclear and conventional weapons in Europe went on unabated. The nub of the security problem for the FRG was that the US nuclear guarantee for Europe had become eroded since, with strategic nuclear parity, Washington would not be inclined to use its long-range nuclear missiles in answer to a regional threat when these would invite its own annihilation. Moreover, because Europe possessed no intermediate-range systems, European Alliance members would become increasingly susceptible to Soviet intimidation. The outcome would be a progressive decoupling of American and European security, and a destabilizing military imbalance which would damage East–West *détente*.[68]

The NATO decision of 12 December 1979 to station Pershing II and Cruise missiles in Europe, including the FRG, with the stated aim of retaining the nuclear umbrella, gave rise to fierce opposition, especially in West Germany, the opposing argument being that the positioning of Intermediate-Range Nuclear Forces (INF) in Europe which threatened the USSR would invite retaliation from Moscow in kind. It would not encourage the US to use its INF weapons any more than its Intercontinental Ballistic Missiles (ICBM) were Europe attacked, so coupling was still in jeopardy.[69] Furthermore, the actual stationinig of missiles in Europe could be interpreted as highly provocative by Moscow, which could respond with a pre-emptive strike on the missiles deployed in the FRG, thus obliterating the country. Secretary General Yuri Andropov confirmed this and the increased threat to West Germany in July 1983,

67. Jack Snyder, 'The Gorbachev Revolution: A Waning of Soviet Expansionism?', *International Security* 12.3 (Winter 1987–8), 93–131.

68. Stephen F. Szabo, *The Changing Politics of German Security* (London, 1990), pp. 28–9.

69. Rudolf Steinke, 'Introduction', in Steinke and Vale, eds, *Germany Debates Defense*, pp. xvi–xix.

when he told Chancellor Helmut Kohl: 'if American missiles are deployed on West German soil, the situation will change. The military threat to West Germany will grow many times'.[70]

The second reason for the rupture in East–West ties and intra-Alliance strife was a combination of the Iranian hostage crisis and the Soviet invasion of Afghanistan in 1979; the introduction of martial law in Poland in 1980; and the advent of Ronald Reagan's presidency in January 1981. These factors were to lead to a marked divergence in security perceptions by the US and the FRG in particular. For Washington, *détente* was not a concept that lent itself to compromise. Moscow's expansionism and violation of sovereignty signalled the termination of East–West cooperation at all levels, including arms control. President Reagan's huge arms build-up, his belligerent rhetoric including a reference to USSR leaders as 'godless monsters', and his talk of limited nuclear war, together with his demand that an embargo be placed on the Soviet–West European gas pipeline, engendered deep concerns about war in the FRG, and worries that Bonn's *Ostpolitik* could be placed in jeopardy.[71] For Bonn, the American zero-sum approach to *détente* was highly counter-productive, and its leaders were not prepared to endorse such an extreme approach. The FRG, having painstakingly achieved a good rapport, both politically and economically, with the USSR and, to a lesser extent, with the GDR, and having secured a workable policy with the Soviets in regard to West Berlin, was in no hurry to sacrifice these gains. A central dilemma for Bonn, as Philip Windsor has explained, was that, arguably, *détente* had made the FRG more vulnerable to Soviet capriciousness, and Berlin's prevailing status, being an outcome of *Ostpolitik*, had 'become a political hostage for the maintenance of détente'. The survival of West Berlin depended upon Alliance solidarity which might itself collapse over Western dissent regarding the maintenance of *détente*.[72]

For Bonn, this was altogether a particularly difficult and testing time, for additional, but related, reasons. First, the FRG's unwillingness to toe the US line on the demise of *détente* brought into question West Germany's loyalty to NATO, and gave a stimulus to Allied suspicions that Bonn was being seduced by the East.[73] Secondly, the FRG perceived

70. Quoted in 'Yuri Andropov's Conversation with Helmut Kohl', *Soviet News* No. 6180, 6/7/1983, pp. 225, 227.

71. Szabo, *Changing Politics*, p. 34; Ekkehart Krippendorf and Michael Lucas, ' "One Day We Americans Will Have to Consider the Destruction of Europe" ', in Steinke and Vale, eds, *Germany Debates Defense*, pp. 33–43.

72. Windsor, 'Germany and the Western Alliance', p. 7.

73. Elisabeth Pond, 'The Security Debate in West Germany', *Survival* XXVIII.4 (July/August 1986), 326.

that its security had been substantially weakened as a consequence of the recent Soviet military build-up in Europe and Moscow's recent displays of aggression, the growing unreliability of the American commitment, the INF crisis and the collapse in *détente* which threatened to damage Bonn's relations with the USSR and, therefore, to impair an important element of its security. Thirdly, inter-German relations had cooled perceptibly, as East Germany, describing NATO as the principal threat to European peace, declared darkly that Bonn's decision with regard to INF would reveal its true priorities as far as its relations with the GDR were concerned.[74] Finally, Bonn had soon to endure a return to frosty relations with Moscow after a break of 12 years, as the USSR once again reverted to its old theme of accusing the FRG of revanchist behaviour.[75] Prior to this diplomatic freeze which commenced in 1984, the Soviet government had made concerted and sustained efforts to induce the FRG to abandon its allies.[76] It is the Soviet attitude towards the FRG in this period that deserves separate analysis at this juncture.

It seems clear that successive Soviet leaders following Khrushchev regarded an East–West military balance that favoured the Soviet side as an important asset in providing Moscow with political leverage over the West, and most notably Bonn. The decision to deploy the SS-20 ICBM was a good example of this. It is likely that this decision was first made on military grounds, to compensate for US forward-based nuclear systems and British and French nuclear forces. However, the fact that the SS-20s could target Western Europe at a stage when the superpowers had reached strategic nuclear parity left the countries of Western Europe feeling extremely vulnerable, and Chancellor Helmut Schmidt, articulating these fears, called for the removal of the 'disparities of military power in Europe parallel to the SALT negotiations'.[77]

By maintaining an inflexible stand on deploying the SS-20s throughout, the Soviet Union apparently hoped to draw the FRG away from NATO by exploiting the deep rifts that had opened up between the Bonn leadership and substantial sections of the FRG population, including a strong and vocal peace movement. Moscow's stance continued to be that the West had no right to deploy Cruise and Pershing missiles, but that the Warsaw Treaty Organization had the right to deploy its SS-

74. See *Tass* statement, *Financial Times*, 12/8/1982.

75. 'Communiqué of the Meeting of the Committee of Ministers of Foreign Affairs of the Warsaw Treaty Member States', *Soviet News* No. 6168, 13/4/1983, pp. 117–18.

76. Smith, 'Soviet Policy', p. 22.

77. Helmut Schmidt, 'The 1977 Alistair Buchan Memorial Lecture', *Survival* XX.1 (January/February 1988), 2–10.

20s.[78] The Soviet Union mounted a sustained two-pronged campaign, directed at the FRG, appealing over the heads of the Bonn government to the people.[79]

While making frequent reference to its own peaceful intentions, Moscow warned, first, of the dire consequences for the FRG if deployment of the NATO missiles was to go ahead.[80] On one occasion, the Kremlin wondered if the FRG populace realized that it would be 'sitting on 2,500 Hiroshimas'.[81] Secondly, the Soviet Union questioned whether the people of the FRG had seriously considered that Bonn's acceptance of the stationing of the missiles would contravene the 1970 Moscow Treaty and, therefore, indirectly damage *Ospolitik*.[82] But, as in the past, the USSR miscalculated the effect its campaign was having in the FRG, for the constant use of intimidatory tactics merely reinforced public belief in Chancellor Kohl's warnings about the Soviet threat and Soviet stubbornness. The fact that Moscow refused to make any concessions whatsoever on the INF issue, for example by offering to reduce the number of warheads on its missiles in Europe, made it easier for the Bonn leadership to agree to the deployment of Cruise and Pershing II missiles.[83]

One result of Moscow's hard-line approach regarding the INF issue was that, following the *Bundestag*'s decision to go ahead with the stationing of the missiles, inter-German relations began to improve, as Erich Honecker insisted on maintaining the progress of *détente* with the FRG. Honecker was in fact annoyed at having to play host to further Soviet missiles in the GDR, and at having to pay for them. He went ahead with arranging a visit to Bonn, but was forced to cancel it because of Moscow's display of extreme displeasure.

If Bonn's security concerns were heightened by INF-related nuclear issues, they were intensified still further by the revelation of the Reagan administration's intention to embark upon the development of the so-called Strategic Defense Initiative (SDI), which became public in March 1983. The revolutionary nature of this programme, which rested upon a purely defensive strategy and envisaged a multi-layered ballistic missile defence shield in space, with the objective of eliminating the need for

78. Spartak Beglov, 'Nuclear Blackmail Won't Pay', *Soviet Weekly*, 25/6/1983, p. 6.

79. 'Nikolai Tikhonov's Reply to Krefeld Initiatives' Appeal', *Soviet News* No. 6220, 18/4/1984, pp. 130–1.

80. See, for instance, *Pravda*, 11/9/1983; also *Izvestia*, 22/9/1983.

81. Colonel-General Nikolai Chernov, 'The USA Has No Constructive Programme for Limiting Nuclear Weapons', *Soviet News* No. 6216, 21/3/1984, p. 96.

82. Spartak Beglov, letter to *The Times*, 'Soviet Response to US Missiles', 25/11/1983.

83. Pond, 'The Security Debate', p. 328.

nuclear deterrence, was a fearful prospect for many Europeans, not least the Germans.[84] The worst fears revolved around the perception that if SDI became fully operational, it would enable the US to retreat behind its defensive shield, a 'fortress America', having relinquished its commitment to its allies; or, conversely, the shield might permit the US to gamble recklessly with Europe's safety.[85] The then FRG Defence Minister, Manfred Woerner, articulated all these anxieties, plus another – that the Soviet Union would shortly reciprocate with its own version of SDI, and Europe would be left unshielded and vulnerable to conventional conflict.[86]

Washington's promise to deploy an anti-tactical missile (ATM) system to protect Europe against Soviet attacks by ICBMs and SLBMs (Submarine Launched Ballistic Missiles) only served to increase *angst* among the European allies. They feared that such a move, even if feasible (which was doubtful), would only encourage Moscow to saturate the system by greatly extending its own deployment of INF systems, and by expanding its Ballistic Missile Defence (BMD) system, which could lower the credibility of British and French nuclear forces.[87] The Soviet Union, which had its own security reasons for being fundamentally opposed to SDI and was determined to find a means of banning space weapons altogether, frequently focused upon the warning that SDI would kill the arms control process, and lead to the abrogation of the ABM (Anti-Ballistic Missiles) treaty.[88] Moscow was well aware of the importance European states attached to agreements to limit arms. It therefore made clear what the implications of the abandonment of the arms control negotiations would mean for the security of Europe, especially the FRG,[89] in further attempts to exacerbate the friction between Washington and Bonn, and to coax West Germany towards neutrality.

This phase in Soviet attitudes towards Germany was one in which Moscow initially believed that the FRG, realizing that its defence and security interests were incompatible with those of the US, especially

84. Werner Kaltefleiter, *The Strategic Defense Initiative: Some Implications for Europe*, Occasional Paper No. 10 (London, 1985), p. 26.

85. Stephen Kirby, 'The Military Uses of Space and European Security', in Stephen Kirby and Gordon Robson, eds, *The Militarisation of Space* (Brighton, 1987), p. 184.

86. Paul Taylor, Reuters, 'NATO Ministers Informed but Not Convinced on Star Wars', Cesme, Turkey, 4/4/1984.

87. Gil Klinger, 'Superpower Arms Control II. Its Impact on the NATO Alliance', in Walter Goldstein, ed., *Fighting Allies: Tensions within the Atlantic Alliance* (New York, 1986), pp. 101–2.

88. Moscow Correspondent, 'Russia Offers Deal on SDI', *The Times*, 17/6/1986.

89. 'USSR–FRG Conference Ends', *Soviet News* No. 6305, 18/12/1985, p. 464.

with regard to the maintenance of *détente* and the avoidance of war, was urgently seeking a measure of political autonomy in order to influence Alliance decision-making.[90] One Soviet author declared that the countries of Western Europe, particularly the FRG, thoroughly disillusioned with Washington's security policy, were well on the way to establishing their own European defence framework to articulate a Europeanist defence approach.[91] But, by the middle of the decade, Moscow was forced to revise these views. The deployment of INF, support for SDI by most European leaders, the tightening of COCOM restrictions and the reduction in export credits led to the belief that intra-Alliance links were in fact being strengthened, and not least because of East–West tensions and Western concerns regarding the Soviet threat.[92] It was these altered perceptions that led Moscow, disappointed with the FRG's subservience to the US, to cease diplomatic dialogue with Bonn, and to indulge in accusations of revived militarist ambitions by the West German CDU/CSU government, while the SPD and the peace movement were praised for their constructive approach.[93] Moscow now concentrated its invective on Bonn's dependence on Washington, declaring that the US was fuelling the FRG's expansionist and militarist tendencies, and that West Germany's military forces were far in excess of what was needed for the country's defence.[94]

THE FINAL PHASE: 1987–90 – THE GORBACHEV INITIATIVES

In the mid-1980s, Gorbachev's rise to power in the Soviet Union was soon followed by 'new thinking' in Moscow's foreign policy. This 'new thinking' was given impetus by a number of factors, arising from the failures of the Brezhnev era, which included: (i) a new and costly arms

90. V. Kniazhinsky, *West European Integration: Its Policies and International Relations* (Moscow, 1984), pp. 346–8; 379–83.

91. R. F. Laird, 'Soviet Perspectives on French Security Policy', *Survival* 27.2 (1985), 70; M. J. Sodaro, 'Soviet Studies of the Western Alliance', in H. J. Ellison, ed., *Soviet Policy towards Western Europe* (Seattle, WA, 1983), pp. 254–5.

92. Neil Malcolm, *Soviet Policy Perspectives on Western Europe* (London, 1989), p. 41.

93. M. J. Sodaro, 'Soviet Studies of the Western Alliance', in Ellison, ed., *Soviet Policy*, p. 257.

94. Valentin Falin, *Mirovain Eknomika i Mezhdunarodnye Otnoshenilia* (*MEMO*) 12 (1987), 77.

race; (ii) an expensive and disastrous Soviet involvement in the Third World (Afghanistan); (iii) domestic economic stagnation; and (iv) low Soviet political standing in the world. These were combined with a recognition that the costs of striving for global military hegemony exceeded the Soviet Union's financial capabilities.[95] This change of direction brought with it an entirely different approach towards the West, based upon a devaluation of ideological preconceptions and constraints and a revised view of capitalism.[96] The emphasis was now on achieving mutual security through negotiation, by reducing confrontation, and by restricting arms to what was required for 'reasonable sufficiency'.[97] It also meant borrowing ideas from the West, through the espousal of the concepts of interdependence and multipolarity, and giving attention to matters such as environmental degradation and world poverty.

In terms of Soviet relations with the FRG, at a general level the Gorbachev era heralded a more realistic assessment of Bonn's ties with the West. Moscow had begun to grasp that Bonn's attachment to the Western Alliance had in no small part been provoked by fears arising from recent Soviet policy, together with anxieties over possible decoupling from the US. It also realized that the tactic of appealing heavily to the West German people over the heads of their governments, as happened under Brezhnev, had not been successful.[98] In addition, the Soviet hierarchy recognized that it was not feasible to expect Bonn (or any of the Western European capitals for that matter) to exert influence on American behaviour, nor was it appropriate to treat the FRG and other Western European states as though they were simply American appendages, whose views could be disregarded. It was necessary to regard European countries as relatively independent actors whose views should not be 'pushed to the sidelines'.[99]

The new Soviet policy towards Western Europe as a whole was one that aimed for the eventual dissolution of both military blocs in return for European neutrality, but which accepted meantime that the NATO alliance was preferable to the option of a German-dominated West European defence system. For Gorbachev, NATO solidarity was compat-

95. Snyder, 'The Gorbachev Revolution', 108–10.

96. Mikhail Gorbachev, Speech to the Central Committee plenum, 18/2/1988, *Pravda*, 19/2/1988.

97. S. Sestanovich, 'Gorbachev's Foreign Policy: A Diplomacy of Decline', *Problems of Communism* 37.1 (January–February 1988), 3.

98. J. Hough, 'Soviet Perspectives on European Security', *International Journal* 12 (1984–5), 36–7.

99. 'Perestroika, the 19th Party Conference and Foreign Policy', *International Affairs* (Moscow) 10 (1988), 10, 37.

ible with pan-European cooperation, for the time being. Ultimately, he envisaged a 'Common European Home', in which all European states would cooperate and live in harmony, from the Atlantic to the Urals, from which the US would be excluded.[100] At the same time, Gorbachev was quite content to continue the old Soviet trick of fomenting divisions and disagreements in Western Europe and NATO, to serve the Soviet Union's traditional purposes.[101] There were thus marked ambiguities in Gorbachev's approach, contrasting the desire to woo Western Europe for its credits, trade, expertise and technology with the wish to exert Soviet hegemony over Europe in its entirety. Pierre Hassner referred to the USSR as still the 'objective Findlandizer'.[102]

More specifically, Moscow's relations with Bonn, which had been cooler than its ties with other Western states for several years, improved rapidly in the second half of 1987. Erich Honecker at last visited Bonn; the FRG extended one billion Deutschmarks of credit to the USSR; Chancellor Kohl offered to dismantle the Pershing II missiles; and Soviet Foreign Minister Shevardnadze visited Bonn in January 1988. In the course of this visit West German Foreign Minister Hans-Dietrich Genscher stated his hope to 'turn a new page in Soviet–West German relations and fill it with a qualitatively new content'.[103] Gorbachev's new *détente* with Bonn was predicated on a policy of appealing to the FRG population at large by pursuing an accommodating and cooperative style with its leaders, taking into consideration popular views in West Germany. This was evident in Gorbachev's response in deference to the opinions of the FRG political left demanding alternative defence strategies founded upon a limitation of military capabilities sufficient for defensive defence alone, as the best means of achieving mutual East–West security.[104] Gorbachev first called for a cut in conventional weapons by both sides to prevent any possibility of a sudden attack.[105] Then, on 29 May 1987, the Warsaw Treaty Organization formally declared its willingness to adopt a policy of retaining only enough forces to allow for defensive action, and suggested that, in future, Eastern Bloc military

100. Hannes Adomeit, 'The Impact of Perestroika on Europe', Paper delivered at the RIIA, December 1988, p. 17.

101. Idem, 'Gorbachev's Policy toward the West: Smiles and Iron Teeth', *Soviet Foreign Policy* (Proceedings of the Academy of Political Science 36.4) (New York, 1987), p. 94.

102. Pierre Hassner, 'Europe between the United States and the Soviet Union', *Government and Opposition*, 21.1 (Winter 1986), 23.

103. *Foreign Broadcast Information Service – Soviet Section* (*FBIS-SOV*), 19/1/1988, p. 41.

104. Gerhard Wettig, ' "New Thinking" on Security and East–West Relations', *Problems of Communism* XXXVII (March–April 1988), 4.

105. *Pravda*, 11/4/1987.

forces would be structured on defensive lines. The communiqué also invited NATO to reciprocate in kind.[106]

However, Moscow's softer and more cordial line towards Bonn generated a negative effect for the USSR. Not only did it not succeed in intensifying neutralism in the FRG, it did not achieve a distancing of relations between Bonn and Washington either.[107] Even more irritating for Moscow was that the new, more open Soviet style simply encouraged Bonn to place demands on the Soviet government that previously it would have considered a waste of time. As an example of this, both Kohl and Genscher urged the Soviet leadership to accept the partitioning of Germany as a temporary phenomenon.[108] However, Moscow's response to such demands was a negative one, on the grounds that the *status quo* had to be upheld.[109]

The radical shift in Soviet foreign policy initiated by Gorbachev was of such magnitude and so profound as to have become, arguably, irreversible by the end of the 1980s, even if Gorbachev had been unseated.[110] It had generated its own momentum. In the USSR, domestic reforms dictated a reconfiguration of the German question. Gorbachev realized that the *status quo* in Eastern Europe could not be maintained if reform was to continue at home as he had decided it should. The satellite states were a drain on the Moscow exchequer, and they too had to undergo reform or be freed.[111] Shevardnadze, speaking in 1990, endorsed this view in retrospect:

> We felt that if serious changes did not take place, then tragic results would ensue. In principle, we sensed this, we knew this. But we could not, proceeding from and guided by the principles of new political thinking, interfere in the affairs of others, the affairs of other states.[112]

Unknowingly, Gorbachev gave an impetus to German unification by dislodging the *status quo* in Europe, and by undermining the position of Stalinist rulers in the Eastern Bloc, particularly Honecker. The latter found himself in an untenable situation, wedged between Kohl and Genscher in Bonn and reformers in Moscow. The downgrading of ideology combined with the emphasis on reconciliation and openness meant that in the changed circumstances the Honecker regime, which

106. 'Warsaw Treaty Political Consultative Committee: Military Doctrine', *Soviet News* No. 6377, 3/6/1987, p. 193.

107. Sestanovich, 'Gorbachev's Foreign Policy', p. 11.

108. *FBIS-SOV*, 19/1/1988, p. 44.

109. Ibid.

110. Malcolm, *Soviet Policy Perspectives*, p. 79.

111. Treverton, *America*, p. 147.

112. *FBIS-SOV*, 5/7/1990, p. 8.

was sustained by ideology, division and Soviet troops, was no longer as relevant as it used to be.

However, the two Germanies themselves advanced the pace towards unification. In the FRG, Foreign Minister Genscher had appreciated early on that Gorbachev was serious in striving for a new era of security in Europe, in order to overcome chronic economic problems at home. He was quick to grasp the opportunities that this change of direction presented for overcoming peacefully the division of Germany and Europe.[113] He was determined that Germany should be at the forefront of the new bridge to be built in Europe, not least because the Germans had been responsible for the Second World War – ultimately the event which had led to the division of the European continent.[114] Genscher earnestly set about this task, assuming that Gorbachev would assist in building a new European architecture in a controlled manner, in which the reunification of Germany could be achieved, but the revolutions of 1989 occurred entirely unexpectedly and exposed the frailty of the political and economic structures of the Eastern Bloc.[115]

In the GDR, events were also hastening the revolutionary process which would culminate in reunification. Despite the erosion of East–West *détente* in the first half of the decade, inter-German political, economic and social ties were intensified throughout the 1980s; the FRG exerted an enormous pull on the population of the GDR. The East German population, 90 per cent of whom could watch FRG television, were attracted by the standard of living and freedom enjoyed by those in the other half of Germany. East Germans were also aware of the moves towards democracy in Hungary and Poland, and the reforms that were taking place in Russia. This exacerbated dissatisfaction with their own regime. In the summer of 1988, 56,000 East Germans emigrated to the FRG. In the summer of 1989, an estimated 100,000 were due to leave. The Honecker regime had lost its legitimacy with the people, particularly after Honecker offered support to Beijing's leaders after the Tiananmen Square massacre in June 1989.

Following the fall of Honecker on 18 October 1989, the opening of the Berlin Wall on 9 November, and the opening of the Brandenburg Gate on 22 December, free elections were promised in the GDR for 18 March 1990. In February 1990, the two-plus-four formula was decided at Ottawa, under which the two Germanies were to arrange their union with the four wartime powers which had to ratify the

113. Hans-Dietrich Genscher, 'Taking Gorbachev at his Word', speech at the World Economic Forum, Davos, Switzerland, 1/2/1987, *Statements and Speeches*, 6/2/1987.

114. Hans-Dietrich Genscher, 'Speech to the Bundestag, 27 April 1989', p. 2.

115. Szabo, *Changing Politics*, p. 133.

agreement. The victory by Kohl's Christian Democrats in the East German elections in March 1990 effectively sealed the union. Until February 1990 Moscow was insistent that Germany should become a neutral country. It was also opposed to a united Germany's membership of NATO. But events moved speedily. By July 1990, Gorbachev had accepted that a reunited Germany would remain in NATO but under certain conditions, and pledged that Soviet forces would be removed from the former GDR by the end of 1994. Bonn promised over $10 billion in aid to the Russians. 'The post-war order was over. Moscow had given up on it.'[116]

CONCLUSION

West Germany was the focus for Soviet policy towards Western Europe from 1945 onwards. Successive Soviet leaders over the period under review attempted to find ways of solving the German question in a way that would ensure that Germany was never again allowed to threaten Moscow. The dominant theme was one in which the FRG had to be contained and the GDR controlled. A lesser theme focused on the idea of a neutral, unified Germany, which could later be brought into the Soviet sphere of influence. But for most of the period 1945–90 (that is, since 1955), the preference was for a permanently divided Germany, for two central reasons: first, to enable the unity of the Eastern Bloc of states to be perserved; and secondly, to exploit West German desires for unification, which could only be fulfilled by Moscow, as a means of providing the Soviet Union with opportunities for influencing East–West relations.

One of the most striking features regarding Soviet policy towards the FRG has been the frequency with which Soviet leaders have engaged in policies which have produced the opposite results to those intended. This was true of the immediate post-war period, when Russia was in a position to achieve a united, neutral Germany, had Moscow only shown more cooperation and a willingness to compromise. It was also the case in the post-*détente* phase when Moscow believed that it could lure the FRG away from American dependence by saturating the population with threats to decimate it if Bonn agreed to proceed with INF deployment. It

116. Treverton, *America*, p. 152.

also applied to the final phase, and this is perhaps the most interesting one. Although it too involved a serious miscalculation, unlike the other occasions which resulted from blinkered vision and/or unclear objectives, this was forced upon the Soviet leadership by desperately serious internal circumstances. It is clear that Gorbachev never envisaged that his policies would lead to the unification of Germany. Even as late as March 1990, he described this scenario as 'totally out of the question'.[117] The maintenance of the GDR was of paramount importance to Moscow for historical, economic, political and military reasons, as Gorbachev acknowledged.[118] However, pressing domestic-economic factors appear to have been the reason why such a risky strategy was deployed, which by 1990 had brought the Soviet Union to crisis point. Shevardnadze admitted in July 1990 that the country was facing economic 'ruin'.[119]

117. Ibid., p. 151.
118. See, for instance, *The Economist*, 12/5/1990, p. 49.
119. *FBIS-SOV*, 5/7/1990, pp. 8–9.

CHAPTER ELEVEN

Germany and the West: the 'Rapallo Factor' in German Foreign Policy from the 1950s to the 1990s

Klaus Larres

On 16 April 1922 German Foreign Minister Walther Rathenau and Soviet Commissioner of Foreign Affairs Chicherin signed the Treaty of Rapallo. Immediately, there arose fears of a powerful bonding of the two spheres of interest which might also be accompanied by a concomitant weakening of German interest in its western neighbours.[1] Thus Rapallo came to symbolize for many the deviousness of a too-independent German foreign policy, as well as that country's unreliability and unpredictable yearning for great-power status. Statesmen everywhere were reminded of earlier prophecies of a Russo-German domination of Europe. This had been gloomily anticipated since the end of the German Wars of Liberation in 1814/15. Ever since, Germany's mythical hankering after a 'special relationship' with Russia has invoked fear and suspicion among its neighbours.[2] Rapallo became synonymous with the Western nightmare of close Soviet–German cooperation,[3] the more so

1. See Peter Krüger, 'A Rainy Day, April 16, 1922: The Rapallo Treaty and the Cloudy Perspective for German Foreign Policy', in Carole Fink, Axel Frohn and Jürgen Heideking, eds, *Genoa, Rapallo, and European Reconstruction in 1922* (Cambridge, 1991), p. 50.

2. See Rolf-Dieter Müller, 'Rapallo–Karriere eines Reizwortes', *Die Zeit* No. 16 (10/4/1992), p. 60.

3. The French but also the Americans were very alarmed, 'suspecting German . . . intentions to monpolize the Russian market'. See Krüger, 'A Rainy Day', p. 57; Hartmut Pogge von Strandmann, 'Rappallo-Strategy in Preventive Diplomacy: New Sources and New Interpretations', in Volker R. Berghahn and Martin Kitchen, eds, *Germany in the Age of Total War* (London, 1981), p. 123. See also Renata Bournazel, *Rapallo, ein französisches Trauma* (Cologne, 1976); Axel Frohn, 'Der "Rapallo-Mythos" und die deutsch–amerikanischen Beziehungen', in Jost Dülffer *et al.*, eds, *Deutschland und Europa: Kontinuität und Bruch* (Frankfurt, 1990), pp. 138–53.

as the treaty seemed to culminate in the Soviet–German non-aggression treaty of 1939 and resulted in Germany's attempted conquest of continental Europe. This, and the fear of another Rapallo, strongly influenced Western policy towards the Federal Republic of Germany immediately after the Second World War. It was once said: 'We all know that the Germans, whenever they join forces with the Russians, are soon afterwards on the outskirts of Paris.'[4]

Following a brief account of the events of 1922, this essay will examine the importance of the 'Rapallo complex'[5] in influencing West Germany's relations with the Western Allied powers in the post-Second World War era. The first, careful steps towards a rapprochement with Moscow were conducted under the chancellorship of Konrad Adenauer in the mid-1950s. Western reaction to Adenauer's Eastern policy, however, has been largely neglected in the literature and will therefore be examined. Western, and particularly American, suspicions that were aroused by Willy Brandt's *Ostpolitik* in the late 1960s and early 1970s and also the initial British and French opposition to the process of German unification in 1989/90 will subsequently be analysed. Since German unification, the Federal Republic has been adopting an ever more active policy towards Eastern Europe. Germany's post-unification *Ostpolitik*, however, is not always regarded uncritically, and old fears and prejudices are sometimes reawakened. In its final part the article will therefore attempt to clarify whether these carefully voiced Western reservations are simply a result of the negative memories of the past or whether there is actually some justification for such fears. Can it be said that Germany is moving towards a policy of building up its Eastern links to the detriment of the country's Western relations? Has the newly united Germany perhaps commenced with a new *Schaukelpolitik* (policy of the swing) between East and West? Are German politicians and intelligentsia seriously reconsidering the usefulness of the Federal Republic's close links with the West as indicated in an influential book in the early 1990s?[6] In short, is the 'Rapallo complex' in Germany's relations with the Western world still a factor?

4. This was uttered by French High Commissioner André François-Poncet. Quoted in Renata Fritsch-Bournazel, 'The French View', in Edwina Moreton, ed., *Germany between East and West* (Cambridge, 1987), p. 74.

5. Eberhard Kolb, *The Weimar Republic* (London, 1988), p. 17.

6. Rainer Zitelmann *et al.*, eds, *Westbindung: Chancen und Risiken für Deutschland* (Frankfurt, 1993).

RAPALLO 1922

The Treaty of Rapallo was signed on the occasion of the Genoa Conference, the world's first economic summit. It brought 28 states to the conference table with the purpose of re-ordering the world's economy, which was still suffering from the devastations and disruption caused by the First World War. The participating nations included Soviet Russia and Germany, who – for the first time since the conclusion of the Versailles Peace Treaty – enjoyed parity with the other states attending the summit.[7] The USA did not attend as the French had insisted that the reparation issue be excluded from the agenda, though Germany hoped it would be able to introduce the topic indirectly. After all, the desire for the economic revival of Eastern and Central Europe was at the heart of the conference. The Poincaré government in France particularly, but also the Lloyd George government in London, which had initiated the Genoa Conference, and also, at times, the German Foreign Minister Walther Rathenau, wished to create an international economic and financial consortium consisting of France, Britain, Germany and Belgium to raise, distribute and control the finances necessary to rebuild Russia. The intention was to establish 'a united front . . . of all European states that had granted credits to pre-revolutionary Russia, or whose nationals had suffered losses due to socialization since the Bolsheviks assumed power'.[8] As this would almost inevitably have led to Soviet dependency on Western goodwill, the Russian government was not in favour of such a consortium. It regarded this multilateral Western attempt to obtain access to Soviet resources as a blatant, imperialist infringement of its sovereignty. The country was therefore keen on driving a rift between the assembled states, particularly between Britain and France, and subsequently concluding separate treaties with individual states.[9]

It is probably not entirely correct to talk of a carefully worked-out,

7. For the conference see Carole Fink, *The Genoa Conference: European Diplomacy, 1921–22* (Chapel Hill, NC, 1984); and the various articles in Fink *et al.*, eds, *Genoa.* For the general background of German foreign policy at this time see Peter Krüger, *Die Aussenpolitik der Republik von Weimar* 2nd edn (Darmstadt, 1993), pp. 132ff., 151ff.

8. Kolb, *Weimar Republic*, p. 43. See also Wolfgang Michalka, 'Deutsche Aussenpolitik 1920–33', in Karl Dietrich Bracher, Manfred Funke and Hans-Adolf Jacobson, eds, *Die Weimarer Republik, 1918–33: Politik, Wirtschaft, Gesellschaft* (Bonn, 1987), pp. 310–11; Karl-Dietrich Erdmann, 'Deutschland, Rapallo und der Westen', *Vierteljahrshefte für Zeitgeschichte* 11 (1963), 105–65.

9. Erdmann, 'Deutschland'; also Theodor Schieder, 'Die Entstehungsgeschichte des Rapallo-Vertrages', in *Historische Zeitschrift* 204 (1967), 555, 559.

'grand strategy' as the basis for German foreign policy at this stage.[10] There were other reasons for Berlin's interest in a rapprochement with Russia, apart from economic and financial ones. Germany wished to break out from its post-war diplomatic isolation. It hoped to obtain a revision of the Treaty of Versailles, for example concerning the territories lost to Poland, through cooperation with Lenin's government. Mutual hostility towards the newly re-created Poland and to the Polish–French alliance was certainly a factor in achieving this aim. A closer understanding with the Soviet Union might also provide useful leverage with the West in the matter of reparation payments. These payments had proved to be a heavy burden on the German economy.[11] Influential advisers in the government like Assistant State Secretary Ago von Maltzan, who was in effect running the German government's eastern policy, and Chief of Staff General Seekt favoured a more active German *Ostpolitik*. They particularly had an eye on closer military cooperation.[12] Moreover, Foreign Minister Rathenau himself was an influential industrialist who was very aware of the economic advantages of a close relationship with the Soviet Union. He had been working for such a development since 1919, though in 1922 Rathenau had continued to express doubts about entering into the treaty, until shortly before it had been signed.[13]

Despite this somewhat strange partnership between Lenin's revolutionary Soviet Union – still intent on exporting communism to the world – and capitalist Germany with its strong, right-wing political leanings, a Russo-German rapprochement should not have come as a surprise. Although events in the recent past had led to the deterioration and eventually cessation of political relations between the two, this development was soon reversed. After the war, both countries realized that they needed to escape from the diplomatic and economic isolation that had been imposed on them by the West in the aftermath of the war. In short, they could not afford to remain on unfriendly terms.[14] Moreover, by February 1920, European powers like Italy, Britain and France had become interested in exploring the huge export potential of Russia's large population. Soon 'the European race for Russia was on'

10. As indicated by Schieder: see 'Entstehungsgeschichte', 558. For a refutation of this view see Krüger, 'Rainy Day', p. 56.

11. See Hermann-Josef Rupieper, *The Cuno Government and Reparations, 1922–1923: Politics and Economics* (The Hague, 1979).

12. See Schieder, 'Entstehungsgeschichte', 549ff.; Marshall M. Lee and Wolfgang Michalka, *German Foreign Policy, 1917–1933: Continuity or Break?* (Leamington Spa, 1987), pp. 50ff.; Pogge von Strandmann, 'Preventive Diplomacy', p. 138.

13. See Krüger, 'Rainy Day', pp. 56, 60.

14. See Lee and Michalka, *German Foreign Policy*, pp. 49ff.; John Hiden, *Germany and Europe, 1919–39* (London, 1977), pp. 86ff.

and Germany made sure that it was 'from the beginning a significant factor in Western economic initiatives in Russia'.[15] Ever-closer economic and, since 1920, increasing, though still limited, military cooperation took place. On 6 May 1921, this culminated in the signing of a Provisional Agreement between Germany and Russia. Almost immediately further attempts to improve relations were embarked upon. In the winter of 1921/22 they almost came to fruition. Unsuccessful negotiations took place in December/January, February and again between 2–4 April 1922 in Berlin. A five-point agreement had been worked out in February but not signed. Because of Germany's hesitation to rule out categorically the country's participation in the envisaged international consortium, the Soviet representative refused to sign. Both Rathenau and Chancellor Wirth were not too upset, not wishing to spoil relations with the Western powers before the Conference of Genoa. At this stage they may have hoped that Germany's membership of the consortium would enable the country to obtain a solution in its favour of the complicated reparation question. However, only two months later the substance of the document drawn up in February would become known to the world as the Treaty of Rapallo.[16]

Still, as Pogge von Strandmann has explained, 'in the last resort neither Rathenau nor Wirth really believed in an international consortium for developing Russia. They put German industry first and exploited the separate dealings of the allies to defend the German action.'[17] At Genoa the German delegation soon realized that negotiations between the Allied powers and the Soviet Union were not progressing too well. An agreement regarding a consortium was not imminent. The Allies might well be on the brink of asking the Germans to join the negotiations. On the insistence of the British Prime Minister, Lloyd George, and contrary to the initial intentions of the Allies, Germany had been excluded from the talks with the Russians. London believed that the envisaged solution involving a mutual renunciation of all Russian and Allied debts might encourage the Germans to ask for the same.[18]

When an invitation to join the negotiations seemed to be imminent, Ago von Maltzan, the mover behind the scenes, acted quickly by immediately approaching the Soviets. The Germans, and not the Soviets as has long been assumed, took the initiative.[19] Germany now declared

15. See Krüger, *Aussenpolitik*, p. 115; Lee and Michalka, *German Foreign Policy*, p. 51.

16. See Schieder, 'Entstehungsgeschichte', 565–6, 589; Pogge von Strandmann, 'Preventive Diplomacy', pp. 124ff.; Lee and Michalka, *German Foreign Policy*, pp. 48ff.

17. Pogge von Strandmann, 'Preventive Diplomacy', p. 137.

18. See Krüger, 'Rainy Day', pp. 53–4.

19. Ibid., pp. 55–6.

it was prepared to sign an agreement based on the Berlin negotiations in February. The German government used the argument that the Allies had been about to sign an agreement with the Soviets that would have left Germany isolated as a pretext for its rapid signing of the treaty. Apart from reasons of economic cooperation, the government in Berlin wanted to demonstrate in a spectacular way that negotiations with the Soviet Union ought not to be conducted without German participation. The country regarded relations with Eastern Europe as its traditional domain. Maltzan had indeed embarked on 'pure power politics'.[20]

However, there were also domestic reasons for concluding the treaty with the Soviets quickly. For the German electorate, the Berlin government was synonymous with the highly unpopular policy of fulfilling the Versailles peace treaty. Demonstrating that it was capable of executing a strong policy which ran counter to the plans of the Allied powers would be much appreciated by the German public.[21] It is still a matter of controversy whether or not the government employed this strategy in the hope of actually signing the treaty in the course of the Genoa Conference, thus creating the strongest impact possible.[22] However, the conclusion of the treaty was 'by no means certain from the beginning and depended on many unforeseeable circumstances'.[23]

When the Treaty of Rapallo was announced to the assembled international gathering and to the world at large, it was a bombshell; it was a sensation which amazed the other participants and almost wrecked the conference.[24] The actual content of the agreement, however, was rather modest and could be regarded as merely representing a belated peace treaty between the Soviet Union and Germany.[25] Both countries abandoned any claims against each other for war damage. Moreover, Germany renounced its claims to all German property that had been nationalized by the Bolshevik government. Russia, on the other hand, would not make use of Article 116 of the Versailles peace treaty which provided for Russian claims for reparations from Germany, albeit in somewhat vague terms. The two countries also entered into full diplomatic relations and agreed to conduct their economic affairs on a most-

20. Pogge von Strandmann, 'Preventive Diplomacy', pp. 123–4, 142–3. The quote is from Krüger, 'Rainy Day', p. 59.

21. See Pogge von Strandmann, 'Preventive Diplomacy', p. 143; Krüger, 'Rainy Day', p. 57.

22. See Pogge von Strandmann, 'Preventive Diplomacy', pp. 123–4, 128ff.; see also note 10 above.

23. Krüger, 'Rainy Day', p. 60.

24. See Pogge von Strandmann, 'Preventive Diplomacy', p. 138; Lee and Michalka, *German Foreign Policy*, p. 56.

25. See Schieder, 'Entstehungsgeschichte', 593, 599–600.

favoured-nation basis.[26] Despite immediate rumours that Russia and Germany had also signed secret military agreements and entered into extensive commercial deals, this was not the case, though subsequently a close and secret military and trade relationship between the two countries began to flourish.[27]

The significance of the Treaty of Rapallo was and still is highly controversial. For the Soviet Union it was for decades the model of how to enter into agreements with capitalist states based on 'peaceful co-existence'. For many Germans it was the first attempt to revise the detested Versailles peace treaty which had demoted Germany, as it was viewed, from its rightful great-power status. This is not the place, however, to enter into a detailed discussion of the relevant literature.[28] It is sufficient to state that Hermann Graml's controversial thesis that the Treaty of Rapallo was meant to destroy the 'policy of fulfilment' and represented in fact 'a German–Soviet "revisionist" conspiracy' directed against the Treaty of Versailles has not entirely stood the test of time.[29] At least partially, Rapallo seems to have been a 'treaty of normalization and liquidation, born of immediate economic and political needs',[30] though whether it was politically in the best interest of the German people to sign the treaty at this point is questionable. It seems, however, to be somewhat of an exaggeration to regard the Treaty of Rapallo as 'one of the major mistakes of German politics which turned the history of Europe into a fateful direction'.[31]

Rapallo was not simply defensive. It was also a preventive treaty. With its dramatic action the Berlin government was pointing out to the Western world that relations with Soviet Russia were predominantly a German matter and that 'the Allies should neither negotiate nor come

26. See Kolb, *Weimar Republic*, p. 43; Karl Dietrich Erdmann, *Die Weimarer Republik*, Gebhardt Handbuch der deutschen Geschichte Vol. 19 (Munich, 1980), pp. 154–5.

27. See Lee and Michalka, *German Foreign Policy*, p. 56; Schieder, 'Entstehungsgeschichte', 550–4; Helmut Heiber, *Die Republik von Weimar* 12th edn (Munich, 1979), p. 108; B. Whaley, *Covert German Rearmameant, 1919–1939: Deception and Misperception* (Frederick, 1984), pp. 77–86; Hartmut Pogge von Strandmann, 'Grossindustrie und Rapallopolitik: Deutsch–sowjetische Handelsbeziehungen in der Weimarer Republik', *Historische Zeitschrift* 222 (1976), 265–341.

28. For a discussion of the literature see the excellent survey in Kolb, *Weimar Republic*, pp. 172–4.

29. See ibid., p. 173; Hermann Graml, *Europa zwischen den Kriegen* 5th edn (Munich, 1982); idem, 'Die Rapallo-Politik im Urteil der westdeutschen Forschung', *Vierteljahrshefte für Zeitgeschichte* 18 (1970), 366–91.

30. See Schieder, 'Entstehungsgeschichte', 549, 551ff., 587ff., 599ff. (English quote from Kolb, *Weimar Republic*, p. 173). See also Michael Laffan, 'Weimar and Versailles: German Foreign Policy, 1919–33', in idem, *The Burden of German History, 1919–45* (London, 1988), p. 89.

31. Müller, 'Rapallo–Karriere eines Reizwortes', p. 60.

to any arrangement with Russia over Germany's head'.[32] The treaty represented Germany's first bid for equality and great-power status since Versailles. This does not mean that it was the beginning of a crudely revisionist anti-Western policy, though it certainly had an adverse effect on the slowly emerging European consciousness and on any plans for European cooperation developed by Lloyd George and others.[33] The 'Rapallo legend' of a conspiratorial Soviet–German deal against the Western world must largely be regarded as a myth, albeit a very influential one. Even today, this legend has proven to be almost indestructible.[34] Still, to a considerable degree the Germans had only themselves to blame for the creation of such a myth. After all, Rapallo was indeed 'a risky gamble that Germany might substantially improve its international position by establishing a special, intimate relationship with Soviet Russia, thereby [at least potentially] continuously threatening other European powers with a close Russo-German tie on all levels and thus demonstrating for domestic as well as international purposes a strong sense of national independence'.[35] Since then, 'Rapallo has been without doubt, in the eyes of the West, a reminder of the possibility of further, separate and perhaps more threatening agreements between Germany and Russia'.[36]

ADENAUER'S VISIT TO MOSCOW IN 1955

In the immediate aftermath of the Second World War, however, the Western Allies had no reason to fear that the West German government would be tempted to do a deal with the Soviet Union in an attempt to unify the divided country. It was well known in Western capitals that Chancellor Adenauer strongly believed in the need for integrating the Federal Republic with the West. He was also a convinced advocate of

32. See Pogge von Strandmann, 'Preventive Diplomacy', pp. 123–4.

33. See Krüger, 'Rainy Day', pp. 63–4; also idem, 'European Ideology and European Reality: European Unity and German Foreign Policy in the 1920s', in Peter M. Stirk, ed., *European Unity in Context: The Interwar Period* (London, 1989), pp. 89–91.

34. See Kolb, *Weimar Republic*, p. 174. It has been rightly said that the real importance of the Treaty of Rapallo lies in the exaggerated significance it has been given generally. See Bernd Martin, *Weltmacht oder Niedergang? Deutsche Grossmachtpolitik im 20. Jahrhundert* (Darmstadt, 1989), p. 83.

35. Krüger, 'Rainy Day', p. 56.

36. Pogge von Strandmann, 'Preventive Diplomacy', p. 123.

a united Europe,[37] and his support led to some notable successes on this path. Above all, France, West Germany and the Benelux countries signed up to the Schumann Plan in 1950, which later resulted in the union of the coal and steel industries.[38] The signing of the Bonn and Paris treaties in May 1952 established the formation of a European Defence Community (EDC) which was meant to provide for peaceful West German rearmament and protection against an invasion from the East. The pursuit of an ever closer political union was also mentioned in this context. The Bonn and Paris treaties guaranteed almost full sovereignty for the West German state once the treaties had been ratified by the national parliaments of the six signatory states.[39]

Without doubt, Adenauer's primary political goals were to obtain full national sovereignty for West Germany and the country's integration with the West as an equal. The Chancellor had little faith in his fellow countrymen and was determined to make it impossible for either the Germans or their future leaders to conduct independent power-politics and thus to embark again upon the path to war or to seek a too-close rapprochement with the USSR.[40] He never admitted this in public. This was for both practical political, as well as for personal, philosophical, reasons. The Chancellor was realistic enough to regard German unification as something which only ought to be achieved in the long run – if at all.[41]

37. See, for example, Werner Weidenfeld, *Konrad Adenauer und Europa: Die geistigen Grundlagen der westeuropäischen Integrationspolitik des ersten Bonner Bundeskanzlers* (Bonn, 1976); Ludolf Herbst *et al.*, eds, *Vom Marshallplan zur EWG: Die Eingliederung der Bundesrepublik Deutschland in die westliche Welt* (Munich, 1990). On Adenauer see above all Henning Köhler, *Adenauer: Eine Politische Biographie* (Frankfurt, 1994); Hans-Peter Schwarz, *Adenauer: Der Staatsmann, 1952–67* (Stuttgart, 1991); and, of course, Adenauer's extensive memoirs: *Erinnerungen* Vols 1 and 2, 4th edn (Stuttgart, 1984).

38. See John Gillingham, *Coal, Steel and the Rebirth of Europe, 1945–1955: The Germans and French from Ruhr Conflict to Economic Community* (Cambridge, 1991).

39. See Saki Dockrill, *Britain's Policy for West German Rearmament, 1950–1955* (Cambridge, 1991); Robert McGeehan, *The German Rearmament Question: American Diplomacy and European Defense after World War II* (London, 1971); Edward Fursdon, *The European Defence Community: A History* (London, 1980).

40. See Public Record Office, London (hereafter PRO): FO 371/118 254/WG 1071/1374, 15/12/1955, conversation between the British Permanent Under-Secretary Sir Ivone Kirkpatrick and the German Ambassador in London, Herwarth von Bittenfeld; also PRO: FO 371/118 183/WG 10338/153, letter Allen (Bonn) to Johnston (Foreign Office, London – hereafter FO), 17/9/1955. See also Peter Bender, *Neue Ostpolitik: Vom Mauerbau bis zum Moskauer Vertrag* 2nd edn (Munich, 1989), p. 41.

41. See Klaus Larres, *Politik der Illusionen: Churchill, Eisenhower und die deutsche Frage, 1945–1955* (Göttingen, 1995), pp. 147ff.; see also the various articles in Josef Foschepoth, ed., *Adenauer und die Deutsche Frage* 2nd edn (Göttingen, 1990).

Due to the French parliament's hesitation in giving up sovereignty over a large part of its military forces, the ratification of the EDC treaty failed in August 1954. However, an alternative route to West German rearmament and integration with the West was found in the autumn. It enabled the Federal Republic to join both the Western European Union and NATO on 5 May 1955 and thereby obtain its sovereignty.[42] Only two weeks later, on 20 May, the Warsaw Pact was founded with the GDR as an integral member. German unification had become even more unlikely to happen than before. While the Federal Republic's integration with the West had now been realized, no genuine rapprochement with Moscow had taken place. Consequently, in the early Cold War years the 'Rapallo factor' did not play a decisive role in West Germany's relations with the wider world. In actual fact, it was generally feared that the Bonn government's accession to NATO might worsen East–West relations further.[43]

This, however, was not the case. Instead, 1955 proved to be a watershed as far as Moscow's policies regarding both the East–West conflict and the German question were concerned. In all likelihood, until the uprising in the GDR in June 1953 the Soviet Union had hoped to be able to prevent the integration of the Federal Republic with the West and thereby to obtain German unification on a neutral basis.[44] When this failed to happen, the USSR gradually began to adopt a strategy which required that Germany should remain permanently divided. Consequently, Moscow needed international recognition of its protegé, the GDR. It also meant that the improvement of relations with the West, particularly with West Germany, would be prudent. After all, apart from the desire to obtain acceptance of the East Berlin government,

42. See Raymond Aron and Daniel Lerner, eds, *France Defeats the EDC* (New York, 1957); Paul Noack, *Das Scheitern der Europäischen Verteidigungsgemeinschaft: Entstehungsprozesse vor und nach dem 30. August 1954* (Düsseldorf, 1977); Rolf Steininger, 'Das Scheitern der EVG und der Beitritt der Bundesrepublik zur NATO', *APUZ* 17 (27/4/1985), 3–18; Köhler, *Adenauer*, pp. 820ff.

43. Adenauer, *Erinnerungen, Vol. 2: 1953–1955*, p. 448.

44. See Klaus Larres, 'Preserving Law and Order: Britain, the United States and the East German Uprising of 1953', *Twentieth Century British History* 5.3 (1994), 320–50; see also Christian Ostermann, *The United States, the East German Uprising of 1953, and the Limits of Rollback* (Cold War International History Project, Woodrow Wilson Center, Washington, DC, 1994). On Moscow's German policy since mid-1953 see Boris Meissner, 'Die deutsch–sowjetischen Beziehungen seit dem Zweiten Weltkrieg', *Osteuropa* (1985), pp. 631–52; Eberhard Schulz, 'Die sowjetische Deutschlandpolitik', in Dietrich Geyer, ed., *Osteuropa-Handbuch. Sowjetunion: Aussenpolitik: 1955–73* (Cologne, 1976), pp. 229–93.

the new Soviet leadership also wished to improve its poor trade relations with the West.[45]

From February 1955 this became an active policy, once Prime Minister Malenkov had been replaced by Bulganin with Khrushchev being the mover behind the scenes. The USSR embarked on a policy of *détente* and peaceful co-existence.[46] As early as 26 March, Bulganin declared that Moscow was quite ready to attend a four-power summit conference to improve international confidence. On 13 June it was announced that such a four-power conference of heads of government would take place in Geneva in the second half of July. By this stage, a particularly impressive demonstration of Soviet interest in the relaxation of the East–West conflict had already occurred. It was the signing of the Austrian State Treaty on 15 May. Austria remained undivided, received its sovereignty on the condition of 'perpetual neutrality' and the Soviet occupation forces left the country.[47] Khrushchev and Bulganin also embarked upon a dramatic rapprochement with Tito by visiting Belgrade between 26 May and 2 June.[48] Then, on 7 June 1955 Adenauer received an invitation to visit Moscow 'in the near future' to 'consider the question of establishing diplomatic and trade relations . . . and to examine the relevant issues'. It was stated that 'no preliminary conditions' for entering into diplomatic relations were deemed necessary. The Soviet Union hoped that 'personal contact' with Adenauer and any of his representa-

45. See Angela Stent, *From Embargo to Ostpolitik: The Political Economy of West German–Soviet Relations, 1955–1980* (Cambridge, 1981), pp. 27–35. See also Gerhard Wettig, 'Die beginnende Umorientierung der sowjetischen Deutschland-Politik im Frühjahr und Sommer 1953', *Deutschland-Archiv* 28.5 (1995), 495–507.

46. In the course of Adenauer's negotiations in Moscow Khrushchev still maintained that NATO was a hostile alliance and the 'Soviet Union was doing everything it could to weaken NATO'. However, the Soviet Union had realized that asking for the dissolution of NATO was 'unrealistic' – the 'important thing was co-existence'. *Foreign Relations of the United State* (hereafter *FRUS*), 1955–57, Vol. 5, p. 576: Bohlen (Moscow) to State Dept., 11/9/1955.

47. It was also agreed that for the purpose of securing neutrality 'in all future times Austria will not join any military alliances and will not permit the establishment of any foreign military bases on its territory'. Royal Institute of International Affairs (hereafter RIIA), ed., *Documents on International Affairs, 1955* (London, 1958), p. 239. See also Günter Bischof, 'Österreichische Neutralität, die deutsche Frage und europäische Sicherheit 1953–1955', in Rolf Steininger *et al.*, eds, *Die doppelte Eindämmung: Europäische Sicherheit und deutsche Frage in den Fünfzigern* (Munich, 1993), pp. 133–76; Rolf Steininger, '1955: The Austrian State Treaty and the German Question', *Diplomacy & Statecraft* 3.3 (1992), 494–522.

48. See Stephen Clissold, ed., *Yugoslavia and the Soviet Union, 1939–1973: A Documentary Survey* (London, 1975); Pierre Maurer, *La reconciliation sovieto-yougoslave, 1954–1958: illusions et desillusions de Tito* (Fribourg, CH, 1991).

tives could be established in the 'interest of peace and European security'.[49]

In the West, the note from Moscow was regarded as 'a diplomatic sensation of the first order'.[50] The general 'vigour and freshness and apparent conciliatoriness of the new Soviet regime . . . gave western statesmen much to think about'.[51] Adenauer, in particular, was confronted with a political dilemma. The new climate of *détente* and the invitation to visit Moscow exposed the inner contradictions in the Chancellor's politics. As early as 1952 Adenauer had hinted that the possibility of entering into closer relations with the Soviet Union and Eastern Europe were part and parcel of West German sovereignty.[52] But it was obvious that such a policy would raise the difficult question of recognizing the GDR, a country which was already represented by an ambassador in the Soviet capital but was regarded as illegitimate by both Bonn and the West. The situation was similar in respect to the Polish border along the Oder–Neisse line which the Adenauer government

49. The note is published in RIIA, ed., *Documents*, pp. 245–8, with quotes on pp. 248, 245. See also *FRUS*, 1955–57, Vol. 5, p. 544: Bohlen (Moscow) to State Dept., 6/8/1955. Regarding Adenauer's invitation and subsequent journey to Moscow see above all Josef Foschepoth, 'Adenauers Moskaureise 1955', *APUZ* 22 (31/5/1986), 30–46; Detlef Felken, *Dulles und Deutschland: Die amerikanische Deutschlandpolitik, 1953–1959* (Bonn, 1993), pp. 320–6; Köhler, *Adenauer*, pp. 872–89; Schwarz, *Adenauer: Der Staatsmann*, pp. 189–222; idem, *Die Ära Adenauer: Gründerjahre der Republik 1949–1957* (Stuttgart, 1981), pp. 273–82; Max Schulze-Vorberg, 'Die Moskaureise 1955', in Dieter Blumenwitz *et al.*, eds, *Konrad Adenauer und seine Zeit: Politik und Persönlichkeit des ersten Bundeskanzlers* (Stuttgart, 1976), I, pp. 651–64; Rainer Salzmann, 'Adenauers Moskaureise in sowjetischer Sicht', in Blumenwitz *et al.*, *Adenauer und seine Zeit*, (Stuttgart, 1976), II, pp. 131–59. See also the memoirs from members of Adenauer's delegation, above all Wilhelm G. Grewe, *Rückblenden, 1976–1951* (Berlin, 1979), pp. 229–51; Herbert Blankenhorn, *Verständnis und Verständigung: Blätter eines politischen Tagebuchs 1949 bis 1979* (Frankfurt, 1980), pp. 224–35; Carlo Schmidt, *Erinnerungen* (Bern, 1979), pp. 564–85; and, of course, Adenauer himself, *Erinnerungen* Vol. 2, pp. 487–556. See also Strobe Talbott, ed., *Khrushchev Remembers: The Last Testament* (London, 1974), pp. 357–62.

50. *Christian Science Monitor*, 8/6/1955, quoted in RIIA, ed., *Survey of International Affairs, 1955–56* (London, 1960), p. 138.

51. RIIA, ed., *Survey*, p. 69.

52. On Adenauer's *Ostpolitik* see Peter Siebenmorgen, *Gezeitenwechsel: Aufbruch zur Entspannungspolitik* (Bonn, 1990); Christoph Klessmann, 'Adenauers Deutschland- und Ostpolitik 1955–1963', in Foschepoth, ed., *Adenauer*, pp. 61–79; Gottfried Niedhart and Normen Altmann, 'Zwischen Beurteilung und Verurteilung: Die Sowjetunion im Urteil Konrad Adenauers', in ibid., pp. 99–117; Boris Meissner, 'Adenauer und die Sowjetunion von 1955 bis 1959', in Blumenwitz *et al.*, eds, *Adenauer* II, pp. 192ff.; Hans-Peter Schwarz, 'Adenauers Ostpolitik', in Wolfram Hanrieder *et al.*, eds, *Im Spannungsfeld der Weltpolitik: 30 Jahre deutsche Aussenpolitik* (Stuttgart, 1981), pp. 207–32; Klaus Gotto, 'Adenauers Deutschland- und Ostpolitik 1954–1963', in Klaus Gotto *et al.*, eds, *Konrad Adenauer: Seine Deutschland- und Aussenpolitik 1945–1963* (Munich, 1975), pp. 156–286.

refused to accept as permanent. Bonn continued to insist on observing that part of the 1945 Potsdam agreement which said that Germany's eastern border was to be decided by a future German peace treaty.[53]

Adenauer had always emphasized that German unification would only come about in a climate of East–West *détente* and disarmament. This, he strongly believed, could only be achieved by a Western policy of strength.[54] Now *détente*, in the form of a personal invitation to Moscow, had arrived. Nevertheless, the Chancellor had no intention of changing his policy. He was deeply distrustful of the Soviet peace initiative.[55] Adenauer was convinced that the Soviet Union was 'now weak and . . . [the West] should not grant them the time to recover'.[56] However, he found himself under increasing pressure to develop a more flexible attitude. German public opinion and the SPD opposition believed very strongly that the Chancellor ought to travel to Moscow as soon as possible.[57] Also the pressure from German business – mostly loyal supporters of the government – to develop much more extensive trade relations with the East was an important factor which Adenauer could not afford to ignore.[58] The next general elections were due in two years' time. To an ever increasing number of people, only normal relations with Moscow would provide a way out of the 'dead end of the cold

53. See Schwarz, *Adenauer: Der Staatsmann*, pp. 177–9.

54. On the West's 'policy of strength' see the standard work by Coral Bell, *Negotiation from Strength: A Study in the Politics of Power* (London, 1962). Regarding Adenauer's anti-communism see, for example, Weidenfeld, *Adenauer und Europa*, pp. 142–79. For the relationship between Dulles and Adenauer see Felken, *Dulles*, pp. 145–50; Hans-Jürgen Grabbe, 'Konrad Adenauer, John Foster Dulles and West German–American Relations', in Richard H. Immerman, ed., *John Foster Dulles and the Diplomacy of the Cold War* (Princeton, NJ, 1990), pp. 109–32; Manfred Görtemaker, 'John Foster Dulles und die Westintegration der Bundesrepublik Deutschland', in Steininger *et al.*, eds, *Eindämmung*, pp. 9–38.

55. In his memoirs Adenauer says: 'It was my conviction that the Soviet Union aimed at a period of détente in order to solve the [inner] problems the Soviet leadership found itself confronted with. Yet, there was no indication that the USSR had changed its inner goal, which was the ambition to conquer and rule the world through communism'. *Erinnerungen*, Vol. 2, p. 491.

56. *FRUS* 1955–57, Vol. 5, p. 226: Conversation Adenauer–Dulles, 13/6/1955.

57. See Salzmann, 'Adenauers Moskaureise', p. 137.

58. See RIIA, ed., *Survey*, p. 140; Stent, *Embargo*, pp. 35–40. In this field, as in others, Adenauer had to be careful not to arouse too much suspicion. For example, Douglas Dodds-Parker, the British Parliamentary Under-Secretary for Commonwealth Affairs, expressed in mid-September 1955 the widely shared opinion: 'Chancellor Adenauer, of course, is definitely pro-West, but Germany has traditional economic ties to Russia in the East. It is the old struggle between the Teutons and the Slavs. Only the fact that neither will allow the other to rule the household prevents a grand alliance against the West'. PRO: FO 371/118 183/WG 10338/161, 13/9/1955. See also Hanna Paul Calm, *Ostpolitik und Wirtschaftsinteressen in der Ära Adenauer* (Frankfurt, 1981).

war'.[59] Most importantly, it was obvious that German unification could only be obtained through discussions with the Soviet Union. Now the Federal government had received the opportunity of talking to Moscow directly for the first time since the war; due to West Germany's newly found sovereignty one did not have to rely on the mediation of the Western Allies any more. Adenauer, therefore, was in no position to decline the invitation. There was also the highly emotive question of the fate of a considerable number of German soldiers and civilian internees who were still captive in the Soviet Union.[60] By early 1955 Moscow was ready to use these captives to make the Bonn government more amenable to Soviet wishes. The Kremlin's strategy was to claim that a solution to the problem could easily be found once Adenauer had entered into negotiations on the issue.[61] Thus, the German public hoped that Adenauer's journey to Moscow would lead to considerable progress in the matter.

There existed, however, yet another potentially difficult issue which the Chancellor had to tackle. This was the relationship with the Western Allies and the suspicion that Adenauer's invitation to Moscow and any arrangements agreed upon with the Soviet government could easily lead to the beginning of a new 'Rapallo policy'.[62] Indeed, the French government's initial reaction to the invitation from the Kremlin was described by British diplomats as 'one of some apprehension'.[63] Adenauer, therefore, had to avoid creating the impression that the German government was about to do yet another secret deal with the Soviet Union. In his memoirs the Chancellor describes his difficult task as follows: 'The prime task of my negotiations in Moscow had to be: absolute loyalty to the West. We could not afford to give rise to the slightest suspicion regarding our firm attachment to the West.'[64] Moreover, because of the general enthusiasm for the Austrian State Treaty,

59. *Rheinische Post* as quoted (without date) in RIIA, ed., *Survey*, p. 140.

60. See Foschepoth, 'Adenauer's Moskaureise', 31–4. See also Dieter Riesenberger, ed., *Das Deutsche Rote Kreuz, Konrad Adenauer und das Kriegsgefangenenproblem: Die Rückführung der deutschen Kriegsgefangenen aus der Sowjetunion (1952–1955)* (Bremen, 1994); and Arthur L. Smith, *Die 'vermisste Million': Zum Schicksal deutscher Kriegsgefangener nach dem Zweiten Weltkrieg* (Munich, 1992).

61. Regarding the German POWs in the Soviet Union see also PRO: FO 371/118 404 (July–December 1955). See also for the GDR: Beate Ihme-Tuchel, 'Die SED und die deutschen Kriegsgefangenen in der Sowjetunion zwischen 1949 und 1955', in *Deutschland-Archiv* 27.5 (1994), 490–503.

62. For the US view in connection with Adenauer's visit to Moscow see *FRUS* 1955–57, Vol. 5, pp. 224–38, 566–601. For the British view see PRO: FO 371/118 178–183 (March–October 1955).

63. PRO: FO 371/118 178/WG 10338/19, Minute Hancock, 8/6/1955.

64. Adenauer, *Erinnerungen* Vol. 2, pp. 493, 449.

Adenauer believed he needed to convince the Allied powers that a similar solution to the German question, namely the creation of a unified but neutral Germany or a belt of neutral states or zones in the middle of Europe, was much too dangerous.[65]

With hindsight, however, it is most unlikely that Moscow was seriously willing to sacrifice the GDR in favour of a solution to the German question modelled on the Austrian State Treaty. In fact, the note to Adenauer indicated that Moscow's aim was to stabilize the *status quo* in Europe. The Soviet Union wished to have 'normal' relations not only with East Berlin but also with Bonn. In all likelihood it was European *détente* and the realization of the 'two-state theory' that were the main reasons for Moscow's approach to Adenauer and not German unification.[66] 'For the next 15 years, the main goal of the USSR's policy vis-à-vis West Germany remained constant: to obtain Bonn's acceptance of both the postwar borders and the permanent division of Germany.'[67] At the time, however, it was hardly surprising that different conclusions were drawn. Adenauer particularly believed very strongly that it was Moscow's intention to woo West Germany and to ascertain whether or not Bonn could be tempted to embark on a 'Rapallo policy'.[68]

Adenauer was therefore careful to consult the Western Allies, above all the USA, about the invitation to Moscow, which had not come entirely as a surprise to them, though it had not been expected that Moscow would react so quickly after the Federal Republic's accession to NATO.[69] On the whole, the American administration believed that the Kremlin did not seriously anticipate reaching an agreement with Adenauer but wanted to manoeuvre him into a position in which he

65. Ibid., pp. 441–6, 449. See also *FRUS* 1955–57, Vol. 5, pp. 225–6: Conversation Adenauer–Dulles, 13/6/1955.

66. See, for example, Foschepoth, 'Adenauers Moskaureise', 34–5; Wettig, 'Die beginnende Umorientierung', 504–7. For a view to the contrary see Salzmann, 'Adenauers Moskaureise', pp. 136–41; Eden, *Full Circle*, p. 294. See also Harold Macmillan's view as expressed in a conversation with Dulles in Paris on 15 July 1955: *FRUS* 1955–57, Vol. 5, p. 320.

67. F. Stephen Larrabee, 'Moscow and the German Question', in Dirk Verheyen and Christian Soe, eds, *The Germans and their Neighbours* (Boulder, Colo., 1993), p. 206.

68. Adenauer, *Erinnerungen* Vol. 2, p. 553; see also Salzmann, 'Adenauers Moskaureise', pp. 135–6.

69. See *FRUS*, 1955–57, Vol. 5, p. 544, note 3; PRO: FO 371/118 178/WG 10338/G, Hayter (Moscow) to FO, No. 555, 8/6/1955. Even before the official invitation, the East had attempted to establish personal contact with the Adenauer government. For example, Finance Minister Schäffer was asked to travel to East Berlin to meet up with an old acquaintance of his, Vinzenz Müller, who was now the supreme commandant of the East German police. Adenauer made sure that the Allied powers were fully informed about this development, which did not lead to any results. See in detail Schwarz, *Adenauer: Der Staatsmann*, pp. 191–3; Adenauer, *Erinnerungen* Vol. 2, p. 450.

would be forced to turn down a Soviet offer of unification and thus become very unpopular at home. The SPD opposition, which regarded a neutral and united Germany as acceptable, would undoubtedly be strengthened by such an event. This coincided with Adenauer's own view.[70] After all, internal politics obliged Adenauer to 'make a determined effort to ensure that the question of German reunification was at least discussed in Moscow'.[71] There remained, however, an element of insecurity. The Soviet Union was always good for a surprise and might well present some genuine proposals to Adenauer. Therefore, the Chancellor was very careful to keep in close touch with the Western Allies.

During the course of a visit to the USA in mid-June, the Chancellor informed President Dwight D. Eisenhower and Secretary of State John Foster Dulles personally. He pointed out that he did not want to travel to Moscow before the four-power heads of government meeting in Geneva that July. This was so that the Western position on German unification could be made clear before the meeting with the Soviet leadership. He also felt that it might be a good idea if any subsequent four-power foreign ministers' meeting could be held after his return from Moscow. The Western Allies would then be able to benefit from his trip. He emphasized that no concessions should be made 'without obtaining German unification in return'.[72] Adenauer also used the opportunity to warn against any ideas of establishing a neutral Germany or neutral zones in Europe.[73] This in particular was the topic of his conversation with British Prime Minister Eden, whom he visited on his way back from the USA.[74]

In August, following the conference which had produced the much-acclaimed 'spirit of Geneva'[75] and a month before Adenauer's visit, the

70. See Adenauer, *Erinnerungen*, Vol. 2, p. 450; PRO: FO 371/118 183/WG 10338/156, letter Beith (Paris) to Johnston (FO), 22/9/1955.

71. PRO: FO 371/118 179/WG 10338/42, Minute Caccia about his conversation with German Ambassador von Herwarth, 15/8/1955.

72. Adenauer, *Erinnerungen* Vol. 2, p. 460.

73. Ibid., pp. 441–6, 455–65. On Adenauer's US visit see also PRO: FO 371/118 151, Hoyer Millar (Bonn) to FO, Nos 301 and 309, 16/6 and 23/6/1955.

74. Eden mentioned in passing that the West had to consider the possibility that Moscow might have lost interest in a united Germany. See Adenauer, *Erinnerungen* Vol. 2, pp. 462–5; see also PRO: PREM 11/905, FO to UK Delegation in San Francisco, No. 13 (PM T (E) 55/55), 21/6/1955.

75. For the Geneva summit conference see Hermann-Josef Rupieper, 'Gipfeldiplomatie 1955: Dwight D. Eisenhower und Georgij Schukow über Europäische Sicherheit und Deutsche Frage', in Rolf Steininger *et al.*, eds, *Eindämmung*, pp. 213–32; Mechthild Lindemann, 'Die Deutschlandfrage auf der Gipfelkonferenz und der Aussenministerkonferenz in Genf 1955', in Dieter Blumenwitz, Karl Wilhelm Fricke *et al.*, eds, *Die Deutschlandfrage vom 17. Juni 1953 bis zu den Genfer Viermächtekonferenzen von 1955* (Berlin, 1990), pp. 177–205.

German ambassador to Washington, Heinz Krekeler, was in constant touch with the American administration. On 10 August the Chancellor expressed his thoughts in a personal letter to Dulles from which the Secretary of State concluded 'that Adenauer obviously felt nervous about his forthcoming Moscow trip'.[76] At the end of the month, Adenauer's close confidant, Herbert Blankenhorn, was dispatched to Paris and London to inform the respective governments there of the Chancellor's thinking.[77] On 31 August, Dulles' trusted adviser, Livingston Merchant, came to Bonn for 'private and informal talks'.[78] Adenauer explained his quite detailed strategy for the negotiations in Moscow. He once again said that he was merely embarking on an 'exploratory' journey and only intended to get to know the Soviet leadership.[79] Without progress over the questions of German unification and the prisoners of war, no diplomatic relations would be entered into.[80] In the event of progress being made, however, which he regarded as most unlikely,[81] Adenauer was still only prepared to exchange 'diplomatic agents' with Moscow and to have political commissions set up to look into issues such as unification, the POWs and diplomatic recognition. As far as economic issues were concerned, 'there was little in the Soviet trade that Germany needed'. Adenauer summarized his strategy by saying, 'There could be no true normalization as represented by full diplomatic relations so long as the Soviet Union maintained the GDR regime.'[82]

Adenauer emphasized that he had 'little hope of success'[83] and that he was quite prepared, if the Russians were intransigent on the return of the POWs, reunification and other issues, 'to break off negotiations and return to Bonn'. Merchant agreed with this strategy. The Chancellor's adviser, Blankenhorn, added 'that it was not the German intention

76. *FRUS*, 1955–57, Vol. 5, p. 546: Conversation Eisenhower–Dulles, 11/8/1955; see also Adenauer, *Erinnerungen* Vol. 2, pp. 478–80.

77. PRO: FO 371/118 180/WG 10338/61, Allen (Bonn) to FO, No. 475, 25/8/1955.

78. *FRUS*, 1955–57, Vol. 5, p. 550: Letter Dulles to Adenauer, 15/8/1955.

79. See PRO: FO 371/118 180/WG 10338/87, FO to British Embassy Bonn, No. 712, 2/9/1955; *FRUS*, 1955–57, Vol. 5, pp. 567, 569: Conversation Adenauer–Merchant *et al.*, 31/8/1955.

80. See *FRUS*, 1955–57, Vol. 5, p. 574: Bohlen (Moscow) to State Dept., 10/9/1955; PRO: FO 371/118 181/WG 10338/94, Minute Kirkpatrick, 8/9/1955.

81. See PRO: FO 371/118 180/10338/80, FO to Bonn, No. 712, on Kirkpatrick's conversation with Blankenhorn in London, 2/9/1955.

82. *FRUS*, 1955–57, Vol. 5, pp. 567–9: Conversation Adenauer–Merchant *et al.*, 31/8/1955.

83. According to the British record, Adenauer said: 'He expected very little, not even agreement on the return of the prisoners of war.' PRO: FO 371/118 180/WG 10338/87, FO to Bonn, No. 712, 2/9/1955.

to reach final decisions'. The realization of a 'middle solution between the two extremes of breaking off negotiations and establishing full relations' might be the best 'means of continuing contact with the Russians'.[84] The British Foreign Office's Permanent Under-Secretary, Ivone Kirkpatrick, also agreed with this strategy. He 'thought it a good thing for the Germans to hold up on the establishment of full diplomatic relations'.[85]

All in all, the Chancellor was careful to give the Western Allies as much information and reassurance as possible prior to his departure for Moscow. Upon arriving on 8 September, Adenauer reported to Dulles 'that nothing has happened to disturb Germany–US relationship'.[86] Soon, however, it became clear that the Chancellor had overestimated his ability to direct the negotiations. He confessed that he 'had taken too stiff a line immediately before . . . [his] visit to Moscow'. In the next few days Adenauer would have to go 'a good deal further down the throat of the Russian bear than he had said he was going to do before leaving Bonn'.[87]

On the whole, the American and British administrations believed in Adenauer's loyalty to the West. The 'Rapallo factor' and the fear of a separate Russo-German special relationship did little to influence Western policy-makers in their view. The only exception was Washington's ambassador in Moscow, Charles Bohlen. Although initially 'confident' that Adenauer would 'not accept' full diplomatic relations, Bohlen had been in favour of postponing the visit.[88] He found it 'difficult to see what advantage there would be . . . by [Adenauer's] personal visit prior to establishing diplomatic relations'.[89] Adenauer's activities in Moscow only confirmed his view. To him, these were equivalent to the 'appeasement' of the Soviet Union.[90] When, late on

84. *FRUS*, 1955–57, Vol. 5, p. 569. Similar statements were made during German State Secretary Hallstein's and Foreign Minister von Brentano's conversations with British officials in Bonn. See, for example, PRO: FO 371/118 180/WG 10338/61, Allen (Bonn) to FO, Nos 475 and 480, 27/8/1955 and 28/8/1955.

85. *FRUS*, 1955–57, Vol. 5, p. 571: Conversation Kirkpatrick–Merchant *et al.* in London, 1/9/1955.

86. Quoted in Felken, *Dulles*, p. 321.

87. PRO: FO 371/118 183/WG 10338/156, letter Beith (Paris) to Johnston (FO), 22/9/1955; ibid., WG 10338/158, Minute Ward, 15/9/1955; ibid., 118 182/WG 10338/142, Jebb (Paris) to FO, No. 371, 21/9/1955.

88. *FRUS*, 1955–57, Vol. 5, p. 575: Bohlen (Moscow) to State Dept., 10/9/1955.

89. Ibid., p. 545: Bohlen (Moscow) to State Dept., 6/8/1955. See also PRO: FO 371/118 180/WG 10338/88, Minute Jellicoe on Bohlen's views, 8/9/1955.

90. Charles E. Bohlen, *Witness to History, 1929–1969* (New York, 1973), p. 387; Grewe, *Rückblenden*, pp. 245–51; PRO: FO 371/118 181/WG 10338/94, Hayter (Moscow) to FO, No. 1025, 13/9/1955.

12 September, Blankenhorn informed him, together with the British and French ambassadors, about a deal on opening diplomatic relations, proposed at the very last minute by the Soviets, Bohlen exploded. The French ambassador also 'became rather excited'.[91]

At a reception for the German delegation in the evening of 12 September, Bulganin and Khrushchev had suddenly suggested entering into a secret 'gentlemen's agreement',[92] involving the 'release of all German nationals at present detained or imprisoned in Soviet Union in return for diplomatic relations with Federal Republic and exchange of ambassadors'. This was 'a complete surprise' to Adenauer, coming as it did after the day's totally 'negative and occasionally acrid discussion'. Blankenhorn expressed the view that despite the dissent of some of the Chancellor's advisers, Adenauer would not be able to refuse the return of the prisoners. Bohlen, however, pointed out to him that the USSR was, in fact, offering the 'prisoners against legalization of the division of Germany' and 'doubted whether any letter of reservation in regard to GDR would change that basic fact'.[93] Bohlen even went so far 'as to say that the next step would be for the Chancellor to agree to Germany leaving NATO in exchange for reunification'.[94]

The British government was less adamant. Although William Hayter, the British ambassador, was much more critical of Adenauer's conduct than his colleagues in London, he did not go as far as Bohlen. Despite some misgivings, in general London viewed with 'equanimity' the establishment of diplomatic relations between Bonn and Moscow. After all, the British had never been very keen on German unification. On the whole they believed that the continued division of Germany would ensure that Europe would be much more stable and peaceful.[95] Furthermore, the government in London had 'little

91. PRO: FO 371/118 181/WG 10338/94, Hayter (Moscow) to FO, No. 1025, 13/9/1955. See also Bohlen, *Witness to History*; *FRUS*, 1955–57, Vol. 5, pp. 579–84.

92. *FRUS*, 1955–57, Vol. 5, p. 582: Bohlen (Moscow) to State Dept., 14/9/1955; PRO: FO 371/118 181/WG 10338/94, Hayter (Moscow) to FO, No. 1025, 13/9/1955. Regarding Moscow's wish to keep the 'bargain' secret see PRO: FO 371/118 181/WG 10339/109, Allen (Bonn) to FO, No. 513, 14/9/1955.

93. PRO: FO 371/118 181/WG 10339/109, Allen (Bonn) to FO, No. 513, 14/9/1955; *FRUS*, 1955–57, Vol. 5, p. 580: Bohlen (Moscow) to State Dept., 13/9/1955. See also Talbott, ed., *Khrushchev Remembers*, pp. 359–60.

94. PRO: FO 371/118 181/WG 10339/109, Allen (Bonn) to FO, No. 513, 14/9/1955.

95. See, for example, the successful attempts by the FO in 1953–55 to 'scupper' Churchill's endeavours to overcome the division of Germany by means of an international summit conference in Larres, *Politik der Illusionen*, pp. 151ff.; see ibid., p. 181, for Minister

doubt that the Chancellor will accept the Russian offer whatever we say'.[96]

However, Adenauer's retreat in Moscow could hardly be overlooked. Despite his strong assurances beforehand – 'firmness was the only thing they understood'[97] – a rapprochement with the 'arch enemy' had actually taken place. The British even spoke of a 'very considerable victory for the Russians'.[98] In return, Adenauer had merely received a verbal promise that Moscow would release all of the remaining 9,626 German 'war criminals' as well as any surviving civilian internees either to East or West Germany depending on where they used to live. During the negotiations, the issue of German unification, which Dulles, particularly, had wished to be at the centre of the discussions, was hardly mentioned. Instead, the Soviet Union adopted a very tough and intransigent stand and advised Adenauer 'to establish contact with [the] GDR' if he wished to bring about German unification.[99] In the end, the German view that, despite entering into diplomatic relations with the Soviet Union, the Federal Republic was still the sole legitimate representative of the whole of Germany was merely communicated as a unilateral statement to Bulganin in the form of a letter. It was also pointed out that Bonn recognized neither the legitimacy of the GDR nor the Oder–Neisse line as Germany's eastern border.[100]

Ambassador Bohlen was convinced that Adenauer's negotiations in Moscow had been 'disastrous'. He believed that the permanent division of Germany and the existence of the GDR were gaining acceptance through the back door – something Bonn had always claimed it would never be prepared to tolerate. Bohlen also 'was exceedingly angry' about the fact that Adenauer had promised the Soviets to have a word with the

---

of State Selwyn Lloyd's famous statement regarding the necessity of the continued division of Germany.

96. PRO: FO 371/118 181/WG 10338/94, Hayter (Moscow) to FO, No. 1025, 13/9/1955.

97. On 11 September he had also told the Western ambassadors in Moscow somewhat prematurely that 'his chief conclusion from the visit was that it was useless to try to deal with these people by amiability'. PRO: FO 371/118 181/WG 10338/93, Hayter (Moscow) to FO, No. 1025, 11/9/1955.

98. PRO: FO 371/118 181/WG 10338/109, Hayter (Moscow) to FO, No. 1039, 14/9/1955.

99. *FRUS*, 1955–57, Vol. 5, p. 575: Bohlen (Moscow) to State Dept., 11/9/1955; PRO: FO 371/118 181/WG 10338/91, Hayter (Moscow) to FO, Nos 1018 and 1019, 10/9/1955, No. 1020, 11/9/1955, on his conversations with Blankenhorn.

100. Adenauer, *Erinnerungen* Vol. 2, pp. 547–51. See also PRO: FO 371/118 181/WG 10338/107, Hayter (Moscow) to FO, No. 1037, 14/9/1955. On the legal implications of the establishment of diplomatic relations see WG 10338/143, Memorandum Fitzmaurice, the Legal Adviser, 15/9/1955.

Americans about balloons which carried US propaganda material into the Soviet Union.[101] The ambassador reported to the State Department a 'complete collapse of the West German position' and spoke of Moscow's 'greatest diplomatic victory in [the] post-war period'. He even claimed that the countries might have entered into a 'more substantial' agreement.[102]

With this statement, the ambassador resurrected the 'Rapallo complex' as a factor in West German–American relations. Indeed, the American administration could not overlook the fact that Adenauer's proposed strategy for the negotiations in Moscow had been discarded entirely; the Chancellor had not been able to stand up to the very skilful Soviet tactics. He had been incapable of foreseeing Moscow's strategy. Adenauer was actually quite 'shocked by [the] toughness' and occasional 'rudeness' of the Russian conduct of the negotiations.[103] This had led him to tell the Western representatives, after the first few days of negotiating, that 'the positions on prisoners and unification were so far apart that there was virtually no chance for agreement'.[104] Within US governmental circles, however, it had been expected that Moscow would use the POW question to 'bribe Adenauer to break away from [the] West' and into entering diplomatic relations with the USSR.[105] At least partially, this was exactly what happened. Bohlen, in fact, thought that such a 'trade' was 'inherent' from the moment Adenauer accepted the invitation, in spite of the fact that the Chancellor had always been strongly 'against such [a] deal unless some satisfaction in regard to unity was obtained'.[106]

On the whole, the American administration received the impression that Adenauer had indeed given in to the Soviet Union. Ambassador Conant in Bonn added to this picture when he reported that Adenauer

101. PRO: FO 371/118 181/WG 10338/111, Hayter (Moscow) to FO, No. 1040, 14/9/1955.

102. *FRUS*, 1955–57, Vol. 5, p. 583: Bohlen (Moscow) to State Dept., 14/9/1955. When Bohlen referred to the likely consequences of this action he meant 'particularly the quasi legalization division Germany inherent in acceptance formal diplomatic relations with Soviet Union, which at the same time maintains to say least full diplomatic relations GDR'. See for this statement ibid., pp. 544–5: Bohlen to State Dept., 6/8/1955. British Ambassador Hayter was sceptical of Bohlen's conviction. See PRO: FO 371/118 181/WG 10338/109, Hayter (Moscow) to FO, No. 1039, 14/9/1955.

103. *FRUS*, 1955–57, Vol. 5, p. 587: Conant (Bonn) to State Dept., 16/9/1955; PRO: FO 371/118 181/WG 10338/98, Allen (Bonn) to FO, No. 508, 12/9/1955.

104. *FRUS*, 1955–57, Vol. 5, p. 577, note 4: Bohlen (Moscow) to State Dept., 12/9/1955. See Foschepoth, 'Adenauers Moskaureise', 41–4.

105. *FRUS*, 1955–57, Vol. 5, p. 320: Beam (Paris) to State Dept., 15/7/1955, on the conversation Dulles–Macmillan in Paris.

106. Ibid., p. 580: Bohlen (Moscow) to State Dept., 13/9/1955.

and his delegation did not seem 'very happy about what had happened'.[107] Washington, however, realized that Moscow's threat to publicly announce their offer had put Adenauer in a bad position: he would have found it very difficult to explain to the West German public that he had refused the release of almost 10,000 men because he did not wish to see the establishment of a Soviet embassy in Bonn. This might easily have backfired during the 1957 elections.[108] Although West German ambassador Krekeler reported from Washington that the Eisenhower administration was not overjoyed with the results of Adenauer's journey, the USA never criticized the Chancellor openly. During as well as after the negotiations, the American administration remained loyal to Adenauer. On 12 September, when the talks in Moscow were entering a difficult phase, Dulles had asked Bohlen to tell Adenauer that his 'handling of [the] discussions inspires every confidence'. A day later, Adenauer was told that the American President 'will stand behind [the] Chancellor in whatever decision [the] Chancellor believes right'. Later Adenauer claimed that Eisenhower's message influenced him in the decision to accept Bulganin's offer.[109] Dulles may have been slightly shocked by the result of Adenauer's negotiations; but he never narrated this fact to the American public. In fact, Dulles did not trust ambassador Bohlen and had only appointed him to the post in Moscow to sideline him. Bohlen's interpretation of Adenauer's motives was therefore regarded with great caution in the State Department.[110]

On 3 October 1955, Dulles attempted to calm Adenauer's still ruffled nerves by expressing the conviction that diplomatic relations between the two countries were 'entirely natural'. He continued by saying 'that we appreciated the difficulties with which you were faced and would stand behind you in whatever decision you believed to be right. It seems to me that it would have been unintelligible to the German people if you had refused the offer with regard to the prisoners of war after the Russians had changed their position on this.'[111] The State Deparatment was 'not unduly worried' about the agreement, which 'in the circumstances' had been the 'only possible decision'. Washington was convinced

107. Ibid., p. 584: Conant (Bonn) to State Dept., 15/9/1955. For a description of the 'varying degrees of gloom' of the Chancellor's advisers see PRO: FO 371/118 181/WG 10338/109, Allen (Bonn) to FO, No. 513, 14/9/1955. For the view of Heinrich von Brentano, Adenauer's Foreign Minister, see Daniel Kosthorst, *Brentano und die deutsche Einheit: die Deutschland- und Ostpolitik des Aussenministers im Kabinett Adenauer 1955–61* (Melle, 1993).

108. *FRUS*, 1955–57, Vol. 5, p. 585.

109. See Adenauer, *Erinnerungen* Vol. 2, p. 547. Quotes from Felken, *Dulles*, p. 324.

110. See Felken, *Dulles*, p. 324.

111. *FRUS*, 1955–57, Vol. 5, p. 611: Letter Dulles to Adenauer, 3/10/1955.

that 'the Germans were sincerely anxious to prove themselves good allies, and . . . the recent decision would cause them to increase their efforts in this direction rather than the reverse'.[112]

The Quai d'Orsay in Paris and the British Foreign Office largely shared this view.[113] The French Foreign Ministry in particular observed that the Soviet Union had given up its aim of reunifying Germany. Instead it was noted in Paris, with satisfaction, that 'the prospect of German reunification remains as remote as ever – possibly more remote than before'.[114] Although the observation was made in London that a direct line to Moscow would make it easier for Adenauer's successors 'to revert to the old game of playing off East against West', it was acknowledged that 'the Rapallo Treaty of 1922 was concluded before the establishment of diplomatic relations between Russia and Germany'.[115] London came to the conclusion that the establishment of diplomatic relations between the two was inevitable. It was pointed out with some relief that 'the visit's most dangerous potentiality . . . namely the creation of a real understanding between Moscow and Bonn behind the backs of the Western Powers' had not materialized.[116] Moreover, the British government had come to the agreeable conclusion 'that exchanging diplomatic relations is to some extent a recognition of the partition of Germany and tends, therefore, in the direction of preserving the *status quo.* But if it is the German Chancellor who himself elects to do this, surely it is not for us to be more royalist than the King?'[117] In addition, London noted with satisfaction that soon the Western powers 'should be relieved of some of the responsibilities which have allowed the Federal Government . . . to make us bear some of their Eastern burdens for them. We might also be able gradually to put our own relationship with the DDR onto a more practical basis. We cannot, however, force the pace on this nor refer to it publicly at present.'[118]

112. PRO: FO 371/118 181/WG 10338/130, Scott (Washington) to FO, No. 546, 17/9/1955, on his conversation with US diplomat Kidd, head of the State Department's German Political Affairs Office.

113. PRO: FO 371/118 181/WG 10338/156, letter Beith (Paris) to Johnston (FO), 22/9/1955.

114. PRO: FO 371/118 181/WG 10338/142, Jebb (Paris) to FO, No. 371, 21/9/1955.

115. PRO: FO 371/118 181/WG 10338/120, memorandum Johnston 'Dr. Adenauer's Visit to Moscow', 14/9/1955.

116. PRO: FO 371/118 182/WG 10338/138, letter Caccia (FO) to Hayter (Moscow), 19/9/1955.

117. PRO: FO 371/118 182/WG 10338/138, Jebb (Paris) to Kirkpatrick (FO), 15/9/1955.

118. PRO: FO 371/118 181/WG 10338/110, Allen (Bonn) to FO, No. 514, 14/9/1955.

Adenauer was held in such high esteem in Western capitals that the announcement of the Soviet–West German agreement to enter into diplomatic relations raised only a few eyebrows. There was little public criticism. The Chancellor's policy of 'Western and European integration first' and 'unification much later' had meant that the 'Rapallo factor' had not played any role whatsoever in the Western reaction to Adenauer's agreement with Moscow. With the exception of ambassador Bohlen and, to some degree, his French and British colleagues in Moscow,[119] the United States, Britain and France never believed that Adenauer was about to do a secret deal with the Soviet Union. After all, Adenauer's Moscow visit had not led to a proper Russo-German rapprochement. Instead, it seemed to have had a sobering effect on the Germans, and made them think about the implications of a deal with Moscow. The Foreign Office in London concluded with relief:

> The fact is that the German Delegation, and not least the Chancellor himself, know that they have been taken for a ride by the Russians, and they know that we know it, and they are not very happy about it, or about the future. They went off determined, so they said, not to give an inch, and not to come back with any agreement (since they saw no prospect of a good agreement). They have come back with an agreement; and the change is due to Soviet blackmail tactics and unscrupulous use of the prisoners. The upshot of it is . . . that the Germans may be wary how they come within reach of the bear's hug again.[120]

WILLY BRANDT'S *OSTPOLITIK*

A decade and a half after Adenauer's journey to Moscow, the West German government was yet again suspected of being prepared to enter into a secret deal with the Soviet Union. In October 1969 the socialist Willy Brandt was elected Chancellor, at the head of a Social Democratic–Liberal coalition government.[121] Almost immediately Brandt and

119. The fact that Bohlen was more or less alone in his sceptical view is confirmed by PRO: FO 371/118 182/WG 10338/138, Caccia, FO to Jebb (Paris), 19/9/1955.

120. PRO: FO 371/118 183/WG 10338/152, letter Allen (Bonn) to Johnston (FO), 16/9/1955.

121. See above all Arnulf Baring with Manfred Görtemaker, *Machtwechsel: Die Ära Brandt–Scheel* (Stuttgart, 1982); also Dennis L. Bark and David R. Gress, *A History of West Germany, Vol. 2: Democracy and its Discontents 1963–1988* (Oxford, 1989), pp. 151ff.

Liberal Foreign Minister Walther Scheel began to embark on their 'new Ostpolitik'.[122] They intended to turn the Federal Republic away from the outdated pursuit of a strongly anti-Eastern and pro-Western Cold War strategy towards a more balanced, more modern and also somewhat more independent and mature foreign policy.[123] After all, by the late 1960s, in Henry Kissinger's words, 'for years, the democracies had paid lip service to the idea of German unity while doing nothing to bring it about. That approach had come to the end of its possibilities. The Atlantic Alliance's German policy was collapsing.'[124]

Brandt was fortunate that his pro-Eastern *Ostpolitik* coincided with the beginning of a general period of East–West *détente*. As early as May 1964, US President Johnson had spoken of the need for 'building bridges', and in October 1966 he advanced the idea of 'peaceful engagement' with the countries of the Eastern Bloc. Even the Harmel Report, approved by the NATO member states in December 1967, spoke explicitly of the Western aim 'to further a *détente* in East–West relations'. During the Council of Ministers' meeting in Rejkjavik in June 1968 all NATO members emphasized their willingness to embark upon East–West negotiations regarding troop reductions in Europe.[125] Thus, as a German official expressed it in the early 1970s: 'The notion that it was the Germans who all of a sudden had this mad lust for dealing with the

122. A considerable amount of literature deals with *Ostpolitik*. Good overviews are given in: William E. Griffith, *The Ostpolitik of the Federal Republic of Germany* (Cambridge, Mass., 1978); Bark and Gress, *Democracy and its Discontents*, pp. 90ff.; Lawrence L. Whetten, *Germany's Ostpolitik: Relations between the Federal Republic and the Warsaw Pact Countries* (London, 1971); Stent, *Embargo*, pp. 154ff.; Peter Borowsky, *Deutschland 1970–76* 4th edn (Hanover, 1983); Bender, *Neue Ostpolitik*, esp. pp. 115ff.; also Manfred Uschner, *Die Ostpolitik der SPD: Sieg und Niederlage einer Strategie* (Berlin, 1991); Horst Ehmke *et al.*, eds, *Zwanzig Jahre Ostpolitik: Bilanz und Perspektiven* (Bonn, 1986); see also the somewhat confusingly structured book by Timothy Garton Ash, *In Europe's Name: Germany and the Divided Continent* (London, 1993). See also Willy Brandt, *Erinnerungen* (Frankfurt am Main, 1989), pp. 168ff. (English abridged version: *My Life in Politics*, London, 1992); Horst Ehmke, *Mittendrin: Von der Grossen Koalition zur Deutschen Einheit* (Berlin, 1994), pp. 53ff., 125ff.; Willy Brandt, *People and Politics: The Years 1960–1975* (London, 1978), pp. 166ff.

123. See Brandt, *Erinnerungen*, p. 192; Ehmke, *Mittendrin*, p. 128; Henry Kissinger, *The White House Years* (London, 1979), p. 389.

124. Henry Kissinger, *Diplomacy* (London, 1994), p. 735; see also idem, *White House Years*, pp. 409–10.

125. See Raymond L. Garthoff, *Détente and Confrontation: American–Soviet Relations from Nixon to Reagan* (Washington, 1994), pp. 123–4, 127–8; also Adrian W. Schertz, *Die Deutschlandpolitik Kennedys und Johnsons* (Cologne, 1992), pp. 437ff.; Seymour M. Hersh, *The Price of Power: Kissinger in the White House* (New York, 1983), p. 416; Helmut Schmidt, *Menschen und Mächte* (Berlin, 1987), p. 187 (paperback edition); Borowsky, *Deutschland*, p. 15.

East is just historically not true.'[126] In the 1950s Adenauer had been able to use the West's policy of containment for his pro-Western strategy of integrating the Federal Republic with the West. Less than two decades later Brandt's new course also followed the general directions which had been emanating from Washington for the previous few years.

However, when Richard Nixon and his National Security Adviser Henry Kissinger moved into the White House in early 1969, it was not *détente* but the war in South-east Asia which was foremost in their minds. Only after observing the successes of Brandt's policy did the Nixon administration embark on a similar course.[127] Still, by early 1970 the US government was keen on becoming involved in East–West preliminary discussions regarding the surface traffic to and from West Berlin and in a European security conference. Kissinger believed that it was necessary to embed *Ostpolitik* 'in a matrix of negotiations that enhanced the bargaining position of the Federal Republic but also set limits beyond which it could not go without an allied consensus'.[128] Washington was careful to prevent the Brandt government from acting too independently.

To discredit Brandt's initiative, a number of ill-disposed foreign observers, predominantly Americans, accused the left-wing government in Bonn of embarking upon a new 'Rapallo' policy and old-style nationalism.[129] In his memoirs, published in 1979, even Henry Kissinger drew attention to the fact that 'from Bismarck to Rapallo it was the essence of Germany's nationalist foreign policy to manoeuvre freely between East and West'.[130] Initially, his suspicions were aroused as the Bonn government seemed to be prepared to accept the division of its country 'in return for nothing more than improvements in the political atmosphere'.[131] However, this conclusion was rather unfair. After all, Kissinger, like most other politicians in both East and West, was glad

126. Quoted in Hersh, *The Price of Power*, p. 416. For a general overview of *détente* in the late 1960s and 1970s see Richard Crockatt, *The Fifty Years War: The United States and the Soviet Union in World Politics, 1941–1991* (London, 1995), pp. 207ff.; Richard W. Stevenson, *The Rise and Fall of Détente: Relaxations of Tension in US–Soviet Relations, 1953–1984* (Basingstoke, 1985), pp. 144ff.; also Keith L. Nelson, *The Making of Détente: Soviet–American Relations in the Shadow of Vietnam* (Baltimore, 1995).

127. See Garthoff, *Détente*, pp. 126–7; Hersh, *The Price of Power*, p. 416.

128. Kissinger, *White House Years*, p. 412, see also p. 530.

129. See Brandt, *Erinnerungen*, p. 192; Douglas Brinkley, *Dean Acheson: The Cold War Years, 1953–71* (New Haven, Conn., 1992), pp. 291–2.

130. Kissinger, *White House Years*, p. 409, see also pp. 529–30. See also Frohn, 'Rapallo-Mythos', pp. 146–8.

131. Kissinger, *White House Years*, p. 824. See also Frank Ninkovich, *Germany and the United States: The Transformation of the German Question since 1945* (Boston, 1988), pp. 150–2.

that West Germany was finally accepting political realities; most of them had realized that *Ostpolitik* 'was more likely to lead to a permanent division of Germany than to healing its breach'.[132] Indeed, the new Chancellor was about to shatter a fundamental illusion prevalent in the Federal Republic: the belief that unification was just round the corner and that the West German state merely constituted a provisional arrangement. With this Brandt began to embark on a policy the West had secretly regarded as necessary for the last ten years, while the East had been demanding it since the mid-1950s.[133]

From the time of Adenauer's Moscow visit in 1955, all West German governments had attempted to achieve better relations with the Warsaw Pact states – without much success, however. Due to the Hallstein Doctrine, which required that the Federal government consider the recognition of the East Berlin government by another state as an unfriendly diplomatic act, and respond accordingly, West Germany had imposed severe foreign policy shackles on itself. It was high time that Bonn took a decisive step to free itself from such an obsolete and unnecessary political constraint. In the face of a loosening of Western policy towards the Soviet Union, the Federal Republic had acquired the reputation throughout the 1960s of being opposed to East–West *détente*, of being more Catholic than the Pope.[134] In the course of the Grand Coalition between 1966 and 1969, when Brandt, as Foreign Minister, had cautiously initiated his new policy, he had realized that Bonn's Western partners would leave it to the West German government to modernize its foreign policy. While they would continue to protect the Federal Republic through NATO, in political matters West Germany had to take the initiative itself.[135] The Soviet Union had been extending more positive feelers for a number of years. Western statesmen assumed that Moscow was worried about its increasingly strained relations with China and therefore wished to improve relations with its western neighbours.[136] Moreover, since the Soviet invasion of Prague in 1968, the USSR had become more intent than ever to 'secure an agreement with the West that would recognize the legitimacy of Soviet

132. Kissinger, *White House Years*, p. 411.

133. See, for example, Bender, *Neue Ostpolitik*, pp. 160ff.

134. Ibid.; also Garthoff, *Détente*, p. 125.

135. Bender, *Neue Ostpolitik*; Brandt, *Erinnerungen*, p. 188; Brian White, *Britain, Détente and Changing East–West Relations* (London, 1992), p. 121.

136. See Kissinger, *White House Years*, p. 966; Stent, *Embargo*, pp. 157–9; Bender, *Neue Ostpolitik*, pp. 154–5.

influence in Eastern Europe and thereby lessen the prospect of another Czechoslovakia'.[137]

Brandt knew, however, that he had to convince the world that *Ostpolitik* did not mean the abandonment of NATO and European integration. He began in December 1969, in the course of an EC summit meeting in the Hague, by persuading French President Pompidou to discontinue France's opposition to Britain's entry to the EEC. It was also Brandt who took the first step towards turning the EC from a purely economic to a more political organization. The EC member states began to co-ordinate their foreign policy in the Council of Ministers. As both Britain and France harboured fears of a resurgent German nationalism, European integration was actually spurred on by *Ostpolitik*.[138] Brandt took every opportunity to assure his Western partners within the NATO Council that the German government was deeply committed to the European Community and NATO and was not considering yet another German *Sonderweg*. Brandt's defence minister Helmut Schmidt – although not involved in *Ostpolitik* himself – was charged with reassuring Western governments by enabling the Brandt administration to announce annually an impressive increase in the West German defence budget, thus displaying Bonn's attachment to the Western Alliance.[139] Moreover, the Chancellor himself was the living symbol of German resistance to communism and loyalty to the West. Brandt, after all, was not only a socialist who had been pursued by Hitler; he had also been prominent during the Berlin blockade when he occupied a leading political position in the city. Moreover, he had been mayor of Berlin when President Kennedy announced his support for the isolated Western enclave by declaring that he was 'ein Berliner'.[140]

In a speech in honour of former Foreign Minister Walther Rathenau, Brandt, however, highlighted the positive 'inner' aspects of the Rapallo treaty signed by Rathenau in 1922. According to the Chancellor the treaty had led to the re-establishment of a normal friendly relationship between Germany and the Soviet Union. Brandt professed to have little time for the totally unrealistic 'recurrent nightmare of Western statesmen'

137. Quote from Stent, *Embargo*, p. 155; Kissinger, *Diplomacy*, p. 734. See also Wjatscheslaw Keworkow, *Der geheime Kanal: Moskau, der KGB und die Bonner Ostpolitik* (Berlin, 1995).

138. See Peter Koch, *Willy Brandt: Eine politische Biographie* 2nd edn (Bergisch-Gladbach, 1992), p. 412; see also Brandt, *Erinnerungen*, p. 188; Kissinger, *White House Years*, p. 422.

139. See Koch, *Brandt*, p. 411; Bender, *Neue Ostpolitik*, p. 160; also Ehmke, *Mittendrin*, pp. 128–9.

140. Ibid. For Kissinger's portrait of Brandt's anti-communism and German nationalism see *Years of Upheaval* (London, 1982), pp. 143–5.

of yet another alleged secret Russo-German deal. Such a policy, he declared, would run counter to the national interest of the Federal Republic. The fundamental interest of any West German government lay in cooperating closely with both West and East while recognizing that the 'partnership' with the West was of an entirely different quality to the 'friendship' with the USSR. While in the 1920s a united Germany had had the option to embark upon a 'Rapallo policy', the western half of a divided nation neither could afford nor had the intention to embark on such a strategy.[141]

Brandt was, of course, quite right. Neither Adenauer before him nor he himself intended (or was in a position) to trade a more normal relationship with the East for the Federal Republic's integration in the West. But if *détente* was to be given a chance it was essential to come to a new understanding with both the Soviet Union and the GDR. This involved the complex issue of German unification and recognition of both the East German government and the post-war European borders. In his inaugural speech in the *Bundestag* following his election as Chancellor, Brandt declared: 'An international recognition of the GDR by the Federal government is out of the question. Although there are two states in existence in Germany, they do not represent foreign territory for each other; their relationship can only be of a special kind.'[142]

With these words, a West German head of government had officially acknowledged the existence of the GDR as an independent state for the first time while not explicitly stating the need for unification. Only when he mentioned the right to self-determination of all the Germans did Brandt hint at this goal indirectly. This, of course, represented a gesture towards Moscow indicating that Bonn was serious about accepting and formalizing the post-war *status quo*.[143] After all, all parties had to be willing to work for a new rapprochement. It was clear that the East would only be prepared to embark on closer relations with the West if it no longer felt threatened politically or militarily, and if its territorial borders were respected. Brandt believed that in the last resort, East–West *détente* would not make any real progress unless Bonn was prepared to come to terms with the division of Germany and the loss of the country's former eastern territories. The *status quo* had to be accepted in order to free *détente* from the German question as much as possible.

The underlying rationale of Brandt's policy was summarized by the Chancellor when he said: 'My government accepts the results of his-

141. Müller, 'Rapallo–Karriere eines Reizwortes', p. 60 (quote from ibid., my translation); Brandt, *Erinnerungen*, p. 187; Koch, *Brandt*, pp. 410–11.

142. Quoted in Koch, *Brandt*, pp. 400–1 (my translation).

143. Ibid., p. 401.

tory.'[144] He acknowledged that the Germans only had themselves to blame for the division of Germany and the loss of the eastern territories. Persuading the West German people to accept this responsibility enabled him to embark upon a realistic political course. Moreover, Brandt hoped that his new policy would also prepare the preconditions for internal changes in the Eastern Bloc. Until then, the threat of the 'German danger' had consolidated Moscow's grip over its satellite states and inhibited any political progress. It was hoped that once this fear had disappeared, the Eastern European states would begin to develop in a much less restricted way. The catchword was '*Wandel durch Annäherung*' (change through rapprochement).[145]

Therefore, Brandt did not hesitate to say that unification had become 'very improbable' – something his predecessors had never dared to say, though even Adenauer had been convinced of this fact. Instead of talking about unification, Brandt emphasized the unity of the nation – the cultural, social, economic and political nationhood as well as the nation based on the common feeling of belonging together. To him 'there could be no return to a nation-state on the 19th century pattern'.[146] Thus Brandt spoke of 'two states but one nation' – a situation which he thought would continue for an indefinite period of time, though he did not want to exclude the possibility of German unity. Brandt used the device of 'treaties of peaceful reconciliation' for the realization of his *Ostpolitik*. However, he emphasized that these treaties were not peace treaties. After all, hardly anybody desired the conclusion of a proper peace treaty. This would almost inevitably have included the withdrawal of all Western and Eastern forces from German territory. Germany – as one or two states – would have been left to its own devices and neither the Western Allied powers nor the Soviet Union wished for this. The governments in both Bonn and East Berlin were not too keen on the idea either.[147]

On 18 November 1969, almost immediately after taking over political responsibility, the Brandt government became a signatory to the nuclear non-proliferation treaty. West Germany thereby renounced all intention of ever owning nuclear weapons – an issue which had been hotly

144. He said this in the course of signing the Warsaw treaty on 7 December 1970. Quoted in Bender, *Neue Ostpolitik*, p. 165 (my translation); see also Koch, *Brandt*, p. 402.

145. See William E. Griffith, 'The American View', in Moreton, ed., *Germany between East and West*, pp. 53–4.

146. Anthony Glees, 'The British and the Germans: From Enemies to Partners', in Verheyen and Soe, eds, *The Germans*, p. 48.

147. Bender, *Neue Ostpolitik*, pp. 163–6.

debated for the last ten years.[148] The official abandonment of the 'Hallstein Doctrine' was another signal to the Soviet Union that the new government was serious about *détente* and its new *Ostpolitik*. All German embassies were told to ask the governments in their respective countries to postpone the recognition of the GDR for a little while. It was explained that Bonn was seeking to conclude a treaty with East Berlin and intended to get both governments accepted as full members of the UN.[149]

For the Brandt government it was sensible to embark upon negotiations with the Soviet Union first before dealing with the other Eastern European states. Instead of attempting to play off the USSR and its satellites, including the GDR, against each other as, until then, had been the case, Bonn intended to come to an arrangement, to the benefit of both East and West, for managing *détente*. Brandt regarded a friendship treaty with the Soviet Union as the basis for a comprehensive policy of *détente* in Europe. He hoped that once the bilateral treaties with Moscow, Warsaw, East Berlin and Prague had been concluded, a multilateral phase could begin. This would include agreements about the mutual reduction of troops and a conference about security and cooperation in Europe. Eventually, he intended to arrive at a point which might lead to German unification, the dissolution of NATO and the Warsaw Pact and the general respect of self-determination and basic human rights.[150]

Egon Bahr, Brandt's trusted adviser in the chancellery, was made responsible for the initial negotiations with Moscow.[151] Foreign Minister Scheel would only become actively involved in the final stages of the talks. It was hoped that the negotiations could be concluded as early as the summer of 1970. Late in 1969 Bonn's ambassador in Moscow, Helmut Allardt, was instructed to hold preliminary talks with Soviet Foreign Minister Gromyko. On 30 January 1970 Bahr himself flew to Moscow and began negotiating in earnest.[152]

Soon, on 26 March 1970, and simultaneously with the bilateral Soviet–West German discussions, negotiations began between the three Western ambassadors accredited to the West German government in Bonn and the Soviet ambassador in East Berlin. These centred on an

148. See, for example, Johannes Steinhoff and Rainer Pommerin, eds, *Strategiewechsel: Bundesrepublik und Nuklearstrategie in der Ära Adenauer–Kennedy* (Baden-Baden, 1992). See also Harold Wilson, *The Labour Government, 1964–70: A Personal Record* (London, 1971), p. 612.

149. See, for example, Koch, *Brandt*, p. 402.

150. See ibid., p. 410; also Kissinger, *Years of Upheaval*, p. 145.

151. For a critical description of Bahr see Kissinger, *Years of Upheaval*, pp. 146–8; idem, *White House Years*, pp. 410–11; see also Dieter S. Lutz, ed., *Das Undenkbare denken. Festschrift für Egon Bahr zum 70. Geburtstag* (Baden-Baden, 1992).

152. See Andrei Gromyko, *Memories* (London, 1989), pp. 197–201.

agreement to alleviate the political complications concerning West Berlin. At issue were, in particular, the unimpeded access to Berlin via the transit ways from the Federal Republic and the legal, political and diplomatic recognition of the city's close ties with West Germany. This was despite the fact that West Berlin was not legally a constituent part of the Federal Republic. After GDR leader Ulbricht's fall from power in May 1971 the quadripartite negotiations progressed well and were initialled in September.[153] Brandt had attempted to avoid any linkage between the Berlin agreement and the Moscow treaty. However, domestic politics and strong American pressure would not allow this. Accordingly, the West German cabinet decided that the Moscow treaty would only be presented to the *Bundestag* for ratification after an agreement over Berlin had been reached. After some hesitation this was accepted by Gromyko but Moscow now insisted on another linkage: the condition that the Berlin agreement could only come into force after the ratification of the West German–Soviet treaty.[154]

Eventually, on 12 August 1970 – almost 31 years after the Stalin–Hitler pact – the non-aggression treaty between Moscow and Bonn was signed in the Soviet capital. It acknowledged the geopolitical realities. From Moscow, Brandt was able to tell the German public: 'With this treaty nothing has been given away which had not already been lost.'[155] Henry Kissinger commented: 'The Federal Republic had crossed its Rubicon: It had accepted the division of Germany; it had sealed the *status quo* in Central Europe.'[156] The treaty with the Soviet Union meant that the West German government officially accepted the consequences of the war. By means of this agreement West Germany hoped to overcome the confrontation of the Cold War and to replace the *status quo* gradually with a policy of *détente* and peaceful co-existence. The treaty included elements which normally would have been part of an all-German peace treaty. Above all, the Soviet–West German agreement referred to the acceptance of the post-war frontiers in Europe including the border between East and West Germany. Recognition of these

153. See Stent, *Embargo*, pp. 181–2; Hersh, *The Price of Power*, pp. 421–2. See also the literature in note 154 and David M. Keithly, *Breakthrough in the Ostpolitik: The 1971 Quadripartite Agreement* (Boulder, Colo., 1986); Andreas Wilkens, *Der unstete Nachbar: Frankreich, die deutsche Ostpolitik und die Berliner Vier-Mächte-Verhandlungen 1969–1974* (Munich, 1990).

154. See, for example, Borowsky, *Deutschland*, pp. 26–34; Koch, *Brandt*, p. 417; White, *Britain*, pp. 121–2, Garthoff, *Détente*, pp. 135–9; Stephen E. Ambrose, *Nixon, Vol. 2: The Triumph of a Politician, 1962–72* (New York, 1989), pp. 464–5; Kissinger, *White House Years*, pp. 530–4, 799ff., 824ff., 966.

155. Quoted in Koch, *Brandt*, p. 423 (my translation).

156. Kissinger, *White House Years*, p. 533.

borders was regarded as the precondition for the continued improvement of Soviet–West German relations. In the near future, it was planned to concentrate on intensifying economic cooperation and cultural links between the two countries. Furthermore, Bahr and Gromyko had worked out a strategy for the forthcoming negotiations with Warsaw, Prague and East Berlin. Both the Soviet Union and the Brandt government regarded *Ostpolitik*'s series of treaties as closely interlinked.[157]

In December 1970 the Brandt government signed the treaty with the Polish government in Warsaw. Among other things, the agreement recognized Poland's post-war borders. Bonn accepted the Oder–Neisse line as Germany's eastern border, thus *de facto* (though not *de jure*) giving up any claim to the territory lost to Poland and the Soviet Union as a result of the Second World War. However, the normalization of the Polish–West German relationship, including the establishment of diplomatic relations, was only to be considered after the ratification of the treaty by the West German *Bundestag*.[158] The *Bundestag* ratified the Moscow and Warsaw treaties on 17 May 1972. They came into force on 3 June 1972 – on the same day the Berlin agreement, initialled in September 1971, was formally signed by the four Allied powers.[159]

From the beginning it had been obvious that the normalization of relations with the GDR would be the most difficult part of *Ostpolitik*. Initially this consisted of two unsuccessful summit meetings between Brandt and East German Prime Minister Willi Stoph in Erfurt and Kassel in March and May 1970.[160] The second, much more successful, part of the inter-German negotiations began in January 1972 when Bahr and East German State Secretary Michael Kohl commenced talks on a traffic agreement between the two countries. The treaty was signed on 26 May. West Germans were now allowed to travel to the GDR several times a year for personal or business reasons. East German citizens could also apply to travel to the West on 'urgent family matters', though whether they would receive permission to visit the FRG was still uncertain. The Federal Republic thus accepted the GDR as a political equal. Bonn, however, had not yet recognized the sovereignty of the East German state with all the consequences regarding the issues of its borders, citizenship, reunification and membership in international organizations. Bonn particularly wished to preserve the notion of a 'special

157. On the Moscow treaty see, for example, Borowsky, *Deutschland*, pp. 19–22.

158. See ibid., pp. 22–4; Koch, *Brandt*, pp. 428–9.

159. Koch, *Brandt*, p. 458. For the texts of the treaties see Bender, *Neue Ostpolitik*, pp. 233ff.

160. See Brandt, *Erinnerungen*, pp. 225–9. Brandt's visit to Erfurt was, however, a huge personal success for him as thousands of GDR citizens welcomed him enthusiastically.

relationship' between Bonn and East Berlin and the concept of 'one German nation'. After all, the responsibility of the four Allied powers for the safety of Berlin rested on the latter. Between June and November 1972 these difficult negotiations took place; the so-called Basic Treaty was signed on 21 December 1972.[161]

This treaty institutionalized the *status quo* of a divided Germany. West Germany now accepted that the GDR was a sovereign and independent country within the German nation; it was acknowledged that the 'zonal frontier' constituted in fact the territorial border of the East German state.[162] This did not mean that the FRG recognized the government in East Berlin as a legitimate administration, though Brandt came close. Bonn tried to keep alive the notion that the GDR did not represent foreign territory and that the German nation, as a whole, continued to exist, for example by insisting on the exchange of permanent representatives and not ambassadors. The chancellery in Bonn and not the foreign ministry was responsible for the new West German permanent representation in East Berlin. Moreover, in the preamble to the Basic Treaty it was explicitly pointed out that both states had 'different views . . . regarding basic questions including the national question'.[163] It was therefore only consistent that the 'letter on German unity' which had been given to the Soviet Union when the Moscow treaty was signed in 1970 was also presented to the GDR. It stated that the Federal Republic had the 'political objective to work for a state of peace in Europe in which the German nation could recover its unity in free self-determination'.[164] The Basic Treaty, however, did not deal with the question of citizenship; for Bonn a separate GDR citizenship did not exist. Still, the Brandt government agreed to give up West Germany's claim to be the sole representative of the German people.

From now on the Bonn government would cooperate increasingly with East Berlin in the economic sphere and it also included the GDR in the further unfolding of the international process of *détente*. The new relationship between Bonn and East Berlin was symbolized by the admission of both German states to the United Nations in September 1973. Much to the satisfaction of East German leader Erich Honecker, Willy Brandt's *Ostpolitik* certainly led to a higher international profile and a considerably wider international recognition of the GDR as an

161. See, for example, Borowsky, *Deutschland*, pp. 25–6, 35–44. The text is published in Bender, *Neue Ostpolitik*, pp. 247–9.

162. Many academics at the time began to regard West Germany almost as a nation-state in its own right. See, for example, Gerhard Schweigler, *West German Foreign Policy: The Domestic Setting* (New York, 1984).

163. Quoted in Borowsky, *Deutschland*, p. 40 (my translation).

164. Quoted in Glees, 'The British and the Germans', p. 48.

independent state.[165] Whether *Ostpolitik* actually prolonged the division of Germany or whether Brandt's strategy helped to overcome it by undermining the political, economic and cultural isolation of the Eastern Bloc was a matter of much contemporary debate. On 27 April 1972 it even led to an attempt by the Conservative opposition in the *Bundestag* to vote Brandt out of office with the help of a 'constructive vote of non-confidence'. Brandt narrowly survived the vote.[166] Ever since – and particularly after the breaching of the Wall in November 1989 and German unification in October 1990 – the controversy surrounding *Ostpolitik* has remained a hotly debated issue between neo-nationalist conservatives (the so-called generation of 1989) and the largely left-wing supporters of *Ostpolitik*.[167]

Ostpolitik's series of bilateral treaties was concluded when Bonn signed a treaty of reconciliation with the Czechoslovak government on 11 December 1973. After that, *Ostpolitik* became fully integrated into the general process of *détente* and East–West disarmament negotiations which had slowly begun in the course of 1970. Its first climax was the signing of the SALT I treaty on 26 May 1972.[168] In November 1972 discussions about a Conference on Security and Cooperation in Europe (CSCE) began in earnest; they would lead to the important Helsinki conference which lasted from 1973 to 1975.[169]

Despite some 'Rapallo' fears, the British and, though somewhat less enthusiastically, the French governments, as well as almost all other NATO member states,[170] were convinced that Brandt's attempts to accept the *status quo* and make progress in the direction of a policy of *détente*

165. This development climaxed more than a decade later when Chancellor Kohl received Honecker in the course of the latter's first and only official state visit to Bonn in 1987. See, for example, Henry Ashby Turner, Jr., *Germany from Partition to Reunification* (New Haven, Conn., 1992), pp. 214–17. See also Franz-Josef Strauss, *Erinnerungen* (Berlin, 1989), pp. 497–508 (paperback edition).

166. On the CDU's attitude towards *Ostpolitik* see Clay Clemens, *Reluctant Realists: The Christian Democrats and West German Ostpolitik* (Durham, NC, 1989).

167. See Klaus Larres, 'A Widow's Revenge: Willy Brandt's Ostpolitik, Neo-Conservatism and the German General Election of 1994', *German Politics* 4.1 (1995), 42–63; Gordon A. Craig, 'Did Ostpolitik Work? The Path to German Reunification (review essay)', *Foreign Affairs* 73.1 (1994), pp. 162–7.

168. See Kissinger, *White House Years*, pp. 534ff.; see also, for example, John Newhouse, *Cold Dawn: The Story of SALT* (Washington, 1989).

169. See on the CSCE and the Helsinki conference Alexis Heraclides, *Security and Co-operation in Europe: The Human Dimension, 1972–1992* (London, 1993).

170. See Kissinger, *White House Years*, p. 411. The Netherlands particularly supported *Ostpolitik*. See the report by Manfred Berg about the conference 'National Interest and European Order: Germany's Role in Europe since the Interwar Period', University of Mannheim, 22–5 March 1995, in *Bulletin: German Historical Institute Washington, D.C.*, No. 16 (Spring 1995), p. 13.

with the East had been more than overdue. While London viewed Brandt's activities between 1969 and 1973 largely with approval, Paris, however, fluctuated considerably 'between friendly understanding and wild speculation'.[171] Although President Pompidou 'had no personal liking for Brandt', on the whole 'he welcomed and supported . . . Ostpolitik because it meant the recognition of realities in Europe'. Nevertheless, Pompidou would always remain slightly 'distrustful toward ulterior motives both in Moscow and in Bonn that might eventually lead to the "Finlandization" of Germany and the expansion of Soviet power in Europe'.[172] Both France and Britain wished to maintain the *status quo*; they had no interest in the unification of the nation and the possibility of 'new German hegemony'.[173] Therefore Britain 'warmly encouraged' the Brandt government's *Ostpolitik*. The attempts to enter into agreements with Moscow and Warsaw were seen by Prime Minister Harold Wilson as 'highly positive and innovative'.[174] Early in 1970 during a visit to Washington Wilson had even 'urged on Nixon the benefits of Brandt's policy as if no other approach were conceivable'.[175] Although the subsequent Conservative government of Edward Heath had a somewhat cooler attitude to *Ostpolitik* than Wilson, it also supported Brandt's initiatives.[176] 'Without doubt . . . [the British] believed that *détente* lessened the risk of war in Europe and in the world. It seems likely, too,

171. Brandt, *My Life in Politics*, p. 175 (*Erinnerungen*, p. 189).

172. Contribution by George Soutou, 'President Pompidou and the Ostpolitik', as summarized in a report by Manfred Berg on the conference 'National Interest and European Order: Germany's Role in Europe since the Interwar Period', p. 12 (see note 170). See also Thierno Dialli, *La Politique étrangère de Georges Pompidou* (Paris, 1992), pp. 56–67; Herbert Tint, *French Foreign Policy since the Second World War* (London, 1972), pp. 101–5; Dirk Buda, *Ostpolitik à la Française: Frankreichs Verhältnis zur UdSSR von de Gaulle zu Mitterrand* (Marburg, 1990).

173. Kissinger, *White House Years*, p. 409. In *Years of Upheaval*, p. 146, Kissinger explains: 'It was a staple of the conversations of Pompidou, Heath, and Nixon that Brandt's Eastern policy would, however unintentionally, sooner or later unleash a latent German nationalism. A free-wheeling, powerful Germany trying to maneuver between East and West, whatever its ideology, posed the classic challenge to the equilibrium for Europe, for whatever side Germany favored would emerge as predominant. To forestall this, or perhaps outflank it, each of Brandt's colleagues – including Nixon – sought to preempt Germany by conducting an active détente policy of its own. In this sense Ostpolitik had effects far beyond those intended. It contributed to a race to Moscow and over time heightened mutual suspicions among the allies.' See also *Years of Upheaval*, pp. 731–2.

174. Quotes from Wilson, *The Labour Government*, p. 765; Glees, 'The British and the Germans', p. 48.

175. Quote from Kissinger, *White House Years*, p. 416.

176. See John Campbell, *Edward Heath: A Biography* (London, 1993), p. 346; Alec Douglas-Home (Lord Home of the Hirsel), *The Way the Wind Blows: Memoirs* (London, 1976), pp. 250–1; also Roger Morgan, 'The British View', in Moreton, ed., *Germany between East and West*, p. 90.

that they believed that, in practical terms, the German Question had been solved.'[177]

After all, West Germany had given up any attempts to revise the results of the Second World War. Instead it had built a bridge to Eastern Europe. Britain realized that it would soon be possible to recognize the GDR diplomatically. In general, the East German economy was much overrated by British politicians. They believed 'that the GDR occupied an important position within the Soviet system and hoped that diplomatic recognition would produce a considerable increase in British exports to the GDR'.[178] In 1981 the then Foreign Secretary, Lord Carrington, summarized the British view of Brandt's *Ostpolitik* in a speech in Stuttgart:

> Your reconciliation with your Eastern neighbours gave great satisfaction to your fellow Europeans. It gave us all a greater sense of security too. The resulting increases in your contacts with Eastern Europe and the Soviet Union enriched the lives of millions and did much to erode the mistrust which divides this continent of Europe.[179]

However, it has also rightly been said that *détente* forced Britain to abdicate its solitary Cold War role as a semi-independent intermediary between the US and the USSR and become a team player within the Western European concert of nations; this soon included membership of the European Community.[180] Moreover, 'a successful Ostpolitik threatened significantly to reduce British influence in Moscow. A normalization of FRG–Soviet relations inevitably reduced Soviet fears of a revanchist Germany. To the extent that Moscow had hitherto looked to the British and the French to restrain the Germans, their value was consequently reduced.' This was one of the reasons why both London and Paris involved themselves closely in the quadripartite Berlin negotiations in 1971. Despite increased competition from Bonn, both countries would insist on their traditional role as global players.[181]

Throughout the negotiations with the Soviet Union, the GDR and other Eastern European nations, there existed what Brandt called in his memoirs a 'carefully hidden mistrust' about what the West Germans were up to and what the consequences would be for the international *status quo*. When the Chancellor, on the invitation of Leonid Brezhnev, travelled to the Crimea in September 1971 'for an unprecedented private

177. Glees, 'The British and the Germans', p. 48.

178. Ibid., p. 49; see also Morgan, 'The British View', pp. 91–2.

179. Quoted in Morgan, 'The British View', p. 92.

180. On Britain's entry into the EC see Campbell, *Heath*, pp. 353ff.; also Uwe Kitzinger, *Diplomacy and Persuasion: How Britain Joined the Common Market* (London, 1973).

181. See White, *Britain*, pp. 130–3 (quote: p. 131); Morgan, 'The British View', p. 91.

meeting' without first having consulted his Western allies, he realized that he had to be 'quick to point out that this meeting did not signify another Rapallo. . . . Brandt always had to find a delicate balance between his independent Ostpolitik and the need to reassure the United States of the FRG's reliability.'[182]

While mistrust did exist in London and Paris, it was most prevalent in Washington. Initially, those Americans who paid attention to the development of *détente* in Europe – mostly old Cold Warriors like Dean Acheson, John McCloy, Lucius Clay, but also Thomas Dewey, George Ball, Kenneth Rush, the American ambassador to Bonn, and of course Henry Kissinger – were 'deeply disturbed' and viewed the developments 'with great alarm'.[183] Perhaps the strongest opponent of *Ostpolitik* was former Secretary of State Dean Acheson. In August 1970 he wrote to a friend: 'My real worries centre about Willy Brandt's foolish flirtations with the Russians. . . .' Acheson believed that *Ostpolitik* represented nothing more than traditional German nationalism: 'Fear I am not sufficiently au courant to see anything new in Ostpolitik or Brandt's Rapallo policy.' He particularly resented the treaties with Moscow and Warsaw as dangerous precedents for a general acceptance of the *status quo*. He advised publicly that 'Brandt should be cooled off' and the 'mad race to Moscow' ought to be slowed down. Many observers suspected that the White House had encouraged Acheson to make these remarks. Only when Acheson became increasingly outspoken and even declared that *Ostpolitik* was merely a domestic political ploy by Brandt to save his coalition from falling apart did Washington rebuke the former Secretary.[184]

At first, Nixon himself disliked Brandt's initiatives.[185] Moreover, Nixon and also most of Brandt's other opponents in Washington, above all Kissinger, strongly distrusted the Chancellor personally.[186] However, in his memoirs Henry Kissinger writes about Brandt: 'I personally liked him – Nixon less so – but his policy worried us both.'[187] He continues by claiming that Brandt was the European statesman whose policy made Nixon 'most uneasy and whose personality was perhaps most

182. Stent, *Embargo*, p. 184.

183. Quotes from Ambrose, *Nixon*, Vol. 2, p. 386; Brinkley, *Acheson*, p. 295.

184. See Brinkley, *Acheson*, pp. 287, 291–6; also Brandt, *Erinnerungen*, pp. 191–2.

185. See Brandt, *Erinnerungen*, pp. 189–93; Kissinger, *White House Years*, pp. 405ff.; Ehmke, *Mittendrin*, pp. 140–2.

186. For example, when Brandt in the course of a meeting with Nixon in December 1971 expressed his gratitude for NATO's support of *Ostpolitik*, according to Kissinger's account, 'Nixon frostily corrected him, saying that the alliance did not object to the policy'. Kissinger, *White House Years*, p. 966.

187. Kissinger, *Years of Upheaval*, p. 143; see also Brinkley, *Acheson*, pp. 293–5.

incompatible with his own'.[188] This clearly contradicts the impressions of other observers. David Binder, a journalist and author of a Brandt biography, quotes one of Kissinger's former advisers. According to this source, Kissinger and his aides Alexander Haig and Helmut Sonnenfeldt (like Kissinger an *émigré* from Nazi Germany) 'intensely disliked Brandt and his chief aide, Egon Bahr'. Roger Morris, a member of Kissinger's staff in the White House until his resignation in autumn 1970, supports this view. He believes that Kissinger 'hated Ostpolitik and Willy Brandt from the beginning', while Nixon 'liked Brandt better than most European politicians'. This led Kissinger to play '[a] charade in which his real feelings and irrational attitude toward Brandt were never transferred upstairs to the Oval Office. With Nixon he couldn't insult the Germans.' Furthermore, Morris is convinced that 'Henry thought the Germans were flirting with historical tragedy; that Ostpolitik would be a prelude to internal fascism, a turn to the right, and the emergence of another Weimar Republic'.[189]

The Nixon administration was certainly worried that *Ostpolitik* would 'finally come together on some nationalist, neutralist program, as Adenauer and de Gaulle had feared'.[190] Moreover, after the French exit from NATO's integrated military command in 1966, de Gaulle's all too obvious rapprochement with the Soviet Union and his talk about the East–West conflict as a predominantly European concern,[191] Washington feared similar developments in Bonn. The Federal Republic might also be tempted to break the 'West's united front toward Moscow' and endanger the Western alliance. Washington had realized that 'there were only three powers capable of disrupting the postwar *status quo* in Europe – the two superpowers and Germany'. The American government believed that, unlike Adenauer, Brandt 'never had an emotional attachment to the Atlantic Alliance' and that Egon Bahr, his closest adviser and, according to Kissinger, 'an old-fashioned German nationalist',[192] 'was also free of any sentimental attachment to the United States'.[193] Brandt's policies were therefore regarded as potentially dangerous.

188. Kissinger, *Years of Upheaval*, p. 155. According to Kissinger, Nixon's 'suspicion of Brandt' never 'abated'. See *White House Years*, p. 416. Brandt seems to have had similar reservations about Nixon. For the Nixon–Brandt relationship see also Richard Barnet, *The Alliance* (New York, 1983), pp. 283–321.

189. Quotes from Hersh, *The Price of Power*, p. 416.

190. Quote from Kissinger, *Diplomacy*, p. 735; see also idem, *White House Years*, pp. 408, 410; idem, *Years of Upheaval*, pp. 144–6.

191. See Garthoff, *Détente*, pp. 124–5; Dialli, *La politique étrangère*, pp. 80ff.; Tint, *French Foreign Policy*, pp. 148ff.

192. Kissinger, *Years of Upheaval*, p. 147.

193. Idem, *White House Years*, p. 411.

It was, however, gradually recognized that *Ostpolitik*'s time had come and that it could not be stopped. Thus, Nixon and Kissinger felt that attempting to obstruct this policy would be equally dangerous. It seemed to be necessary to accept *Ostpolitik* in order to avoid 'the risk of cutting the Federal Republic loose from the bonds of NATO and the restraints of the European Community'.[194] Moreover, Kissinger soon sought to capitalize on the developments. *Ostpolitik* gave the USA the opportunity of ending the permanent crisis over Berlin. He was convinced that it was only his insistence on a linkage between *Ostpolitik* and free access to Berlin that had led to the success of the negotiations and the Berlin Agreement of 1971/72. He wrote proudly: 'Berlin disappeared from the list of international crisis spots.'[195] According to the White House, it was its Eastern policy which prevented the nationalistic elements in Brandt's *Ostpolitik* from coming to the surface: 'Our role was decisive for the ultimate success of Ostpolitik and the Berlin negotiations.'[196] Although this claim is doubtful, it is true to say that the signing of the Berlin Agreement did much to lessen the Nixon administration's antagonism towards *Ostpolitik*.[197]

While many American foreign policy experts were sceptical towards Brandt's *Ostpolitik* on principle, the US administration was not fundamentally opposed to the general direction of Willy Brandt's policy.[198] After all, global *détente* was more or less the one foreign policy area in which glory was heaped on the American government. It is obvious that Nixon and Kissinger disliked the independence and confidence with which the West Germans pursued their new foreign policy. Washington was of the opinion that if anyone was to initiate a serious East–West *détente* it should be the USA. This factor contributed considerably to the suspicion with which Brandt's policy was regarded by the Nixon administration.[199] It is therefore not surprising that in his memoirs Kissinger does not forget to emphasize that despite all obstacles he managed to uphold the process of 'close consultation' with Bonn and was able to influence the Brandt government's policy. He does, however, admit that 'the new German government informed rather than

194. Quotes from Kissinger, *Diplomacy*, pp. 735–6. See also Ambrose, *Nixon*, Vol. 2, pp. 386–7; Kissinger, *White House Years*, pp. 410–11; idem, *Years of Upheaval*, p. 146.

195. Quote from Kissinger, *Diplomacy*, p. 736. See also Ambrose, *Nixon*, Vol. 2, pp. 464–5; Hersh, *The Price of Power*, pp. 415–22.

196. Kissinger, *White House Years*, p. 381.

197. See Schmidt, *Menschen und Mächte*, p. 187.

198. Brandt, *Erinnerungen*, p. 190; Schmidt, *Menschen und Mächte*, p. 187.

199. Brandt, *Erinnerungen*, pp. 189, 192; Hersh, *The Price of Power*, p. 416; Ehmke, *Mittendrin*, p. 128.

consulted. They reported progress; they did not solicit advice.'[200]

The Rapallo factor was occasionally mentioned when suspicion about the 'nationalistic undercurrents' in Brandt's *Ostpolitik* was voiced in the United States and elsewhere, particularly in 1970.[201] While neither London nor Paris seriously believed that West Germany was about to break away from the Western camp, Washington at times expressed strong reservations. The view that West Germany was developing a new *Schaukelpolitik* between East and West was not always dismissed. While in 1955 the British and the French had been most mistrustful of the West German government's intentions, in 1970 it was the US administration which was very sceptical. However, once the United States had itself become actively involved in *Ostpolitik* by partaking in the Berlin Agreement and negotiating the SALT I Treaty, 'Rapallo' ceased to be an issue. The situation in 1955, when Adenauer established diplomatic relations with the Soviet Union, was similar to the era of *Ostpolitik* insofar that, after an initial period of heightened mistrust, the 'Rapallo factor' played only a minor role in Germany's relations with the West.

The Western powers, particularly London and Paris, had realized with relief that Brandt's policy, like Adenauer's strategy in the 1950s, would not lead to unification in the short run. Only in the USA did politicians find it difficult to understand that the Brandt government was not seeking a quick route to unification any more. The general Cold War view was still widely shared that it would be an 'illusion of peace' if there was a 'settlement based on the *status quo*'.[202] However, Kissinger and others later realized that 'insisting on German reunification against the wishes of the German government' made little sense; 'we could not be more German than the Germans'.[203] Eventually even Henry Kissinger admitted that 'it was to Brandt's historic credit that he assumed for Germany the burdens and the anguish imposed by necessity'.[204] However, in principle – and in stark contrast to London and Paris – Washington never wavered in its support for the desire of many Germans to

200. Quotes from Kissinger, *White House Years*, pp. 411, 530. In his memoirs Kissinger expresses great pride in his skill at bypassing the State Department and developing a backchannel with Bahr and Soviet ambassador Dobrynin 'by which we [the White House] could stay in touch outside the formal procedures'. See ibid., pp. 411–12 (quote: p. 411); also Hersh, *The Price of Power*, pp. 417ff.; Walter Isaacson, *Kissinger: A Biography* (London, 1992), pp. 322–7.

201. Quote from Kissinger, *White House Years*, p. 799.

202. John Foster Dulles said this during a speech to the Amerian Society of Newspaper Editors on 18 April 1953. Quoted in Larres, *Politik der Illusionen*, p. 124.

203. Kissinger, *White House Years*, p. 530.

204. Ibid., p. 410; see also idem, *Years of Upheaval*, p. 145.

unify their nation. This explains to some extent the different reactions in the Western capitals to the events of 1989/90.

CONCLUSION: UNIFICATION AND AFTER

It is well known that, following the breaching of the Berlin Wall in November 1989, only the United States expressed full, though qualified, support for German unification.[205] British Prime Minister Thatcher, French President Mitterrand and also President Gorbachev in Moscow were much less enthusiastic about having to deal with a united Germany of 80 million people.[206]

In late 1989, when events were assuming an altogether unexpected pace, it was Margaret Thatcher, above all, who wished to prevent or at least 'slow down' unification. She believed that a 'truly democratic East Germany would soon emerge and that the question of reunification was a separate one, on which the wishes and interests of Germany's neighbours and other powers must be fully taken into account'.[207] She reprimanded her Trade and Industry Secretary, Nicholas Ridley, when, during an interview in July 1990, he declared that Germany was about 'to take over the whole of Europe' – albeit reluctantly. Ridley thought that relinquishing part of British sovereignty to the EC was tantamount to handing it to Adolf Hitler. He implied that Hitler was preferable to Kohl: 'I am not sure I wouldn't rather have the shelters [of World War II] and the chance to fight back.'[208] Similarly, the comments by Lord Rees-Mogg, who expected a 'German Age' but hopefully without swastikas and concentration camps, and by Conor Cruise O'Brien, predicting a rehabilitation of racial theories and a rise of respect for Hitler, seemed to reflect the thinking of much of the Anglo-Saxon

205. See Peter H. Merkl, *German Unification in the European Context* (University Park, Penn., 1993), pp. 5–6, 315–18; Gregory F. Treverton, *America, Germany and the Future of Europe* (Princeton, NJ, 1992), pp. 180–3; Philip Zelikow and Condoleeza Rice, *Germany United and Europe Transformed. A Study in Statecraft*, Cambridge, Mass, 1995.

206. On the British and French attitude see Merkl, *German Unification*, pp. 318–25.

207. Quotes from Margaret Thatcher, *The Downing Street Years* (London, 1993) (paperback edition), pp. 797–8, 792; see also pp. 813–15.

208. Quoted in Merkl, *German Unification*, p. 4; see also Renata Fritsch-Bournazel, 'German Unification: Views from Germany's Neighbours', in Wolfgang Heisenberg, ed., *German Unification in European Perspective* (London, 1991), pp. 75–6; Thomas O. Hueglin, 'Gross-Deutschland in Europe', in William D. Graf, ed., *The Internationalization of the German Political Economy: Evolution of a Hegemonic Project* (Basingstoke, 1992), pp. 285ff.

political elite.[209] Moreover, it soon became known that in March 1990, Thatcher herself had convened an academic seminar in Chequers to be briefed 'on the many undesirable attributes of the "German character" '.[210] In late 1990, after 40 years during which the West had never stopped criticizing the Soviet Union for preventing the democratic unification of Germany, the British Prime Minister was convinced that unification had arrived 'prematurely'.[211]

In 1990 it was generally feared that unification would produce an economic superpower which might well either turn its back on both European integration and the Western security system or assume the domination of western Europe and antagonize the United States.[212] Neither Thatcher nor anybody else foresaw the enormous economic and social difficulties inherent in unification. These problems would ensure that in the immediate post-Cold War years Germany would be entirely occupied with its domestic problems to the exclusion of all else.[213] Moreover, the Gulf War of 1991 and the UN peacekeeping activities in the early 1990s showed that, in purely power-political terms, united Germany was similar to West Germany. There was no will to dominate its European partners. Instead, 'a desire for national continuity rather than the dominance of others' could be observed. The hasty German recognition of Croatia in 1992 seems to have been a sad exception to this general tendency.[214]

Initially, there was also some fear 'that Germany – first under the spell of Mr Gorbachev and later with the lure of reunification – might . . . [move] away from the Western alliance towards neutralism'.[215] But once Gorbachev had, in February 1990, in exchange for the promise of a considerable amount of financial aid to the Soviet Union, declared that German unity should be decided by the Germans themselves and had

209. See Merk, *German Unification*, p. 323.

210. Ibid., pp. 4–5.

211. Thatcher, *Downing Street Years*, p. 814.

212. Ibid., pp. 813–15.

213. Regarding Germany's economic problems see, for example, Gerlinde Sinn and Hans-Werner Sinn, *Jumpstart: The Economic Unification of Germany* (Cambridge, Mass., 1992), pp. 19ff.

214. See *Financial Times*, 24/9/1994 (article by David Marsh); see also David Marsh, *Germany and Europe: The Crisis of Unity* (London, 1994). On the recognition of Croatia see Philip H. Gordon, *France, Germany, and the Western Alliance* (Boulder, Colo., 1995), pp. 53–66; and on the country's new international role in general see Lothar Gutjahr, *German Foreign and Defence Policy after Unification* (London, 1994), pp. 94ff. For authors who call for a more prominent German role in world politics, see, for instance, Hans-Peter Schwarz, *Die Zentralmacht Europas: Deutschlands Rückkehr auf die Weltbühne* (Berlin, 1994).

215. Thatcher, *Downing Street Years*, p. 783.

also given his public consent to a united Germany being a member of NATO, this fear was not significant any more. The 'Rapallo factor' did not detrimentally influence the process of German unification in 1990 to any considerable extent.[216] With American and Soviet agreement to changing the *status quo* of the Cold War, it had become clear to the dissenting junior partners in London and Paris 'that there was nothing we could do to halt German reunification'.[217]

While even Thatcher came to believe that talk about 'Germany loosening its attachment to the West was greatly exaggerated',[218] there was a widespread belief in 1990 that the Germans would soon dominate eastern Europe economically if not territorially. Mitterrand and Thatcher were genuinely worried about 'the Germans' so-called "mission" in central Europe'. The united German nation, they believed, would be able to use its economic power to have an almost exclusive influence over countries like Poland, Hungary and the Czech Republic. Thatcher came to the conclusion: 'we must not just accept that the Germans had a particular hold over these countries, but rather do everything possible to expand our own links there'.[219] Thus by the time of German unification the Rapallo factor had undergone a considerable transformation. A German *Schaukelpolitik* between East and West or a German–Soviet rapprochement and a simultaneous weakening of Germany's ties with the West were no longer feared. Rather, the fear of German economic hegemony (followed by political dominance) in both the new capitalist states in the east and the European Union in the west has become the dominant issue.

There can indeed be no doubt that since the 1970s and 1980s the Federal Republic has been the prime beneficiary of the EC system. Its penetration of EC export markets enabled it to obtain by far the largest market share. It outsold its major European rivals both globally and regionally. The Federal Republic was therefore the only EC country able to accumulate persistently huge trade surpluses. Thus by 1989, West German economic influence in the EC was clearly dominant.[220] During the same decades West Germany had also obtained considerable eco-

216. For a good overview see Stephen F. Szabo, *The Diplomacy of German Unification* (New York, 1992). For Kohl's and Gorbachev's 'deal' see the memoirs of a former West German government minister: Hans Klein, *Es begann im Kaukasus. Der entscheidende Schritt in die Einheit Deutschlands* (Berlin, 1991).

217. Thatcher, *Downing Street Years*, p. 798.

218. Ibid., p. 784.

219. Ibid., p. 798.

220. See Andrei S. Markovitz and Simon Reich, 'Should Europe Fear the Germans?', in Michael G. Huelshoff *et al.*, eds, *From Bundesrepublik to Deutschland: German Politics after Unification* (Ann Arbor, Mich., 1993), pp. 277–8.

nomic influence in Eastern Europe. This applied at the micro as well as the macro level. Particularly since the early 1970s the FRG has become Eastern Europe's most important Western trading partner: 'one would find it extremely difficult to find any category of commerce and trade in which the Federal Republic has not consistently been the most important Western presence in Eastern Europe'.[221] *Osthandel*, the economic and commercial side of *Ostpolitik*'s strategy of *détente*, 'most certainly gave the Germans a running start in Eastern Europe for the post-cold war era'.[222]

Since 1989/90 Germany's influence in eastern Europe has grown even more. Almost all of the new eastern European capitalist states view Germany's historic *Wirtschaftswunder* (economic miracle) and the country's successful transition to liberal democracy and prosperous capitalism in the post-war years as a role model.[223] They consequently believe that advice and investment ought to come from there. In stark contrast to Margaret Thatcher's and Milton Friedman's uninhibited free market philosophy, the Federal Republic's much more restricted and controlled (and more successful) so-called 'social market economy' appeals to most of the former socialist states. Moreover, the traditionally strong German cultural and linguistic influence in eastern Europe has re-emerged and has contributed to the huge German economic penetration of these countries.[224]

While there is, of course, resentment and some fear of united Germany's potentially powerful economic position in both western and eastern Europe, any expectations regarding German military domination and future territorial conquest are unjustified. The Kohl government in Bonn is certainly not interested in the military domination of any other nation; the Federal Republic is probably not even intent on achieving economic hegemony. However, as countries to the west and particularly to the east 'are busily immersing themselves in a web of relations' with the Federal Republic, this may well be the outcome.[225] Geir Lundestad's expression 'empire by invitation', which referred to the American role

221. Ibid., p. 283. In 1989 West German trade to all Eastern European countries except the USSR was almost four times greater than Italy's and still larger than those of Italy, the US and France combined. Regarding the USSR, West Germany's sales exceeded those of the US, the runner-up, by almost 50 per cent (see ibid.).

222. Quote from ibid., p. 283.

223. On the development and characteristics of the social market economy see Anthony J. Nicholls, *Freedom with Responsibility: The Social Market Economy in Germany, 1918–1963* (Oxford, 1994).

224. See Markovitz and Reich, 'Should Europe Fear the Germans?', pp. 284–7; also the various articles in Heinz D. Kurz, ed., *United Germany and the New Europe* (Aldershot, 1993), pp. 89ff.

225. Markovitz and Reich, 'Should Europe Fear the Germans?', p. 286.

in Western Europe during the Cold War, may soon describe the Federal Republic's position in eastern Europe, at least in the economic and financial field.[226]

Still, unlike the United States during the Cold War, Germany both before and after unification has not been actively looking for a political (and certainly not military) leadership role. Such a tendency may, however, emerge in the future. During the five years since unification, the government in Bonn, however, has been very hesitant to contradict France's traditional though somewhat illusionary conviction that Paris is the natural leader in the EU. Germany is very reluctant about assuming a greater leadership role.[227] This, however, may gradually be changing; economic ascendancy almost inevitably leads to at least some degree of political dominance. Germany's insistence on a seat in the UN Security Council and the decision by the German supreme court that participation in international UN peacekeeping missions and NATO activities out of area do not contradict the Basic Law show this. It is true that the domestic debate in the Federal Republic about 'Germany's national identity, its national interests, and its proper international role, is still unresolved' – but the Germans will soon find it impossible to avoid these issues any longer.[228] At the moment the united nation is still following a policy well summarized by Renate Schmidt, a Social Democratic member of parliament: 'We want to harness ourselves in Europe. We don't want to dominate. . . . We don't want to be a great nation. We want our economic power to be controlled within Europe.'[229] Former Chancellor Helmut Schmidt thinks that this is not necessarily a purely altruistic strategy but also serves 'to prevent coalitions against Germany from ever happening again'. Germany clearly wants to maintain a balance of power in Europe by binding itself into a greater entity.[230]

This, of course, corresponds to the wishes of both France and Britain.

226. See Geir Lundestad, *America, Scandinavia and the Cold War, 1945–49* (New York, 1980), chapter 6.

227. See *Financial Times*, 27/1/1995 (Michael Stürmer), p. 16; ibid., 18/1/1995 (Ian Davidson), p. 20; *Washington Post*, 22/6/1995 (Rick Atkinson), p. A24. See also Gordon, *France, Germany*, pp. 83ff.

228. Quote from the *Financial Times*, 21/11/1994 (Quentin Peel), p. xvi. On 4/6/1994 Peel wrote in the same paper (p. xv): 'Germany's reemergence as the dominant economic power in Europe has been accompanied by a great inner search for a new national identity and pride, a debate about the dangers of nationalism and a huge effort to find its proper equilibrium in the centre of Europe.' See also Lothar Gutjahr, 'Stability, Integration and Global Responsibility: Germany's Changing Perspectives on National Interests', *Review of International Studies* 21.3 (1995), 301–17.

229. *Financial Times*, 4/6/1994 (Peel), p. i; also 21/11/1994 (Peel), p. xvi.

230. Ibid., 4/6/1994, p. i. See also Helmut Schmidt, *Handeln für Deutschland: Wege aus der Krise* (Berlin, 1993), pp. 198ff.

After all, the Maastricht Treaty of 1991 had the hidden agenda of binding Germany, more populous and, as was suspected, economically stronger than ever, into an even more closely integrated Europe. The western European nations had no alternative but to agree to German unification in 1990, but decided to anchor the Germans firmly into the EU while at the same time 'domesticating' the Deutschmark and breaking 'Germany's de facto dominance of European monetary affairs by emasculating and (later) scrapping the D-Mark'.[231] Bonn had agreed to this in return for unification. But it also pressed for the development of a closer political European union.[232] The German government hoped that this would create a new equilibrium in Europe in general, and also balance the Franco-German partnership much better.[233] 'Ever closer integration into the European Union . . . was seen as the other side of the coin of German unification, the essential reassurance for the rest of Europe that a unified Germany would be no threat.'[234]

Since then, Germany has not only remained an advocate of deepening the EU. It has also come out strongly in favour of widening the EU by offering full membership not only to Austria and the Scandinavian countries, but also to Poland, Hungary, the Czech Republic, Slovakia, Bulgaria and Romania, and possibly even the Baltic states and Slovenia.[235] Many observers are convinced that eastern enlargement (like the entry of Austria, Sweden and Finland in January 1995) would only strengthen Germany's economic position in the EU further. However, others like Britain plainly believe that such a course would dilute the EU's supranationalism and should therefore be welcomed. London is in favour of merely concentrating on eastern enlargement and against proceeding with the deepening of the EU. The French would be happy to make progress with the deepening of the Union while ignoring the pressure of admission from the eastern European states. In contrast, Germany is the only member of the EU which is 'equally committed to widening and deepening simultaneously'. General disagreement exists about the actual pace of reforming the EU.[236] The German view was well summarized in a policy paper entitled 'Reflections on European Policy' which was drawn up by the CDU group in the *Bundestag* in November 1994:

231. *Financial Times*, 13/3/1995 (Marsh), p. 10.
232. Ibid., 23/1/1995 (Lionel Barber), p. 16.
233. Ibid., 27/1/1995 (Stürmer), p. 16.
234. Ibid., 21/12/1994 (Peel), p. xvi.
235. Ibid., 12/12/1994 (Barber), p. 2.
236. Ibid., 21/11/1995 (Peel), p. xvi; ibid., 16/12/1994 (leading article), p. 19. If there was a decision to welcome eastern enlargement, Paris would almost certainly insist on balancing any such policy by a Mediterranean strategy.

> The only solution which will prevent a return to the unstable pre-war system, with Germany once again caught between East and West, is to integrate Germany's central and eastern European neighbours into the (West) European post-war system, and to establish a wide-ranging partnership between this system and Russia. . . . Germany has a fundamental interest both in widening the EU to the East, and in strengthening it through deepening. Indeed, deepening is a precondition for widening. Without such further internal strengthening, the Union would be unable to meet the enormous challenge of eastward expansion. It might fall apart, and once again become no more than a loose grouping of States unable to guarantee stability.[237]

Political and economic stability, not hegemony and dominance, is what united Germany is most interested in. It therefore hopes that the 1996 EU intergovernmental conference in Turin will mean another 'big step towards European integration' – this time, though, to appease the British, in a somewhat more pragmatic way.[238] While in the post-Cold War world the 'Rapallo factor' so far has not seriously affected Germany's relations with the West, the country will still not be able to ignore its traditional role on the European continent. Germany can escape neither its history nor its geography:

> Germany will be the swing power in Europe, involved in an eternal balancing act between east and west, seeking to reconcile and integrate. It will do so with one hand still tied behind its back. For it will still be loath to lead, and merely seek to react to the initiatives of others.[239]

One can be more optimistic, however. After all, multinational corporations are paying less and less attention to national boundaries. Ever-increasing globalization may well mean that it will soon be impossible 'to talk of countries running dominant economic policies'. Moreover, when the eastern enlargement of the EU is eventually realized, the original rationale for monetary union may well become obsolete and the old concept of differentiating between eastern and western Europe may lose all relevance. Soon, it may not even be feasible to embark on a 'Rapallo policy' any more:

> There is no longer a need . . . to 'bind' Germany to western Europe to stop it turning eastwards. The idea of Europe being divided into east and west

237. Ibid., 21/11/1994 (Peel), p. xvi.
238. Ibid.
239. Ibid.; see also Fritsch-Bournazel, 'German Unification', pp. 73–4.

> is outdated. Poland and the Czech Republic will soon become normal countries.[240]

If this was to come true, the Rapallo factor in Germany's relations with the West would have been laid to rest for good. Throughout the Cold War and in the post-1990 world – despite occasional ill-founded fears and suspicions – 'Rapallo' and its associations with an aggressive, expansionist Germany, cooperating closely with Russia and not being averse to plotting against the West, never played a genuinely influential role in Germany's relations with the Western world. 'Rapallo' nevertheless serves as a useful reminder that united Germany ought not to aspire to become too powerful. It would do no harm to observe, at least to some degree, a healthy balance of power within an enlarged European Union. It is true, in the current transitionary phase of world politics, that Germany has developed more of a 'special relationship' with both Russia and the other eastern European nations than anyone else in the West. But any government in Bonn or Berlin would do well to remember that ultimately the roots of post-Cold War Germany's stability, security and prosperity lie in its close cooperation with the USA, Britain and France. As the United States may well be on the way towards relative 'splendid isolation', in European affairs a *ménage à trois* of Germany, France and Britain in the economic, political and security field would best ensure that renewed suspicion about German intentions is avoided.[241]

In this respect, post-1989/90 Europe is not that different from the Europe of the Cold War: the hegemony or dominance of any one European country is not required; desirable are cooperation and integration. A policy is called for which is firmly rooted in the former Western Europe but is open-minded and equally cooperative regarding the countries of what used to be referred to as Eastern Europe. United Germany's foreign policy ought not to be characterized by impulsive swings. Rather, in order to incorporate the new and complex post-Cold War developments without destabilizing the European continent, continuity and reliability must be the order of the day. If this is realized, then the lessons of 'Rapallo' and the widespread suspicions connected with this word in the post-1945 world will have been learned.

240. *Financial Times*, 24/9/1994 (Marsh), p. i. See also Hélène Seppain, 'European Integration, German Unification and the Economics of Ostpolitik', in Kurz, ed., *United Germany*, pp. 73–86.

241. For Anglo–German–French cooperation in the security field see above all Gordon, *France, Germany*, pp. 31ff.; *Financial Times*, 27/1/1995 (Stürmer), p. 16; ibid., 18/1/1995 (Davidson), p. 20; ibid., 20/1/1995 (Dominique Mosi), p. 14.

Maps

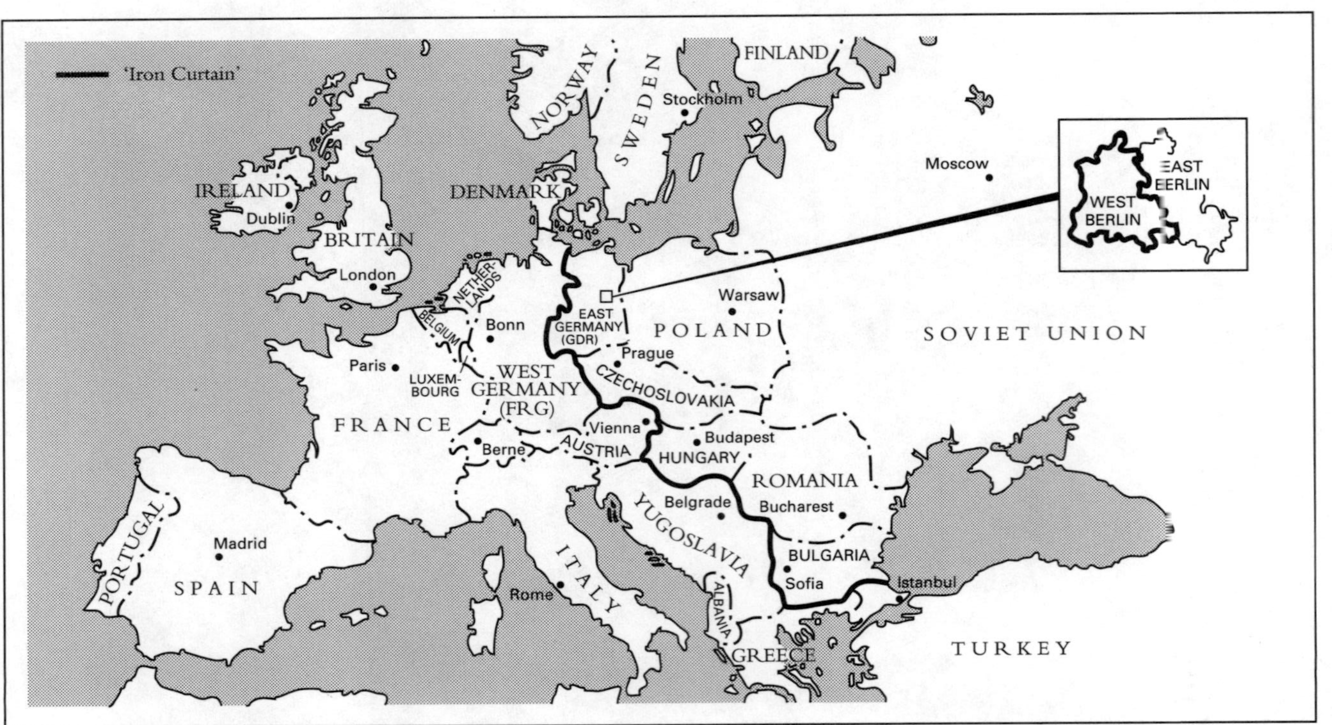

Map 1: Europe, 1949–90

Map 2: Europe, 1995

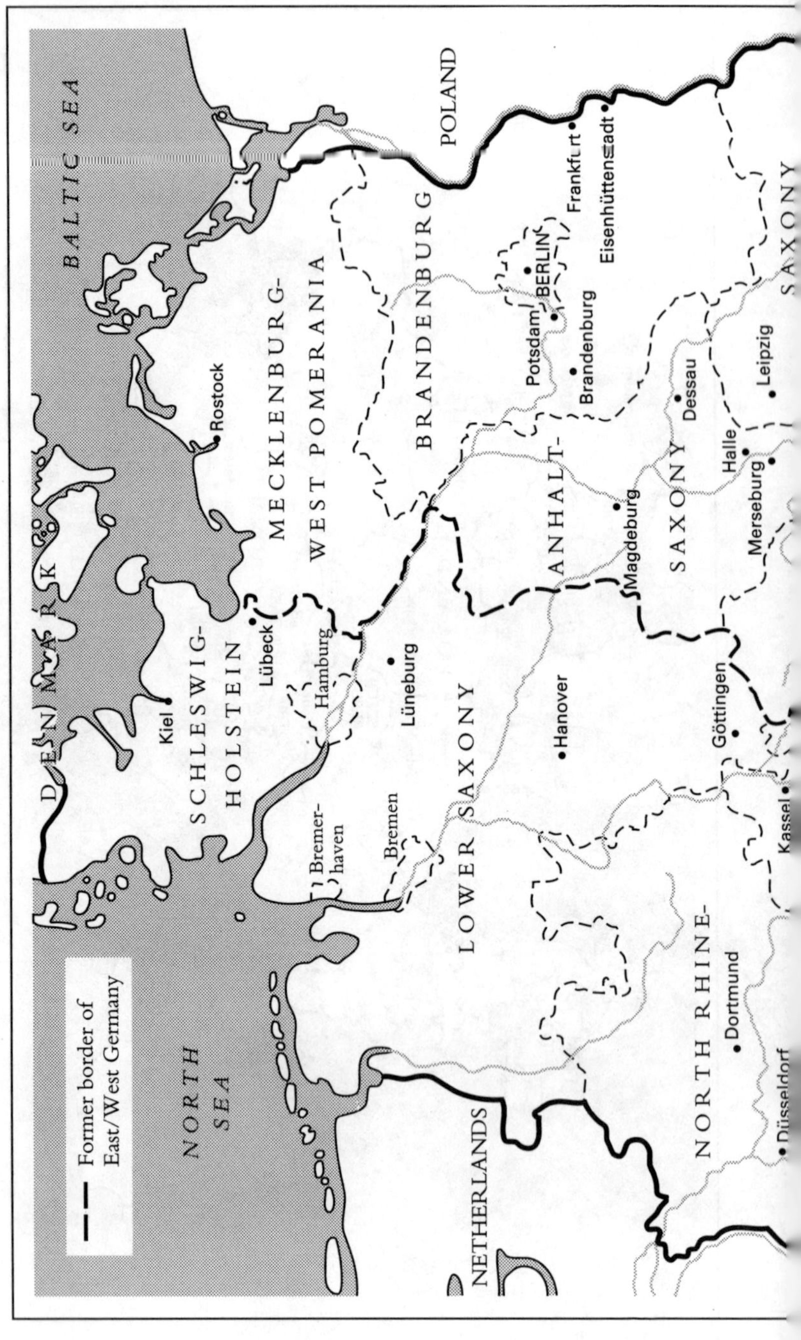
Former border of East/West Germany
NORTH SEA
BALTIC SEA
DENMARK
NETHERLANDS
POLAND
SCHLESWIG-HOLSTEIN
MECKLENBURG-WEST POMERANIA
BRANDENBURG
LOWER SAXONY
SAXONY-ANHALT
NORTH RHINE-
SAXONY
Kiel
Lübeck
Rostock
Hamburg
Lüneburg
Bremer-haven
Bremen
Hanover
Göttingen
Kassel
Dortmund
Düsseldorf
Magdeburg
Potsdam
BERLIN
Brandenburg
Frankfurt
Eisenhüttenstadt
Dessau
Halle
Merseburg
Leipzig

Map 3: Unified Germany

Index